Current Research in Puerto Rican Linguistics

T0358852

Current Research in Puerto Rican Linguistics is an edited collection of original contributions which explores the idiosyncratic grammatical properties of Puerto Rican Spanish.

The book focuses on the structural aspects of linguistics, analysed with a variety of frameworks and methodological approaches, in order to present the latest advances in the field of Puerto Rican and Caribbean linguistics.

Current Research in Puerto Rican Linguistics brings together articles from researchers proposing new, challenging, and ground-breaking analyses on the nature of Spanish in Puerto Rico and Puerto Rican Spanish in the United States.

Melvin González-Rivera is Associate Professor of Linguistics in the Department of Hispanic Studies at the University of Puerto Rico at Mayagüez.

Routledge Studies in Hispanic and Lusophone Linguistics
Series Editor: Dale Koike
University of Texas at Austin

For a full list of titles in this series, please visit www.routledge.com

The *Routledge Studies in Hispanic and Lusophone Linguistics* Series provides a showcase for the latest research on Spanish and Portuguese Linguistics. It publishes select research monographs on various topics in the field, reflecting strands of current interest.

Titles in the series:

Contact Phenomena and Linguistic Interfaces: Aspects of Afro-Andean Spanish *(forthcoming)*
Sandro Sessarego

Current Research in Puerto Rican Linguistics
Edited by Melvin González-Rivera

English Lexical Borrowings and Spanish in New York City *(forthcoming)*
Rachel Varra

Fonologia del las vocales del español: descripción y análisis *(forthcoming)*
Fernando Martinez-Gil

Lusophone, Galician and Hispanic Linguistics: Bridging Frames and Traditions *(forthcoming)*
Edited by Fernando Tejedo-Herrero and Gabriel Rei-Doval

Research on Caribbean Spanish in the United States: Dialects from Tropical Islands *(forthcoming)*
Edited by Wilfredo Valentin-Marquez and Melvin González-Rivera

Spanish in Healthcare: Policy, Practice and Pedagogy *(forthcoming)*
Glenn Martinez

U.S. Mexican Spanish: A National Language West of the Mississippi *(forthcoming)*
Daniel Villa

Current Research in Puerto Rican Linguistics

Edited by
Melvin González-Rivera

Routledge
Taylor & Francis Group

LONDON AND NEW YORK

First published 2018
by Routledge

2 Park Square, Milton Park, Abingdon, Oxfordshire OX14 4RN
52 Vanderbilt Avenue, New York, NY 10017

Routledge is an imprint of the Taylor & Francis Group, an informa business

First issued in paperback 2019

British Library Cataloguing-in-Publication Data
A catalogue record for this book is available from the British Library

Library of Congress Cataloging-in-Publication Data
A catalog record for this book has been requested

ISBN: 978-1-138-29266-6 (hbk)
ISBN: 978-0-367-88654-7 (pbk)

Typeset in Times New Roman
by Apex CoVantage, LLC

This book is dedicated to my parents, Johnny González Báez and Carmen Rivera Cruz.

Contents

Contributors

Laurel Abreu is an Associate Professor of Spanish at the Department of Foreign Languages and Literatures at the University of Southern Mississippi, USA. She holds a Ph.D. in Hispanic Linguistics from the University of Florida. Dr. Abreu teaches intermediate and advanced undergraduate Spanish courses, in addition to graduate courses in Spanish and linguistics for the Master of Arts in the Teaching of Languages program. Her research has centered on Puerto Rican Spanish; she also studies second language acquisition from a variationist perspective. Her most recent projects have focused on the pedagogy of linguistics, as well as the creation of community among language learners through social media tools. She has presented at the Hispanic Linguistics Symposium, the American Council on the Teaching of Foreign Languages (ACTFL) Annual Convention, and the Southern Conference on Language Teaching (SCOLT). Her work has appeared in *The Journal of Effective Teaching*, the Selected Proceedings of the 14th Hispanic Linguistics Symposium, *Dimension*, *NECTFL Review*, *Hispania*, and *Foreign Language Annals*.

Jeroen Claes holds a Ph.D. in Hispanic Linguistics awarded in 2014 by the University of Antwerp (Belgium) for a dissertation on the pluralization of presentational *haber* in Caribbean Spanish, which was published with De Gruyter as the monograph *Cognitive, Social, and Individual Constraints on Linguistic Variation*. He has performed extensive fieldwork in Havana, Santo Domingo, and San Juan. He has published articles in leading general linguistics, sociolinguistics, and Hispanic linguistics journals and he is a member of the editorial board of the *Oxford Research Encyclopedia of Romance Linguistics* (Oxford University Press). His current research continues to focus on the variable morphosyntax of (Caribbean) Spanish, but he also explores publicly available corpora, online Big Data, and text mining techniques. Through the study of alternations, he investigates the question as to which cognitive, social, and individual factors shape linguistic variation in general. By investigating this question, he attempts to establish whether the analytical tools provided by Cognitive Linguistics allow us to formulate a psychologically adequate theory of the constraints that govern morphosyntactic variation.

Juan Pablo Comínguez is a full-time faculty member in the Department of Latin American and Iberian Cultures at Columbia University in the city of New York, USA. He obtained his M.A. and Ph.D. in Spanish Bilingualism and Second Language Acquisition, as well as a Certificate in Cognitive Science, from Rutgers University. He conducts research on monolingual and bilingual sentence processing, syntactic and pragmatic variation in Spanish, and second language acquisition and linguistic theory. His research program articulates the domains of theoretical syntax, psycholinguistics, bilingualism, and cognitive science to seek a unitary explanation of native and non-native language variation.

Edward G. Contreras is an instructor at the University of Puerto Rico, Mayagüez and a Ph.D. candidate at the University of South Florida in the field of Second Language Acquisition with Instructional Technology. His current line of research focuses on translanguaging practices and international graduate teaching assistants' language practices at the student and instructor level. In addition, he is collaborating with Dr. Rosita Rivera and is currently co-coordinator and instructor of the Institute for the Teaching and Study of Language and Assessment (ITSLA). Some of his research interests include second language acquisition, computer mediated communication (CMC) and language learning, and the development of ESL and test preparation courses. Contreras's teaching interests include second-year English composition, elevator pitches, incorporation of podcast as a form literature, and compare-and-contrast plays with television adaptation. In collaboration with Dr. Rosita Rivera, Contreras has also created a course titled "English for Science" that focuses on teaching research skills to science majors at UPRM.

Nydia Flores-Ferrán received her B.A. from the University of Puerto Rico and her M.A. at Temple University, USA. She holds a Ph.D. in linguistics from The Graduate Center of the City University of New York, where she specialized in Hispanic linguistics. In particular, her work has centered on variationist socio-linguistic research among Spanish speakers in New York City and New Jersey. In her most recent work, she has also investigated several pragmatic features such as the use of subject pronouns, deixis, and mitigating strategies employed by Spanish speakers. Among her most prominent work is the variable use of subject pronouns in Puerto Rican speakers of New York City. She currently holds a joint appointment at Rutgers University School of Arts and Sciences in the Department of Spanish and Portuguese, where she teaches in the Ph.D. program of Bilingualism and Second Language Acquisition, and The Graduate School of Education, Department of Learning and Teaching, Language Education Program, where she teaches courses in Spanish in context, language in society, introduction of linguistics, etc. She also serves as a member on several doctoral dissertations and chairs research in various aspects of Spanish-speaking communities and Spanish language learners.

Melvin González-Rivera is an associate professor of Spanish Linguistics in the Department of Hispanic Studies at The University of Puerto Rico at Mayagüez. He specializes in Spanish syntax, semantics, pragmatics, and their interfaces.

Kenneth V. Luna was born and raised in Ponce, Puerto Rico. He holds a Ph.D. in Hispanic Languages and Literatures with specialization in Linguistics from the University of California, Los Angeles, USA. He is an associate professor in the Department of Modern and Classical Languages and Literatures, as well as the Department of Linguistics/TESL, at California State University, Northridge, where he teaches phonetics, phonology, acoustics, language and culture, dialectology, Romance linguistics, and historical linguistics. He is also the director of the Barbara Ann Ward Language Center, an Academic Technology Fellow, the campus's Quality Assurance Faculty Lead for Online and Blended Courses and Chancellor's Office liaison, and a mentor for the Clinton Global Initiative University. His research focuses on the phonetics, phonology, and intonation of Spanish and he has published various articles about the Spanish of Puerto Rico. His research interests also include dialectology, Caribbean linguistics, Romance linguistics, historical linguistics, and linguistic typology, as well as the use of technology in the letters and sciences. Before his career in linguistics, Dr. Luna studied Industrial Microbiology at the University of Puerto Rico, Mayagüez. He is fluent in Spanish, Portuguese, and French, and is also a professional in the fields of subtitling, closed captioning, and translation.

Alicia Pousada received her B.A. in Languages and Literature (Honors Program) in 1976 from Hunter College, CUNY, USA, and her M.A. and Ph.D. in Educational Linguistics in 1978 and 1984, respectively, from the University of Pennsylvania, USA. During her career, she has carried out sociolinguistic research in the Puerto Rican communities of North Philadelphia and East Harlem, taught linguistics and language pedagogy in numerous colleges in New York and New Jersey, served as Title VII Bilingual Program Evaluator in New York City public schools, and worked as an ESL Instructor in Adult Basic Education, community college, and private tutoring programs. Since 1987, she has been a professor of linguistics in the English Department of the College of Humanities at the University of Puerto Rico, Río Piedras, and she has directed the Richardson Seminar Room, a graduate research library, since 2007. Her publications and presentations focus on the areas of language policy and planning, multilingualism, and teaching of English as a second language worldwide.

Julia Oliver Rajan teaches Spanish, Hispanic Linguistics, and Spanish for Heritage Speakers at the University of Iowa, USA. She is from Puerto Rico and has dedicated most of her academic research to the linguistic variations and social changes of the coffee zone of her native island. She is currently enhancing a bilingual digital archive about the coffee culture of Puerto Rico called Coffee Zone: Del cafetal al futuro. She has a Ph.D. in Hispanic Linguistics from the University of Illinois at Chicago, where she also coordinated a federally funded project at the College of Education for bilingual children in the Chicago Public Schools. She taught at a variety of national and international institutions prior to arriving at the University of Iowa.

Rosita L. Rivera is a professor in the Department of English at the University of Puerto Rico, Mayagüez Campus, where she teaches ESL and applied linguistics courses. She holds a Ph.D. in Curriculum and Instructions with emphasis in Applied Linguistics from Penn State University, USA. She is a Certified ESL Specialist and designs curriculum and assessment for ESL/ELL courses. She has extensive experience teaching and designing curriculum for bilingual students in different contexts. Her current research interests are in the areas of curriculum development and dynamic assessment in the L2 classroom, non-literal use of language, pragmatics, and discourse analysis. She coordinates the Institute for the Teaching and Study of Language Assessment (ITSLA). As part of the institute, she designs and oversees language instruction for international and local students at the University of Puerto Rico in Mayagüez.

Yolanda Rivera Castillo is a full professor at the University of Puerto Rico, Río Piedras, in the Ph.D. program in Creole languages and literatures. Her main areas of research include Creole languages, prosodic systems, and the phonology-syntax connection. Her research also comprises other areas of inquiry, such as Caribbean Spanish phonology and historical linguistics. She is currently working on the creation of web-based corpora for different Creole languages, such as Papiamentu, Palenquero, and Limonese.

Alma Simounet is Professor of English and Linguistics at the Department of English of the College of Humanities, University of Puerto Rico, Río Piedras Campus, and a member of the teaching staff in the Programa Graduado de Lingüística at the same university. She earned a B.S. in Special Education from the University of Michigan, USA, an M.A. in English from the University of Puerto Rico, and an Ed.D. in Second Language Teaching from Inter-American University. Living in St. Croix, US Virgin Islands, for 30 years has given her access to the socio-linguistic characteristics of the group of Puerto Ricans that moved to this Anglophone island from the Hispanophone Puerto Rican island of Vieques. The lengthy contact with this community became the basis for a number of papers that she presented and published concerning identity, language, culture, language maintenance and loss, among others. She has read papers at international conferences in the Netherlands, Spain, France, Greece, Australia, Cuba, Colombia, Argentina, Chile, Latvia, and the United States in the areas of ethnolinguistics, bilingualism, language and identity, discourse analysis, and intercultural communication. Her published papers reflect the areas mentioned above. At present, she is the Director of the English Department.

M. Emma Ticio is an associate professor in the Department of Languages, Literatures, and Linguistics at Syracuse University, USA. Professor Ticio's research areas are syntax, semantics, and first language acquisition. Her main line of research has focused on the structure of nominal expressions in Romance languages and particularly in Spanish. Among some other topics, she has examined in detail the parallelism between nominal and clausal structure, the possibility of movement in the nominal domain and its locality, the cliticization processes and ellipsis, and the distinction argument/adjunct in nominal expressions. This line of research has led to several papers, book chapters, and conferences on the topic and to a research monograph.

Diane R. Uber is Professor of Spanish Language and Linguistics at The College of Wooster in Wooster, Ohio, USA, where she teaches beginning and intermediate Spanish language, Spanish phonology, the structure of modern Spanish, applied linguistics for language teaching, and a seminar on language, culture, and social identity. She also directs required senior independent study theses on the above topics. She holds a B.A. in Spanish from The College of Wooster, an M.A. in Linguistics from The Pennsylvania State University, and a Ph.D. in Linguistics from The University of Wisconsin-Madison. She has carried out research on topics in sociolinguistics, phonology, morphosyntax, pragmatics, and discourse in the workplace. Her current project deals with forms of address in the discourse of business and in marketing and advertising documents in Latin America and Spain.

Acknowledgements

I would like to thank the panel of scholars who reviewed the chapters and provided valuable feedback for the authors: Catherine Mazak, Juliana de la Mora, Iván Ortega-Santos, J. César Félix-Brasdefer, Sandro Sessarego, Javier Gutiérrez-Rexach, Wilfredo Valentín-Márquez, Julio Villa-García, Daniel Villa, Jennifer Barajas, Rebeka Campos-Astorkiza, Antonio Medina-Rivera, José Camacho, Diane R. Uber, and Michelle Ramos-Pellicia. I also owe a debt of gratitude to all the authors whose works appear in this volume.

Very special thanks to the University of Puerto Rico at Mayagüez (UPRM), the *Centro de Investigaciones Lingüísticas del Caribe* (CILC), and the Faculty of Arts and Sciences at UPRM for their support, which made this publication possible. I also wish to thank Samantha Vale and the publishing team of Routledge for their professionalism and help with the publication of this study.

Introduction

Melvin González-Rivera

The present volume is an edited collection of original contributions that all deal with the idiosyncratic grammatical properties of Puerto Rican Spanish (hereafter PRSp). The issue brings together scholars working on linguistic analyses of PRSp in and outside the island, providing a forum for sharing findings, exploring issues, and keeping us all informed of advances in the fields of Caribbean linguistics and Puerto Rican linguistics. The focus of this edited volume lies primarily, but not exclusively, on the structural aspects of linguistics – phonetics, phonology, morphology, syntax, pragmatics, and language variation – analyzed within a variety of frameworks and methodological approaches. A section on applied linguistics is also included.

In Chapter 1, Julia Oliver Rajan provides an account of vowel raising in the highlands of Puerto Rico. The process of raising mid vowels /e/ to [i] and /o/ to [u] in Puerto Rico is like those found in Spain and other American Spanish dialects, but this distinctive feature has evolved independently from the associations of other languages or dialects in contact. The author argues that vowel raising in Puerto Rico is governed by a lexical rule and this feature is tightly intertwined with the coffee zone, an area in the western mountainous area of the island. She further claims that vowel raising is slowly disappearing because of the physical and social mobility happening in the coffee zone. This drifting is endangering vowel raising, a cultural identifier of this centuries-old community bounded by coffee farming.

In Chapter 2, Yolanda Rivera Castillo describes the mechanisms of hiatus resolution in PRSp within the Optimality Theoretic Framework. The chapter includes a phonetic study of spontaneous speech samples, including six speakers – three men and three women – recorded as part of the PRESEEA project. Hiatus sequences are analyzed for duration and formant height and are compared to individual vocoids as well as to regular diphthongs. Findings indicate that Puerto Rican Spanish resorts mainly to three of the five types of resolution strategies proposed by Casali (1997, 1998): diphthong formation, glide formation, and vowel elision. The study of the second strategy, in the case of mid vowels, provides novel information on Puerto Rican Spanish. These results also demonstrate that, in this variety, markedness constraints are ranked higher than faithfulness constraints that require keeping the same number of segments in the output and that alignment constraints encode restrictions imposed by prominence on hiatus resolution.

In Chapter 3, Kenneth V. Luna examines the allophonic variation of voiceless dental fricative /s̪/ in PRSp. The author proposes an acoustic study of this phoneme with the goal of understanding it better and, at the same time, comprehending its phonology. In this study of the Spanish of Ponce, Puerto Rico, he finds that speakers aspirate /s̪/ consistently in stressed syllabic coda; however, the aspiration undergone by this phoneme is primarily voiced and does not follow voicing assimilation rules. In addition, instead of aspirations, the author consistently finds elisions with compensatory lengthening before voiced obstruents, but not necessarily before sonorants. Furthermore, he provides examples of an additional allophone, rarely documented in PRSp and never before reported in the Spanish of the city of Ponce: a glottal stop [ʔ] (cf. Valentín-Márquez 2006).

In Chapter 4, Juan Pablo Comínguez reports experimental evidence on the existence of non-pronominal preverbal subjects in wh-questions in PRSp. Results show that both preverbal and postverbal subjects are available in the grammar of PRSp speakers, regardless of the status of the wh-operator (argumental versus non-argumental). The syntactic difference between this variety and General Spanish is accounted for in terms of the ways in which C's [uT] is valued by T in the sense of Gallego (2010), which are associated with pragmatic effects. Building on previous research, preverbal subjects are advanced to be topics in PRSp wh-questions.

In Chapter 5, M. Emma Ticio investigates the properties of PRSp lexical subjects and contrasts them with the different properties of these subjects in non-Caribbean dialects. To do so, the study examines the influence of factors such as information structure in PRSp overt subjects. Thus, the study gives us a clearer picture of the overall properties of overt subjects, not only in PRSp and Standard Spanish, but also in our theory of grammar.

In Chapter 6, Laurel Abreu examines the production of subject personal pronouns (SPPs) in spoken PRSp by considering multiple linguistic constraints simultaneously. Along with person and number, switch-reference (i.e., a change in referent from one clause to the next in discourse) has frequently been cited as one of the most important factors in the expression of SPPs by native speakers of Spanish. Another factor group that has been identified as influencing SPP expression in Spanish is priming, or repetition effects. Findings from such studies indicate that speakers are more likely to express an optional subject when the referent differs from the previous one or when the same subject form has recently been produced in the discourse. Results in this study confirm the importance of person and number as a constraining factor in pronominal expression, followed by reference relations, verb tense, aspect, mood, priming, and the presence of a reflexive verb. In contrast to most studies, this study examines the rate of overt SPPs and related underlying constraining factors for a group of speakers outside the well-studied San Juan metropolitan area. Implications are also identified for the analysis of priming effects, which were identified for individual speakers, as well as between interlocutors.

In Chapter 7, Jeroen Claes studies the pluralization of presentational *haber* (*había/habían fiestas* 'there were parties') in PRSp by examining the following cognitive constraints: markedness of coding, statistical preemption, and structural priming. The author briefly introduces these constraints and the way they condition *haber* pluralization and then uses a conditional inference tree model to investigate if and to what extent they interact. Using the conditional permutation of factors in a random forest model of the variation, Claes also determines the relative contributions of the cognitive constraints to explaining the variation. Statistical preemption emerges as the most potent constraint from both procedures. The results suggest that this factor incites speakers to stick to the usage patterns they have observed, whereas markedness of coding and structural priming encourage speakers to extend the agreeing presentational *haber* construction to more and new conceptualizations.

In Chapter 8, Nydia Flores-Ferrán investigates mitigating strategies (e.g., bushes, epistemic disclaimers, parenthetical verbs, and proverbs) in Puerto Rican, Dominican, and Mexican Spanish in an institutional discursive setting using a sociolinguistic-pragmatic lens. The main goal of this study is to determine whether pragmatic variation is evidenced in the discourse of clients who are being treated for depression. Several studies that have investigated mitigation in Spanish have attested to pragmatic variation regarding ways in which mitigation and indirectness are expressed. Given these studies, this study in using a mixed-method approach reveals how mitigation and indirectness are realized. Findings obtained at the macro level point to similar uses of linguistic mitigating strategies among the three dialects and subtle to no pragmatic variation. However, the study reveals that the Puerto Rican clients employ a range of devices while the other two groups tend to exhibit preferences in the use of several strategies.

In Chapter 9, Diane R. Uber examines examples from marketing and advertising documents and signs in Mayagüez, Puerto Rico to illustrate the different usages of *tú* and *usted* geared toward different audiences. Norms of politeness dictate that one should be accommodating toward the addressee. This politeness can be manifest in the form of the respectful, deferential *usted*. Alternatively, politeness also can dictate informal usage (*tú*) toward those sharing equal social status or to show confidence and solidarity toward the consumer in business encounters. Ads directed to business executives, wealthier clients, to mature or elderly people tend to use *usted*, to show respect. *Usted* is also used in signs on store doors and signs issuing direct orders (prohibiting certain activities or behavior). *Tú* tends to be used for public service announcements, ads directed toward local consumers or in-group members, and ads directed toward women, young people, students, or families. Switching between *tú* and *usted* is also found in PRSp, which may be explained by ideological conflicts in Puerto Rico.

In Chapter 10, Edward G. Contreras and Rosita L. Rivera study the use of Spanish and English in text messages by different English level groups at the University of Puerto Rico-Mayagüez Campus. Despite the recent trend in text messaging as a phenomenon, few studies have examined text messaging and language. Network technology has found its way into the language classroom, with recent attention given to incorporating synchronous computer mediated communication technology (CMC), or chatting, into foreign language study. Computer mediated communication via telecommunications technology has been embraced by the youth and young adults and related studies examining the differences in males and females regarding mobile phones have been issued.

In Chapter 11, Alicia Pousada explores the most pressing language policy issues confronting educators in Puerto Rico today, the strategies devised to tackle them, and the persistent problems of implementation and assessment. Among the principal matters discussed are: the development of English proficiency among the students without endangering their native Spanish, the mastery of academic discourse structures (especially written skills) in Spanish, the eradication of functional illiteracy among school dropouts and adults, and the appropriate education of immigrants (e.g., Dominicans and Haitians) and return migrants who utilize language varieties different from those envisioned in the Puerto Rican school curriculum. The article also considers common concerns about the effects of the language contact situation, the concept of "Puerto Rican English," and the prospects for teaching additional foreign languages on the island. Throughout the piece, the need for improved language planning is emphasized.

In Chapter 12, Alma Simounet looks at the origins and characteristics of Puerto Rican Spanish in St. Croix, US Virgin Islands, describes its development and current use, and examines the various factors that have contributed to its maintenance, notwithstanding the plurilingual demographics of the island, the community's long-standing use of English for centuries, the initial rejection to the use of Spanish in school settings, a strong encouragement of the use of English by school officials, and the occurrence of continuous processes of alterity (otherness) directed at the newly arrived foreign language speakers.

Bibliography

Casali, R. F. (1997). Vowel Elision in Hiatus Contexts: Which Vowel Goes? *Language*, 73:3, 493–533.

Casali, R. F. (1998). *Resolving Hiatus*. New York/London: Garland Publishing, Inc.

Gallego, Á. (2010). *Phase theory*. Amsterdam/Philadelphia: John Benjamins Publishing Company.

Valentín-Márquez, W. (2006). La oclusión glotal y la construcción lingüística de identidades sociales en Puerto Rico. In N. Sagarra & A. J. Toribio (Eds), *Selected Proceedings of the 9th Hispanic Linguistics Symposium* (pp. 326–341). Somerville, MA: Cascadilla Proceedings Project.

Phonetics/phonology

1 Vowel raising and identity in the highlands of Puerto Rico

Julia Oliver Rajan

1 Introduction

Vowel raising is a well-known phonological process in Peninsular Spanish and Navarro Tomás (1948) was the first to document its existence in Puerto Rico. This feature has received attention in the last decades by Holmquist (1998, 2001, 2003, 2005) and my own research (2007, 2008), which was the first one to combine impressionistic evaluations with acoustic analysis and sociolinguistic methodologies to evaluate vowel raising in Puerto Rico. Most recently, the island's coffee industry has suffered many economic mishaps as a consequence of hurricanes, climate changes, a debauched government, and an overall weak economy (Oliver Rajan 2016). People in the coffee zone are moving to urban coastal cities where their rural dialect is mocked and the pressure to advance in the new metropolitan environment makes them disregard their distinctive rural dialect. In the western mountainous area of Puerto Rico, which is considered the coffee zone, the mid vowels /e/ and /o/ raise to high vowels [i] and [u] by the people who live and work there. Vowel raising in Puerto Rican Spanish has been historically attributed to a linguistic vestige left behind by Spaniard ancestry; however, I have found that the vowel raising is prompted by a lexical rule affecting the unstressed vowels within a word boundary. Similarly, Barajas (2014) documented that vowel raising in Colongo, Mexico, is due to devoicing of unstressed vowels, which she refers to as the "Weakening Hypothesis." In the Andes, language contact with Quechua and other indigenous tongues seems to affect vowel systems (Guion 2003; Delforge 2008), but this is also attributed to the unstressed vowel devoicing, a phonological pattern shared by Spanish dialects in Mexico and South America.

Vowel raising can also be found in centuries-old vernaculars such as Judeo-Spanish and modern Spanish parlances in the Southwest of the United States. This feature is also common in Peninsular Spanish and other Romance languages found in Italy and Brazil. Even though vowel raising is spread throughout the world, social and topographical isolation are common denominators across languages with this feature. In fact, closed social networks have been noteworthy predictors of increased vowel raising frequencies among communities. In a study on linguistic variations of a rural community in North Carolina, "cultural identity" is an added sociolinguistic aspect involving the speakers' individuality in relation to their local and extended communities (Hazen 2002). In this chapter, I will show that vowel raising in the highlands of Puerto Rico is governed by a lexical rule and it is also a linguistic emblem of the coffee zone's community of practice.

The present chapter provides a detailed description of vowel raising in Puerto Rican Spanish. First, I give an overview of vowel raising in Puerto Rico based on previous research about this topic. Then I offer a summary of the universal tendencies of vowels and how these are connected to vowel raising in general. In the third section, I provide an outline of vowel raising in other Spanish dialects to introduce the theoretical framework involved in the process found in Puerto Rican Spanish. The proposal in Section 4 illustrates that this feature has evolved organically, prompted by linguistic economy. In summation, I postulate that vowel raising might be absent in some individuals, but in those who preserve this feature, it becomes an emblem of identity, connected to a tight community of practice.

2 Vowel raising in Puerto Rico

Navarro Tomás's studies initiated the research associated with vowel raising in the Americas and his inquiry serves as a starting point to better define the developments of vowel raising in the coffee zone of Puerto Rico. In his book, *El Español en Puerto Rico* (1948), he indicates that the people in the western-central mountainous zone of the island tend to raise the final mid vowels /e/ to [i] and /o/ to [u]. He also found that the area with the highest occurrence of vowel raising lies between the municipalities of Ciales and Aguada, which is known as the coffee zone and spans the inner mountainous part of Puerto Rico, as shown by the shaded area in Figure 1.1. Holmquist (1998) confirmed Navarro Tomás's findings when he examined the unstressed word-final mid vowel variables in the recorded speech of 60 farmers in Castañer. He found that raised vowel variants reached 55 percent for front vowel /e/ and 52 percent for back vowel /o/. Holmquist concludes that the raising of mid vowels is not an isolated linguistic feature and it is apparently associated with vowel harmony and other consonantal distinctive characteristics.

Puerto Rican Spanish shares many characteristics with other dialects of Spain. Features such as *seseo*, which is the lack of differentiation between /θ/ and /s/, aspiration of /s/ at the end of syllables, neutralization of syllable-final liquid consonants, *yeísmo* or no distinction between /j/ or /ʎ/, consonant weakening, and elision are some of the features shared with Andalusian Spanish. This is not surprising because the majority of Spaniards who first came to the Caribbean were indeed from the Canary Islands and from the South of Spain, especially from Andalusia. Henríquez Ureña (1921) was the first to document the different Spanish dialects of Latin America and established the origin of each dialect based on the immigration patterns of Spaniards into the New World. He concluded that Puerto Rican Spanish inherits most of its linguistic characteristics from Andalusian Spanish. Yet this hypothesis was not clearly supported by the first research on Puerto Rican Spanish conducted by Navarro Tomás from 1927 to 1933.

Navarro Tomás only concurs with Heríquez Ureña on the fact that Puerto Rican Spanish shares many of the features of the Caribbean Spanish dialect.

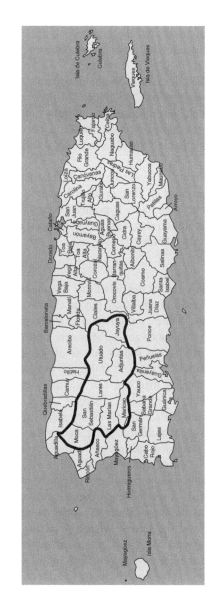

Figure 1.1 Coffee zone of Puerto Rico

Even though there is a tense/lax harmony system in Andalusian Spanish, Navarro Tomas' (1948: 170) findings show a high/mid parameter on unstressed final vowels in the dialect of the west mountainous area. His work identifies two positions that are particularly favorable for high vowel usage: the first one occurs after a preceding stressed high vowel, and the second one after a preceding palatal or high front consonant. Based on this observation, Navarro Tomás wrote:

> no existe aún ninguna demostración convincente de que las modificaciones fonéticas en que se asemejan el andaluz y el hispanoamericano se produjeran en Andalucía antes que en América. La hipótesis más acertada parece ser la que considera tales cambios como resultado de una evolución que fue operándose de manera coincidente y simultánea en los dos campos mencionados.

> there is still no convincing evidence that the phonetic changes that Andalusian and American Spanish have produced were in Andalusia before they were in America. The most likely hypothesis seems to be that such changes are a result of an evolution that was being operated simultaneously and by coincidence in these two fields.

> (1948: 196)

Navarro Tomás not only rejects the belief that one dialect is solely responsible for the linguistic variation in Puerto Rico, but he also disagrees with the general credence of homogeneous dialect zones. Heríquez Ureña proposes that Spanish in America is divided into five major zones: Mexican, Caribbean, Central, Andino, and Platense. Yet Navarro Tomás shows that small geographical areas such as the tiny island of Puerto Rico (which is 100 miles long and 36 miles wide) can have more linguistic diversity than one can fathom. Further research confirms this diversity across Puerto Rico. Vowel raising is one of the many phonological characteristics of a Spanish dialect full of history and dynamic changes propelled by a rapid social and physical mobility among Puerto Ricans.

In a former analysis on vowel raising in Puerto Rico (Oliver Rajan 2007), a total of 986 tokens were raised out of 6,900 words: 427 from /e/>[i] and 559 from /o/>[u]. These results were derived from 69 interviews in which 29 females and 40 males participated. Vowel raising frequencies in this study indicate that mobility turned out to be the most influential social factor affecting this phonological feature. Gender had the second biggest impact on vowel raising in this area: older- and middle-aged women in general displayed more vowel raising than men. Males have had more physical mobility in this area, while women tend to stay local, thus preserving the vowel raising feature of the area and passing it on to younger generations. Traditionally, coffee picking has been a man's occupation, but now with new roads the coffee zone has easier access to coastal towns providing the men with better-paying jobs. In the absence of men, older- and middle-aged women have taken the role of coffee pickers, which has reinforced the local dialect. However, the migratory patterns of this zone in the past two decades is making younger women search for different paths aside from the traditional role of wife and mother. Labov (1994) determined that women tend to lead sound changes that are not stigmatized; as such, women who have lived in urban areas understand that vowel raising is a stigmatized feature, which explains their decreased vowel raising frequencies when compared to men who have been out of the coffee zone. Females in the coffee zone are the ones leading this change: those who stay in the coffee zone preserve vowel raising and those who move away reject it.

3 Vowel raising and the universal tendencies of vowels

The Origins of Vowel System created by DeBoer (2001) explains the general patterns of vowel systems in human languages. This is a large inventory of phonemes with 451 samples of the world's languages. Of the 921 segments, 652 are consonants, 180 are vowels, and 89 are diphthongs. In the case of vowels, [i] appears in 87 percent of the languages, [a] in 87 percent, and [u] in 82 percent; in contrast, vowels [y], [œ], and [ɯ] appear in only 5 percent, 2 percent and 9 percent of the languages, respectively (DeBoer 2001: 8). The vast majority of vowel systems conform to the Vowel Dispersion Principle, which states that vowels have the tendency to be evenly distributed in the perceptual space or within the limitations of a particular language (Lindblom 1986). In other words, a vowel system that has [e] most probably will have a back counterpart [o]. Some languages do not follow the aforementioned principle and their vowel systems are called *defective*. An example of a defective vowel system is one containing [e a u]. Here the mid front vowel /e/ and the high back vowel /u/ have no match in the opposite space. In the Phonological Segment Inventory Database of UCLA, approximately 14 percent of the vowel systems are defective. According to Ashby and Maidment (2005) the most commonly missed vowels are [e], [o], and [u]. High frontal vowel [i] and low-central [a] are more likely to occur than [e], but mid frontal [e] and mid back [o] are more likely to occur than the high back vowel [u].

In summary, quantum vowels [a], [i], and [u] proliferate in most languages because these have a significant distance between them and create a clearer perception of sounds, making these three vowels sort of a template for most languages. The majority of languages from around the world start with the basic [a], [i], and [u] system and then add other vowels; reversing the normal action of the lips creates [ɛ], [æ], [c] and [ɑ], but most languages do not have these secondary cardinal vowels. According to Roca and Johnson (1999) one plausible reason for the prevalence of the quantum vowels could be that they are easier to articulate. However, minimizing articulatory effort cannot be the only consideration for the selection of sounds in languages; if this was the case then vowels [a], [i], and [u] would be in all languages universally, but there are some languages such as Pirahã, Ubykh, and Arrernte having [a], [i], and [o]. Still, the consensus is that vowels [a], [i], and [u] are almost universal and there is a tendency to have reduced complex vowel systems neighboring these three.

3.1 Vowel raising in Romance languages

Llorente (2001: 12) uses Advanced Tongue Root [ATR] to explain the parasitic harmony among vowels in the evolution of Spanish. The forward movement of the tongue root is captured by the distinctive feature [ATR]. An [+ATR], or tense vowel, will have more pharyngeal space, and a lax vowel, or [-ATR], will have less space in the pharyngeal area. In Latin, only [-ATR] stressed vowels diphthongized, creating the following pattern:

(1)   i← e← ɛ ← a ɔ→ o → u

As shown in (1), the formation of a vowel system from Latin to Spanish has had a tendency to raise vowels. Llorente (2001: 185) indicates that more or less any Proto-Spanish vowel, except for /a/, was raised by a form of *yod*.

This tendency of eliminating vowels is universal. Martinet (1955) says that vowel systems have functional economy, and it is reflected in the way they shift in the oral cavity to preserve the capacity to distinguish words. Labov (1994) maintains that there are three universal principles of vowel shifting: long vowels rise, short vowels fall, and back vowels move to the front. The latter principle has to do with the physiology of the human oral cavity and the symmetric pattern of vowel systems. Martinet (1955) states that the front articulatory space has four degrees of height and the natural behavior of vowels will be to arrange the same degrees in the back. However, there is limited space in the back and the overcrowding vowels will move to the front. This type of behavior among vowels has been stable in the progression of Spanish: central vowel /a/ in Vulgar Latin changed to /e/: *lacte* > *leche* 'milk', and mid back vowel /o/ moved to a /u/: *multum* > *mucho* 'a lot'. Similar changes in the vowel systems of other Romance languages have been observed. Bisol (1989) states that languages originated from Latin have shown a long history of variation in the unstressed mid vowels /e/ and /o/. Her study on the Gaucho dialect of the Brazilian state of Rio Grande do Sul suggests that stress has an important role in the phonological system of this dialect. She concludes that the process of vowel harmony in the Gaucho dialect involves raising of the pretonic mid vowels when a high vowel occurs in the immediate following syllable, as in *pepino* [pepínu > pipínu] 'cucumber'. When a stressed vowel assimilates to the postonic vowel, it creates a pattern of height harmonies or metaphony.

Penny (1969) was among the first to study the harmonic pattern between vowels caused by the [+/- high] features across the word domain of the Pasiego dialect of Spain. Penny reserves the term metaphony to indicate the harmony process initiated by the final, high, and non-stressed vowel in a word domain. Penny (2002) later concludes that the trigger of metaphony in Pasiego is a word-final high vowel. For example, in the word *lobo* [lóβu] ~ [lúβu] 'wolf', the final vowel causes metaphonic raising of the tonic vowel. Metaphony could be also a morphological process. For example, final /o/ marks the masculine plural of count nouns such as *pelo* [pélo] 'hair' versus *pelos* [pélu] ~ [pílu] 'hairs'. A morphemic vowel raising process is also observed by Barnes (2013) in Asturias, Spain. In this Spanish dialect the masculine singular suffix /-o/ has a tendency to raise to [-u] and the feminine plural -/as/ advances to [-es] most of the time. Holmquist (1998) has also found results similar to Penny's and Barnes's when he studied a community of farmers in Castañer, Puerto Rico. He found that high final vowels are relatively rare outside the nominal and verbal categories, but other studies on American Spanish dialects (Oliver Rajan 2008; Barajas 2014) were unable to find a strong indication that morphological categories control vowel raising. Likewise, Hualde (1998) argues that metaphony in Lena Bable is a phonological process rather than an alternation induced purely by a grammatical category.

Vowel raising is found not only in Spanish dialects: other Romance languages such as Vedeto and Grado, which are both Italian dialects, have shown this phonological feature. These two dialects have a metaphonic pattern in which the final, high and non-stressed vowel extends its features to the stressed vowel or vowels in a word (Maiden 1991). In Vedeto, high postonic vowels cause raising in height in stressed mid vowels /e/ and /o/. This indicates that vowels with the dorsal features [+/-high] are sensitive to their position in the domain. Maiden (1991) also indicates that in Veneto and Grado the postonic syllables govern the prosodic domain. Metaphony in Veneto is associated with 'rural speech' and these vowel variations are not found in urban cities such as Venetia.

A similar process is observed in the Judeo-Spanish dialect of Monastir, in modern-day Macedonia, and the conversations of Judeo-Spanish speakers in New York. In the analysis of these two records, Luria (1930: 99–100) finds that pre-tonic vowels /e/ and /o/ were raised as follows: *decir > dizir* 'to say' and *comer > cumer* 'to eat'. He also indicates that mid final vowels tend to raise in open syllables or after consonants /s/ or /n/. Lax vowels are also observed in similar environments in Sanders's (1998) study on some plural nouns and verbal forms in Andalusian Spanish, a dialect with aspiration of /s/ in the coda location; similarly, Puerto Rican Spanish also has aspiration and deletion of /s/ in coda position. Even though my earlier study on vowel raising in Puerto Rico does not show a strong correlation between raised vowels and the grammatical category of words, it shows that 21 percent of vowel raising was for the back mid vowel /o/ in a setting of mostly open syllables (Oliver Rajan 2008). However, Lipski (1990: 1) indicates that "reduction and elision of unstressed vowels is frequent in Andean Spanish, particularly in contact with /s/". On the other hand, Barajas (2014) found that in Colongo, Mexico, the syllable type (open/closed) was not a substantial pointer of vowel raising for /e/. Barajas's (2014: 232) interpretation of these results is that /e/ is in a further advanced stage of the raising process than /o/ and "it is less sensitive to the influence of external and internal factors". Further research linked to the vowel raising in American Spanish dialects is needed to demonstrate any relationship between morphological or word categories.

3.2 Vowel raising in the Americas

Shifts in vowel quality are also found in Colombia, Dominican Republic, Mexico and the Andean region. Garrido (2007) observes raised vowels as a resolution in hiatus contexts in Colombian Spanish. This diphthong formation [e.o] > [jo] is common in most Spanish dialects, especially in rapid speech. Roca (1991: 609) designed the Syllable Merger Rule as shown in (2) to explain this process:

(2)

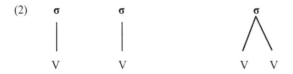

In slow speech, vowels tend to be realized in hiatus. In casual or rapid speech, the merger rule in (2) occurs following both universal and language-specific sonority guidelines as illustrated in (3):

(3)   a. *te hundió*   t[ju]ndió   'he/she sank you'
      b. *lo hiló*   l[wi]ló   'he/she spun it'
      c. *porque Ana*   porqu[já]na   'because Ana'
      d. *peor*   p[jó]r   'worst'

D'Introno, Del Teso, and Weston (1995: 218–222) summarize the process in (2) with two rules:

(4)   [mid] → [+high]/ {_____$ V   or   V $_____
                                  [+stress]   [+stress]

(5)   V → G/{ _____ V   or   V _____
              [+high]   [+high]

Rule (4) indicates that an unstressed syllable final mid vowel becomes high when it is next to a stressed vowel. Then this [+high] vowel becomes a glide when it is next to another vowel. Both rules, (4) and (5), apply at the postlexical level within a phono-logical word or between words in a phonological phrase. Rules (4) and (5) basically depend on the speech rate in which the phonological utterance is made by the speaker.

On the other hand, Hutchinson (1974) indicates that there is no need for order-ing rules in this process. She proposes an analysis based on phonetic evidence in which contiguous vowels undergo vowel sandhi. According to Hutchinson, vowel sandhi occurs in part to comply with the CV syllable structure, but this is dependent on the type of speech style used. Syllable-timing is independent from stress but is dependent on speech style and it varies from careful to casual. In the former, the speaker pays attention to whatever he or she is saying, but in a casual style, the speaker's attention is minimal. Willis (2008) shows that in the casual speech of Dominican Spanish, the atonic /e/ and /o/ overlap with the high vowels /i/ and /u/. Similarly, Bullock, Toribio, and Amengual (2010) have studied the post-tonic vowel reduction via raising in rural Dominican Spanish. A comparable vowel overlay is present in the southwestern region of San Juan de la Maguana in Dominican Republic and Cibaeño Spanish (R. Núñez-Cedeño, personal communication, May 15, 2007). Yet research related to the production and perception of vowel raising in the Dominican Republic needs additional developments.

Hasegawa (1979), Ramsaran (1978), and Siptár (1991) maintain that speaking styles are highly correlated with the social demands and the situation that the speaker has with the listener rather than speed. In cases of language contact, a speaker's first language (L1) can affect the production of the second language (L2), and this pattern as shown by Flege, Bohn, and Jang (1997) is dependent on personal experiences and social interactions. Vowel differences are also observed in Chicano Spanish in the United States, pointing to vowel deletion in casual or allegretto speech (Salcedo 2010). In a similar study, Willis (2005) also found that the /u/ in Southwest Spanish speakers is more forward compared to Mexican Spanish. Diverse Spanish dialects from different areas demonstrate that vowel quality can be affected by the speaker's speech style.

Vowel quality, reduction, raising, and ultimately elision have been documented by Lipski (1990), Guion (2003), Delforge (2008), and O'Rourke (2010), among others. Quechua (in most of the Andes) and Kichwa (in Ecuador) have a vowel system of three /i, a, u/. Guion (2003) compared the vowel systems of simultaneous and late Kichwa and Spanish bilinguals in Ecuador and found that simultaneous and early bilinguals have a five vowel system in Spanish, while late and mid bilinguals have a tendency to reduce Spanish vowels to [i, a, u]. While the link between vowel raising and social identity among speakers is observed in most of the presented studies, there are differences in the phonological rules leading this feature depending on the dialectal variation. Barajas (2014) found that vowel raising in Colongo, Mexico is due to a *weakening process* proposed in her "Weakening Hypothesis" that affects the vowel quality. In the same way, Delforge (2008: 122) and Lipski (1990: 13) conclude that vowel raising is governed by a model of feature geometry called unstressed vowel devoicing (UVD) and unstressed vowel reduction (UVR), respectively. These processes of reduction occur mainly in Spanish dialects where final /s/ or /s/ in a coda position is preserved as those in Andean and Mexican varieties. Delforge (2008) indicates that Mexican and Andean UVR have a tendency to weaken mid vowels /e/ and /o/ when consonant /s/ is in coda position. Lipski (1990: 6) affirms that vowel /e/ is more affected in this model because "UVR occurs when the Place node associated with the front vowel is delinked from its Root node, and linked to the Root node of /s/." Lipski also found that UVR is more constant in closed syllables than in open syllables. In Cusco, the same pattern is observed, but Delforge (2008) wonders if the UVD of mid vowels is caused either by the contact with Quechua or by an independent evolution of vowels in Spanish. I can also attest that vowel raising in Puerto Rico has evolved independently in this community of practice and it is considered a symbol of rurality or *hablar jíbaro*, which means "country talk". The term *jíbaro* in Puerto Rican Spanish usually refers to a person from the countryside or the mountains, and occasionally it is also used as a synonym for *puertorriqueñidad* or "being a very proud Puerto Rican".

Lipski (1994: 321) also notes that vowel "neutralization" between mid and high vowels across the Andean region is highly stigmatized and "it is above the level of awareness", making it a social trademark among speakers. This negative stigma is also observed in Puerto Rico when people from urban coastal areas associate the distinctive feature of vowel raising with rurality. López Morales (1983) confirms differences between the Spanish of people from San Juan and of those from rural regions. He states that it is not unusual to hear people from San Juan or other parts of the island mocking people from Lares (see Figure 1.1) when they say: *La genti di Larih toma lechi di poti*, 'People from Lares drink canned milk.' Furthermore, Barajas (2014: 222) also found that "speakers in closed networks have had little exposure to other dialects of Mexican Spanish and may not be aware of the possible stigma associated with vowel raising." In Puerto Rico, participants in Oliver Rajan's (2008) study mentioned that people from urban coastal areas tend to mock the way they speak with the popular phrase cited by López Morales (1983), but they only noticed these differences when they were out of the coffee zone. Other interviewees who have lived in urban areas for long periods of time said that when they talked to friends and family from the coffee zone, their *hablar jíbaro* reappears, ratifying a sense of pertinence and belonging through language.

4 High vowels in the highlands of Puerto Rico

Both Navarro Tomás and Holmquist indicate that vowel raising rates occurring in final position are more frequent when the neighboring consonant is a palatal as shown in (6):

(6)   a.   *ocho*/óʧo/ → [óʧu] 'eight'
      c.   *puño*/púɲo/ → [púɲu] 'fist'
      d.   *amarillo*/amaɾíjo/ → [ãmaɾíju] 'yellow'

Final vowels also have the tendency to raise when /a/ is the stressed vowel: *padre* [páɖɾi], *carro* [káRu] 'car', *brazo* [bɾásu] 'arm'. Holmquist (1998:75) finds that variation seldom occurs in adverbs such as *últimamente* 'finally'; in discourse, pauses using *dónde* 'where'; *pero* 'but'; or *este* 'this'; and in the neutral pronouns *eso* 'that'. However, Navarro Tomás contradicts these findings when he documented various individuals in the town of Ciales (see Figure 1.1) who raise the final vowel in demonstratives used as pronouns, such as: *ése* [ési] 'that' and *éste* [ésti] 'this'. Most of Navarro Tomás's and Holmquist's examples are words with two syllables, but I have also found evidence of vowel raising in previously unexplored contexts including articles, clitics, pre-tonic position, closed syllables, and polysyllabic words such as: *después* [dih.pwéh] 'after', *de agua* [djá.ɣwa] 'of water', *el saco ese* [il.sà.kwé.si] 'that bag', and guayánd**o**lo [gwa.ján̩.du.luh] 'shredding them' (Oliver Rajan 2008: 201–204). Similar findings occur in

Peninsular Spanish, and example (7) taken from Hualde (1989: 795) shows vowel raising towards the left and the right:

(7) *el miedo* /el miédo/ → [il mjéu̯] 'the fear'

Example (7) shows that height spreads to the left and suggests that height harmonies can be bidirectional. On the other hand, Hualde (1989) says that if the spreading of [+high] were bidirectional there will be examples such as *el húmedo* *[il úmiḍu] 'the wet', and this does not occur in Peninsular dialects. This phonological word raises only in the article and in the unstressed final mid vowel such as *el húmedo* [il úmeḍu]. The same pattern is observed in Puerto Rico and I have hypothesized that vowel raising in the coffee zone of Puerto Rico is formed by the application of a lexical rule as shown in (8):

(8) Stress Dependent Vowel Raising Rule (SDVRR)

$$V \rightarrow [\text{+high}]/ \quad \perp \#$$

$\quad$[-low]　　　　　Σ

$\quad$[+ATR]

$\quad$[-stress]

The rule above indicates that unstressed mid vowels will raise in the last foot of a word, consistent with the results of vowel raising in American Spanish dialects and in Spain. The rule in (8) shows that unstressed mid vowels raise when they are located in the last metric foot of a word domain and Σ indicates a metric foot as used by Roca and Johnson (1999). The metrical model to assign stress comes from Hayes's (1995) Uneven Syllabic Trochee theory, and the framework to explain vowel raising in Puerto Rican Spanish is based on the theories of Lexical Phonology (Mohanan 1982). More evidence that vowel raising is a lexical rule can be found in Antworth (1991), and Bye (2011: 164) adds that, "Raising, which doesn't look beyond the word for its context, is lexical."

Derivation (9) shows that the proposed rule in (8) is a cyclic rule that raises the unstressed mid vowel on the last metric foot of the lexicon. Postlexical rules such as aspiration of /s/ will affect the original form. The rule presented in (8) can also predict vowel raising in tokens with clitics such as verb [gwajáⁿduluh] 'shredding them':

(9) [[guaja][ndo]] [[lo][s]]
Lexical stratum
Level I

[[guája][ndo]] [[lo][s]]	Stress assignment
(*　*)	
*	
[guajándo] [[lo][s]]	Affixation of gerund and de-accenting rule
[guajándo] [[lo][s]]	Metric re-footing
(*)(*　*)	
*	
[guajándu] [[lu][s]]	SDVRR

Level II

[guajándu] [lus]   Affixation of plural /s/

_____   SDVRR

Level III

_____   SDVRR

Postlexical stratum

[guajándulus]   Affixation of clitic /los/

[guajánduluh]   Aspiration of /s/

[gwajánduluh]   Gliding

[gwajáṇduluh]   Surface form

The SDVRR rule raises the unstressed mid vowel placed in the last metric foot of a word. As shown in derivation (9), direct object pronouns (as well as indirect object pronouns) are often found in Spanish as enclitics. Clitics are treated as independent categories and they are later attached to the main word at the postlexical level to become one-word phrases. Examples such as *guayándolos* are actually phrases in the same way that *me dice* and *díceme* 'he/she says to me' are phrases (J. Guitart, personal communication, October 7, 2007). In derivation (9) both the clitic and the derived verb are treated as separated words in the lexical stratum. It is only at the postlexical level that clitics can arise syntactically as a one-word phrase.

Compound words work differently compared to cliticized verbs or one-word phrases. Kenstowicz (1994: 222) indicates that, in Spanish, compound words such as *hierbabuena* 'peppermint' composed of noun *hierba* 'grass' and adjective *buena* 'good' are formed in Level III, as shown in derivation (9). Each word has an independent paroxytone stress; however, in Level III the word boundaries among them disappear. The compounding action triggering the de-accenting rule that erases the stress of *hierba* /iérba/ toward the rightmost segment is proof of this process. As indicated by Mascaró (1976), when a stressed affixation is added, the stem loses its stress and the rightmost accent surfaces. In the case of *hierbabuena*, the compound is considered headless because the adjective is not transferring its characteristics to the noun; it is creating a new word with a different meaning. On the other hand, in a compound word such as *camposanto* 'cemetery', *campo* 'field' receives sacred characteristics from the adjective on the right *santo* 'saint' (Núñez Cedeño 1991: 592). According to the proposed rule (8), vowel raising could be possible in both the noun and the adjective of *camposanto* such as [kàmpusáṇtu] because both elements are separate words and have the environment for SDVRR to be applied in Levels I and II. As opposed to compound words, enclitics can only arise at the postlexical level.

5 Vowel raising and identity in the coffee zone

Vowel harmony is not one of those features that shows up only in rapid speech or in other stylistically governed phenomenon (Anderson 1980). In Puerto Rico, this happens to be the case: vowel raising in the coffee zone occur in both careful and casual speech. The conversation samples in (10) were extracted from an interview with a woman from the coffee zone who talks about her supernatural beliefs and how she predicted her mother's death. Dialogue (10a) was taken from the first 10 minutes of the interview and (10b) after 45 minutes.

(10) a. Que venían para adentro por las . . . y cosas así. Que las brujas salían de noche.
      'That they used to come inside by the . . . and things like that. That the witches used to come at night.'
      [ke.βe.ní.an.pa'.**ðéṉ.t̞u**.pol.lah.i.kó.sah.a.sí.ke.lah.βrú.hah.sa.lí.aṉ.de.**nó.ʧĩ**]

      b. Yo cuando oigo las gallinas cantando . . . cacareando. Digo: "Se va a morir alguien." Y al minuto . . . cuando la mamá mía se murió.
      'When I hear the hens singing . . . cackling. I say: "Someone is going to die." And a minute went by . . . when my mother died.'
      [ʝ̑jo.kwáṉ.dói̯.yo.lah.ya.jí.nah.**kaṉ.táṉ.du.ka.ka.rjáṉ.du.dí.yu**.se.βá.mo.rí.lál.yjen.jal **mĩ.nú**.tu.kwáṉ.do.la.mã.má.mí.a.se.mu.rjó]

One can see that there is no significant difference between the tokens raised in the first 10 minutes and the last minutes of the conversation. Therefore, vowel raising could be considered a local characteristic, and in the case of this interviewee, part of her linguistic range. This is further exemplified by the participant's obliviousness about the negative stigma that vowel raising has outside this mountainous area. The woman in example (10) answered questions about the language of her area and she did not know that vowel raising was "bad Spanish", as she expressed. Therefore, the interviewee in example (10) employs this feature to conform to this community of practice and I hypothesize that vowel raising is her emblem of belonging to the coffee zone.

Eckert and McConnell-Ginet (2003) state that everyday performances build up stable social routines and one person's way of speaking could eventually become the rule in that particular community. The language used by a particular community is shaped by many extralinguistic variables, such as social class, education, economic background, ethnicity, gender, age, speech style, religious beliefs, or political ideas. Barajas (2014: 223) notices that for people who leave Mexico (to work in the United States) and return back, vowel raising appears to become "a way of reasserting his Colongo identity after having been away for so many years". Likewise, for those who have lived outside the coffee zone, vowel raising in Puerto Rico seems to reiterate a person's rural identity or connection with the coffee industry. However, almost a decade ago, vowel raising was disappearing among younger generations due mostly in part to the rapid physical mobility to other coastal areas. Further investigation on how this feature has changed over time is currently in progress and available through a digital archive (Oliver Rajan 2016). Newer inquiries will provide a clear interpretation of vowel raising as part of the social identity within the coffee zone.

6 Summary

Phonological theories alone are not sufficient to interpret vowel raising in the coffee zone of Puerto Rico. Linguistics systems become alive when people use them to create their communities and their way of life. I have shown that there is no particular rule that can largely explain vowel raising in all the dialectal varieties of Spanish. Each parlance has other progressions that are elicited by following sounds, previous consonants, speech style and a sum of social factors. Still, vowel raising in the Americas as well as in Spain has the tendency to reduce a five vowel structure to a more discerning and economical three vowel system. Even though the processes governing vowel raising in the presented Spanish dialects can be slightly different, there is a continuous and undeniable pattern: vowel raising becomes an identifier by outsiders, and a membership tool for insiders in a community of practice.

Bibliography

Anderson, S. R. (1980). Problems and perspectives in the description of vowel harmony. In R. M. Vago (Ed.), *Issues in vowel harmony* (pp. 1–48) Amsterdam: John Benjamins.

Antworth, E. L. (1991). *Introduction to two-level phonology*. Retrieved from SIL International: http://www-01.sil.org/pckimmo/two-level_phon.html.

Ashby, M., & Maidment, J. (2005). *Introducing phonetic science*. Cambridge: Cambridge University Press.

Barajas, J. (2014). *A sociophonetic investigation of unstressed vowel raising in the Spanish of a rural Mexican community* (Doctoral dissertation). Retrieved from https://kb.osu.edu/dspace/handle/1811/59931

Barnes, S. (2013). *Morphophonological variation in urban Asturian Spanish: Language contact and regional identity* (Doctoral dissertation). Retrieved from https://etd.ohiolink.edu/pg_10?0::NO:10:P10_ACCESSION_NUM:osu1371475793

Bisol, L. (1989). Vowel harmony: A variable rule in Brazilian Portuguese. *Language Variation and Change, 1*, 185–98.

Bullock, B. E., Toribio, A. J., & Amengual, M. (2010). Reduction ad absurdu(m): Posttonic phrase final vowel reduction in rural Dominican Spanish. Paper presented at the *14th Hispanic Linguistics Symposium*, Indiana University Press, Bloomington.

Bye, P. (2011). Derivations. In N. C. Kyla, B. Botma & K. Nasukawa (Eds.), *The Bloomsbury Companion to Phonology* (pp. 135–173). New York: Continuum International Publishing Company.

DeBoer, B. (2001). *The Origins of Vowel Systems*. Oxford: Oxford University Press.

Delforge, A. M. (2008). Unstressed vowel reduction in Andean Spanish. In L. Colantoni & J. Steele (Eds.), *Selected Proceedings of the 3rd Conference on Laboratory Approaches to Spanish* 260 *Phonology* (pp. 107–124). Somerville, MA: Cascadilla Proceedings Project.

D'Introno, F., Del Teso, E., & Weston, R. (1995). *Fonética y fonología actual del español*. Ediciones Cátedra: Madrid.

Eckert, P., & McConnell-Ginet, S. (2003). *Language and Gender*. Cambridge: Cambridge University Press.

Flege, J. E., Bohn, O., & Jang, S. (1997). Effects of experience on non-native speakers' production and perception of English vowel. *Journal of Phonetics, 25*, 437–70.

Garrido, M. (2007). Diphthongization of Mid/Low Vowel Sequences in Colombian Spanish. In J. Holmquist, A. Lorenzino, & L. Sayahi (Eds.), *Selected Proceedings of the Third Workshop on Spanish Sociolinguistics* (pp. 30–37). Somerville, MA: Cascadilla Proceedings Project.

Guion, S. G. (2003). The vowel systems of Quichua-Spanish bilinguals. *Phonetica*, *60*, 98–128.

Hasegawa, N. (1979). Casual speech vs. fast speech. In P. R. Clyne, W. F. Hanks, & C. L. Hofbauer (Eds.), *Papers from the Fifteenth Regional Meeting of the Chicago Linguistic Society* (pp. 126–137). Chicago: Chicago Linguistic Society.

Hayes, B. (1995). *Metrical stress theory*. Chicago, IL: University of Chicago Press.

Hazen, K. (2002). Identity and language variation in a rural community. *Language*, *78*(2), 240–257.

Henríquez Ureña, P. (1921). Observaciones sobre el español de América. *Revista de Filología Española*, *8*, 357–90.

Holmquist, J. (1998). High lands-high vowels: A sample of men's speech in rural Puerto Rico. In C. Paradis, D. Vincent, D. Deshaies, & M. LaForest (Eds.), *Papers in Sociolinguistics: NWAVE-26 a l'Université Laval* (pp. 73–79). Quebec: Université Laval.

Holmquist, J. (2001). Variación vocálica en el habla masculina de Castañer, PR. *Cuaderno internacional de estudios hispánicos y lingüística*, *1*, 96–103.

Holmquist, J. (2003). Coffee farmers, social integration and five phonological features: Regional socio-dialectology in West-Central Puerto Rico. In L. Sayahi (Ed.), *Selected proceedings of the first workshop in Spanish sociolinguistics* (pp. 70–76). New York: Cascadilla Proceedings Project.

Holmquist, J. (2005). Social stratification in women's speech in Rural Puerto Rico: A study of five phonological features. In L. Sayahi (Ed.), *Selected proceedings of the first workshop in Spanish sociolinguistics* (pp. 109–119). Somerville, MA: Cascadilla Procedings Project.

Hualde, J. I. (1989). Autosegmental and metrical spreading in the vowel – harmony systems of northwestern Spain. *Linguistics*, *27*, 773–805.

Hualde, J. I. (1998). Asturian and Cantabrian metaphony. *Rivista di Linguistica*, *10*, 99–108.

Hutchinson, S. (1974). Spanish vowel Sandhi. In A. Bruck, R. A. Fox, & M. W. La Galy (Eds.), *Papers from the Parasession on natural phonology* (pp. 109–119). Chicago, IL: Chicago Linguistic Society.

Kenstowicz, M. (1994). *Phonology in generative grammar*. Oxford: Blackwell.

Labov, W. (1994). Principles of linguistic change: Internal factors (Vol. 1). Oxford: Blackwell.

Lindblom, B. (1986). Phonetic universal in vowel systems. In J. Ohala, & J. Jaeger (Eds.), *Experimental phonology* (pp. 13–44). New York: Academic Press.

Lipski, J. (1990). Aspects of Ecuadorian vowel reduction. *Hispanic Linguistics*, *4*, 1–19.

Lipski, J. (1994). *Latin American Spanish*. London & New York: Longman.

Llorente, L. (2001). Vowel raising in Spanish historical phonology: A feature geometry analysis. Muenchen: Lincom Europa.

López Morales, H. (1983). *Estratificación social del español de San Juan de Puerto Rico*. Editorial Universitaria: Universidad Nacional Autónoma de México.

Luria, M. A. (1930). A study of the Monastir dialect of Judeo-Spanish based on oral material collected in Monastir, Yugo-Slavia. New York: Instituto de Las Españas en Los Estados Unidos.

Maiden, M. (1991). Interactive morphology: Metaphony in Italy. New York: Routledge.

Martinet, A. (1955). *Économie des changements phonétiques*. Berne: A. Francke.

Mascaró, J. (1976). *Catalan phonology and the phonological cycle* (Doctoral dissertation). MIT Press, Cambridge, MA.

Mohanan, K. P. (1982). *Lexical phonology* (Doctoral dissertation). MIT Press, Cambridge, MA.

Navarro-Tomás, T. (1948). *El español en Puerto Rico: Contribución a la geografía lingüística hispanoamericana*. Puerto Rico: Editorial Universitaria, Universidad de Puerto Rico.

Núñez-Cedeño, R. (1991). Headship assignment resolution in Spanish compounds. In H. Campos & F. Martínez-Gil (Eds.), *Current studies in Spanish Linguistics* (pp. 447–473). Georgetown University Press.

Núñez-Cedeño, R. (2007, May 15). Personal communication.

Oliver Rajan, J. (2007). Mobility and its effects on vowel raising in the Coffee Zone of Puerto Rico. In J. Holmquist, A. Lorenzino, & L. Sayahi (Eds.), *Selected proceedings of the third workshop on Spanish sociolinguistics* (pp. 44–52). Somerville, MA: Cascadilla Proceedings Project.

Oliver Rajan, J. (2008). *Vowel raising in Puerto Rican Spanish* (Doctoral dissertation). Retrieved from ProQuest http://gradworks.umi.com/33/16/3316757.html

Oliver Rajan, J. (2016). *Del cafetal al futuro/From the Coffee Fields to the Future*. Retrieved from http://coffeezone.lib.uiowa.edu

O'Rourke, E. (2010). Dialectal differences and the bilingual vowel space in Peruvian Spanish. In M. Ortega-Llebaria (Ed.), *Selected proceedings of the 4th conference on laboratory approaches to Spanish phonology* (pp. 20–30). Somerville, MA: Cascadilla Proceedings Project.

Penny, R. (1969). El habla pasiega: Ensayo de dialectología montañesa. London: Tamesis Books Limited.

Penny, R. (2002). *A history of the Spanish language*. Cambridge: Cambridge University Press.

Ramsaran, S. M. (1978). Phonetic and phonological correlates of style in English: A preliminary investigation (Doctoral dissertation). London, England: University of London.

Roca, I. 1991. Stress and Syllables in Spanish. In H. Campos, & F. Martínez-Gil, F. (Eds.), *Current Studies in Spanish Linguistics* (pp. 599-635). Washington: Georgetown University Press.

Roca, I., & Johnson, W. (1999). *A course in phonology*. Oxford: Blackwell Publishers.

Salcedo, C. S. (2010). The phonological system of Spanish. *Revista de Lingüística y Lenguas Aplicadas, 5*, 195–209.

Sanders, B. P. (1998). The Eastern Andalusian vowel system: Form and structure. *Rivista di Linguistica, 10*, 109–135.

Siptár, P. (1991). Fast-speech processes in Hungarian. In M. Gósy (Ed.), *Temporal factors in speech: A collection of papers* (pp. 27–62). Budapest: Research Institute for Linguistics, Hungarian Academy of Science.

Willis, E. (2005). An initial estimation of Southwest Spanish vowels. *Southwest Journal of Linguistics, 24*(1&2), 185–98.

Willis, E. (2008). No se comen, pero sí se mascan: Variación de las vocales plenas en la República Dominicana. Paper presented at the *XV Congreso Internacional de la Asociación de Lingüística y Filología de América Latina (ALFAL)*. Montevideo, Uruguay.

2 Hiatus resolution in Puerto Rican Spanish and language typology

Yolanda Rivera Castillo

1 Hiatus resolution in Spanish

Hiatus resolution consists on reorganizing adjacent vowels belonging to different syllables as a tautosyllabic group, or a diphthong (Carreira 1991). Casali (1997: 497–8) identifies five types of hiatus resolution among languages, as shown in the following examples: (a) diphthong formation, or "syllabifying the two vowels into the nucleus of a single syllable" (1a); (b) glide formation, or a situation in which "the first of two adjacent vowels surfaces as a glide" (Casali 1998) (1b); (c) vowel elision (1c); (d) epenthesis (1d); and (e) coalescence, or "the replacement of a vowel sequence by a third vowel sharing features from both original vowels" (1e):[1]

	Language	Initial sequence		Hiatus resolution
(1a)	Ngiti:	izo ɔkʊ	→	i.zo̳o̳.kʊ ('reed sugarcane')
(1b)	Igede:	gu ɔba	→	gwɔ̳.ba ('wave a mat')
(1c)	Igede:	da eɲi	→	de̳.ɲi ('to rain')
(1d)	Axininca:	no n pisi̳ i̳	→	nom.pi.si̳.tiu ('I will sweep')
(1e)	Anufɔ:	fa i	→	fɛ̳ɛ̳ ('take it')

Senturia (1998: 20–21) adds labialization and palatalization to this list. For the most part, Casali's description applies to syllabification across morphological boundaries. However, these strategies also apply to morpheme internal vowel groups. Languages resort to hiatus resolution mainly to eliminate onsetless syllables and comply with Onset constraints.

A phonological hiatus in Spanish includes combinations of two non-high vowels or a non-high vowel plus a stressed high vowel, rendering an onsetless syllable beginning with the second vowel. Hiatus resolution eliminates the onsetless syllable and, in many cases, leads to glide formation. It does not introduce novel phonemic distinctions between different types of vowels since vowels and glides do not constitute different phonemes. Only in a handful of cases in which a morpheme boundary separates vowels into different feet, such as in *pjá.ra/pi.á.ra*, a distinction between these segments seems to play a phonemic role (Roca 1997: 234, 251–252; Rosenthal 1994). However, following Hualde (1999), we argue below that these glides are positional variants of vowels and that syllable or morpheme boundaries correlate to the distribution of vowel allophones. There are also allophonic alternations between vowels, palatals, and glides according to positional and morphological restrictions: *creía, creyó* (not **crejó*); *él i Pedro, yo i él; rej/reyes* (Espinosa 1930: 58). In some varieties, glides are interchangeable with laterals and trills in post-nuclear position (Dominican Spanish), they can change the point of articulation of a preceding or following consonant (palatalization and velarization), and substitute intervocalic voiced palatals (Southwestern US Spanish).

Malmberg (1965: 26) indicates that, historically, groups of vowels followed by consonants become falling diphthongs, but groups including a glide followed by another vowel in syllable initial position become a consonant+vowel group (Torreblanca 1989). Harris (1980, 1985) has discussed similar phenomena in Modern Spanish (MS). Hiatus resolution has been attested historically as well. It is also subject to great register and diatopic variation. In fact, it generally, but not always, indicates differences between formal and vernacular registers.

In Puerto Rican Spanish (PRSp), hiatus resolution applies, as shown below, morpheme internally [(2a)-(2c)] and across morpheme boundaries [(2d)-(2e)], and includes the following strategies: (a) diphthong formation (requiring stress shift) (2a); (b) glide formation [(2b), (2c) and (2d)] (sometimes requiring a shift in stress position); and (c) vowel elision (2e) (for mid vowels with the same feature value for [±back]):[2]

	Initial sequence		Hiatus resolution
(2a)	pe.rí.o.do	→	pe.rjo.do ('period')
(2b)	a.é.re.o	→	a.é.reo ('airborne')
(2c)	o.cé.a.no	→	o.cja.no ('ocean')
(2d)	pelear	→	peljar ('to fight')
(2e)	kré.e	→	kré ('she/he believes')

Glide formation operates in three ways: (a) mid vowel shortening (2b); (b) stress shift followed by vowel raising (2c); and (c) raising the first vowel in a set of non-high vowels.

There is a strong preference for rising diphthongs in this variety. In fact, in the case of two mid vowels (2b), the first mid vowel might be raised too: a.é.rjo. Since early studies, such as Navarro Tomás's (1948) description of PRS, it is evident that glide formation targets the first vowel in a group. Indeed, if the second vowel is higher than the first, there is hiatus preservation (Navarro Tomás 1966: 55): "A hiatus is more resistant to change when the order of vowels constitute a falling sequence: *cae, traen, comae, tocao*."[3]

Other vernacular varieties, such as New Mexican Spanish, have cases of stress shift (3a) resulting in diphthong formation, glide formation (3b), vowel raising (3c), vowel elision (3d), and epenthesis (3e) (Espinosa 1930: 97):[4]

	Standard Spanish		Vernacular Spanish
(3a)	pa.ís	→	pájs ('country')
(3b)	te.á.tro	→	teá.tro ('theater')
(3c)	ko.é.te	→	kwé.te ('rocket')
(3d)	kré.e	→	kré ('she/he believes')
(3e)	ka.ér, ve.a, pú.a, desnú.o	→	ka.yér, ve.ya, pu.ya, desnu.yo

Jenkins (1999: 19–20) indicates that, in New Mexican Spanish, the deletion of the first vowel also applies to a set of homorganic vowels such as /ou/ and /ei/.[5]

Hiatus resolution applies also across word boundaries as well in Spanish for groups of two vowels. This is called *sinalefa* by traditional grammars (Bakovic 2007):

(4a)	mi amigo	→	mja.mi.go ('my friend')
(4b)	mi hebra	→	mjé.bra ('my hair strand')
(4c)	mi obra	→	mjó.bra ('my creation')
(4d)	pague ocho	→	pa.gjó.cho ('pay eight')
(4e)	porque a veces	→	por.kja.ve.ces ('because sometimes')

In sequences of three vowels, these are tautosyllabic if the vowel in the middle is lower than the vowels on the group edges (Quilis & Fernández 1982: 150; Núñez-Cedeño & Morales Front 1999: 187):

	Tautosyllabic	Heterosyllabic
(5a)	/eae/ área espada	/aoa/ esta o aquella
(5b)	/eai/ muerte airada	/aie/ apaga y enciende
(5c)	/iou/ sitio umbroso	/euo/ siete u ocho

Vowel height is a key element in determining syllabic organization and an important component of our analysis. Also, stress plays a role in hiatus conservation across word boundaries. Souza (2010:2) provides examples of conservation when one of the vowels is stressed:

(6a)	se áman	→	se.á.man ('they love each other')
(6b)	comí otro	→	co.mí.o.tro ('I ate another one')

Chitoran and Hualde (2007: 57) find a correlation between duration and stress, such that we should expect those sequences of hiatus involving stressed syllables to have longer duration than diphthongs and other hiatus sequences with unstressed components.

In the case of Spanish, although hiatus resolution has been typically associated with Vernacular Spanish, it is also attested in formal varieties. Matluck's study (1994: 286) indicates that it is frequent among speakers of formal varieties of Spanish ("hablantes cultos") at the word level, and across word boundaries with a total of 54 percent resolution, and 46 percent hiatus conservation. There is a lower percentage of resolution among groups of mid vowels as compared to the case of vowels of different height, but it still comprises a large percentage of cases (40 percent). Moreover, speakers of formal registers typically reject diphthongization word-internally (*sinéresis*), but they produce diphthongs across word boundaries (Matluck 1994: 283).[6]

On the other hand, cases of stress shift resulting in diphthong formation are attested in numerous dialects, including Peninsular Spanish (Lapesa 1986: 479–80). Similar alternations are attested in Bogotá, México, Chile, Aragón, Andalucía, and Buenos Aires, and other dialects (Navarro Tomás 1977; Espinosa 1930; Rosenblat 1930).

The next section includes a description of the conditioning features for hiatus resolution. It also summarizes some of the analyses of this phenomenon from previous studies.

1.1 Glides and vowels

Based solely on height, and according to standard Spanish syllabification, there are 14 diphthongs in the language, including: (a) [+high] and [-high] vowels {ai, ia, ei, ie, oi, io, au, ua, eu, ue, ou, uo}; and (b) [+high] and [+high] vowels {iu, ui}. In traditional descriptions, diphthongs comprise one nuclear element and a non-nuclear [+high] vocoid on the right or left edge of the nucleus. This chapter proposes that the non-nuclear component is [-low] instead of [+high] in PRSp. Vowel height determines the selection of edges (glides) or nuclei. Casali's (1998: 125) Standard Height Theory proposes two height distinctions, which would accommodate PRSp nuclear vowels, as shown in Table 2.1:

Table 2.1 Height distinctions according to Standard Height Theory (Casali 1998)

	+high	i u
	-high	e o
Low		a

Only the vowels in the highlighted cells can constitute glides in PRSp. Glides include high and mid vowels, since the latter might occupy the same position as glides in a shortened vowel group, as shown below. Quilis (1981), Aguilar (1999), and Face and Alvord (2004: 561) demonstrate that hiatus sequences are longer than diphthongs in other varieties of Spanish. Face and Alvord (2004) also demonstrate that speakers perceive accurately the difference between hiatus and diphthongs.

Phonetically, glides have less lip rounding or tongue height than nuclear vowels. Their features include a change or shift in formant height during phonation and short duration with respect to the nucleus. In prenuclear position, in onsetless syllables, these become approximants with perceptible friction, unlike nuclear vowels (Núñez Cedeño & Morales Front 1999: 31).

From a phonological perspective, Spanish glides are not consonants, unlike English /j/ and /w/, since these exhibit positional restrictions, such as never being placed in onset position.[7] Among structural components of the syllable, glides only occur as members of vocalic clusters, never as part of onset or coda clusters in Spanish (Martínez-Celdrán 2004: 206): "On the other hand, Spanish does not admit consonant groups in syllable onset, except for those formed by a stop or [f] plus {l, r}, so [sj] cannot be a syllable onset group."

Senturia (1998) discusses the problems associated with using only phonetic criteria to distinguish glides from vowels. Indeed, Senturia (1998: 9) recognizes "that vowels and glides are similar, except for duration (and perhaps some degree of constriction)". In diphthongs, Quilis and Fernández (1982: 65) define glides as the non-nuclear vowel with less articulatory energy in the group. These are phonetic correlates associated to positional differences. This interpretation is supported by the fact that morphologically related words might exhibit glide/nuclear variants of the same vowel. There are alternations between tautomorphemic glides and vowels in lexemes related by inflectional processes (Senturia 1998: 183): *ma-ú-lla/maw-ll*ar. Moreover, Cressey (1978: 27–28), following Navarro Tomás (1977: 67), indicates that /e/, and /o/ can be analyzed as non-high glides (/o̯/, /e̯/).

Our study does not describe hiatus conservation. Lexical specifications can override postlexical restrictions across morpheme boundaries in the case of vowels prespecified as nuclear components, such that diphthongization (or hiatus resolution) does not apply. Examples follow in Table 2.2 for combinations of non-high vowels and high vowels in some dialects that do not constitute diphthongs (Bakovic 2007; Colina 1999: 122–123; Hualde 1999; Quilis & Fernández 1982: 71, Harris 1980):

Table 2.2 Canonical hiatus at morpheme boundaries

With prefix	*With suffix*	*Compounds*
a-unar	afectu-oso	boqui-abierto
anti-ácido	defectu-oso	electro-imán
auto-inducido	actu-al	estado-unidense
contra-indicación	usu-al	franco-hispano
intra-uterino	virtu-al	mani-atar
pluri-empleado	jesu-ita	mono-usuario
pre-universitario	pi-ar	veinti-uno
re-unificar		
semi-experto		
sobre-humano		

These have the structure of a hiatus with two adjacent nuclear vowels. These stems, disyllabic prefixes and stressed suffixes, behave as phonologically autonomous units, such that the contiguous vowels at morpheme edges belong to different syllables. In the case of compounds, these originate in combinations of independent lexemes. Each component is a PWord and, therefore, has an autonomous foot structure, which explains hiatus in these cases. On the other hand, it is possible to apply contrastive stress to the listed affixes in Table 2.2. This contrastive stress assignment suggests that these are phonologically autonomous affixes.

Hualde (1999) has indicated that Spanish restricts the presence of glides (*w+V) before morphological boundaries. In other languages, bound morphemes exhibit phonological independence as well. Prefixes can carry pitch accent or stress in focused structures (Wennerstrom 1993: 313; Raffelsiefen 1999). For example, Raffelsiefen (1999) proposes that, historically, stressed prefixes in English meet Minimal Word Requirements.

Quilis (1981: 179) provides some minimal pairs with stressed and unstressed vowels at morpheme boundaries (Stressed [+high]V and Unstressed [+high]V), and morpheme internal unstressed glides (Unstressed [+high]G):

	Stressed [+high]V	Unstressed [+high]V	Unstressed [+high]G
(7a)	pí-e	pi-é	pjé
	'that it chirps'	'I chirped'	'foot'
(7b)	fí-e	fi-é	fjés-ta
	'that he lay-away it'	'I lay-away it'	'party'

In some cases, a phonological hiatus (8a) has reflexes in derivationally related words, even if stress position supports the structure of a diphthong (8b):

(8a) dí.a 'day'
(8b) di.á.rio 'daily'

Still hiatus resolution is possible at morpheme boundaries in other cases (Bakovic 2007), although it is not the preferred context for it. Resolution applies only if the second vowel is stressed. In fact, stress is an important component of syllabification. A stressed [+high] vowel never constitutes a glide in a vowel group, such that it is always syllabified in a different syllable:

(9a) rí.o   versus   *río   ('river')
(9b) a.í   versus   *aí   (*ahí*, 'there')
(9c) bú.o   versus   *búo   (*búho*, 'owl')
(9d) ba.úl   versus   *baúl   ('chest')

The facts discussed above suggest that vowels and glides do not constitute different phonemes. As indicated by Colina (1999), glides are variants of regular vowels. She proposes that there is correspondence between stressed and unstressed [+high] vowels, and between vowels and glides.

In Sections 2 to 2.2, we demonstrate that duration and formant distance distinguishes traditional hiatus from diphthongs in PRSp. The data also show that some hiatus groups exhibit durations that are not significantly different from that of traditional diphthongs in PRSp, indicating that the latter have undergone hiatus resolution. Cases of hiatus resolution including only mid vowels and diphthongs display similar duration. Likewise, formant distance is significantly different between etymological diphthongs and hiatus groups. Mean formant distance is also very similar between etymological diphthongs and cases of resolution. We believe that this shows that PRSp resorts to vowel shortening and modulation in formant transition to create novel types of diphthongization with mid vowels.

Finally, we demonstrate that differences between glides and vowels, especially in the case of mid vowels, depend on constraints on possible vowel sequences and on the requirement that syllables have onsets. These constraints (Section 3.1–3.3) eliminate the need for the partial prespecification of syllable structure (Hayes 1989, 1990; Hualde 1991; Harris 1995; Roca 1997) or the use of features such as [±syllabic] to distinguish vowels from glides.

2 Data analysis

This phonetic analysis includes spontaneous speech samples from six Puerto Rican speakers recorded through the PRESEEA project (Morales & Ortiz López 2001) in 1996. The group includes three female and three male speakers selected from recordings of spontaneous speech samples with the lowest noise levels. This project follows a standard methodology, and all interviews were conducted in familiar settings for speakers.

For this chapter, the set of speakers included: one speaker per generation/gender (only three generations included in PRESEEA) and two schooling levels per gender. Due to the noise levels in some recordings, we had to limit the set of interviews used for this analysis. Including the same number of females and males is important in the study of phonetic features, as indicated by Himmelman and Ladd (2008: 265).[8]

Unlike other studies, which include reading samples as well as spontaneous speech samples (Aguilar 1999; Garrido 2007), this study only includes spontaneous speech samples. Due to the nature of spontaneous speech data, we cannot predict the number of tokens that speakers would produce. In the case of this study, with only six speakers, there are 178 tokens in the sample: 48 monophthongs, 56 diphthongs, 64 cases of hiatus (22 diphthongs resulting from diphthong and glide formation), and 10 cases of vowel elision. We selected diphthongs and monophthongs in stressed syllables only, which further reduced the number of tokens. By measuring stressed forms only, we avoid the effect of stress on the duration of vowel groups (Chitoran & Hualde 2007). In the case of hiatus, at least one vowel would constitute the nucleus of a stressed syllable. Since previous studies have demonstrated significant differences in duration between diphthongs and hiatus (Quilis 1981; Aguilar 1999; Face & Alvord 2004), our main goals are to provide evidence that:

(10a)   there are significant differences between the duration of diphthongs and hiatus in PRSp, as shown for other dialects;

(10b)   reduced groups of mid vowels or reduced sequences of mid low vowels (where the mid vowel is first) and diphthongs are comparable in duration;

(10c)   in some combinations of /a/ and a stressed [+high] vowel, there is vowel shortening (hiatus resolution) due to stress shift;

(10d)   groups of identical vowels, where the first vowel is stressed, undergo reduction;

(10e)   differences in formant distance match differences in duration between hiatus and cases of hiatus resolution.

In fact, smoother formant transitions between vowels and shorter duration than a regular hiatus co-occur in 22 vowel sequences in the data. Sets of individual vowels and vowel sequences have been analyzed for duration and formant frequency and transition. Garrido (2007) found the same differences in duration in other varieties of Caribbean Spanish. She found no significant differences in duration between sequences of mid vowels (/eo/) and etymological diphthongs (/jo/) in pretonic position in Caribbean Spanish; while she found significant differences for Andean speakers (Garrido 2007: 33). Garrido (2007: 33) also measured first formant height in groups of mid low vowels (/eo/) and found that Caribbean speakers exhibited a lower F1 than Andean speakers, indicating that /e/ has values closer to those of high vowels (/i/), suggesting that there is diphthongization in /eo/ groups. Our analysis determines formant transition between vowels instead of differences in absolute formant values between vowels and glides. We aim to compare the formant transition in cases of etymological diphthongs versus hiatus. We compare these transitions also to formant height variation within single vowels.

This chapter compares the duration of individual vowels to that of lexical diphthongs, diphthongs resulting from hiatus resolution, and hiatus. Vowel duration measurements were performed based on auditory identification and the visual inspection of formants, using the PRAAT software.

The formant analysis includes PRAAT listing of formant values at 20 percent and 80 percent of the vowel and vowel group duration. This is a standard way of comparing diphthongs and monophthongs, since formant movement starts at about 30 percent of segment duration. The analysis includes calculating the distance in formant movement using a formula for the absolute Euclidean distance between the nucleus 1st and 2nd formant values and the offglide/onglide values. Monophthongs typically show no considerable differences in values since there is minimal formant movement. A diphthong exhibits considerable differences but less than a comparable hiatus given the fact that coarticulation operates within the vowel group.

Final results for duration and formant transition are compared with an analysis of variance (one-way ANOVA calculated with SPSS).

2.1 Results from data on PRS: duration

According to Romeo (1968: 43), vowel duration distinguishes diphthongs from hiatus: "The diphthong is realized only when one of the two vowels is short and weak in relation to the other and is under the M-point (muscular tension)." Experiments on diphthong identification with synthetized vowel groups (Bond 1978) also indicate that glide duration is a determining factor in the identification of diphthongs versus hiatus in English.[9] Finally, there are no tense/lax phonemic distinctions in Spanish, so duration does not correspond to these differences. Tenseness is partly subordinated to stress and intonation contours (Navarro Tomás 1917: 371). In fact, Spanish vowels are described as generally tense (Quilis 1981; Navarro Tomás 1917a, b; Núñez Cedeño & Morales Front 1999: 31). We propose that differences in duration indicate whether a group is tautosyllabic or not.

Souza (2010: 72) has found a correlation between speech rate and the duration of vowel groups. We have not included speech rate in our study. However, Souza's (2010: 73) study also shows that vowel sequences in highly frequent lexical items exhibit longer duration. Given the nature of our data, the lexical items included in our study are vernacular forms.

After completing all duration measurements, we divided the group of etymological hiatus into two groups based on mean duration measurements (Tables 2.3 and 2.4). Mean vowel duration in our data provides evidence of these differences, with closer durations between lexical diphthongs and diphthongs resulting from hiatus resolution:

Table 2.3 Mean durations diphthongs versus hiatus in ms

Diphthong	Hiatus	Hiatus resolution
112.86	227.42	120.73

Groups of identical mid vowels (stress in the first vowel), two mid vowels and a mid vowel followed by a low vowel, and stress shift from a high to a low vowel exhibited shorter duration. Similarities in duration between single vowels (monophthongs) and some hiatus groups with identical vowels also showed interesting results:

Table 2.4 Mean durations vowels and vowel sequences in ms

Vowel	Hiatus resolution =Monophthong
58.16	74.8

Differences between these monophthongs (74.8ms) resulting from resolution and hiatus sequences (227.42ms) are even greater. However, identical vowel reduction only applied when the first vowel was in a stressed syllable: *cré.e* → *cré*.

The results show that there are statistically significant differences between groups $(F(1,182) = 187.80)$, $p = .000$. A Tukey Post-Hoc test indicates that differences in duration between diphthongs and hiatus are significant ($p \geq .000$). The same results apply when the data include hiatus and diphthongs resulting from vowel raising and vowel reduction ($p \geq .000$), but not when lexical diphthongs and diphthongs resulting from resolution are compared ($p \geq 1.00$). All vowel groups have significantly longer duration than single vowels: (a) vowels-diphthongs ($p = .008$); (b) vowels-hiatus ($p = .000$); and (c) vowels-hiatus resolution ($p = .049$).[10] However, differences are not significant when single vowels are compared to single vowels resulting from identical vowel reduction ($p = .996$).

There were no differences associated with the effect of intrinsic vowel duration. Typically, /a/ is longer than other vowels. As indicated by Delattre (1969), in vowel reduction, Spanish vowels are stable and show minimal differences.

These results are consistent with descriptions from previous studies. Stressed diphthongs are longer than stressed monophthongs (Navarro Tomás 1917: 407). Moreover, a sequence of two adjacent vowels with no glides is significantly longer than a sequence with a glide. Quilis (1981: 176–188) shows that the proportion between [ua], [wa], and [ba] is 6:2:1; and that the transition between vowels in a diphthong like [wa] is different from cases in which a vowel such as [u] precedes [a]. The same applies to sequences with /i/. For Spanish, in heterosyllabic sequences, a high vowel shows longer duration than glides in tautosyllabic sequences (Quilis 1981: 181): hacja/hací.a, and cwatro/situ.ado. This is also the case for sequences in which both vowels are high (Quilis 1981: 176–184): vjuda/di.urno. Aguilar's (1999) study shows similar results.

For example, for Speaker 2, the hiatus /a.í/ in the word *ahí*, 'there', has a duration of 256ms, while this sequence in cases of stress shift (/áj/) has a duration of 193ms. The following figures illustrate differences in duration between the hiatus (Figure 2.1) and the diphthong, and the reduction of the glide (Figure 2.2):

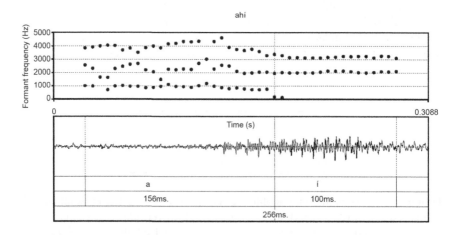

Figure 2.1 Lexical hiatus in *ahí*, 'there'

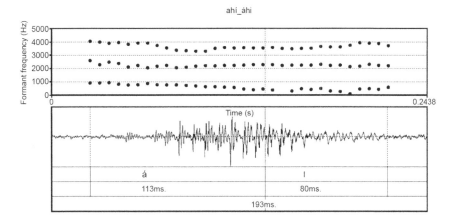

Figure 2.2 Stress shift for *ahí*, 'there'

It is interesting to notice that the stressed /a/ in Figure 2.2 is shorter than the unstressed /a/ in Figure 2.1. This is evidence that /a/ is the only syllabic component in the first case, while it is one of two components in the rhyme in Figure 2.2.

The data on duration support the descriptions in (10a) through (10d). Vowel reduction, stress shift, and vowel raising in the data result in shorter durations comparable to those of lexical hiatus. The following section describes data on formant distance.

2.2 Results data on PRS: formant distance

The same tokens were compared for formant distance. We measured the height of the first and second formants for each vowel in vowel groups and for single vowels as well. The transition between two components in the diphthong should produce greater numbers in terms of the Euclidean distance than those obtained from single vowels. Likewise, the transition in a hiatus group should show greater differences than in the case of a diphthong because the transition between vowels in the hiatus is more abrupt.

The results show that there was a statistically significant difference between groups as determined by a one-way ANOVA analysis *(F(1,160) = 142.10), p = .000)*. A Tukey Post-Hoc test indicates that differences in formant distance between diphthongs and hiatus are significant. However, there are no significant differences between hiatus and diphthongs resulting from vowel raising and vowel reduction. These results suggest that hiatus resolution triggers vowel shortening but not the same degree of coarticulation attested in lexical diphthongs.

On the other hand, mean formant distance indicates that lexical diphthongs and diphthongs resulting from hiatus resolution have similar values, as seen in Table 2.5:

Table 2.5 Mean formant distance in vowels and vowel sequences

Vowel	Hiatus resolution-monophthong	Hiatus	Diphthong	Hiatus resolution
219.5	130.80	354.04	302.10	310.90

These are still closer in mean formant distance than hiatus and diphthongs. Differences in formant distance between all vowel groups and single vowels are significant, including those monophthongs resulting from resolution.

The data analyzed indicate that PRSp speakers distinguish hiatus from diphthongs with regard to duration and formant distance. However, those diphthongs resulting from resolution are significantly different from hiatus groups regarding duration but not with respect to formant distance. Therefore, the data do not support the statement in (10e). It seems that the main phonetic correlate of hiatus resolution is shorter vowel duration. However, the analysis of a larger set of data is necessary to confirm these results.

These phonetic results correspond to system internal constraints on vowel groups and syllabic constituency. The following sections (3 and 3.1) describe the interaction of constraints and restrictions that license these vocalic sequences.

3 An account of syllabification of contiguous vocoids

The spontaneous speech data analyzed in this chapter provides evidence of the three strategies described in Section 1.1, above: (a) diphthong formation (requiring stress shift) (11a); (b) glide formation, including vowel raising [(11b) – (11e)] (sometimes requiring a shift in stress position); and (c) vowel elision (11e) (for mid vowels when the second vowel is unstressed):

(11a)	di.rí.a	→	di.rjá
(11b)	ma.es.trí.a	→	maes.trí.a
(11c)	cré.o	→	creo
(11d)	á.re.a	→	á.rja
(11e)	cré.o	→	créw
(11f)	lé-e	→	lé

Stress shift (11a) places stress on the lowest element among contiguous vowels. Similarly, reduction[11] [(11b) and (11c)] and raising [(11d) and (11e)] select the highest and/or unstressed component in a group. If two contiguous vowels have the same height, the unstressed vowel undergoes reduction or raising (11f).

On the other hand, vowel elision applies when a vowel in second position is unstressed if both vowels share three feature-values (12a) to (12c) ([±high, ±low, ±back]). It does not apply when the second vowel has a different value for back [(12b) and (12d)] or if it is stressed [(12e) through (12h)]. The data also show elision in lexical diphthongs comprising vowels with the same feature-value for [±back] (13):

(12a)	cré.e	→	cre
(12b)	cré.o	→	creọ
(12c)	maní.es	→	manís
(12d)	mangó.es	→	mangós
(12e)	cre.ér	→	cre.ér (not *crér)
(12f)	cre.í	→	cre.í (not *crí)
(12g)	cre.é.mos	→	cre.é.mos (not *crémos)
(12h)	cre.ó	→	cre.ó (not *cró)

(13)	experịencia	→	experẹncia

Vowel elision is conditioned by the vowels' feature specifications and by stress position.

All these conditioning features determine which sequences undergo resolution and which do not. The constraints described below must account for:

(14a) structural restrictions to avoid onsetless syllables [(11a)-(11f)];
(14b) positional restrictions requiring that nuclei are first in sequences of mid vowels;
(14c) OCP restrictions against sequences of identical vowels (11f);
(14d) height restrictions to raise the highest vowel in a group [(11d) & (11e)].

This analysis concurs with previous analyses concerning the role ONSET plays in hiatus resolution. Hiatus sequences include onsetless syllables that violate this constraint (McCarthy 1993; Boroff 2003; Bakovic 2006). Therefore, ONSET is highly ranked in PRSp. Our constraint-based account includes constraints that have been provided by previous descriptions:

(15) ONSET (Prince & Smolensky 1993): syllables must have onsets.

(16) DEP$_{IO}$ (Baird Senturia 1998: 80): every segment of the output has a correspondent in the input (no epenthesis).

(17) MAXμ: do not delete input morae (Keer 1999: 10).

Consonant insertion is not a preferred option in PRSp; therefore, DEP$_{IO}$ is highly ranked as well. MAXμ restricts the application of vowel deletion, a resolution strategy that applies only to sequences of identical or nearly identical vowels. Both DEP$_{IO}$ and MAXμ are faithfulness constraints, while ONSET is a markedness constraint.

We need a constraint that requires the presence of glides among tautosyllabic vowels. Only head components (nuclei) in the syllable bear main stress, so glides must be unstressed due to positional restrictions. Glides are on the right side of the following ranking of headhood and saliency:

(18)   [+low]   << [-low, -high]   << [-low, +high]
       /a/   << /e, o/ ∧ /e̜, o̜ /   << /i, u/ ∧ /j, w/

There is preference for non-low vowels as glides, in non-nuclear position. In the examples provided above [(11a) and (11d)], /a/ is always in nuclear position, never an edge component. We need to include a constraint that licenses variation of high glides (/j, w/) with mid glides (/e̜, o̜ /), as attested in the data [compare (11d) and (11e)]:

(19)   GLIDEHOOD (Casali's 1998: 29): a glide must be [-low] and either [front] or [round]

This constraint originates in Casali's (1998) GLIDEHOOD constraint, which requires glides to be non-low and either [front] or [round]. The data analyzed indicates that there is variation in cases of vowel raising, so raised vowels alternate with mid glides. This constraint, along with ONSET, licenses a stress shift since the [-low] vowel in a group should be a glide, and the [+low] vowel, the nucleus. Stress is always assigned to nuclei, not to rhyme edges.

Finally, we have to account for positional restrictions. In a group of vowels, the nuclear component is always lower than the edge component in Spanish. Additionally, there is a preference for the reduction or deletion of the second component in groups of vowels of equal height. In these cases, we need an alignment constraint as well as a restriction on groups of identical vowels. Vowel elision only applies under identity but it is conditioned by the position of stressed vowels [see example in (11e)]. Bakovic (2006) proposes a restriction on sequences of identical vowels resulting in long vowels: NoLONG. It originates in Keer's (1999: 118) NoLONGVOWEL constraint:

(20)   NoLONGVOWEL: do not have a surface long vowel

Spanish does not have long vowels and there is no coalescence either. This constraint accounts for vowel deletion but it does not account for the positional restrictions in cases of deletion, so we need an alignment constraint:

(21)   NUCL1RSTMIDVS [ALIGN -V_1[-high, -low]V_2[-high, -low] (V_1, N)]: in tautosyllabic sequences of mid vowels, the nuclear vowel is the first

The first component in groups of identical vowels must be the nucleus. This explains why the first vowel is stressed in tautosyllabic sequences of identical vowels. This constraint also applies to phrasal domains in Spanish since there are other cases of vowel elision with identical vowels across word boundaries: *está hablando* ◊ *establándo*.

These constraints provide the mechanisms to select candidates in cases of stress shift, vowel reduction, vowel raising, and vowel deletion. We provide the ranking that licenses two examples of stress shift below: one traditional shift from vernacular varieties (*perí.odo*◊ *perjódo*) and one attested in the data from PRSp (*dirí.a*◊ *dirjá*):[12]

Tableau 1a Stress shift

CANDIDATE	Dep_{io}	Onset	GlideHood
+pe.rjó.do			
pe.río.do			*
pe.rí.o.do		*	
pe.rí.yo.do	*		

Tableau 1b Stress shift

CANDIDATE	Dep_{io}	Onset	GlideHood
+di.rjá			
di.ría			*
di.rí.a		*	
di.rí.ya	*		

The winning candidate is the one that complies with the glide restriction and ONSET. In the case of vowel reduction (shortening), the data exhibits reduction in combinations of two [-low, -high] vowels:

Tableau 2 Vowel reduction

CANDIDATE	Dep_{io}	Onset	GlideHood
+creo̯			
créo			*
cré.o		*	
cré.yo	*		

As in the case of stress shift, *creo̯* does not violate the glide restriction and ONSET.

When the mid vowel undergoes vowel raising, there is no violation of the highest ranked restrictions either. "Correspondence" relations (Colina 1999) can explain the association between vowels of different height given that some form of lexical redundancy statements complements the correspondence constraint. However, the mid short and high vocoid alternate in this variety:

Tableau 3 Vowel reduction and raising

CANDIDATE	Dep_{io}	Onset	GlideHood
créw			
créǫ			
créo			*
cré.o		*	
cré.yo	*		

We propose that there is no winning candidate in the case of *crew* and *créǫ*.

There are two additional constraints that play a role in explaining vowel elision in groups of identical mid vowels: NoLong and Nucl1rstMidVs.

Tableau 4 Vowel elision

CANDIDATE	Dep_{io}	Onset	GlideHood	Nucl1rstMidVs	NoLong	Maxμ
+cré						*
créę					*	
creę́				*	*	
cree			*		*	
cré.e		*				
cré.ye	*					

Finally, the following constraint ranking describes hiatus resolution in PRS:

(22)   Dep$_{io}$ <<Onset << GlideHood << Nucl1rstMidVs << NoLong << Maxμ

4 Conclusions

The data analysis and phonological description suggests that the most important difference between vernacular and formal registers is the ranking of Onset. This constraint must be lower in the ranking for speakers in formal contexts. On the other hand, the phonetic data suggests that PRSp does not have systematic resolution and that some resolution strategies might be optional, such as vowel raising.

This chapter proposes that the main difference between vowels and glides is the position each one occupies in the syllable. By default, non-nuclear vowels are shorter than nuclear vowels. This is a subphonemic difference that licenses the correct syllabification of segments in different registers and across morpheme boundaries. A distinction based on positional restrictions allows us to eliminate the need for mechanisms such as partial prespecification of syllable structure (Hayes 1989; Hualde 1991; Harris 1995; Roca 1997) or the need for features such as [syllabic] to distinguish vowels from glides.[13]

This chapter describes hiatus resolution and preservation in vernacular varieties of Puerto Rican Spanish, provides evidence that this dialect is not exceptional among other Spanish varieties, and matches similar phenomena in other languages.

Notes

* I would like to thank the University of Puerto Rico for its continuous support and my research assistant, Camille Wagner, for her help in revising the final version of this chapter.

1 Casali (1997) also includes hiatus preservation (heterosyllabification) as a strategy.

2 We represent high glides with the traditional IPA symbol and non-syllabic mid vowels with a diacritic (e̯) for convenience. However, we do not concur with interpretations of glides as members of the set of consonants due to the distributional restrictions already stated above.

3 "El hiato se mantiene también con notoria resistencia cuando la disposición de las vocales da al grupo un orden descendente: *cae, traen, comae, tocao*" (our translation).

4 Coalescence, labialization, and palatalization are attested historically. Coalescence is not common in PRSp (Gold 2012).

5 Epenthesis is uncommon in PRSp:

   (i)   mangóes →   mangoses (not the same register)
   (ii) maníes   →   manises (not for all speakers)
   (iii) púa   →   puya (different meanings for different speakers)

6 The University of Texas database of the Hispanic Cities Project: *Estudio coordinado de la norma lingüística culta de las principales ciudades de Iberoamérica y de la Península Ibérica.* Matluck (1994) did not distinguish between registers in his study, and the data was collected from 10 speakers of a formal variety from different Spanish-speaking countries.

7 In some Southwest Spanish varieties, these can be in onset position.

8 Himmelman's and Ladd's (2008) methodological proposals address issues regarding research on F0. However, some have suggested that formant height also correlate to gender distinctions. On the other hand, we chose the same number of males and females, and we expect homogeneity within each group (González 2004: 284).

9 In Bond's (1978: 258) experiment, even glides of "0" duration triggered the identification of an item as a "diphthong." Notice that differences between English /o/ and /e/ tense vowels in final position and Spanish /e/ and /o/ require that vowel tension increases for Spanish, but decreases in English forms ending in a glide (Quilis & Fernández 1982: 59).

10 This includes identical vowel reduction.

11 "Reduction" is a cover name for shortening, since this variety has no phonemic [±ATR] distinctions. There are no phonemic distinctions between long and short vowels either, so "short" is a subphonemic property.

12 For practical purposes, we eliminate the constraints that are not relevant to individual tables, although that does not change the ranking.

13 Additionally, we avoid using circular definitions of syllabicity. It is only necessary to know whether a vowel is adjacent to another vowel and its relative height to determine whether it has shorter duration than a nuclear vowel. This is the classic separation of dominance and linear constraints from Phrase Structure Grammars.

Bibliography

Aguilar, L. (1999). Hiatus and Diphthong: Acoustic cues and speech situation differences. *Speech Communication, 28,* 57–74.

Bakovic, E. J. (2006). Hiatus resolution and incomplete identity. In F. Martínez-Gil & S. Colina (Eds.), *Optimality theoretic studies in Spanish phonology* (pp. 62–73). Amsterdam: Benjamins Pu.Co.

Bond, Z. S. (1978). The effects of varying Glide durations on Diphthong identification. *Language and Speech*, *21*(3), 253–263.

Borroff, M.L. (2003). *Against an ONSET Analysis of Hiatus Resolution*. Retrieved from https://pdfs.semanticscholar.org/0a27/af514a106032c7a15ebb282a12ded69492cf.pdf?_ga=2.241475906.1588146049.1495570095-472833369.1495570095

Carreira, M. (1991). The alternating Diphthongs in Spanish: A paradox revisited. In H. Campos & F. Martínez-Gil (Eds.), *Current studies in Spanish linguistics* (pp. 407-446) Washington, DC: Georgetown University Press.

Casali, R. F. (1997). Vowel Elision in Hiatus contexts: Which vowel goes? *Language*, *73*(3), 493–533.

Casali, R. F. (1998). *Resolving Hiatus*. New York & London: Garland Publishing, Inc.

Chitoran, I., & Hualde J. I. (2007). From Hiatus to Diphthong: The evolution of vowel sequences in Romance. *Phonology*, *24*(1), 37–75.

Colina, S. (1999). Reexamining Spanish glides: Analogically conditioned variation in vocoid sequences in Spanish dialects. In J. Gutiérrez-Rexach & F. Martínez-Gil (Eds.), *Advances in Hispanic linguistics: Papers from the 2nd Hispanic linguistics symposium* (Vol. 1, pp. 182–197). Somerville, MA: Cascadilla Press.

Cressey, W. W. (1978). *Spanish phonology and morphology: A generative view*. Washington, DC: Georgetown University Press.

Delattre, P. (1969). An acoustic and articulatory study of vowel reduction in four languages. *IRAL*, *7*(4), 295–325.

Espinosa, A. (1930). *Estudios sobre el español de Nuevo México. Parte 1: Fonética*. Buenos Aires: Instituto de Filología de la Facultad de Filosofía y Letras de la Universidad de Buenos Aires.

Face, T. L., & Alvord S. M. (2004). Lexical and acoustic factors in the perception of the Spanish Diphthong vs. Hiatus Contrast. *Hispania*, *87*(3), 553–564.

Garrido, M. (2007). Diphthongization of mid/low vowel sequences in Colombian Spanish. In J. Holmquist (Ed.), *Selected proceedings on the third workshop on Spanish sociolinguistics* (pp. 30–37). Somerville, MA: Cascadilla Proceedings Project.

Gold, D. L. (2012). The Politicization of a Monophthong (A refutation of all Puerto Rican myths about the native Spanish place name Porto Rico). In F. Rodríguez González (Ed.), *Estudios de lingüística española: Homenaje a Manuel Seco* (pp. 215–268). Alicante, España: Universidad de Alicante.

González, J. (2004). Formant frequencies and body size of speaker: A weak relationship in human adults. *Journal of Phonetics*, *32*, 277–287.

Harris, J. W. (1995). Projection and edge marking in the computation of stress in Spanish. In J. A. Goldsmith (Ed.), *The handbook of phonological theory* (pp. 867–887). Cambridge, MA: Blackwell Publishers.

Harris, J. W. (1985). Spanish Diphthongization and stress: A paradox resolved. *Phonology Yearbook*, *2*, 31–45.

Harris, J. W. (1980). *Spanish phonology*. Cambridge, MA & London: MIT Press.

Hayes, B. (1989). Compensatory lenghtening in moraic phonology. *Linguistic Inquiry*, *20*, 253–306.

Hayes, B. (1990). Precompiled phrasal phonology. In S. Inkelas & D. Zec (Eds.), *The phonology-syntax connection* (pp. 85–108). Chicago & London: University of Chicago Press.

Himmelman, N., & Ladd, D. R. (2008). Prosodic description: An introduction for fieldworkers. *Language Documentation and Conservation*, *2*(2), 244–274.

Hualde, J. I. (1999). Patterns in the Lexicon: Hiatus with unstressed high vowels in Spanish. In J. Gutiérrez-Rexach & F. Martínez-Gil (Eds.), *Advances in hispanic linguistics:*

Papers from the 2nd hispanic linguistics symposium (Vol. 1, pp. 182–197). Somerville, MA: Cascadilla Press.

Hualde, J. I. (1991). On Spanish syllabification. In H. Campos & F. Martínez-Gil (Eds.), *Current studies in Spanish linguistics* (pp. 475–493). Washington, DC: Georgetown University Press.

Jenkins, D. L. (1999). Hiatus resolution in Spanish: Phonetic aspects and phonological implications from Northern New Mexican data (Doctoral dissertation). University of New Mexico, Albuquerque, NM.

Keer, E. W. (1999). *Geminates, the OCP, and the Nature of CON* (Doctoral dissertation). New Brunswick, NJ: Rutgers University.

Lapesa, R. (1986). *Historia de la lengua española* (9th ed.). Madrid: Editorial Gredos.

Malmberg, B. (1965). *Estudios de Fonética Hispánica*. Madrid: Consejo Superior de Investigaciones Científicas.

Martínez-Celdrán, E. (2004). Problems in the classification of approximants. *Journal of the International Phonetic Association, 34*(2), 201–210.

Matluck, J. H. (1994). Hiato, sinéresis y sinalefa: A Sociolinguistic Updating. In P. Hashemipour, R. Maldonado, & M. van Naersen (Eds.), *Studies in language learning and Spanish linguistics* (pp. 280–289). New York, San Louis, San Francisco, Auckland, & Bogotá: McGraw-Hill, Inc.

McCarthy, J. 1993. A case of surface constraint violation. *Canadia Journal of Linguistics, 38,* 127–153.

Morales, A., & Ortiz López, L. (2001). *PRESEEA: Proyecto para el studio sociolingüístico del español de España y de América (San Juan de Puerto Rico)*. Alcalá de Henares: Universidad de Alcalá. Retrieved from junio 2014, http://preseea.linguas.net/Equipos/SanJuandePuertoRico.aspx

Navarro Tomás, T. (1977). *Manual de pronunciación* española (15th ed.). Madrid: Consejo Superior de Investigaciones Científicas.

Navarro Tomás, T. 1966/1948. *Estudios de Fonología Española*. New York: Las American Publishing Company.

Navarro Tomás, T. (1917a). Cantidad de las vocales inacentuadas. *Revista de Filología Española, 4,* 371–388.

Navarro Tomás, T. (1917b). Cantidad de las vocales acentuadas. *Revista de Filología Española, 5,* 387–408.

Núñez Cedeño, R. A., & Morales-Front, A. (1999). *Fonología generativa contemporánea de la lengua española*. Washington, DC: Georgetwon University Press.

Prince A., & Smolensky, P. (1993). *Optimality theory: Constraint interaction in generative grammar*. Manuscript RuCCS-TR-2; CU-CS-696–93. Retrieved from http://roa.rutgers.edu/files/537-0802/537-0802-PRINCE-0-0.PDF

Quilis, A., & Fernández, J. A. (1982). *Curso de fonética y fonología españolas*. Madrid: Consejo Superior de Investigaciones Científicas.

Quilis, A. (1981). *Fonética Acústica de la Lengua Española*. Madrid: Editorial Gredos.

Raffelsiefen, R. (1999). Diagnostics for Prosodic words revisited: The case of historically prefixed words in English. In T. A. Hall & U. Kleinhenz (Eds.), *Studies on the phonological word* (pp. 133–201). Amsterdam/Philadelphia: John Benjamins Publishing Company.

Roca, I. (1997). There are no "Glides," at least in Spanish: An optimality account. *Probus, 9,* 233–265.

Romeo, L. (1968). The economy of Diphthongization in early romance. The Hague/Paris: Mouton.

Rosenblat, A. (1930). Notas. In A. Espinosa (Ed.), *Estudios sobre el español de Nuevo México. Parte 1: Fonética Estudios sobre el español de Nuevo Méjico, Parte I.* Fonética: Buenos Aires: Instituto de Filología de la Facultad de Filosofía y Letras de la Universidad de Buenos Aires.

Rosenthall, S. (1994). *Vowel/glide alternation in a theory of constraint interaction* (Doctoral dissertation). University of Massachusetts, Amherst.

Senturia, M. B. (1998). *A prosodic theory of Hiatus resolution* (Doctoral dissertation). University of California, San Diego.

Souza, B. J. (2010). *Hiatus resolution in Spanish: An experimental study* (Doctoral dissertation). University Park, The Pennsylvania State University.

Torreblanca, M. (1989). De fonosintaxis histórica española: la ausencia de diptongación de ĕ˜ y ŏ˜ latinas no condicionada por palatal. *Journal of Hispanic Philology, 14*(1), 61–77.

Wennerstrom, A. (1993). Focus on the prefix: Evidence for Word-internal Prosodic Words. *Phonology, 10*, 309–324.

3 Phonetics and phonology of /ṣ/ in the Spanish of Puerto Rico

Aspiration, elision with compensatory lengthening, and glottalization

Kenneth V. Luna

1 Introduction

A very important segment, and perhaps one of the most interesting and distinctive in the Spanish-speaking world, is the voiceless dental fricative /ṣ/, not only in modern phonetic and phonological frameworks, but also in the field of historical linguistics. The historical changes that led to our modern /ṣ/ and its complexity go back to the times of Medieval Spanish, whose sound inventory contained six sibilants that were in phonological opposition: /t͡s/, /d͡z/, /ṣ/, /ẓ/, /ʃ/, and /ʒ/ (Lapesa 1981; Parodi 1995; Penny 2002). In Castile, a deaffrication of the affricates and a loss of the voicing opposition left the language with only three phonemes: /s̪/, /ṣ/, and /ʃ/. Due to the perceptual ambiguity and acoustic proximity caused in part by the crowding of these sounds in front of the oral cavity, in order to make a better and more efficient use of the articulatory space, /s̪/ was fronted to [θ] and /ʃ/ retracted to /x/. The velar sound /x/ was further retracted to a uvular articulation /χ/, perhaps because of the acoustic proximity that was still felt between the voiceless apico-alveolar fricative /ṣ/ (whose acoustic quality is closer to [ʃ]) and the voiceless velar fricative /x/. This created modern Castilian /θ/, /ṣ/, and /χ/.

In Andalusia, the developments were slightly different. After the deaffrication of /t͡s/ and /d͡z/, the dialect was left with /s̪/, /ẓ/, /ṣ/, /ẓ/, /ʃ/, and /ʒ/. In a step that did not occur in the Castilian dialect, there was a merger of /s̪/ into /ṣ/ and of /ẓ/ into /ẓ/, which left the system with /ṣ/, /ẓ/, /ʃ/, and /ʒ/. A subsequent step resulted in the loss of the voicing contrast in favor of the voiceless correlates, which only left /ṣ/ and /ʃ/. As in the rest of the Iberian Peninsula, /ʃ/ was retracted to /x/; however, /x/ was eventually relaxed and further retracted to /h/.

It is a common assumption that the development of the sibilants in Andalusia was transplanted to America. This is an overgeneralization of the facts and represent an erroneous view of the reality in the Americas. Parodi (1995), in her book *Orígenes del español americano*, provides evidence that the development of the sibilants – and of Latin American Spanish in general – took a slightly different course. Although Latin American Spanish has an undeniable Andalusian base, Castilian Spanish also influenced it and this can be seen in the development of the sibilants. Parodi demonstrates that for /ṣ/, /ẓ/, /s̟/, and /z̟/, both /ẓ/ and /z̟/ merged into /ṣ/ after a loss of voicing. This left /ṣ/ and /s̟/, which then merged and left the system with only /ṣ/. As for /ʃ/, they were pronounced in Latin America as /x/ or /h/.

In modern terminology, the phonological process in which the distinction between /θ/ and /s/ (whether apico-alveolar or dental) is lost in favor of /s/ (as in Andalusia, Canary Islands, and Latin America) is termed SESEO. In addition, there is an opposite process, ceceo, in which the distinction between /θ/ and /s/ is lost in favor of a slightly different variant of [θ], namely, a dentalized version [θ̪]. The first process, seseo, is widespread throughout the Spanish-speaking world, except in the Castilian standard, and it is an accepted and valid pronunciation in the educated norm of Hispanic America. The second process, limited to small enclaves of the Hispanic world – namely, Granada and certain areas of El Salvador and other, mostly Central American, countries – is not accepted by the educated norm of any region of the Spanish-speaking world and carries a heavy stigma.

In Andalusia, in the Canary Islands, and in the lowlands of Hispanic America, there is a further development in the pronunciation of /ṣ/. When /ṣ/ is in syllable coda, it undergoes a process termed ASPIRATION, in which /ṣ/ is realized as a voiceless glottal fricative, or aspirate, [h]. This voiceless realization is typically found before voiceless consonants and word-finally:

(1)   /ˈpaṣta/ → [ˈpahta̯]   pasta   'paste'
      /ˈniɲoṣ/ → [ˈniɲoh]   niños   'children'

Before voiced consonants, the aspiration is realized as a voiced glottal fricative [ɦ]:

(2)   /ˈiṣla/ → [ˈiɦla]   isla   'island'
      /ˈmiṣmo/ → [ˈmiɦmo]   mismo   'same-masc.sing.'

Sometimes, an otherwise aspirated /ṣ/ can get to the point of being elided, though usually leaving a trace of its existence – through changes in quality or lengthening – in the pronunciation of a preceding vowel or a following consonant:

(3)   /ˈniɲoṣ/ → [ˈniɲoː] ~ [ˈniɲɔ]   niños   'children-masc.'
      /ˈmiṣmo/ → [ˈmimmo]   mismo   'same-masc.sing.'

As will be seen below, the issue of aspiration and elision of coda /ṣ/ in the dialects of Spanish have been thoroughly documented and studied (Henríquez Ureña 1921, 1930; Menéndez Pidal 1957, 1968; Lapesa 1964, 1981; Canfield 1981; Moreno de Alba 1988; Granda 1994). Unfortunately, due to the degree of variability among the dialects, the study of these phenomena has been inconclusive and our understanding of it is incomplete. Since there is no clear phonological explanation, and the contexts in which the process is realized are not systematic, the process has also been studied in a sociolinguistic context without any fruitful results. The sociolinguistic results are too scattered and reach a point where there is almost no systematicity. In order to provide some insight into the long-standing problem of aspiration and elision of coda /s̺/, I submit these phenomena to an acoustic study, in this case, using data from the Spanish of Ponce, Puerto Rico, a dialect for which this had not been done previously.

This study will (1) describe and analyze the acoustic nature of the realizations of /s̺/ in the Spanish of Ponce, Puerto Rico; (2) contest the idea that the only transformations are aspiration and elision with, perhaps, compensatory lengthening or change of vowel quality, by reporting a glottal stop realization of /s̺/; and (3) demonstrate, as postulated by Moraic Theory, that compensatory lengthening is obligatory in cases of elision due to the fact that Spanish codas are moraic.

2 Methods

A total of nine native speakers of Puerto Rican Spanish were interviewed and recorded (see Table 3.1): five males and four females of middle/upper-middle class, three of which were in their late teens/twenties, four in their forties/fifties, and two in the seventies range, all from the city of Ponce. They were all chosen at random from among friends and acquaintances of mine, my family, and friends.

Speakers were interviewed with a 26-question questionnaire. The questionnaire asked for biographical information, as well as information and anecdotes about their childhood, adolescence, and adulthood, in order to get them to elicit as much speech as possible. The speakers were also told to speak as if they were in a regular conversation with someone. By talking about topics that are known to them and to which they can relate, the speakers relax if not forget about the fact that they are being interviewed and, hence, produce natural speech.

Words containing aspirated /s̺/ in stressed syllable coda were isolated from the middle of the speech sample. The first and third thirds of the recording were avoided whenever possible in order to control for overemphasis and effortlessness in the speech. If the middle did not yield the amount of required tokens, the search was extended towards the edges of the recording. The first

Table 3.1 Summary of speakers' information

Speaker	Gender	Age
KGLS	Male	20
KASC	Male	21
KSC	Female	19
SISV	Female	50
JVLL	Male	56
ICC	Female	45
KASV	Male	44
VVA	Female	72
WSP	Male	74

10 examples of one kind of aspiration – either [h] or [ɦ] – were isolated per speaker, making sure to note any other allophones or processes in the course of isolating these 10.

Spectrograms were produced and frequency measurements were taken from the middle of the segment using Praat. The duration of the segment was also recorded. For the segmentation of vowels, specifically before /s̪/, instead of the conventional ending cutoff point at the offset of higher-frequency components, I did so at the point of amplitude change. This was done because there was a consistent change of amplitude after vowels followed by an /s̪/ that was aspirated. Such consistent change in amplitude is evidence of a segmental change, in this case, the cue for a voiced glottal fricative or murmur. Failure to see this – in addition to the murmur's also being audible – would have required me to include the amplitude-changing portion as part of the vowel segment, in essence, arguing, incorrectly, for the elision of /s̪/. The measurements were imported into Microsoft® Excel®, where descriptive statistics were calculated.

3 Results, analysis, and discussion

The following figure illustrates the standard voiceless dental fricative pronunciation of /s̪/ (Figure 3.1):

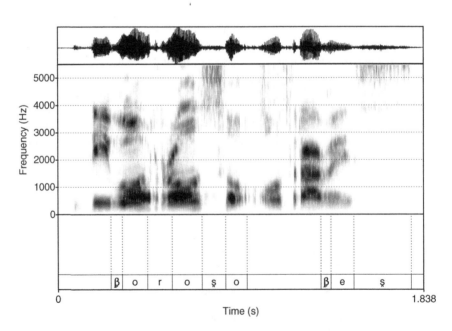

Figure 3.1 Spectrogram of the words <u>borroso</u> [βoˈros̪o] 'blurry' and <u>vez</u> [ˈβes̪] 'time' as part of the sentence <u>Di "borroso" otra vez</u> 'Say "borroso" again', illustrating the standard pronunciation of /s̪/ (→ [s̪]) as produced by SISV

As it can be seen in Figure 3.1, the spectrum of [ṣ] is characterized by aperiodic frequencies or noise above the 4,000 Hz area. The absence of a voicing bar at the bottom indicates that the sound is voiceless. As it will be seen below, the most common allophones of /ṣ/ in coda in the Spanish of Ponce, Puerto Rico look very different to this.

3.1 Voiced aspiration

As mentioned above, 10 tokens of the same kind of aspirated /ṣ/ – that is, voiceless or voiced – in stressed syllable coda were isolated from the data per speaker, for a total of 90 tokens. One hundred percent of the informants consistently aspirate stressed syllable coda /ṣ/. However, the default aspiration is realized with a voiced glottal fricative [ɦ] (see Table 3.2). Traditional accounts on the subject document a voiced aspiration only before voiced consonants, as in (2) above, as a result of a voicing assimilation process regularly undergone by /ṣ/ even in non-aspirating dialects (e.g., General Spanish /'desde/ → ['dezðe] desde 'from'; /'mismo/ → ['mizmo] mismo 'the same'). In the Spanish of Ponce, Puerto Rico, this voiced allophone is realized regardless of the voicing of the following segment:

(4) a. ['pueṣ] → ['pueɦ] pues 'so' (KSC)
     b. ['aṣta] → ['aɦta] hasta 'until' (SISV)
     c. [ma'eṣtro] → [ma'eɦtro] maestro 'teacher' (JVLL)
     d. [deṣko'noṣko] → [deɦiko'noɦiko] desconozco 'I don't know' (KASC)
     e. ['dezðe] → ['deɦde] desde 'from' (VVA)[1]

Examples (4a-e) show a realization of /ṣ/ as [ɦ] in all coda environments: word-finally (a), before voiceless consonants (b-d), and before a voiced consonant (e). This, as surprising as it may seem given the voicing of /ṣ/ even before voiceless segments, had already been documented by Navarro Tomás when he stated: "*A veces se percibe cierto rehilamiento o resonancia sonora como elemento adherido al timbre de la referida vocal*" 'Sometimes one perceives a sort of voiced vibration or resonance as an element attached to the timbre of said vowel' (1948: 73). As reported in Table 3.2, the average duration of the voiced aspiration is 42.4ms. The aspiration, however, could be a short as 12.2ms and as long as 123ms.

Table 3.2 Descriptive statistics for duration of the voiced glottal fricative [ɦ]

Voiced aspiration [ɦ]	
	duration (s)
Mean	0.042389764
Median	0.03610489
Standard deviation	0.021853455
Minimum	0.012249559
Maximum	0.122968494
Count	90

Information and statistics on spectral frequency are not given due to the fact that, in the case of glottal fricatives, their frequencies depend on the adjacent vowel and, thus, are not self-defining in and of themselves. Figures 3.2a–b illustrate the voiced aspiration [ɦ] as enunciated in the data:

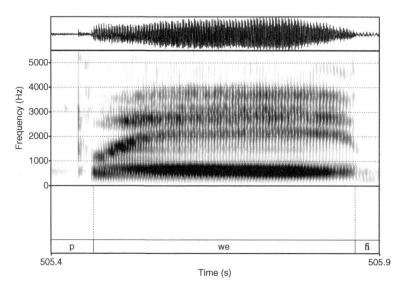

Figure 3.2a Spectrogram of the word <u>pues</u> [ˈpweɦ] 'so', illustrating the voiced glottal fricative [ɦ] as produced by KSC

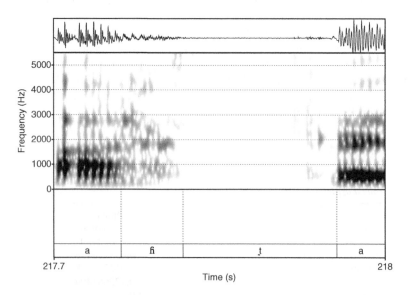

Figure 3.2b Spectrogram of the word <u>hasta</u> [ˈaɦt̪a] 'until', illustrating the voiced glottal fricative [ɦ] as produced by SISV

Both figures show a voiced element, as evidenced by the voice bar, in stressed syllable coda, which, rather than a friction, would be more accurately described as a murmured or breathy voiced glottal. Such a description of the voiced glottal fricative as a transitional state of the glottis with no manner of articulation other than its phonation type has already been given by phoneticians (Laufer 1991; Ladefoged 2001), and represents the general and standard notion of the sound. The sound could be fairly strong (Figure 3.2b) or rather weak (Figure 3.2a), but still under the category of a murmur. Figure 3.2b is clear evidence of a voiced aspiration even before a voiceless consonant such as [ţ].

According to Spanish syllabification and sandhi rules, the aspiration should be blocked because of the fact that /ş/ would go from being a coda to being the onset of the following syllable, and the phonological transformation could no longer apply:

(5)   /ˈmaş aˈmoɾ/ → [ˈma şaˈmoɾ]   más amor   'more love'

As expected for this dialect, the data shows that the phonological process is, in fact, not blocked:

(6)   a. [ˈmaş aˈşi] → [ˈmafi aˈşi]   más así   'more like that'   (KSC)
      b. [inteˈreş en] → [inteˈɾefi en]   interés en   'interest in'   (SISV)
      c. [şi ˈβaş al] → [şi ˈβafi al]   si vas al   'if you go to the' (KASV)

Evidence as in (6) suggests that, in this dialect, the original syllable boundary takes precedence over the new syllable boundary produced by (re)syllabification rules (cf. Figure 3.3a–b below). The syllable boundary at the lexical level, therefore, seems to be the triggering and relevant factor in these cases of aspiration of /ş/. Any dissolution of codas as in (5) is the product of a postlexical syllable boundary that yields the utterance ineligible as an input for the transformation.

These spectrograms are evidence that, in this dialect, resyllabification and sandhi rules, according to which /ş/ should resyllabify to become the onset of the following syllable, do not block the application of the aspiration phonological rule. The fact that the aspiration still surfaces is an indication that the original – that is, the lexical syllable/word boundary – is the triggering environment for the aspirations of /ş/. In earlier rule-based phonological accounts, this outcome was the product of rule ordering: the aspiration rule would apply before the resyllabification rule. However, examples such as (5), in which resyllabification seems to have applied before aspiration, although less frequently, can still be reported in this dialect. This simply points to a process of free variation.

Based on (4a-e), the phonological rule for the aspiration of /ş/ in this dialect would be:

(7)   /ş/ → [ɦ]/_____]σ

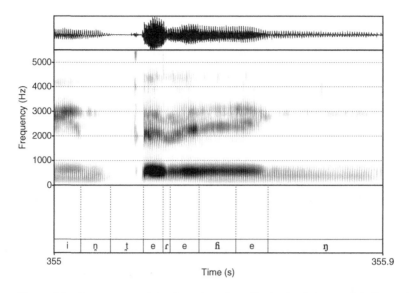

Figure 3.3a Spectrogram of the phrase <u>interés en</u> [ɪɲteˈɾeɦ eŋ] 'interest in', illustrating the voiced glottal fricative [ɦ] across word boundary before a vowel as produced by SISV

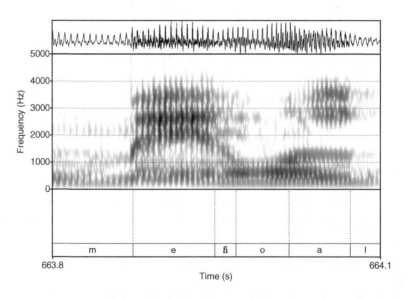

Figure 3.3b Spectrogram of the phrase <u>mes o al</u> [ˈmeɦ o al] 'month or to the', illustrating the voiced glottal fricative [ɦ] across word boundary before a vowel as produced by WSP

That is, the voiceless dental fricative /ṣ/ becomes a voiced glottal fricative [ɦ] in syllable coda. Formalizing (7) yields (8):

(8) Aspiration of /ṣ/

$$/ + \text{strident}/ \rightarrow \begin{bmatrix} -\text{consonantal} \\ +\text{spread glottis} \\ -\text{coronal} \\ +\text{voice} \end{bmatrix} / \underline{\hspace{2cm}}]_\sigma$$

Although the present analysis focuses on stressed syllables, a look at stressless syllables indicates that they are also consistently aspirated by all speakers. An analysis of the aspiration of /ṣ/ in stressless syllables specifically is, however, left for a future study.

3.2 Other realizations of /ṣ/

As part of the analysis in the present study, any other realizations of /ṣ/ in the process of collecting the 10 stressed-syllable aspiration tokens per speaker were noted. There were a total of 135 realizations of /ṣ/ that were recorded, including the 90 voiced aspiration ones described above. Thus, there were 45 tokens of other realizations of /ṣ/ in the data, which accounts for 33 percent of data (Figure 3.4 below). This is to say that, for every 10 tokens, three will be other than the voiced glottal fricative [ɦ] discussed in the previous section, which is the most common realization of the phoneme.

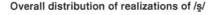

Overall distribution of realizations of /ṣ/

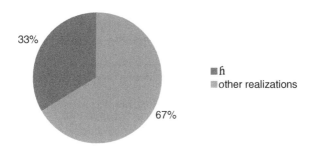

Figure 3.4 Chart reflecting the distribution of [ɦ] and other realizations of /ṣ/

3.2.1 Voiceless aspiration

There were several voiceless glottal fricative [h] realizations of /s̬/ found in the data. Out of the 45 non-[ɦ] realizations, 14 tokens were [h] as in (9):

(9)   a. [ˈes̬te] → [ˈehte]   <u>este</u>   'um …'   (KSC, KGLL, VVA, WSP)
      b. [ˈtʃis̬te] → [ˈtʃihte]   <u>chiste</u>   'joke'   (KGLL)
      c. [ˈmas̬] → [ˈmah]   <u>más</u>   'more'   (WSP)

This pronunciation was only documented before a voiceless dental stop [t̪] as in (9a-b) and in absolute final position as in (9c). No other context surfaced in the 14 examples of [h] found in the data; however, it could be assumed that the same realization would surface before other voiceless stops. Since a voiced aspiration is also possible in these contexts as seen in (4) above, voiceless aspirations such as those in (9) should be considered to be in free variation with voiced aspirations.

Combined with the 90 tokens of [ɦ], there were 104 total stressed syllable aspiration tokens in the data. The descriptive statistics for duration of [h] are shown in Table 3.3. This means that, for every 10 stressed syllable voiced aspirations, one stressed syllable voiceless aspiration will be produced. In terms of the speakers, seven out of the nine speakers exhibited at least one voiceless aspiration in the portion of the recording that was analyzed.

As Table 3.3 indicates, the average duration of the voiceless aspiration is 39.3ms, but actual duration can be anywhere between 17.6ms and 81.1ms. Figures 3.5a-b illustrate the spectra of such aspirations as exhibited in the data.

The first thing that should be noted in the above figures is the absence of a voice bar, which indicates that the sound in question is voiceless. This is the primary difference between the Figures 3.3a–b and 3.5a–b. As with glottal fricatives in general and as mentioned in the previous section, their frequencies are dependent on the surrounding vowel; and so, in these figures, any visible formant frequencies are the same as those of the preceding vowel.

Table 3.3 Descriptive statistics for duration of the voiceless glottal fricative [h]

Voiceless aspiration [h]	
	duration (s)
Mean	0.039324627
Median	0.035188933
Standard deviation	0.017148024
Minimum	0.017556725
Maximum	0.081132919
Count	14

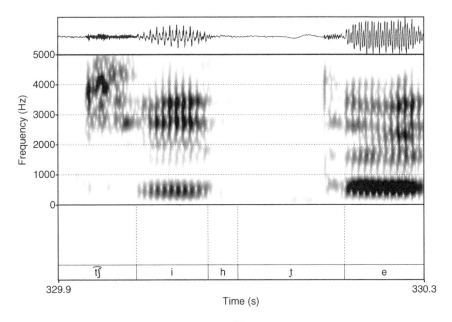

Figure 3.5a Spectrogram of the word <u>chiste</u> [ˈt͡ʃĩhte̥] 'joke', illustrating the voiceless glottal fricative [h] as produced by KASC

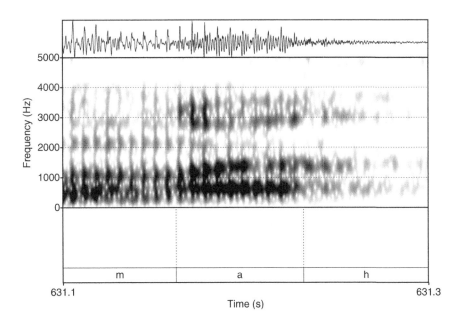

Figure 3.5b Spectrogram of the word <u>más</u> [ˈmah] 'more', illustrating the voiceless glottal fricative [h] as produced by WSP

3.2.2 Elision and compensatory lengthening

Another portion of the 45 non-[ɦ] realizations of /s̪/ constituted what seems to be anticipatory assimilations, that is, assimilations to the following segment. There were 18 of these: five to a following stop, 12 to a following nasal, and one to a following affricate as in (10):

(10) a. [ˈmaz̪ ð̪e] → [ˈmad̪ d̪e]　　　　más de　'more of' (VVA)
　　 b. [ˈmiz̪mo] → [ˈmimmo]　　　　mismo　'same-masc.
　　　　　　　　　　　　　　　　　　　sing' (KGLL)
　　 c. [ð̪es̪ˈpwez̪ je̝ˈɣe] → [ð̪eɦˈpweɟ͡ʝ ɟ͡ʝeˈɣe]　después llegué　'afterwards
　　　　　　　　　　　　　　　　　　　　　　　　　　I arrived' (KSC)

What all these examples and the rest of the tokens recorded in the data have in common is that they are followed by a voiced sound. Although examples before a voiced bilabial stop [b], a voiced velar stop [g], and an alveolar lateral [l] were not available from the section of data analyzed, it can be assumed that the phonological process will occur in those cases as well.

It seems that what this dialect does before a voiced consonant with what should have been a voiced aspiration according to (8) is assimilate to the following segment. However, this assimilation is only apparent. An assimilation account is highly implausible, as having a segment such as /s̪/ change all or most of its features to become a completely different, unrelated sound goes against assimilatory behavior typologically. For example, in order to assimilate to [b], /s̪/ has to change its place feature, manner feature, and laryngeal feature from [+coronal], [+continuant], and [-voice] to [+labial], [-continuant], and [+voice]. The situation is the same with the other voiced sounds [d̪, g, m, n, l, ɟ͡ʝ]. In the cases of [m, n, l], there additionally would be a major class feature change of [-sonorant] to [+sonorant]. These changes are too drastic to be accepted as valid natural phonological processes, and so an assimilatory transformation should not be considered a viable explanation.

Such phenomena can be better explained as being the result of the elision of segment /s̪/, which, according to Moraic Theory (Hyman 1985; Hayes 1989), triggers the compensatory lengthening of a surrounding segment. Based on this, (10) above would be the result of an elision rule:

$$(11) \quad / + \text{strident} / \rightarrow \emptyset / \underline{\hspace{1cm}} \begin{bmatrix} +\text{consonantal} \\ +\text{voice} \end{bmatrix}$$

That is, the voiceless dental fricative /s̪/ is elided before voiced consonants. This is in turn followed by the compensatory lengthening of a surrounding segment to fill the space left by the deleted /s̪/. According to Moraic Theory, the prosodic or moraic structure of a language varies in whether or not it assigns a mora to codas. When a language assigns a mora to codas, if a coda gets deleted, its corresponding mora is stranded. Since prosodic positions cannot be deleted, one of the surrounding segments has to spread to fill the stranded mora slot (Hayes 1989). By virtue of the phenomena in (10) above, we can conclude that codas in the Spanish of Ponce, Puerto Rico are indeed moraic. This would explain the long consonants, or geminates, in such instances. An example such as (10b) is explained as follows:

(12)

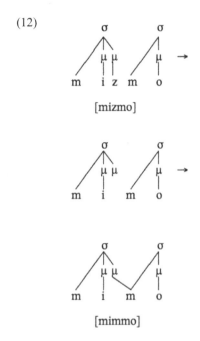

In this example, the [z] in [mizmo] has been deleted and it would have left its mora stranded. Since a mora, as a prosodic position, cannot be deleted, one of its surrounding sounds has to spread to fill the empty position. This was accomplished by the following consonant, which yielded a geminate.

Such an analysis is not unprecedented. Hammond (1986) and Núñez Cedeño (1988) had already discussed compensatory lengthening in Cuban Spanish. Núñez Cedeño's account treats the issue through a framework very similar to Moraic Theory, as he postulates that the process is triggered at the autosegmental level. In addition, more recently and under current theoretical frameworks, a detailed acoustic compensatory lengthening account for elided codas has been given for a Spanish dialect very similar to the dialect under study, namely, Eastern Andalusian Spanish (Gerfen 2002). Such an analysis for the behavior of /ṣ/ in the Spanish of Ponce, Puerto Rico is, then, well within the scope of Spanish phonology.

Figures 3.6a-b are examples of this phenomenon. Figure 3.6a shows no traces of /ṣ/, not even as an aspiration. It can be seen, however, how the function of /ṣ/ is

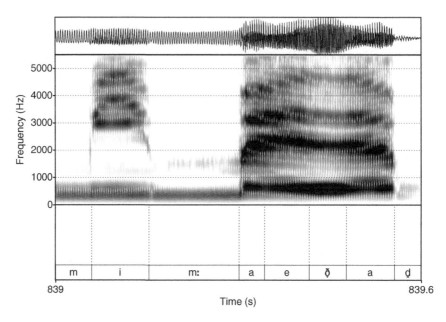

Figure 3.6a Spectrogram of the phrase <u>misma edad</u> [ˈmimma eðað] 'same age', illustrating a geminate [mm] product of compensatory lengthening as produced by ISC

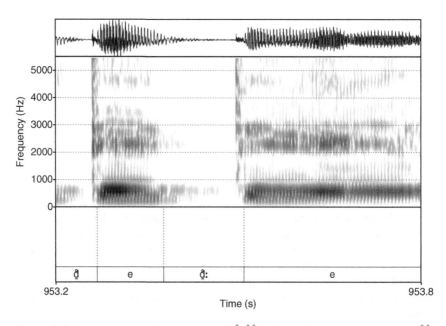

Figure 3.6b Spectrogram of the word <u>desde</u> [ˈdedde] 'from', illustrating a geminate [dd] product of compensatory lengthening as produced by VVA

accomplished, per Moraic Theory, by a lengthening of the following consonant, in this case [m]. This [m] is clearly much longer than the [m] in the stressed syllable, which, by virtue of being in a stressed syllable, should be longer than the following [m] in the stressless syllable. The reason for the unusual length of [m] in the stressless syllable is that, after /s̠/ was elided, [m] lengthened to take over the stranded mora left by the deleted /s̠/ and is now both the onset of its own syllable and the coda of the previous syllable. Measurements of both [m] segments reveal that the [m] from the stressed syllable is 53ms long, whereas the lengthened [mm] is 131ms long; that is, well over twice the length of the non-lengthened [m]. The same is true for Figure 3.6b, where [d̥]² lengthened to take over the stranded mora left by /s̠/ when it was deleted. Compared to the non-lengthened [d̥] at the beginning of the word, which has a VOT of -69ms, the lengthened [d̥d̥] has a VOT of -132ms.

The acoustic evidence, therefore, clearly points to cases of compensatory lengthening in the dialect of Ponce, Puerto Rico. These results follow Gerfen's (2002) evidence of compensatory lengthening in Eastern Andalusian Spanish. However, unlike the Andalusian cases of compensatory lengthening, in which traces of an aspiration are found, in the dialect under study, such remnants of /s̠/ aspiration were not documented.

Statistically, since the 18 cases of compensatory lengthening were registered in the process of documenting the 90 tokens of stressed-syllable voiced aspirations, these results mean that approximately two cases of compensatory lengthening in stressed syllable due to elision will be produced for every 10 stressed syllable voiced aspirations.

It is important to mention that no cases of the elision in final absolute position in stressed syllable were found in data. This may be due to the scarcity of such a context in spontaneous conversation. In such a situation, since there is no following segment available to lengthen and take over the stranded mora, Moraic Theory predicts that the preceding segment would then have to lengthen to perform this task. Future insight into this topic, especially in the context of stressless syllables, being a far more common context, is necessary.

3.2.3 Glottalization

In the course of the data gathering for the analysis of /s̠/ herein, a realization of /s̠/, already reported by Valentín-Márquez (2006) for Puerto Rican Spanish, but otherwise not well documented in the literature on coda /s̠/ in Spanish dialects,³ surfaced and stood out very distinctively. It was the production of a glottal stop [ʔ] in lieu of an aspiration – or a regular [s̠] – at the end of a word when the following word started with a vowel:

(13) a. [de̞ˈmas̠ amis̠ˈta̞ðe̞s̠] → [de̞ˈma̞ʔ a̞mifiˈta̞ðefi] <u>demás amistades</u> 'rest of
          the friends'   (KSC)
      b. [ˈpwe̞s̠ a] → [ˈpwe̞ʔ a]   <u>pues a</u>   'so to . . . '   (VVA)
      c. [ˈkos̠as̠ i] → [ˈkos̠aʔ i̞]   <u>cosas y</u>   'the Americans' (KASC)
      d. [los̠ ˈaŋxele̞s̠] → [lo̞ʔ ˈaɲfiele̞fi] <u>Los Ángeles</u> 'Los Angeles' (KGLL)

The realization of /s̰/ as a glottal stop was so novel that even examples from stress-less syllables were noted in order to validate its attestation and aid in its description. Examples (13a-d) show that the glottal stop can surface both in stressed (13a-b) or stressless (13c-d) syllables. As in (13a, c, and d), sometimes the sounds that surround the glottal stop can be realized with a creaky voice as a result of coarticulation. There were a total of 11 glottalizations in the data.

Figures 3.7a-b show neither aspirations nor compensatory lengthening as allophones of coda /s̰/ as it has been described in the previous sections; rather they represent examples of a glottal stop [ʔ] as a realization of /s̰/. In both figures, a period of silence and a transient typical of a glottal stop release can be observed. In addition, creaky or unstable voice quality, signaled by separated or irregular glottal pulses, can be seen in the spectrum of the previous (Figure 3.7a) and following (Figure 3.7b) vowels, which is the result of coarticulation due to a contiguous glottal stop and which further emphasizes its acoustic output and perception.

Such a realization of /s̰/ is not well documented in other dialects of Spanish. Whereas aspirations and geminations have been documented and are fairly common in the lowlands, instances of glottalization are yet to be described in this area and certainly in the Caribbean, traditionally known for the innovative nature of its processes. The glottal stop is thus another device used by speakers to represent and cue the phoneme /s̰/ in Spanish.

The phonological process undergone by these tokens is summarized in (14):

(14)   /s̰/ → [ʔ]/_____]$_\sigma$ V

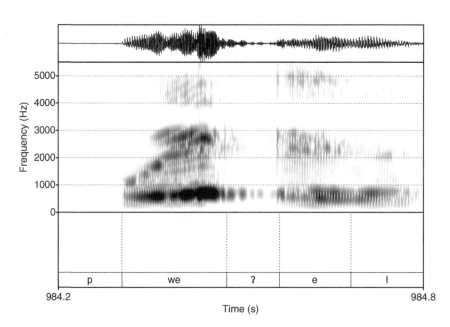

Figure 3.7a Spectrogram of the phrase <u>pues el</u> [ˈpweʔ el] 'so the', illustrating a glottal stop [ʔ] as produced by VVA

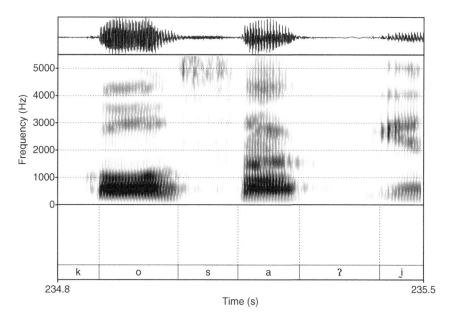

Figure 3.7b Spectrogram of the phrase <u>cosas y</u> [ˈkoʂaʔ i̯] 'things and', illustrating a glottal
stop [ʔ] as produced by SISV

That is, the voiceless dental sibilant /ʂ/ becomes a glottal stop [ʔ] at the end of a
syllable followed by a vowel. This rule is not obligatory, but rather it is in free
variation with an aspiration – rule (8) – or even with an actual realization of [ʂ].
As (13) shows, neither the stress of the syllable or word containing the glottal stop
nor the stress of the following syllable in the next word are relevant in the transformation. Stress has been posited as the determining factor for cases of retention
of /ʂ/ versus aspiration or elision in Dominican Spanish (Alba 1982). In this dialect and for this phonological process, however, this is not the case.

All the examples in (13) could very well have been produced with a voiced
aspiration [ɦ], since, as it was previously shown, this is the standard, most common transformation undergone by /ʂ/ in this dialect. The fact that this is not
what happened is simply a matter of free variation. Formalizing (14) above
yields (15):

(15)   Glottalization of /ʂ/

$$/ + \text{strident}/ \rightarrow \begin{bmatrix} +\text{constricted glottis} \\ -\text{continuant} \\ -\text{delayed relaease} \\ -\text{coronal} \end{bmatrix} / \underline{\hspace{2cm}}]_\sigma \text{ V}$$

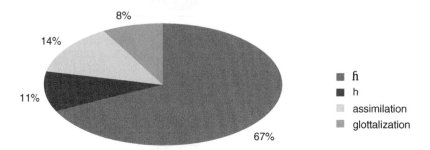

Figure 3.8 Chart reflecting the distribution of all realizations of /ş/ found in the present study

A total of 11 glottalizations in the course of 90 stressed syllable voiced aspirations means that approximately one glottalization will occur for every 10 stressed syllable voiced aspirations.

Figure 3.8 summarizes all the realizations of /ş/ exhibited in this dialect and discussed in this study.

As it can be seen from the chart, any other realization of /ş/ besides the most common [ɦ] will surface approximately 10 percent of the time or, in other words, at a rate of one in every 10 utterances. This is, of course, only in the context of stressed syllables, except for the glottalizations, which included both stressed and stressless syllable tokens.

4 Summary

An analysis of the behavior of the voiceless dental fricative /ş/ in stressed syllable coda in the dialect of Ponce, Puerto Rico has been pursued throughout this study. The gathered data reveal three main transformations in the realization of this phoneme: aspiration, compensatory lengthening due to elision, and glottalization.

The main transformation undergone by /ş/, accounting for 78 percent of the total analyzed data, is aspiration. Two types were documented: a voiced one (voiced glottal fricative [ɦ]) and a voiceless one (voiceless glottal fricative [h]). The most common or "standard" aspiration in this dialect, with 67 percent of the total analyzed tokens, is not voiceless as previously thought and as long reported in the bibliography, but rather voiced. This realization of /ş/ occurs even in environments where a voiceless aspiration is expected and documented in other aspirating dialects – before a voiceless consonant. Not only does the aspiration occur in stressed-syllable coda before a consonant, it is also operative across word boundary before a vowel. This means that regular resyllabification due to sandhi, through which coda /ş/ in the last syllable of a word becomes the onset of the first syllable of the following word, must happen after the aspiration has operated. Otherwise, aspiration could not occur due to the fact that /ş/ would no longer be a coda, but an onset. Spectrograms of the voiced aspiration [ɦ] clearly show a voice bar, and the spectra can be identified as those of glottal fricatives. The average duration of the voiced aspiration is 42.4ms; however, voiced aspiration as short as 12.2ms and as long as 123ms were documented.

There were also cases of voiceless aspiration [h], but they formed 11 percent of the total analyzed tokens. Since they occurred in contexts in which a voiced aspiration also surfaces, voiceless aspirations are considered to be in free variation with the voiced aspiration. Since the only difference between [h] and [ɦ] rests on their voicing, the phonological rule for the voiceless aspiration would be the same as (8) above, but with a [-voice] feature. The spectrum is similarly identifiable as that of a glottal fricative, but in contrast with the voiced aspiration, the voice bar is absent. The average duration for the voiceless aspiration is 39.3ms, but actual duration can be anywhere between 17.6ms and 81.1ms.

Even though the analysis of aspiration was limited to stressed syllables, aspiration also occurs in stressless syllables. A preliminary look seems to indicate that, as with stressed syllables, the default aspiration in stressless syllables is also the voiced glottal fricative [ɦ].

Elisions are also part of the phonological repertoire of /ş/ in the Spanish of Ponce, Puerto Rico. Cases of elision accounted for 14 percent of analyzed data, and they are limited in their occurrence to cases in which /ş/ is followed by voiced consonants. Although at first sight this process involved may seem like one of assimilation to the following segment, a closer look through a more theoretically sound lens points to cases of /ş/-elision that subsequently trigger compensatory lengthening of the following consonant. According to Moraic Theory, the elision of a moraic coda such as /ş/ in this dialect would leave its mora stranded. Since prosodic or metrical positions such as the mora cannot be deleted, the position needs to be filled by the lengthening of one of the surrounding sounds. In this dialect, the following consonant takes on that role, which spreads to the left to fill the empty mora slot, thus yielding a geminate consonant. The spectrograms show no signs of an aspiration. Instead, they show a considerably long consonant with a duration of approximately 130ms where [ş] – or [ɦ, h] – should have been versus a normal consonant duration of approximately 50–70ms for the specific examples given (Figures 3.6a–b).

The final realization of /ş/ documented in the data is as a glottal stop. Due to the small amount of instantiations of this allophone, stressless syllables were also included in the analysis. Glottalizations of /ş/ accounted for 8 percent of the data analyzed. The spectrograms show a transient typical of glottal stops. In addition, the surrounding vowels occasionally show glottal stop coarticulation effects by exhibiting a creaky voice quality, which could be claimed to enhance the effects and the perception of the glottal stop.

Notes

1 This dialect undergoes a separate strengthening process in which the voiced approximants [β, ð̞, ɣ, ʝ] become [b, d̪, g, ɟ͡ʝ], respectively, after an aspiration, hence the change
   [ð̞] → [d̪] in this example. This process can also be found in the rest of the Caribbean,
   in Colombia (except Nariño), El Salvador, Honduras, and Nicaragua (Canfield 1981).
2 The speaker exhibits devoicing of [d̪] → [d̪̥] in this example.
3 See Cortés Gómez (1979) for data related to the west of Spain.

Bibliography

Alba, O. (Ed.). (1982). *El español del Caribe: ponencias del VI Simposio de Dialectología.*
    Santiago, Dominican Republic: Universidad Católica Madre y Maestra.
Canfield, D. L. (1981). *Spanish pronunciation in the Americas.* Chicago, IL: University of
    Chicago Press.
Cortés Gómez, E. (1979). *El habla popular de Higuera de Vargas.* Badajoz, Spain:
    Diputación provincial.
Gerfen, C. (2002). Andalusian codas. *Probus, 14,* 247–277.
Granda, G. de. (1994). Español de América, español de África y hablas criollas hispánicas.
    Madrid, Spain: Gredos.
Hammond, R. M. (1986). En torno a una regla global en la fonología del español de Cuba.
    In R. A. Núñez Cedeño, I. Páez Urdaneta & J. M. Guitart (Eds.), *Estudios sobre la
    fonología del español del Caribe* (pp. 31–39). Caracas, Colombia: La Casa de Bello.
Hayes, B. (1989). Compensatory lengthening in moraic phonology. *Linguistic Inquiry, 20,*
    253–306.
Henríquez Ureña, P. (1921). Observaciones sobre el español en América I. *Revista de
    Filología Española, 8,* 357–390.
Henríquez Ureña, P. (1930). Observaciones sobre el español de América II. *Revista de
    Filología Española, 17*(1), 277–284.
Hyman, L. M. (1985). *A theory of phonological weight.* Dordrecht, Netherlands: Foris.
Ladefoged, P. (2001). *A course in phonetics* (4th ed.). Fort Worth, TX: Harcourt College
    Publishers.
Lapesa, R. (1964). El andaluz y el español de América. *Presente y Futuro de la Lengua
    Española, 2,* 173–182.
Lapesa, R. (1981). *Historia de la lengua española* (9th ed.). Madrid, Spain: Gredos.
Laufer, A. (1991). The 'glottal fricatives'. *Journal of the International Phonetic Associa-
    tion, 21*(2), 91–93.
Menéndez Pidal, R. (1957). Sevilla frente a Madrid: algunas precisiones sobre el español
    de América. In D. Catalán (Ed.), *Miscelánea homenaje a André Martinet: estructural-
    ismo e historia* (pp. 99–165). La Laguna, Spain: Universidad de La Laguna.
Menéndez Pidal, R. (1968). *Orígenes del español.* Madrid, Spain: Espasa-Calpe.
Moreno de Alba, J. G. (1988). *El español en América* (2nd ed.). Mexico, DF, Mexico:
    Fondo de Cultura Económica.
Navarro Tomás, T. (1948). El español en Puerto Rico: contribución a la geografía lingüística
    hispanoamericana. San Juan: Editorial de la Universidad de Puerto Rico.
Núñez Cedeño, R. A. (1988). Alargamiento vocálico compensatorio en el español cubano:
    un análisis autosegmental. In R. M. Hammond & M. C. Resnick (Eds.), *Studies in Car-
    ibbean Spanish dialectology* (pp. 261–285). Washington, DC: Georgetown University
    Press.

Parodi, C. (1995). *Orígenes del español americano*. México, DF, Mexico: Universidad Nacional Autónoma de México.

Penny, R. (2002). *A history of the Spanish language* (2nd ed.). Cambridge, United Kingdom: Cambridge University Press.

Valentín-Márquez, W. (2006). La oclusión glotal y la construcción lingüística de identidades sociales en Puerto Rico. In N. Sagarra & A. J. Toribio (Eds.), *Selected proceedings of the 9th hispanic linguistics symposium* (pp. 326–441). Somerville, MA: Cascadilla Proceedings Project.

Syntax

4 The nature and position of subjects in Puerto Rican Spanish wh-questions

Empirical evidence and theoretical implications

Juan Pablo Comínguez

1 Introduction

Interrogative wh-movement in Caribbean varieties of Spanish (CS) exhibits a distinctive syntactic characteristic regarding the position of subjects. By contrast to General Spanish (GS), CS allows the occurrence of preverbal subjects (e.g., Bergen 1976; Davis 1971; Lantolf 1980; Lipski 1977; Navarro Tomás 1948; Quirk 1972; among others). Whereas in GS subjects cannot surface preverbally like in (1b), this is not the case in CS, where subjects seem to freely occur post- and preverbally as in (2a) and (2b).

(1) General Spanish
      a.   ¿Qué dices tú?
           what say-2ps you
           'What do you say?'
      b.   *¿Qué tú dices?
           what you say-2ps
           'What do you say?'

(2) Caribbean Spanish
      a.   ¿Qué dices tú?
           what say-2ps you
           'What do you say?'
      b.   ¿Qué tú dices?
           what you say-2ps
           'What do you say?'

Despite the fact that the existence of preverbal pronominal subjects as *tú* in wh-questions in Puerto Rican Spanish (PRSp) is a well-known phenomenon, the extent to which subjects in this variety can surface preverbally in these constructions is still far from being clear. On the one hand, some researchers showed that preverbal subjects are unmarked (Lizardi 1993; Suñer & Lizardi 1995), but others found exactly the opposite (Brown & Rivas 2011; Gutiérrez-Bravo 2008a). On the other hand, the data in those studies is inconsistent with regard to whether or not non-pronominal subjects can occur preverbally.

For these reasons, this chapter experimentally explores the extent to which non-pronominal subjects can surface preverbally in PRSp wh-questions. In order to do so, an experiment aimed at eliciting knowledge of non-pronominal subject positions in argumental and non-argumental wh-questions was conducted with native speakers of PRSp living in San Juan. These experimental data are supplemented with further non-experimental data obtained through the judgments of some of the subjects who participated in the original study. This supplement is aimed at providing a more accurate description of the syntactic options available in this variety of Spanish.

This work also accounts for the obtained data along the lines of the Minimalist Program (Chomsky 1995 and much subsequent work). This new account for the syntax of wh-questions in PRSp seeks to reduce dialectal syntactic variation to the set of available syntactic operations of the computational system for human language such as Agree and Move (Chomsky 2000, 2001, 2004). Other previous generative approaches to the syntax of PRSp wh-questions cannot account for the empirical evidence reported in this chapter (Gutiérrez-Bravo 2008a), or have to stipulate the weakening of language-specific rules or conditions in order to account for it (e.g., Suñer 1994).

This chapter is organized as follows: Section 2 reviews previous approaches to the position and nature of subjects in PRSp interrogative wh-movement; Section 3 describes the methodology employed in the experiment and also provides the results; Section 4 accounts for the attested data in an analysis couched within the Minimalist Program (Chomsky 1995 and subsequent work); Section 5 is about the discourse effects associated with preverbal and postverbal subjects in PRSp wh-questions; Section 6 concludes with final remarks and directions for further research.

2 Previous studies on subjects and interrogative wh-movement in Puerto Rican Spanish

Since Navarro Tomás (1948), the existence of preverbal subjects in wh-questions has been advanced to be a phenomenon characterizing the variety of Spanish spoken in Puerto Rico. Data obtained from the administration of a questionnaire to native Puerto Ricans in the 1920s led Navarro Tomás to observe that only first and second person subject pronouns could occur preverbally in PRSp wh-questions. Furthermore, he noticed an asymmetry between matrix and embedded interrogatives according to which second person subject pronouns predominantly surfaced in matrix questions, whereas their embedded counterparts exhibited more variability as first person subject pronouns were also available in that position.

The extent to which other pronominal and non-pronominal subjects were able to surface preverbally in CS wh-questions – including the Puerto Rican variety – was extensively debated in a series of papers published in the 1970s (Bergen 1976; Davis 1971; Lipski 1977; Quirk 1972). However, these scholars were unable to determine whether third person subject pronouns and full DPs such as proper names could occur preverbally in that type of interrogatives, perhaps due to their lack of empirical research. A pioneering empirical study conducted by Lantolf (1980) with speakers of PRSp living in Rochester, New York revealed the existence of a hierarchy concerning the type of subjects allowed to occur in a preverbal position: informal second person singular pronoun (*tú*) > first person singular pronoun (*yo*) > proper names (*Juan*) > formal second person singular pronoun (*usted*) > first person plural pronoun (*nosotros*) > third person singular pronoun (*él*). A remarkable finding of this study is the participants' preference for preverbal subjects in the case of proper names such as *Juan*, something advanced not to be possible by previous researchers, especially in the case of Lipski (1977).

More contemporary research utilizing oral corpora revealed further contradictory findings. Lizardi (1993) and Suñer and Lizardi (1995) found that preverbal subjects in wh-interrogatives were unmarked since overt subjects surfaced more preverbally than postverbally.[1] Specifically, Suñer and Lizardi (1995) analyzed 572 tokens of wh-questions obtained from conversations and TV and radio shows. Their analysis revealed that pronominal subjects targeted the preverbal position 83 percent of the time, and non-pronominal subjects (full DPs) did so 59 percent of the time. The postverbal position was occupied 17 percent and 41 percent of the time by pronominal subjects and non-pronominal subjects, respectively. From these patterns shown in Table 4.1, Suñer and Lizardi (1995) pointed out that, despite the fact that both types of subjects showed a solid tendency to occur preverbally in wh-questions, the pronominal ones surfaced preverbally more often than their non-pronominal counterparts.

Along these lines, Lizardi (1993) analyzed 1,912 tokens of wh-interrogatives and found that preverbal subjects were unmarked. Her analysis including null subjects revealed that 44 percent of the subjects were overt and appeared preverbally, overt postverbal subjects occurring only 17 percent of the time. In addition, null subjects occurred 39 percent of the time. Once null subjects were removed from the sample, 72 percent of the subjects were preverbal, only 28 percent of them being postverbal, as illustrated in Table 4.2.

Table 4.1 Position and type of subjects in wh-questions (Suñer and Lizardi 1995)

Type of subject	Preverbal position (%)	Postverbal position (%)
Pronominal	83	17
Non-pronominal	59	41

Table 4.2 Position of subjects in wh-questions (Lizardi 1993)

Preverbal position (%)	Postverbal position (%)
72	28

In the studies by Suñer and Lizardi (1995) and Lizardi (1993), an asymmetry concerning subject position and type of subject (pronominal and non-pronominal) was found when the distinction between argumental and non-argumental wh-operators was taken into account. This distinction refers to a well-known phenomenon existing in GS interrogative wh-movement, which was theoretically addressed for the first time by Torrego (1984) and further explored by Suñer (1994), among many others.[2] The contrast between (3) and (4) illustrates this phenomenon. Whereas preverbal subjects cannot surface with argumental wh-operators as in (3), the opposite is found with non-argumental wh-operators, which allow the occurrence of preverbal subjects in wh-questions as in (4). Examples in (4) are from Torrego (1984, 106).

(3)   *¿Qué María dijo?
          what María said-3ps
          'What did María say?'
(4) a.   ¿En qué medida la Constitución ha contribuido a eso?
          in what measure the Constitution has-3ps contributed to that
          'In what sense has the Constitution contributed to that?'
     b.   ¿Por qué Juan quiere salir antes que los demás?
          for what Juan wants-3ps leave before that the others
          'Why does Juan want to leave before the others?'

Once the distinction between argumental and non-argumental wh-words was taken into account in PRSp, the unmarked status of preverbal subjects still held in the data analyzed by Suñer and Lizardi (1995) and Lizardi (1993). For example, Lizardi (1993) reported that 64 percent of subjects occurred preverbally with argumental wh-operators, whereas the 80 percent of them did so with non-argumental wh-words, as Table 4.3 shows.

However, when the pronominal and non-pronominal nature of subjects was taken into account, the percentages changed. Pronominal subjects overwhelmingly surfaced preverbally with either argumental wh-words (88 percent) or non argumental wh-words (95 percent), as displayed in Table 4.4. By contrast, non-pronominal subjects surfaced preverbally 51 percent of the time with non-argumental wh-words, but only 9 percent of the time with argumental wh-operators (see Table 4.5 below). In other words, the nature of subjects (pronominal versus non-pronominal) had an impact on whether or not they could surface preverbally with argumental wh-operators.

Table 4.3 Position and type of wh-operator in wh-questions (Lizardi 1993)

Type of wh-operator	Preverbal subjects (%)	Postverbal subjects (%)
Argumental	64	36
Non-argumental	80	20

Table 4.4 Type and position of subjects in argumental wh-questions (Lizardi 1993)

Type of subject	Preverbal position (%)	Postverbal position (%)
Pronominal	88	12
Non-pronominal	9	91

Table 4.5 Type and position of subjects in non-argumental wh-questions (Lizardi 1993)

Type of subject	Preverbal position (%)	Postverbal position (%)
Pronominal	95	5
Non-pronominal	51	49

A similar pattern was found by Suñer and Lizardi (1995). They reported that pronominal preverbal subject occurred 77 percent of the time with argumental wh-operators and 89 percent of the time with non-argumental wh-words. Instead, non-pronominal subjects appeared preverbally 69 percent of the time with non-argumental wh-words, and 32 percent of the time with argumental operators. These patterns are illustrated in Tables 4.6 and 4.7.

Finally, Lizardi (1993) remarked two relevant phenomena. On the one hand, some subject pronouns tended to occur more preverbally than others. For instance, second person singular subject pronouns tended to occur preverbally almost 97 percent of the time with both argumental and non-argumental wh-operators, but third person singular pronouns only did so 64 percent of the time. On the other hand, whereas there were no differences between matrix and embedded interrogative clauses with pronominal subjects, which overwhelmingly tended to occur preverbally, there was a significant difference between these types of clauses with non-pronominal subjects. In matrix clauses, this type of subjects occurred preverbally 27 percent of the time. However, the same type of subjects occurred preverbally 43 percent of the time in embedded wh-questions. These two phenomena remarked by Lizardi (1993) suggest that even the type of pronominal subject has an impact on the extent to which it can surface preverbally, and that embedded questions seem to allow non-pronominal subjects to occur both pre- and postverbally.

In sum, the studies by Suñer and Lizardi (1995) and Lizardi (1993) revealed that preverbal subjects are unmarked in matrix interrogative wh-movement in PRSp, the pronominal nature of subjects having a stronger occurrence in that position than their non-pronominal counterparts. In addition, this asymmetry between pronominal and non-pronominal subjects tended to vanish in embedded interrogatives, since non-pronominal subjects seem to be able to occur either pre- or postverbally.

In contrast to these findings, two more recent studies found that both pronominal and non-pronominal preverbal subjects in PRSp wh-questions were the marked option. Gutiérrez-Bravo (2008a) reported a preliminary text count of PRSp

Table 4.6 Type and position of subjects in argumental wh-questions (Suñer & Lizardi 1995)

Type of subject	Preverbal position (%)	Postverbal position (%)
Pronominal	77	23
Non-pronominal	32	68

Table 4.7 Type and position of subjects in non-argumental wh-questions (Suñer & Lizardi 1995)

Type of subject	Preverbal position (%)	Postverbal position (%)
Pronominal	89	11
Non-pronominal	69	31

wh-interrogatives, which was based on an oral corpus of formally educated speakers from San Juan (Morales & Vaquero 1990). The text count showed that wh-questions exhibited only 10 percent of preverbal subjects, most of which tended to be pronominal. From these findings, Gutiérrez-Bravo (2008a) concluded that preverbal subjects in PRSp interrogative wh-movement were the marked option.

More recently, Brown and Rivas (2011) analyzed 882 wh-questions taken from an oral corpus and found that subjects surfaced only 14 percent of the time in preverbal position, which was interpreted by the researchers as evidence of the marked status of preverbal subjects in wh-interrogatives in this variety of Spanish. With a focus on matrix wh-questions and without distinguishing between argumental and non-argumental wh-operators, Brown and Rivas (2011) reported that lack of subject-verb inversion took place with 86 percent of first and second person singular pronouns, and only with 19 percent of third person singular pronouns and 4 percent of full DPs. In addition, 55 percent of the subjects occurred in a preverbal position with rhetorical and quotative questions, and only 15 percent with authentic questions. From these findings, Brown and Rivas (2011) concluded that non-inversion in wh-questions is not prevalent in this variety of Spanish, and associating PRSp with lack of subject-verb inversion in wh-questions is a sociolinguistic stereotype (Brown & Rivas 2011: 35).

With the exception of Brown and Rivas (2011), who associated the existence of preverbal subjects with a linguistic change consisting in PRSp becoming a rigid SVO language, Suñer and Lizardi (1995), Lizardi (1993), and Gutiérrez-Bravo (2008a) analyzed the existence of this phenomenon as a topicalization strategy available in this variety. More specifically, they argued that preverbal subjects were salient topics, the asymmetry between pronominal and non-pronominal preverbal subjects resulting from the fact that pronouns are better elements to convey this pragmatic function than full DPs.

To sum up, the existing evidence on the nature and position of subjects in PRSp wh-questions is inconclusive. Whereas some studies showed that preverbal subjects are unmarked (Lizardi 1993; Suñer & Lizardi 1995), others found the opposite (Brown & Rivas 2011; Gutiérrez-Bravo 2008a). In the light of these findings, an experiment aimed at eliciting native judgments on the position of subjects in PRSp wh-questions was conducted in San Juan, Puerto Rico.

3 The study

3.1 Participants

Twenty-nine native speakers of Puerto Rican Spanish living in San Juan participated in the study. The group comprised a total of 18 females and 11 males, with a mean age of 26 (range: 18–59). All of them had a similar educational background, as they held undergraduate and graduate degrees in a wide variety of disciplines. All of them were born in Puerto Rico and spent their entire lives there, with the exceptions of two participants who reported having spent between seven months and a year in the United States. The other participants stayed in countries where Spanish was not spoken (United States, as well as European and African countries) in periods ranging from days to two months.

Most of the participants reported using Spanish at home, at work, and with family and friends, with the exception of eight of them, who reported using English at work. In some cases, they had to read papers in that language or interact with native speakers of English. All the participants had some knowledge of a second language, to which they were exposed and learned during primary and secondary school, or college. Besides English, subjects reported having some knowledge of Romance languages such as Italian and French. However, all the participants included in the sample considered themselves not to be bilinguals, their dominant language being Spanish, the language with which they felt more comfortable.

3.2 Methods

All the participants completed a consent form, in addition to a questionnaire about their personal information (e.g., age, sex, level of formal education, etc.). Moreover, the questionnaire asked the participants to provide information about their knowledge of first and second languages; how, where, and for how long they learned them; as well as the situations in which they normally used them, including information about study abroad experiences.

After the completion of the aforementioned forms, subjects took part in the experiment, which is described in the next subsection. The experiment was administered to the participants in places that were convenient for them and in which they felt comfortable. All the subjects received monetary compensation for their participation in the study. The entire session lasted around 60 minutes in total.

3.3 The experiment: an acceptability judgment task

Participants completed a paper-based acceptability judgment task in order to obtain data regarding knowledge of interrogative wh-movement and the position of non-pronominal subjects. The test constructions of this study were interrogative sentences with argumental and non-argumental wh-operators, and non-pronominal preverbal and postverbal subjects. The reasons for only including non-pronominal subjects were three: first, including pronominal subjects in the experiment would have increased the quantity of experimental sentences to a number such that participants would have become exhausted during the completion of the task, results being uninformative. Including the 10 subject pronouns used in Puerto Rican Spanish and non-pronominal subjects would have resulted in a total of 264 experimental sentences (six tokens per each of the four experimental conditions and 11 types of subjects; see the details below about the experimental conditions). The experimental sentences added to an equivalent number of fillers would have given a total of 528 sentences used in the task, which is unfeasible to administer to subjects in one experimental session. Second, having reduced the number of tokens per condition and types of subject would have rendered any statistical analysis on the results useless, as a consequence of lack of statistical power. From this, the analysis and interpretation of results and any variability found in them would have been inconclusive. Finally, only non-pronominal subjects were included under the rationale that if they could occur preverbally, their pronominal counterparts would also be able to do so, but not vice versa (see Ordóñez & Olarrea 2006, who found that Dominican Spanish only allows pronominal preverbal subjects, but not their non-pronominal counterparts).

As for the experimental design, there were two independent variables in the study. Variable A (subject status) distinguishes non-pronominal preverbal subjects from non-pronominal postverbal subjects. Variable B (wh-operator) distinguishes questions with argumental wh-operators from questions with non-argumental wh-operators. This gives rise to four conditions. There were questions with argumental wh-operators and preverbal subjects (first condition), questions with non-argumental wh-operators and preverbal subjects (second condition), questions with argumental wh-operators and postverbal subjects (third condition), and questions with non-argumental wh-operators and postverbal subjects (fourth condition).

There were six tokens per condition, giving rise to a total of 24 stimuli. The sentence subjects were balanced with regard to gender, non-pronominal status (proper and common names), and animacy and humanity (two proper names, two common animate names, and two common inanimate names). The wh-operators utilized in the experimental sentences were *qué* 'what' as the argumental wh-word, and *cuándo* 'when' and *dónde* 'where' as the non-argumental wh-phrases. The non-argumental wh-operators were counterbalanced with the questions containing preverbal (three questions with *cuándo* and three with *dónde*) and postverbal subjects (three questions with *cuándo* and three with *dónde*). All the verbs were transitive, belonged to different endings, and were in the preterit, present, and future tenses. All lexical items were compatible with the lexical idiosyncrasies of the Puerto Rican variety.

In addition to the stimuli, there were 24 fillers so that participants would not realize what kind of data the study was trying to elicit. These 24 fillers were divided into 12 ungrammatical questions and 12 grammatical questions (yes/no questions, and questions with null subjects). In total, there were 48 items, which were randomized following usual procedures in experimental studies. Three lists with the same sentences in different random orders were created, and subjects were randomly assigned to one of these lists in a balanced way so that the same amount of subjects would read each list.

The experimental method consisted of having subjects read a short paragraph of around 50 words, which provided participants with a context. After this, they had to determine how acceptable the following question was with regard to that context. Subjects had to assign a numeric value indicating the level of acceptability of that question according to their native intuitions. The value was assigned by expressing the judgment within a range from 0 (*totally unacceptable*) to 100 (*totally acceptable*). There were two references (one grammatical; another ungrammatical) provided in the task with respect to *totally unacceptable* and *totally acceptable*. These references were meant to work as clear scale anchors. In (5) there is a sample of the task.

(5)   Sample of the experimental task:

Últimamente, el gobierno está muy preocupado por las noticias que publican los grandes medios de comunicación. En particular, la preocupación viene del diario más importante del país, donde su director siempre escribe editoriales en contra del gobierno. Tal es así que la primera pregunta que se hacen los ministros al reunirse cada mañana es:

¿Qué el director escribió en el editorial?

De acuerdo con su juicio, determine un puntaje de aceptabilidad para esta oración en ese contexto.

0	10	30	50	70	90	100

completamente   completamente
inaceptable   aceptable

Puntaje: _____

'Lately, the government is very concerned about reports that mainstream media publish. In particular, their concern is about the most important newspaper in the country, where his manager always writes editorials against the government. For this reason, the first question that ministers ask every morning when they meet is:

What did the manager write in the editorial?

According to your judgment, determine an acceptability score for this sentence in this context.

0	10	30	50	70	90	100

completely   completely
unacceptable   acceptable
                                                              Score: _____'

Before beginning the actual eliciting task, subjects had to read the instructions and complete a training session with eight training items.

3.4 Results

Table 4.8 shows the acceptability means for all the experimental items; namely, the fillers (grammatical and ungrammatical questions) and stimuli (wh-questions with preverbal and postverbal subjects). It reveals that wh-questions with preverbal subjects were highly accepted by participants, but at a slightly lower rate than their counterparts with postverbal subjects and grammatical fillers. Importantly, the rate of acceptability of wh-questions with preverbal subject is much higher than the rate for ungrammatical questions.

The results in Table 4.8 indicate that wh-questions with preverbal subjects are acceptable in the grammar of these speakers, but to a slightly lesser extent than wh-questions with postverbal subjects and yes-no questions.

Table 4.9 represents the means of acceptability for all the four experimental stimuli, namely; argumental wh-questions with preverbal subjects, non-argumental wh-questions with preverbal subjects, argumental wh-questions with postverbal subjects, and non-argumental questions with postverbal subjects. It shows the existence of differences regarding acceptability scores between conditions. Wh-questions with preverbal subjects obtained lower – but still high – scores than their counterparts with postverbal subjects. Moreover, argumental wh-questions with preverbal subjects received a lower score than their non-argumental counterparts. Finally, argumental wh-questions with postverbal subjects received higher scores than their non-argumental counterparts.

A two-way repeated measures ANOVA with a 2 (subject status) x 2 (wh-operator) factorial design revealed a significant main effect for subject status, $F(1, 28) = 15.319$, $p. <.01$. However, there was no significant effect for wh-operator,

Table 4.8 Means of the experimental items (fillers and stimuli)

Type of item	Mean
Grammatical fillers	94.43
Ungrammatical fillers	2.49
Wh-questions with preverbal subjects	80.65
Wh-questions with postverbal subjects	92.17

Table 4.9 Means and standard deviations of the experimental stimuli

Type of stimulus	Mean	Standard deviation
Preverbal subjects with argumental wh-operators	78.78	23.08
Preverbal subjects with non-argumental wh-operators	82.6	14.61
Postverbal subjects with argumental wh-operators	93.93	6.94
Postverbal subjects with non-argumental wh-operators	90.13	11.92

$F(1, 28) = .000, p > .05$, and no significant interaction between subject status and wh-operator, $F(1, 28) = 3.816, p > .05$. Pairwise comparisons showed that the difference between argumental and non-argumental questions with preverbal subjects was not significant ($p = .219$). In contrast, the comparisons revealed that the difference between argumental questions with preverbal subjects and argumental questions with postverbal subjects was significant ($p = .001$), which suggests that argumental wh-questions with postverbal subjects are slightly more preferred than their preverbal counterparts. Furthermore, the difference between non-argumental questions with preverbal subjects and argumental questions with postverbal subjects was significant ($p = .010$), which suggests that non-argumental questions with preverbal subjects are slightly less preferred than argumental questions with postverbal subjects. Finally, the pairwise comparisons showed that the difference between argumental and non-argumental questions with postverbal subjects was not significant ($p = .108$).

To sum up, the statistical analysis revealed that wh-questions with preverbal subjects were highly accepted but at a slightly lesser extent than wh-questions with postverbal subjects, regardless of the argumental status of the wh-operator.

3.5 Discussion

The results from the acceptability judgment task reveal that preverbal subjects in wh-questions are highly accepted by native speakers of PRSp, which indicates that this syntactic option is available in the grammar of these speakers. However, as mentioned above, the postverbal option seems to be slightly more preferred than its preverbal counterpart. In this respect, this pattern is similar to the one found by Lizardi (1993) in embedded wh-questions. In her study, in spite of existing a slightly higher occurrence (53 percent versus 47 percent) of non-pronominal postverbal subjects, their preverbal counterparts occurred at a high rate. From this, Lizardi (1993) concluded that the non-pronominal subjects could occur either pre- or postverbally. Furthermore, she pointed out that her findings showed a novel phenomenon in embedded contexts when compared to what Navarro Tomás (1948) had found; namely, the existence of non-pronominal preverbal subjects. The data reported in this chapter is consistent with Lizardi's (1993) findings on embedded interrogatives, but in this case at the matrix level. In this respect, these experimentally obtained data reveal a novel pattern according to which non-pronominal preverbal subjects can appear in PRSp matrix interrogatives.

One issue that needs to be addressed is why preverbal subjects are slightly less preferred. Existing accounts (Gutiérrez-Bravo 2008a; Lizardi 1993; Suñer & Lizardi 1995) for the asymmetry between pronominal and non-pronominal subjects in their preverbal occurrence proposed that it was an epiphenomenon of the pragmatic function associated with preverbal subjects in wh-questions – that is, they are topics. In particular, as PRSp has been shown to have an increasing loss of the pragmatic differences associated with null and overt subject pronouns in null-subject languages (Morales 1999; among others), overt subject pronouns in PRSp have been argued to have taken over the pragmatic functions associated with null subjects (Morales 1999; among others). Instead of only employing null pronominal subjects to realize discourse topics in the topichood dimension of information structure as in General Spanish (Gutiérrez-Bravo 2008b; Casielles-Suarez 2004; among others), PRSp also employs overt subject pronouns (Morales 1999; among others).

For this reason, if preverbal subjects in PRSp wh-questions are interpreted as topics or sentence themes (Gutiérrez-Bravo 2008a; Lizardi 1993; Suñer & Lizardi 1995), it follows that pronominal subjects are more preferred than their non-pronominal counterparts when they occur preverbally, something that is attested in oral corpora. This is because full DPs are restricted to introduce new discourse topics or realize topic shifts in the topichood dimension of information structure, whereas overt pronominal subjects can also express topic continuity, as they have taken over the pragmatic functions associated with null subjects in other Spanish varieties (Morales 1999).

Building on these previous accounts for the asymmetry between pronominal and non-pronominal preverbal subjects in PRSp wh-questions, it can be entertained that the slightly lower acceptability scores for preverbal subjects reported in this chapter is a performance epiphenomenon resulting from the fact that in PRSp that is a position more targeted by pronominal subjects, due to their pragmatic functions in the topichood dimension of information structure. In other words, whereas any type of subject (i.e., pronominal or non-pronominal) can surface preverbally in PRSp wh-questions from a syntactic point of view, native differences in the use and experimental acceptance of the type of subject results from the pragmatic functions related to full DPs and overt subject pronouns in this variety of Spanish.

4 The syntax of subjects and interrogative wh-movement in PRSp

This section reviews the existing theoretical accounts for PRSp wh-questions couched within the generative framework.

4.1 The weakening of the Argumental Agreement Licensing (Suñer 1994)

Suñer (1994) put forth the idea that the existence of preverbal subjects in wh-questions is the consequence of PRSp experiencing linguistic change. More specifically, PRSp is exhibiting a weakening of the Argumental Agreement Licensing condition, which is described in (6).

(6)   Argumental Agreement Licensing (AAL)
    a. Argumental wh-phrases must be licensed through symmetric Arg-agreement between α (=SpecC) and β (=C).
    b. β Arg-agrees with γ (=V) only if β and γ are Arg-marked and no other Arg-marked element is closer to γ. (Suñer 1994: 361)

The AAL is a Spanish-specific condition advanced in order to account for the asymmetry between argumental and non-argumental wh-operators and the existence of preverbal subjects in GS wh-questions:

(7) a. ¿Qué dice María?
    what says-3ps María
    'What does María say?'
  b. *¿Qué María dice?
    what María says-3ps
    'What does María say?'

(8) a. ¿Por qué comió Pedro la torta?
    for what ate-3ps Pedro the cake
    'Why did Peter eat the cake?'
  b. ¿Por qué Pedro comió la torta?
    for what Pedro ate-3ps the cake
    'Why did Peter eat the cake?'

Whereas (7a), (8a), and (8b) comply with the AAL, (7b) does not. This is because there is an argument (the subject DP *María*) between the argumental wh-operator and INFL. This is illustrated in a clearer way in (9b), in which the occurrence of the subject DP in [Spec, TP] gives rise to intervention effects between the argumental wh-operator in [Spec, CP] and INFL. By contrast, in (9a) there is no such intervention effect due to the fact that there is no constituent in [Spec, TP]. For this reason, the AAL is satisfied in (9a).

(9) a. $[_{CP}$ ARG WH $[C°$ $[_{TP}$ $[V+INFL]$ ...
      ^_____ ^_____ ^
  b. $[_{CP}$ ARG WH $[C°$ $[_{TP}$ DP $[V+INFL]$ ...
      ^_____ ^____X__^

(Zagona 2002: 246)

According to Suñer (1994), Caribbean Spanish in general and PRSp in particular is showing weakening of agreement all across the board, the AAL being one such case. For this reason, preverbal subjects can surface with argumental wh-operators in PRSp Spanish.

4.2 The Interrogative Clause Condition (Gutiérrez-Bravo 2008a)

Gutiérrez-Bravo (2008a) put forward the idea that interrogative clauses are obtained via the Interrogative Clause Condition (ICC), which is illustrated in (10):

(10) ICC
     A clausal Extended Projection is interrogative iff the head of the highest phrase in the Extended Projection bears the feature [Q]. (228)

In this approach, the difference between PRSp and GS is reduced to the way in which the ICC is satisfied. In this respect, PRSp projects either a TP or a CP in matrix clauses, their heads being assigned the feature [Q] in a Spec-Agreement fashion by a wh-operator in their specifier position. The same options are available in embedded clauses. By contrast, GS only projects a TP in matrix clauses, for which reason it does not allow preverbal subjects in matrix interrogative wh-movement. This is because, in this variety, [Spec, TP] is the landing site of wh-operators (but see Villa-García 2015, among others, for an analysis against this proposal). Moreover, GS also allows a CP to be projected in embedded clauses, as both preverbal and postverbal subjects are attested in this interrogative context according to Gutiérrez-Bravo (2008a).

In PRSp, either a TP or CP can be projected in both embedded and matrix interrogative contexts, the ICC being satisfied by a wh-operator in either [Spec, TP] or [Spec, CP]. For this reason, the word order WH-S-V is available in PRSp. Importantly, in this analysis, PRSp resorts to projecting a CP in whose specifier position the wh-phrase can land when there are two phrases that must be fronted to the left periphery of the sentence. That is, in PRSp when a subject and another constituent have to undergo movement to the left-periphery of the sentence, they compete for landing in [Spec, TP]. For instance, when a subject targets [Spec, TP] then the wh-operator has to land in [Spec, CP] in order to comply with the ICC; this gives rise to the order WH-S-V. In contrast, when the wh-operator lands in [Spec, TP] the subject is an adjunct to TP, which gives rise to the order S-WH-V as in (11) below. What triggers movement to the left-periphery in the case of DPs is the need to value a [topic] feature.

(11)   ¿Tú qué haces?
       you, what does-2ps
       'You, what do you do?'

As mentioned above, preverbal subjects in PRSp wh-questions are topics in Gutiérrez-Bravo's (2008a) analysis. Crucially, in his analysis, the existence of two possible projections (TP and CP) in which the ICC is satisfied in PRSp predicts that constituents such as clitic-doubled left dislocations (CLLDs) can intervene between the wh-operator and the verb. This is because the [Spec, TP] position is also a target landing site for CLLDs, as they have to undergo movement to that position to value the [topic] feature. Taking some examples such as (12) from Suñer (1994), Gutiérrez-Bravo (2008a) shows that this prediction seems to be borne out in PRSp.

(12)   ¿Qué al Rafo le han hecho?
       what to-the Rafo CL-3ps-DAT have-3ppl done
       'To Rafo, what have they done? (Suñer 1994: 367)

However, native informants who participated in the study reported in this chapter, and who accept non-pronominal preverbal subjects in wh-questions, reject

CLLDs intervening between the wh-operator and the verb as in (12). According to their judgments, CLLDs can only appear in the left periphery of the sentence preceding the wh-operator as in (13c) and (13d). Finally, the only argument that can occur between the wh-operator and the verb is the subject as shown in (13).

(13) a. *¿Qué a Pedro le dijo?
      what to Pedro CL-3ps-DAT told-3ps
      'To Peter, what did (s)he say?'
   b. *¿María qué a Pedro le dijo?
      María what to Pedro CL-3ps-DAT told-3ps
      'María, to Pedro, what did she say?'
   c. ¿A Pedro qué María le dijo?
      to Pedro what María CL-3ps-DAT told-3ps
      'To Pedro, what did María say?'
   d. ¿A Pedro qué le dijo?
      to Pedro what CL-3ps-DAT told-3ps
      'To Pedro, what did (s)he say?'

By taking into account these data from PRSp informants who accept preverbal subjects in wh-questions, the analysis put forth by Gutiérrez-Bravo (2008a) is not supported, since it predicts that constituents carrying a [topic] feature can land in [Spec, TP], an order WH-CLLD-V being possible, which is not.

In sum, existing generative analyses of PRSp wh-questions have to either resort to a language-specific stipulation to account for the existence of preverbal subjects (Suñer 1994) or their theoretical machinery makes predictions that are unsupported by data elicited from native informants (Gutiérrez-Bravo 2008a). For these reasons, the next section proposes a new theoretical account for the syntax of PRSp wh-questions.

4.3 A minimalist approach to the syntax of interrogative wh-movement in PRSp

In order to avoid language-specific conditions, and to gain enough empirical coverage of the phenomena under consideration, this chapter builds on previous work on T-to-C movement in General Spanish by Gallego (2004, 2006a, 2006b, 2006c, 2007, 2010). Before proposing this new approach, a description of Gallego's (2004, 2006a, 2006b, 2006c, 2007, 2010) analysis of GS interrogative wh-movement is provided.

4.3.1 The syntax of interrogative wh-movement in GS

Gallego (2004, 2006a, 2006b, 2006c, 2007, 2010) puts forth the idea that T-to-C movement is obligatory in GS wh-questions as a consequence of Phase Sliding in Romance Null Subject Languages.[3] Building on Chomsky's Phase Theory (2000, 2001, 2008), Phase Sliding refers to the hybrid phasal domain (v*-T_sP) obtained

after v*-to-T movement, which increases the "amount of structure that is trans-
ferred in the first phase" (Gallego 2010: 111). As a result of this process, the v*P
phase is lifted to T_sP, after which T_sP exhibits phase effects.[4] Once v* moves to T_s,
the complex v*-T_sP is created, T_sP inheriting the phase effects.

Along the lines of Grimshaw's (1991) Extended Projection, Gallego advances
that C is an extension of T_s and v* such that that they conform an abstract unit
within a phase form (Gallego 2010: 81). The C-T-v* abstract unit is argued to
share Tense features that must be valued between C and v* and T_s.[5] Despite the
fact that they form an abstract unit, they constitute different phases. Whereas the
first phase v*P is pushed up to T_sP, which results in the complex v*P-T_sP being the
first phasal domain, CP is the second phase in the syntactic derivation of Romance
Null Subject Languages. This is the only difference with respect to other language
types, in which just v*P is the first phase and CP is the second one.

Phase Sliding is developed by Gallego by resorting to Pesetsky's and Torrego's
(2001, 2004, 2006, 2007) Case system, in which Case is understood as tense.
More precisely, Case is the result of DPs bearing a [uT] feature, which must be
valued by T_s in order to be deleted. In addition to valuing DPs' [uT], T_s also has to
value [uT] features borne by C. In Pesetsky's and Torrego's system (2001), this is
what triggers T-to-C movement.

For instance, (14) illustrates how interrogative wh-movement in GS involves
T-to-C movement in order to value C's [uT].

(14) $[_{CP}$ Qué$_{i [Wh]}$ dijo$_{j [T]}$ C$_{[trF, EPP] [uWh, EPP]}$ $[_{TP}$ María$_{k [uF]}$ T$_{j[T]}$ $[_{VP}$ **t$_k$ t$_j$ t$_i$**$]$ $]]$?
       'What did María say?'

In (14) C bears two kinds of uninterpretable features that must be deleted: [uWh]
and [uT]. One way for them to be deleted is by movement of constituents containing compatible features. For this reason, the wh-phrase *qué* and the inflected verb
dijo in T undergo movement to the specifier of CP and C, respectively.

By contrast, the reason for sequences such as (15) and (16) not triggering T-to-
C movement is accounted for by the nature of the prepositions pied-piped by
wh-adjuncts.

(15)   ¿Por qué Pedro comió la torta?
       for what ate-3ps Pedro the cake
       'Why did Pedro eat the cake?'

(16)   ¿En qué medida la Constitución ha contribuido a esto?
       in what measure the Constitution has-3ps contributed to that
       'In what sense has the Constitution contributed to this?'

According to Gallego (2007, 2010), in all these examples the adjunct pied-piping
a preposition prevents T-to-C movement, since prepositions are species of T, as
Pesetsky and Torrego (2004) claim. This means that they are endowed with an
interpretable [T] feature. For this reason, the complex wh-phrase pied-piping a
preposition can value C's [uT] in a Spec-Head configuration.

To sum up, wh-questions in GS require T-to-C movement so that C's [uT] are valued by T. When the wh-adjunct pied-pipes a preposition, C's [uT] can be valued by the preposition since they are endowed with [iT] in Gallego's (2007, 2010) analysis.

4.3.2 Interrogative wh-movement in PRSp: a proposal

Building on the existence of T-to-C movement in GS interrogative wh-movement, it is possible to reduce the difference between GS and PRSp to the ways in which C's [uT] is valued by T. In accordance with Chomsky (2000, 2001, 2004), uninterpretable features can be valued via Move or Agree, two available syntactic operations of the computational system for human language. From this, it is advanced that C's [uT] in PRSp is valued via T-to-C movement (Move) or via Agree in a probe-goal relation between C and T. These two mechanisms involved in valuing C's [uT] are illustrated in (17a) and (17b).

(17) a. ¿Qué dijo María?
          'What did María say?'
          $[_{CP}$ Qué$_{i \, [Wh]}$ dijo$_{j \, [T]}$ C$_{[u\text{T}, \, EPP] \, [u\text{Wh}, \, EPP]}$ $[_{TP}$ María$_{k \, [u\text{F}]}$ T$_{j[T]}$ $[_{VP}$ **t**$_k$ **t**$_j$ **t**$_i$]]] ?
      b. ¿Qué María dijo?
          'What did María say?'
          $[_{CP}$ Qué$_{i \, [Wh]}$ C$_{[u\text{F}] \, [u\text{Wh}, \, EPP]}$ $[_{TP}$ María$_{k \, [u\text{F}]}$ dijo$_{j \, [T]}$ $[_{VP}$ **t**$_k$ **t**$_j$ **t**$_i$]]] ?
          |_____AGREE_____|

What makes PRSp different is the fact of employing Agree to derive questions that do not involve wh-adjuncts pied-piping a preposition. In (17b), instead of valuing C's [uT] through the movement of T to C, C acts as a Probe and searches for a Goal within a local domain. This process results in having C's [uT] valued, the derivation converging at the interfaces.

In this variety of Spanish, valuing C's [uT] via Agree takes place in matrix, as well as in embedded clauses such as (18).

(18) a. Ellas no saben qué ese método les está haciendo.
          they no know-3ppl what that method CL-3ppl-DAT is-3ps doing
          'They do not know what that method is doing to them.'
                                                        (Suñer 1994: 366)
      b. Yo no sé qué la muchacha quería.
          I no know-1ps what the girl wanted-3ps
          'I do not know what the girl wanted.'
                                                (Suñer & Lizardi 1995: 195)

This analysis predicts that other instances of wh-movement (Chomsky 1977 and much subsequent work), such as exclamative sentences and relative clauses, should also display preverbal subjects. This prediction is borne out in data from oral corpora (Morales & Vaquero 1990), as well as in judgments from PRSp native speakers who participated in the study reported in this chapter. The sentences in (19) show that pronominal and non-pronominal preverbal subjects can surface preverbally in exclamatives. Example (19a) is taken from Morales and Vaquero (1990: 68).

(19)   a.   ¡Pero mira cómo yo estoy!
              but look-2ps how I am-1ps
              'But look how I am!'
        b.   ¡Qué linda María es!
              what pretty María is-3ps
              'How pretty María is!'

In addition, as pointed out by Morales (1999), relative clauses in PRSp display a higher occurrence of preverbal than postverbal subjects, which contrasts with the preferred default word order in GS. According to Gutiérrez-Bravo (2002), the default order in GS relative clauses is VS.

Taken together, all the available data on PRSp wh-movement suggest that Agree is an available option to value C's [uT], which gives rise to the existence of both pronominal and non-pronominal preverbal subjects occupying [Spec, TP] in wh-questions, exclamatives, and relative clauses. Note that these patterns are consistent with Ticio's proposal (see Chapter 5 this volume), who argues and demonstrates that preverbal and postverbal subjects in PRSp are in the same structural position. The next section advances another proposal according to which the different syntactic outputs obtained via Agree or Move are associated with different information structure effects.

5 Syntax and information structure: theme-rheme relations in PRSp wh-questions

As put forth by Suñer and Lizardi (1995: 196), preverbal subjects in PRSp wh-questions are sentence themes, whereas their postverbal counterparts are rhemes. More specifically, they argue that themes are outside the scope of the assertion, whereas the rhemes are under its scope (Suñer 1982). This distinction was further explored by Gutiérrez-Bravo (2008a). In his approach, preverbal subjects in wh-questions are topicalized constituents endowed with a [topic] feature, which must undergo movement to the left-periphery for pragmatic reasons.

Capitalizing on those approaches to discourse effects of subjects in PRSp wh-questions, this chapter proposes that the outputs of the syntactic operations Agree and Move are related to pragmatic effects. On the one hand, subjects obtain a theme interpretation when the valuing process takes place via Agree, and they end up surfacing in a preverbal position. In other words, subjects are salient topics and constitute what the sentence is about when C's [uT] is valued via Agree with T. On the other hand, subjects get a rheme interpretation when C's [uT] is valued via T-to-C movement, and they end up surfacing in a postverbal position. The interpretation that subjects obtain is not the result of their landing site, or the syntactic mechanisms involved in valuing C's [*u*T]. Instead, the interpretations result from the scope relations between the subject DP and the predicate. To be more specific, the interpretations are obtained depending on whether the subject DP grounds the predicate, or vice versa, as shown below.

Following a syntactic approach to theme/rheme relations along the lines of Chomsky's Minimalist Program (1995), Raposo and Uriagereka (1995) advance that differences in interpretation can be obtained by purely syntactic devices. Thus, semantic and discourse interpretations follow from syntactic mapping.

That is the case of categorical and thetic interpretations (Kuroda 1972; Milsark 1977). In the case of categorical interpretations, the proposition is about a prominent argument, which is highlighted by the grammar by different means (e.g., phrasal arrangement). Roughly speaking, a categorical judgment depicts the subject as a salient topic that is what the proposition is about. In the case of thetic interpretations, the subject of the proposition is a mere event participant, since the proposition is not about a salient topic. Raposo and Uriagereka (1995) account for both interpretations in configurational terms. In categorical interpretations the subject has scope over the predicate and, therefore, the subject is not grounded in the context of the main predicate. In thetic interpretations, the subject is within the scope of the predicate, the latter gaining scope over the rest of the expression. As proposed by Gallego (2010), the scope depends on c-command relationships. If the subject c-commands the verb, the proposition gets a categorical interpretation, the subject being a prominent participant. If the verb c-commands the subject, the proposition gets a thetic interpretation, the subject being a mere event participant.

Building on this approach to theme/rheme relations, it is possible to revamp Suñer and Lizardi's (1995) ideas on the different pragmatic effects associated with preverbal and postverbal subjects in PRSp wh-questions, as well as Gutiérrez-Bravo's (2008a) analysis of preverbal subjects as topics. The ways in which C's [*u*T] is valued in PRSp wh-questions can be analyzed by resorting to a configurational approach along the lines of Raposo and Uriagereka (1995). As mentioned above, when C's [*u*T] is valued via Agree, preverbal subjects are interpreted as salient topics. On the other hand, when C's [*u*T] is valued via Move, postverbal subjects are interpreted as mere event participants. In (20), it is possible to appreciate the role of preverbal subjects as salient topics.

(20)　A:　Mira a ese tipo. . .
　　　　　look-2ps to that guy
　　　　　'Look at that guy . . . '
　　　C:　Dios mío, pero mira. . .
　　　　　god mine, but look-2ps
　　　　　'My god, but look . . . '
　　　E:　¿y qué él se cree que tiene?
　　　　　and what he CL-3ps-REFL believes-3ps that has-3ps
　　　　　'And what does he think that he has?'

(Suñer & Lizardi 1995: 197)

Notice that using a full DP such as *ese tipo* again would turn the sentence pragmatically anomalous. Instead, employing a preverbal overt subject in a variety that has been argued to have lost the pragmatic division of labor between null and overt pronominal subjects (Morales 1999) is not anomalous. If the analysis on the pragmatic effects associated with preverbal subjects in PRSp wh-questions is on the right track, then the reported asymmetry between pronominal and non-pronominal preverbal subjects follows. This is because pronouns can convey this pragmatic function with salient topics better than full DPs. Hence, it is not surprising to find fewer cases of non-pronominal subjects surfacing preverbally. Finally, this might also explain why native speakers rated non-pronominal postverbal subjects slightly higher than their preverbal counterparts in the experiment reported in this chapter.

6 Conclusions

This chapter provided experimental evidence about the existence of non-pronominal preverbal subjects in PRSp interrogative wh-movement regardless of the argumental status of the wh-operator. In addition to the experimental findings, this chapter advanced a novel approach to the syntax of interrogative wh-movement in PRSp. More specifically, the source of divergence between GS and PRSp is reduced to the syntactic procedures involved in valuing C's $[uT]$. Whereas GS involves obligatory T-to-C movement in interrogative wh-movement in order to value that uninterpretable feature, PRSp also does so via Agree in a probe-goal relation between C and T. This approach to the syntax of PRSp wh-questions allows us to gain descriptive adequacy without positing language-specific conditions. Finally, the ways in which C's $[uT]$ is valued have discourse effects. Building on previous proposals about the information status of subjects in PRSp wh-questions (Gutiérrez-Bravo 2008a; Suñer & Lizardi 1995), preverbal subjects have been argued to be salient topics, whereas their postverbal counterparts are rhematic elements.

Further experimental research investigating the TP and CP fields in PRSp is needed. It is necessary to determine what kind of constituents (e.g., adverbs) can intervene between the wh-operator and preverbal subjects. Moreover, a detailed mapping of the positions of hanging topics, topicalized (e.g., CLLD) constituents, and focused constituents remains to be explored in order to have further empirical evidence regarding the landing sites of wh-operators, subjects, and other constituents in the left periphery of PRSp sentences. Along these lines, a deeper examination of the information effects associated with subjects is still to be developed in order to determine the exact nature of their theme/topic nature. In other words, it has to be investigated whether preverbal subjects can work as familiar topics, contrastive topics, and/or topic shifts (Frascarelli 2007; among others).

Notes

1 The work by Suñer and Lizardi (1995) was originally presented at the 22nd Linguistic Symposium on Romance Languages, which took place in El Paso/Cd. Juarez in February of 1992. However, it was not published until 1995. This is the reason for presenting their findings before those of Lizardi's (1993).

2 See Section 4 of this chapter in order to find a detailed description of Suñer's (1994) account of the argumental and non-argumental asymmetry regarding wh-operators in GS interrogative wh-movement.

3 The existence of T-to-C movement in interrogative wh-movement in GS is controversial. For analyses arguing against it, see the work by Suñer (1994), Ordóñez and Olarrea (2006), Buesa-García (2008), and Villa-García (2015), among others.

4 T_sP is the maximal projection of T_s, which is the head in charge of assigning Nominative Case to subject DPs. Following Pesetsky and Torrego (2004), there are two kinds of T. In addition to T_s, there also is T_o, the head in charge of assigning Accusative to DPs in a lower domain of the sentence.

5 There are two kinds of tense features: [tense] and [T]. The former is understood as a deictic anchor, whereas the latter is structural Case in Pesetsky's and Torrego's (2001) approach. On the other hand, [tense] is related to v*-to-T_s movement so that C can value its own [tense] feature with v*. [T] is an interpretable feature borne by T_s that values [uT] in subject DPs and C.

Bibliography

Bergen, J. J. (1976). The explored and unexplored facets of questions such as "qué tú tienes?". *Hispania, 59*(1), 93–99.

Brown, E. L., & Rivas, J. (2011). Subject-verb word order in Spanish interrogatives: A quantitative analysis of Puerto Rican Spanish. *Spanish in Context, 8*(1), 23–49.

Buesa-García, C. (2008). The subject-gap restriction in Spanish wh-questions: Some empirical and theoretical consequences (Ms.). Storrs, CT: University of Connecticut.

Casielles-Suarez, E. (2004). The syntax-information structure interface: Evidence from Spanish and English. New York: Routledge.

Chomsky, N. (1977). On wh-movement. In P. Culicover, T. Wasow & A. Akmajian (Eds.), *Formal syntax* (pp. 71–132). New York: Academic Press.

Chomsky, N. (1995). *The minimalist program*. Cambridge, MA: MIT Press.

Chomsky, N. (2000). Minimalist inquiries: The framework. In R. Martin, D. Michaels, & J. Uriagereka (Eds.), *Step by step: Essays on minimalist syntax in honor of Howard Lasnik* (pp. 89–155). Cambridge, MA: MIT Press.

Chomsky, N. (2001). Derivation by phase. In M. Kenstowicz (Ed.), *Ken Hale: A life in language* (pp. 1–52). Cambridge, MA: MIT Press.

Chomsky, N. (2004). Beyond explanatory adequacy. In A. Belletti (Ed.), *Structures and beyond* (pp. 104–131). Oxford: Oxford University Press.

Chomsky, N. (2008). On Phases. In R. Freidin, C. P. Otero & M. L. Zubizarreta (Eds.), *Foundational issues in linguistic theory: Essays in honor of Jean-Roger Vergnaud* (pp. 133–166). Cambridge, MA: MIT Press.

Davis, J. C. (1971). Tú, ¿qué tú tienes? *Hispania, 54*(2), 331–333.

Frascarelli, M. (2007). Subjects, topics and the interpretation of referential pro: An interface approach to the linking of (null) pronouns. *Natural Language and Linguistic Theory, 25*, 691–734.

Gallego, Á. (2004). T-to-C and Σ-to-C movement in (Peninsular) Spanish and Catalan. Paper presented at the *XIV Colloquium on Generative Grammar*. Universidade do Porto, Porto, Portugal.

Gallego, Á. (2006a). *Phase sliding* (Unpublished manuscript), Universitat Autonoma de Barcelona, Barcelona, Spain/University of Maryland, MD.

Gallego, Á. (2006b). Phase effects in Iberian romance. In N. Sagarra & J. Almeida Toribio (Eds.), *Selected proceedings of the 9th hispanic linguistics symposium* (pp. 43–55). Somerville, MA: Cascadilla Proceedings Project.

Gallego, Á. (2006c). *T-to-C movement in relative clauses* (Unpublished manuscript), Universitat Autonoma de Barcelona, Barcelona, Spain.

Gallego, Á. (2007). *Phase theory and parametric variation* (Unpublished doctoral dissertation). Universitat Autonoma de Barcelona, Barcelona, Spain.

Gallego, Á. (2010). *Phase theory.* Amsterdam/Philadelphia: John Benjamins Publishing Company.

Grimshaw, J. (1991). Extended projection. Ms., Brandeis University, Waltham, MA.

Gutiérrez-Bravo, R. (2002). *Structural markedness and syntactic structure* (Unpublished doctoral dissertation). University of California, Santa Cruz, CA.

Gutiérrez-Bravo, R. (2008a). Topicalization and preverbal subjects in Spanish *wh*-interrogatives. In J. B. de Garavito & E. Valenzuela (Eds.), *Selected proceedings of the 10th hispanic linguistics symposium* (pp. 225–236). Somerville, MA: Cascadilla Proceedings Project.

Gutiérrez-Bravo, R. (2008b). La identificación de los tópicos y los focos. *Nueva Revista de Filología Hispánica, 56,* 362–401.

Kuroda, S.-Y. (1972). The categorical and the thetic judgment. *Foundations of Language, 9,* 153–185.

Lantolf, J. P. (1980). Constraints on interrogative word order in Puerto Rican Spanish. *Bilingual Review/La Revista Bilingüe, 7*(2), 113–122.

Lipski, J. M. (1977). Preposed subjects in questions: Some considerations. *Hispania, 60*(1), 61–67.

Lizardi, C. (1993). Subject position in Puerto Rican wh-questions: Syntactic, sociolinguistic and discourse factors (Unpublished doctoral dissertation). Cornell University, Ithaca, NY.

Milsark, G. (1977). Toward an explanation of certain peculiarities of the existential construction in English. *Linguistic Analysis, 3,* 1–29.

Morales, A. (1999). Anteposición de sujeto en el español del Caribe. In L. Ortiz López (Ed.), *El Caribe hispánico: Perspectivas lingüísticas actuales* (pp. 77–98). Frankfurt: Vervuert Verlag.

Morales, A., & Vaquero, M. (1990). *El habla culta de San Juan.* Río Piedras, PR: Editorial de la Universidad de Puerto Rico.

Navarro Tomás, T. (1948). *El español en Puerto Rico: Contribución a la geografía lingüística hispanoamericana.* Río Piedras, PR: Editorial de la Universidad de Puerto Rico.

Ordóñez, F., & Olarrea, A. (2006). Microvariation in Caribbean/Non-Caribbean Spanish Interrogatives. *Probus: International Journal of Latin and Romance Linguistics, 18*(1), 59–96.

Pesetsky, D., & Torrego, E. (2001). T-to-C movement: Causes and consequences. In M. Kenstowicz (Ed.), *Ken Hale: A life in language* (pp. 355–426). Cambridge, MA: MIT Press.

Pesetsky, D., & Torrego, E. (2004). Tense, case, and the nature of syntactic categories. In J. Guéron & J. Lecarme (Eds.), *The syntax of time* (pp. 495–537). Cambridge, MA: MIT Press.

Pesetsky, D., & Torrego, E. (2006). Probes, goals and syntactic categories. In Y. Otsu (Ed.), *Proceedings of the seventh annual Tokyo conference on psycholinguistics* (pp. 25–60). Tokyo: Hituzi Syobo Publishing Company.

Pesetsky, D., & Torrego, E. (2007). The syntax of valuation and the interpretability of features. In S. Karimi, V. Samiian, & W. K. Wilkins (Eds.), *Phrasal and clausal architecture* (pp. 262–294). Amsterdam: John Benjamins.

Quirk, R. J. (1972). On the extent and origin of questions in the form "¿qué tú tienes?". *Hispania*, *55*(2), 303–304.

Raposo, E., & Uriagereka, J. (1995). Two types of small clauses. In A. Cardinaletti & M. T. Guasti (Eds.), *Syntax and semantics: Small clauses* (pp. 179–206). London: Academic Press.

Suñer, M. (1982). The syntax and semantics of presentational sentence-types in Spanish. Washington DC: Georgetown University Press.

Suñer, M. (1994). V-movement and the licensing of argumental wh-phrases in Spanish. *Natural Language and Linguistic Theory*, *12*, 335–372.

Suñer, M., & Lizardi, C. (1995). Dialectal variation in an argumental/non-argumental asymmetry in Spanish. In J. Amastae, G. Goodall, M. Montalbetti, & M. Phinney (Eds.), *Contemporary research in Romance languages* (pp. 187–203). Amsterdam: John Benjamins.

Torrego, E. (1984). On inversion in Spanish and some of its effects. *Linguistic Inquiry*, *15*, 102–129.

Villa-García, J. (2015). *The syntax of multiple-que sentences in Spanish. Along the left periphery*. Amsterdam/Philadelphia: John Benjamins Publishing Company.

5 On Puerto Rican Spanish subjects[1]

M. Emma Ticio

1 Introduction

Since Chomsky (1981) and Rizzi (1982), formal grammars typify languages as null- or non-null-subject languages. Languages that display rich verbal morphology along with absence of overt expletives and reduced occurrences of overt nominal expressions in the subject position are considered consistent null-subject languages (Barbosa 2009; see also Camacho 2013 for discussion on the different types of null-subject languages). Spanish is recurrently mentioned as a prototypical example of consistent null-subject language. Nevertheless, at least since Navarro (1948), several authors have noticed the divergent behavior of subjects in the Caribbean varieties of Spanish and have made an effort to streamline the properties of subjects in these varieties (e.g., Camacho 2013; Comínguez 2013; Gutiérrez-Bravo 2008; Morales 1986, 2007; Suñer 1986; Ticio 2004; Toribio 2000; Villa-García, Snyder, & Riqueros-Morante 2010). Frequently, the study of these properties has not considered the intradialectal richness of Caribbean Spanish and has assumed all Caribbean dialects to share similar subject properties. In this study, I analyze in detail the properties of Puerto Rican Spanish (henceforth, PRSp) subjects, and discuss how they can affect the characterization of PRSp as a consistent null-subject language.

To do so, this study is organized as follows. Section 2 examines the properties of consistent null-subject languages, exemplified by Standard Spanish (SS),[2] against the behavior of PRSp subjects. The results of this comparison show that PRSp departs from the behavior of consistent null- languages in some relevant respects. Section 3 explores whether the different characteristics of PRSp subjects grant the inclusion of this variety in some other types of null-subject languages, namely, discourse-related null-subject languages such as Chinese and Japanese or partial null-subject languages such as Brazilian Portuguese (BP). This section concludes by denying such a possibility and assuming that PRSp can still be characterized as a consistent null-subject language with specific processes affecting its subject properties. Section 4 focuses on the position of pre- and postverbal overt subjects to refine the particular properties of PRSp subjects and their positions. After reviewing the evidence put forward to locate pre- and postverbal overt subjects in SS, Section 3 concludes that no different positions can be postulated for pre- and postverbal overt subjects in PRSp. Finally, Section 4 details a proposal to account for the differences seen between SS and PRSp subjects based on the different properties of their D feature in T and on the relevance of the lack of morphological uniformity displayed in PRSp. This proposal can explain the abundant use of overt subjects in PRSp, along with the possibility of still having some null-subjects. Likewise, the lack of discursive features on many of the overt preverbal subjects and the lack of differences between pre- and postverbal subjects in this variety of Spanish are taken as support for the proposal in this section.

2 On the properties of consistent null-subject languages and PRSPp

This section reviews the behavior displayed by PRSPp subjects[3] regarding a limited number of properties that any consistent null-subject language must satisfy to be included in this category.

The possibility of silencing their subjects is a crucial property to characterize null-subject languages. As known, SS displays null- thematic and expletive subjects and has only overt thematic subjects. This property is also shared by PRSp, as illustrated in (1).[4]

(1) a.   (Él) Ha llamado por teléfono $_{PRSp}$[5]
          (he) has-3ps called by phone
          'He has called by phone'
     b.   Él ha llamado por teléfono $_{PRSp}$
          He has-3ps called by phone
          'He has called by phone'
     c.   (Expletivo) Llueve $_{PRSp}$.
          (It) rains
          "It is raining."
     d.   *Ello llueve. $_{PRSp}$
          it rains

As shown in (1), PRSp thematic subjects (1a-b), along with nonthematic subjects (1c), can be omitted. Furthermore, against the situation found in some other varieties of Spanish, such as Dominican Spanish (see Camacho 2013; Muñoz-Pérez 2014; Toribio 2000), expletives must be null in PRSp (1d).

A closer look at the behavior of overt and covert thematic subjects reveals the first difference between SS and PRSp; whenever the alternation null-subject/overt subject is possible, PRSp requires or prefers the explicit subject over the unpronounced subject option. This is precisely the opposite situation found in consistent null-subject languages, which are constrained by the Avoid Pronoun Principle (Chomsky 1981) that primes the null-subject option over the unpronounced subject option in these languages. In fact, the presence of overtly realized subjects in languages such as SS is only justified if it is associated with some additional meanings,[6] such as the expression of a contrastive meaning (a change of topic) by these elements. This is not the case in PRSp, and several authors (e.g., Navarro 1948; Morales 1986, et seq.; Toribio 2000) have noticed a strong preference for the use of the overt subjects in PRSp. In addition, the higher rate of expressed subjects, apart from being the generalized option in PRSp, does not require any contrastive meaning, as the examples in (2) illustrate.

(2) a. **Yo** no pude estar allí, **yo** oí la gritería, pero **yo** estaba en mi oficina en una reunión

I not could be there, I heard the cries, but I was in my office in a meeting

y **(yo)** los oí gritando (SJ, MI)

and (I) CL$_{acc}$ heard yelling

  b. Bueno es que . . . **yo** . . . cuando me acuerdo . . . cómo eran las cosas . . . cuando **yo** era

Well, is that . . . I . . . when (I) CL$_{dat}$ remember . . . how were the things . . . when I was

estudiante y cómo son ahora, pues, es que **yo** me acuerdo . . . por ejemplo,

student and how (they) are now, well, is that I CL$_{dat}$ remember . . . for example,

que nosotros aceptábamos el Rotecé voluntario, mejor dicho obligatorio,

that we accepted the Army ROTC program optional, better said mandatory,

y nunca recuerdo **yo,** nunca recuerdo **yo,** que esto se cuestionase, nunca hubo

and never remember I, never remember I, that this was questioned, never was

un grupo de muchachos que dijera, bueno, pero esto hay que acabarlo (SJ, MI)

a group of guys that said, well, but this has to be finished

(Morales 2007: her (2) and (3))

This property of PRSp subjects is directly linked to one of the prototypical properties of consistent null-subject languages such as SS. Namely, these languages do not use their subject pronouns in the same contexts in which one would use them in non-null-subject languages such as English or French.

Putting aside the different meanings of overt subjects, null and overt pronominal subjects differ substantially with respect to their interpretation in a number of ways. For instance, overt pronominal subjects in languages such as SS abide by Montalbetti's (1984) Overt Pronoun Constraint,[7] which explains the grammaticality differences in (3).

(3) a. Muchos chicos$_i$ dijeron que (ellos$_j$) no lo habían hecho $_{ss}$

many children said that (they) NEG CL$_{acc}$ have done

b. *Muchos chicos₁ dijeron que ellos₁ no lo habían hecho ₛₛ
many children said that (they) NEG CL_acc have done
'Many children said they didn't do it'

This constraint, which prevents the overt pronoun from being bound by the quantifier, does not seem to operate in the following PRSp examples:

(4) a. Muchos chicos₁ dijeron que (ellos₁) no lo habían hecho _PRSp
many children said that (they) NEG CL_acc have done
b. Muchos chicos₁ dijeron que ellos₁ no lo habían hecho _PRSp
many children said that (they) NEG CL_acc have done

PRSp speakers confirm that not only can the null pronoun but also the overt pronoun be bound by the quantificational phrase *muchos chicos* (many children), which annuls one of the differences between null- and overt subjects.

Another divergent behavior between some PRSp and SS subjects was observed in Morales (1988) and Suñer (1986), who note that PRSp is among the varieties of Spanish that allow overt pronouns with infinitives, as in (5).

(5) Al estar ella₁ trabajando, María₁ no podrá venir el viernes _PRSp
To be she working, María NEG can-fut come the Friday
'As she is working, Mary will not be able to come on Friday'

Note that in (5), the pronoun *ella* (she) can precede its antecedent, María. However, as discussed in Luján (1987), SS opts for the use of the null-pronoun in cases where pronouns linearly precede their antecedents.

Similarly, Cominguez (2011) analyzes the differences between the use of null and overt subjects in SS in cases such as (6a-b) with "when"-clauses preceding the main clause, and contrast them with the PRSp cases, which display the behavior of pronouns in non-null-subject languages (cf. English, 6c).

(6) a. Cuando (él₁) trabaja, Juan₁ no bebe ₛₛ
When (he) works, John NEG drinks
b. *Cuando él₁ trabaja, Juan₁ no bebe ₛₛ
c. When he₁ works, John₁ does not drink

Thus, the last three sets of examples demonstrate the similarities between null- and overt subjects in PRSp, which set this Spanish variety apart from SS, a prototypical consistent null-subject language. Despite the differences between SS and PRSp subjects, PRSp still displays properties strongly associated with consistent null-subject languages. For instance, overt pronominals cannot be interpreted with arbitrary reference, as seen in (7) (cf. Jaeggli 1986; Suñer 1983).

(7) a. (ellos) Dijeron que habían venido.
(they) said that had come
"They (specific or arbitrary) said that they had come." _PRSp and SS

  b.   Ellos dijeron que habían venido.
      they said that had come
      "They (specific only) said that they had come." _{PRSp and SS}

As shown in the interpretations of (7), PRSp and SS speakers alike report that the sentence in (7b) cannot have an arbitrary reading for them.

Returning to the overall characteristics of such languages, another crucial property of consistent null-subject languages is the possibility of having what has been traditionally referred to as free subject inversion in simple sentences. The examples in (8) show the different word orders and the judgments in both SS and PRSp.

  (8)   a.   Juan compró el carro SVO _(SS/PRSp)
           Juan bought the car
       b.   Compró el carro Juan VOS _(SS/*PRSp)
           Bought the car Juan
       c.   Compró Juan el carro VSO _(SS/PRSp)
           Bought Juan the car
           'John bought the car'

As shown in (8), PRSp allows for the possibility of having a subject either pre-ceding or following the verbal predicate[8]; however, Puerto Rican word order is more restrictive and does not accept the VOS easily. Although there is (to our knowledge) no detailed study on the word order in adult PRSp,[9] the occurrence of preverbal subjects in interrogative wh-movement has been extensively studied. As many authors have noticed (e.g., Comínguez 2013; Gutiérrez-Bravo 2008; Lizardi 1993; Morales 1999), PRSp interrogatives do not require the subject to appear in postverbal position; in fact, the speakers of this variety consider the postverbal position of subjects ungrammatical.

  (9)   a.   ¿Qué tú haces?_{PRSp}
           What you do
       b.   *¿Qué haces tú? _{PRSp}
           What do you
           'What do you do?'

As recently analyzed in Comínguez (2013), PRSp's lack of inversion occurs not only in pronominal subjects but also in full nominal expressions and irre-spective of the type of wh-question (i.e., argumental or not) involved. This is also a relevant difference with respect to SS, which crucially requires inver-sion in direct questions (i.e., the grammatical differences in (9) are reversed in SS).

Despite of the different behavior of subjects in PRSp and SS interroga-tive sentences in the previous examples, PRSP and SS interrogative sentences also share some important properties. For instance, contrary to the situation of non-null-subject languages, PRSp and SS allow for the presence of overt complementizers in *[*that*-trace] contexts, such as:

(10) a. ¿Quién piensas que vendrá? PRSp/SS
          Who you think that will come
      b. ¿Quién piensas tú que vendrá? *PRSp/SS
          Who think you that will come
      c. ¿Quién tú piensas que vendrá? PRSp/*SS
          Who you think that will come

To summarize, a brief review to the main properties characterizing consistent null-subject languages shows mixed results.[10] On the one hand, PRSp presents consistent null-subject language properties such as the lack of expletives or the possibility of dropping subjects; however, the similarities between covert and overt subjects and word order restrictions distance this language from this typological category.

This section has compared PRSp subjects with consistent null-subject languages such as SS. Nevertheless, there are languages that omit subjects on a regular basis but do not belong to the consistent null-subject language category. The next section explores some other types of null-subject languages to determine whether PRSp can be characterized as one of them.

3 PRSPp and non-consistent null-subject languages

A long tradition of research on the topic (cf. Barbosa 2009; Camacho 2013 for a summary) has attributed the absence of subjects in consistent null-subject languages to particular properties of their "rich" verbal agreement morphology. Thus, consistent null- languages satisfy their subjects' requirements, by means of their strong verbal agreement system. However, languages such as Chinese or Japanese are also characterized by omitting their subjects while not possessing strong verbal agreement morphology. Given the frequent reports regarding PRSp losing its verbal morphology (cf. Morales 2007; Navarro 1948; Toribio 2000), a possibility to explore here is that PRSPp null-subjects show differences with respect to consistent null-subject languages because they find their licensing via other mechanisms. This section capitalizes on this idea and contrasts the behavior of PRSPp subjects with some crucial properties displayed by some other types of null-subject languages.

Japanese-type languages are characterized by dropping subjects that can be recovered by discursive or contextual information (cf. Huang 1984). These languages are also called "topic-drop languages" because it is assumed that an operator, conveying the topic information and hosted along the left periphery of the sentence, is coindexed with the null-subject, which legitimizes it.

PRSp displays some properties that constitute strong evidence against a topic-drop analysis of PRSPp subjects.[11] First, examples such as (2) above, repeated here again as (11), show that the topic of the discourse is constant and the subject is overtly expressed. This evidence undermines this 'topic-drop' approach to PRSPp subjects.

(11) Yo no pude estar allí, yo oí la gritería, pero yo estaba en mi oficina en una reunión
      I neg could be there, I heard the cries, but I was in my office in a meeting
      y (yo) los oí gritando (SJ, MI)
      and (I) CLacc heard yelling

Furthermore, languages that license referential null-subjects via a discourse operator cannot systematically drop the most embedded referential subject, since the discourse operator can only access the less embedded subjects. However, as sentences such as (12) show, PRSp allows for this type of situation.

(12) a. ¿tú sabes a quién (yo) vi ayer? $_{PRSp}$
          you know to whom (I) saw yesterday
          'do you know whom I saw yesterday?'
      a'. ¿(tú) sabes a quién (yo) vi ayer? $_{PRSp}$
          you know to whom (I) saw yesterday
          'do you know whom I saw yesterday?'
      b. (expletivo) parece que (él/ella) llegó ayer $_{PRSp}$
          (it) seems that (s/he) arrived yesterday
          'it seems that s/he arrived yesterday'

In addition, as also shown in (12a'), PRSp allows for more than one referential null-subject in the same sentence, and these null-subjects can have different referents. This behavior is also contrary to the prototypical behavior of topic-drop languages, which display a unique discourse operator, licensing all null- elements in the sentence.

Based on these important empirical differences, it seems inadequate to pursue a classification of PRSp as a language that only legitimates null-subjects via discourse operators.

Another mechanism to license referential null-subjects has been postulated in order to explain the inconsistency of null-subjects in languages such as BP (cf. Barbosa 2009 for discussion on BP null-subjects' properties). Works such as Rodrigues 2004 or Toribio 2000 claimed that some languages have the possibility of identifying referential null-subjects with a c-commanding nominal expression. Unfortunately, PRSp does not seem to fit into this category either, as the contrast in the constructions in (13) illustrate.

(13) a. (expletivo) parece que (él/ella) ha llamado por teléfono $_{PRSp}$
          (it) seems that (s/he) has called by phone
          "it seems that s/he has phoned"
      b. O João$_i$ disse que (ele)$_{i/*j}$ vende sorvete
          'the João said that (he) sells ice cream
          "John said that he sells ice cream"

As the example in (13) shows, PRSp can have referential null-subjects (*él/ella*) in cases where there is no proper linguistic antecedent *c*-commanding the expression. Note that this is not the case in BP, as the ungrammaticality of (13b) with a referentially independent interpretation shows.

Similarly, the grammaticality of the sentences in (14) and (15) below make it untenable to follow a c-commanding nominal expression analysis for PRSp null-subjects. First, note the grammaticality of (14) with the coindex 1, which illustrates that a c-commanding nominal expression can intervene between the null- referential subject and its antecedent without leading to ungrammaticality.

(14) a. $Juan_1$ dijo a $Pedro_2$ que $(él_{1/2})$ ha llamado a Ivis $_{PRSp}$
      b. $Juan_1$ dijo a $Pedro_2$ que $él_{1/2}$ ha llamado a Ivis $_{PRSp}$
          'John said to Peter that (he) has phoned to Ivis'

Second, (15) also raises serious issues for this line of analysis. This is so because, in (15), the referents of the null-subject are both "Juan" and "María"; namely, (15) illustrates a case of "split antecedents."

(15) $Juan_1$ dijo que $María_2$ piensa que (ellos $_{1+2}$) son inteligentes $_{PRSp}$
      John said that Mary thinks that (they) are intelligent-pl
      'John said that Mary thinks that they are intelligent'

In addition to the previous empirical evidence furnished against this line of analysis, it seems that PRSp presents important differences with the kind of null-subjects typically allowed in languages characterized as partial null-subject languages. Among these differences, the most important seems to be that person or syntactic position does not restrict PRSP null-subjects. In other words, the so-called partial null-subject languages are characterized by dropping some types of subjects but not others. For instance, in languages such as Hebrew (Shlonsky 2009), only first and second person subjects can be null, while in languages such as Shipibo (Camacho & Elías-Ulloa 2010), only embedded subjects that are controlled can be unpronounced. No single morphological, semantic, or syntactic property seems to be useful in isolating banned cases in PRSp, and the properties and proliferation of PRSp null-subjects resemble more those of consistent null-subject languages than partial null-subject languages. Given the available evidence, there is no reason to conclude that PRSp does not belong to the consistent null-subject language category, although a detailed explanation of the divergences found is necessary.

The next section examines what has been considered as the most important architectural characteristic of consistent null-subject languages; namely, the differences between preverbal and postverbal subjects, with the goal of improving understanding of PRSp subjects and finding an explanation of the differences found so far.

4 On the location of PRSp preverbal and postverbal subjects

Lexical subjects in consistent null-subject languages display a number of well-documented semantic and syntactic asymmetries, depending on the linear position they occupy relative to the verb, which ultimately informs us about their structural position. This section examines the behavior of PRSp lexical subjects against these asymmetries.

Since Pollock (1989), adverb position has been used as a diagnostic to determine subject and verb positions cross-linguistically. Consider the examples in (16):

(16)   a.   Yo ya lo vi SS
              I already CL saw-1SG
         b.   ya lo vi yo
              already CL saw-1SG I
              "I already saw it"

The relative word order shown in the examples in (16) illustrate that two different structural positions for subjects can be necessary in Spanish. In other words: assuming that adverbs such as 'ya' (already) are immobile and attached to the TP projection, preverbal subjects in Spanish seem to appear in a higher position, within the CP field, while postverbal subjects originate in a lower TP position, probably as the Spec,TP.

Crucially, the corresponding PRSp preverbal subject in (17) does not precede linearly the adverb, which points to a different position for preverbal subjects in PRSp.

(17)   Ya yo lo vi $_{PRSp}$
         already I CL saw-1SG

Interestingly, recent research (Villa-García 2013) has provided additional tests to discriminate whether preverbal subjects can be in a lower position in SS. According to this author, the possibility of constructions such as (18) in SS illustrates that preverbal subjects can occupy a TP specifier position.

(18)   ¡Que los que maten se mueran de miedo! $_{SS}$
         that the that kill cl. die3.PL-Subj. of fear
         'I hope those who kill will die of fear.'
                                         (Noches de Boda, Spanish song by Joaquín Sabina 1990)
                                                                    (Villa-Garcia 2013, his (11c))

The example in (18) shows that the preverbal subjects *los que maten* (those who kill) can appear in desiderative constructions following the complementizer *que* (that) and preceding the subjunctive verb in SS. This grammaticality contrasts with the behavior of topics and clitic left dislocated material that do not exhibit the same distribution, as evidenced in (19), and that are assumed placed in a peripheral position along the CP:

(19)   a.   ¡El tenedor, que lo cojan! $_{SS}$
              the fork that cl. take3.PL-Subj.

b.   *¡Que *el tenedor* lo cojan! ₛₛ
　　that the fork cl. take3.PL-Subj.
　　'I demand that they grab the fork.'
　　　　　　　　　　　　　　　　(Villa-García 2013, his (7c) & (8c))

Villa-García (2013), among others, concludes that preverbal subjects can occupy lower positions in SS. Crucially, examples such as (18), with preverbal subjects in desiderative constructions, are also found in PRSp, cf. (20) below, which points to the possibility of preverbal subjects occupying lower positions in the TP/inflectional domain in PRSp as well.

(20)　. ¡Que Dios me los bendiga! ₚᵣₛₚ
　　　That God Dat Acc bless
　　　'(I wish) that God blesses you'
　　　　　　　　　　　　　　(Valió la pena, PRSp song by Marc Anthony 2013)

Furthermore, Ticio (2004) noted that PRSp preverbal subjects do not behave as SS preverbal subjects when considering some tests with certain left dislocated elements in the literature. For instance, the contrasts in (21) below show the incompatibility of having a Negative Polarity Item (NPI) as a left dislocated element in constructions with an overt preverbal subject in SS. This incompatibility was explained (cf. Ordóñez & Trevino 1999, for discussion of this and other similar tests) as the result of both elements competing for the same position.

(21)　a.　*A nadie [Juan (le) debe la renta] ₛₛ
　　　　　To nobody Juan CL owes the rent
　　　b.　A nadie [(le) debe Juan la renta] ₛₛ
　　　　　To nobody CL owes Juan the rent
　　　　　'John does not owe the rent to anybody'

Note that the corresponding example in PRSp is correct, as shown in (22a), and PRSp preverbal subjects can also appear in cases such as (22b-c), in which another quantificational left dislocated element is already present in the structure. Examples (22b-c) are considered deviant in SS.[12]

(22)　a.　A nadie [Juan (le) debe la renta] ₚᵣₛₚ
　　　　　To nobody Juan CL owes the rent
　　　　　'John does not owe the rent to anybody'
　　　b.　A cualquiera tu madre pone contento ₚᵣₛₚ
　　　　　To anybody your mother make-2ps happy
　　　　　'your mother makes happy to anybody'
　　　c.　A todo el mundo la prensa ha aceptado ₚᵣₛₚ
　　　　　To everybody the press have-3ps accepted
　　　　　'the press have accepted to everybody'

Consequently, the examples above show that it cannot be maintained that PRSp preverbal subjects compete with certain XPs for peripheral positions along the CP.

According to the evidence offered so far, preverbal subjects in SS can (but need not) occupy a CP specifier position in addition to the more canonical subject position Spec, TP. Contrary to this, PRSp preverbal subjects do not occupy a peripheral position in the CP but only a lower one within the TP functional projection. Moreover, the previous discussion also goes against the claim that PRSp pre-verbal subjects are structurally higher than PRSp postverbal subjects, and points to the conclusion that preverbal subjects in PRSp are in the same position as postverbal subjects.

An additional series of properties differentiating PRSp and SS subjects seem to validate the last claim. For instance, the above-mentioned Montalbetti's (1984) Overt Pronoun Constraint (OPC), which establishes that an overt pronominal must not have a quantified antecedent, holds only for subjects that appear in the preverbal position in SS.

(23) a. *Muchos chicos$_i$ dijeron que ellos$_i$ no lo habían hecho $_{SS}$
      many children said that they NEG CL$_{acc}$ have done
   b. Muchos chicos$_i$ dijeron que no lo habían hecho ellos$_{i\,SS}$
      many children said that NEG CL$_{acc}$ have done they
      'Many children said they didn't do it'

The differences in bound readings are an indication of placement of the different types of subjects in these types of languages. This way, preverbal subjects, which cannot be bound, should be placed in a position outside of the scope of the quantified antecedent. In return, postverbal subjects, which can be bound in the same type of constructions, should be placed in positions accessible to the quantified antecedent, and therefore are structurally lower than preverbal subjects.

Remarkably, the examples in (24) illustrate the data cannot be replicated in PRSp; namely, the subject can be bound in the preverbal position in this variety of Spanish.

(24) a. Muchos chicos$_i$ dijeron que ellos$_i$ no lo habían hecho $_{PRSp}$
      many children said that they NEG CL$_{acc}$ have done
   b. ??/*Muchos chicos$_i$ dijeron que no lo habían hecho ellos$_{i\,PRSp}$
      many children said that NEG CL$_{acc}$ have done they
      'Many children said they didn't do it'

Following the previous line of reasoning, overt preverbal subjects in PRSp do not need to occupy a position as high as the position occupied by overt preverbal subjects in consistent null-subject languages.[13]

Similarly, another semantic property that differentiates pre- and postverbal subjects in SS, cf. Uribe-Etxebarria (1991), is that subjects in Spanish have differences regarding their quantification scopes, as illustrated in (25):

(25)   Algún estudiante sacó prestado cada libro _{SS}
       Some student took lent each book
       a.   *Each book was borrowed to some student (narrow scope)
       b.   A (specific) student borrowed each book (wide scope)

This type of evidence supports the proposal for a CP domain position of preverbal subjects in SS, as preverbal subjects produced the highest scope allowed. Remarkably, the contrast is not found in PRSp and, as (26) illustrates, both scopes are possible.

(26)   Algún estudiante sacó prestado cada libro _{PRSp}
       Some student took lent each book
       a.   Each book was borrowed to some student (narrow scope)
       b.   A (specific) student borrowed each book (wide scope)

As shown, the different scopal facts just introduced, which supported a different position for preverbal subjects and postverbal subjects in SS, cannot be replicated in PRSp. This grammaticality difference points to a similar position for pre- and postverbal PRSp subjects, hosted both within the TP field.

To summarize: this section has illustrated that preverbal PRSp and SS subjects do not behave similarly on most occasions, with preverbal subjects in PRSp displaying a behavior closer to postverbal subjects in both dialects. The properties discussed here seem to point to a TP position for pre- and postverbal subjects in PRSp. The next section formalizes these observations within a minimalist framework.

5 Formalization of the proposal

This study has shown evidence that PRSp is a consistent null-subject language, apparently affected by some circumstances that hinder its subject properties and derive the peculiar properties of PRSp subjects. Furthermore, the data in Section 3 revealed that PRSp and consistent null-subject languages' lexical subjects occupy different positions, with PRSp subjects consistently located in canonical Spec TP positions. This section formalizes a proposal to account for the differences seen between SS and PRSp.

Generative research has always assumed the position of subjects is regulated by the Extended Projection Principle (EPP). The universal EPP[14] can be satisfied by different elements in languages. A large body of research on consistent null-subject languages (cf. Camacho 2013 for a summary of these proposals) has claimed that verbal morphology satisfies the EPP in languages such as SS, which forces lexical subjects to appear in higher topic-like positions. The evidence provided in previous sections showed that lexical subjects do not occupy a CP field position, which would imply that PRSp verbal morphology does not suffice to satisfy the EPP in some circumstances.

To reformulate this long tradition of research under minimalist premises (cf. Chomsky 1995) and to accommodate the peculiar behavior displayed by PRSp, the current proposal assumes that cross linguistic differences can be traced back to lexical differences. This is so because, under minimalist assumptions, lexical items are formed by bundles of features that trigger the universal operations Merge and Agree. Different compositions in the bundle of features contained in lexical items will then result in different derivational properties.

Recent research on consistent null-subject languages (cf. Roberts 2010 and references therein) postulate that null-subjects are actually the result of a deletion process. According to these proposals, null-subject languages are able to delete subject pronouns, which surface as null-subjects. This deletion process is enabled by the identification of the phi-features of the unpronounced pronoun and by its legitimation/valuation via Agree between the D-feature in T and the D feature in the pronoun. The formal mechanism can be then depicted as in (27), where only the relevant structure is detailed.

(27)   a.   (él) Salta $_{SS}$
         . . . [TP pronoun $_{(phi\text{-}3ps'\ D)}$ [T' [T $_{(phi\text{-}3ps'\ D)}$ [VP [. . . salta. . .]]]]]
       b.   Identification of phi-features and valuation of D feature
         . . . [TP pronoun $_{(\overline{phi3ps'\ D})}$ [T' [T $_{(phi\text{-}3ps'\ D)}$ [VP [. . . salta. . .]]]]]
       c.   Deletion process
         . . . [TP ~~pronoun~~$_{(\overline{phi3ps'\ D})}$ [T' [T $_{(phi\text{-}3ps'\ D)}$ [VP [. . . salta. . .]]]]]
       d.   Pronounced result
         (él) Salta (he jumps)

As illustrated in (27b-c), the legitimation of null-subjects is based (cf. Roberts 2010) on the idea that T bears a particular D-feature, which values the D feature carried in the pronoun and enables the deletion in the language given that all the features are checked at that point of the derivation.

Under this approach, the presence of additional features in the pronoun should cancel the possibility of deletion if they are not licensed by the features in T. Following this reasoning, the additional semantic notions involved in some overt pronominal subjects in SS are the reason that prevents the deletion process. Thus, the derivation, cf. (28), contains a contrastive Focus feature that will not be checked against T and prevents the deletion process.

(28)   a.   Él salta SS
         . . . [TP pronoun (phi-3ps, D, Focus) [T' [T (phi-3ps, D) [VP [. . . salta. . .]]]]]
       b.   Identification of phi-features and valuation of D feature
         . . . [TP pronoun (~~phi3ps, D~~, Focus) [T' [T (~~phi-3ps, D~~) [VP [. . . salta. . .]]]]]
       c.   Deletion process-unsuccessful
         . . . [TP pronoun (~~phi3ps, D~~, Focus) [T' [T (~~phi-3ps, D~~) [VP [. . . salta. . .]]]]]
       d.   Pronounced result
         él$_F$ Salta (he jumps)

As depicted in (28), the lack of identity between T and the pronominal subject invalidates the deletion operation in (28c) due to the presence of additional features in the pronoun that need to be checked against some other functional category.

Keeping this in mind, note that the lack of identity between T and a pronominal subject caused by the impossibility of checking some of the pronominal features present in (27) against the features in T should also prevent the deletion process. This is precisely our proposal for the overuse of overt pronominal subjects in PRSp. In other words: PRSp pronominal subjects cannot be deleted in some cases due to the lack of some features in the functional head T. Thus, the current proposal assumes a direct link between rich verbal agreement and recoverability of null-subjects (cf. Cole 2010 and references therein for an extensive discussion of this link), capitalizes on the well-documented erosion of the PRSp morphological verbal paradigm (attested since Navarro 1948), and assumes that T in PRSp can enter the derivation with or without a D feature. Then, the presence or absence of D in T will determine the presence or absence of the lexical subject in PRSp. Under this proposal, four logical outcomes are available for PRSp subjects. First, if the subject is a pronoun and T carries the D feature, the pronoun can be deleted and we have a case of a null-subject, cf. (27), as it is the standard case in SS, repeated here for convenience as (29).

(29) a. (él) Salta $_{\text{PRSp}}$
       . . . [TP pronoun $_{\text{(phi-3ps, D)}}$ [T' [T $_{\text{(phi-3ps, D)}}$ [VP [. . . salta. . .]]]]]
   b. Identification of phi-features and valuation of D feature
       . . . [TP pronoun $_{\text{(phi3ps, \overline{D})}}$ [T' [T $_{\text{(phi-3ps, D)}}$ [VP [. . . salta. . .]]]]]
   c. Deletion process
       . . . [TP ~~pronoun~~$_{\text{(phi3ps, \overline{D})}}$ [T' [T $_{\text{(phi-3ps, D)}}$ [VP [. . . salta. . .]]]]]
   d. Pronounced result
       (él) Salta (he jumps)

Second, if the subject is a pronoun and T does not carry a D feature, then the pronoun will not be legitimated and the deletion will not be possible, cf. (30).

(30) a. él Salta $_{\text{PRSp}}$
       . . . [TP pronoun $_{\text{(phi-3ps, D)}}$ [T' [T $_{\text{(phi-3ps)}}$ [VP [. . . salta. . .]]]]]
   b. Identification of phi-features and valuation of D feature
       . . . [TP pronoun $_{\text{(phi3ps, D)}}$ [T' [T $_{\text{(phi-3ps)}}$) [VP [. . . salta. . .]]]]]
   c. Deletion process-unsuccessful
       . . . [TP pronoun $_{\text{(phi-3ps, D)}}$ [T' [T $_{\text{(phi-3ps)}}$) [VP [. . . salta. . .]]]]]
   b. Pronounced result
       Él salta (he jumps)

This is the situation that triggers a higher percentage of overt subject pronouns in PRSp without any additional meaning associated to them.

Third, if the subject is a lexical NP and T does not carry D, then no derivational crash will happen, as only pronominal subjects can be deleted via this mechanism (cf. 31).

(31)   a.   Juan salta
    ... [TP Juan $_{(phi\text{-}3ps, D)}$ [T' [T $_{(phi\text{-}3ps)}$ [VP [... salta...]]]]]
    b.   Identification of phi-features and valuation of D feature
    ... [TP Juan $_{(phi3ps; D)}$ [T' [T $_{(phi\text{-}3ps)}$ [VP [... salta...]]]]]
    c.   Deletion process-unsuccessful
    ... [TP Juan $_{(phi\text{-}3ps; D)}$ [T' [T $_{(phi\text{-}3ps)}$ [VP [... salta...]]]]]
    d.   Pronounced result
    Juan salta (Juan jumps)

Finally, given the overall weakening tendency of PRSp verbal morphology, the proposal assumes that a fourth possibility with T carrying D and a lexical subject, although logically possible, is not feasible.

Additionally, note that the previous evidence illustrated that preverbal subjects are not generated in a higher position (i.e., within the CP periphery) in any case. PRSp preverbal subjects are in Spec, TP. This is expected since PRSP lexical subjects do not display any additional meaning, which could trigger their movement to a CP peripheral position to check the additional meaning feature. Hence, the similar behavior of null- and non-null-subjects of preverbal and postverbal PRSp subjects discussed in the previous section is fully predicted, as the only difference is the presence or not of phonetic features in the pronoun.

Furthermore, this line of analysis is also able to account for cases in which PRSp subjects do carry additional meanings. These cases have been pointed out by authors such as Gutiérrez-Bravo 2008 in relation to examples such as (32):

(32)   ¿Qué tú a mí me vas a dar?
    What you to me CLdat go-2SG to give
    'What are you going to give to me?'

Examples such as (32) illustrate that PRSp subjects in wh-questions are topical, as witnessed by their ability to occur above topics in these structures. The current proposal accounts for these data and the unusual position of the PRSp preverbal subject in these structures by assuming that the pronoun carries a Topic feature that ultimately triggers the movement of the subject to the CP periphery and avoids its deletion.

To conclude, the current proposal can explain the abundant use of overt subjects in PRSp, along with the possibility of still having some null-subjects as the result of the presence/absence of D in T, which is traced back to the particular properties of PRSp verbal morphology. Assuming a deletion approach to null-subjects (cf. Roberts 2010), the current proposal makes two defining properties of PRSp crucial to explaining the peculiar behavior of PRSp subjects; namely, the weakening of verbal morphology and the different placement of subjects in PRSp. As for the lack of discursive features on the overt pre-verbal subjects and the differences between pre- and postverbal subjects in this variety of Spanish, the proposal assumes they are derived from the different lexical composition of subjects in PRSp.

Notes

1 Thanks are due to Melvin González-Rivera for his invaluable help with judgments. Thanks are also due to all my informants, both on the island and in the Syracuse area. I am indebted to two anonymous reviewers for their insightful comments and suggestions, which have greatly improved this study. All remaining errors are mine.

2 The dialectal judgments reported as Standard Spanish have been typically based on the Peninsular Spanish variety in the relevant previous literature. In this study all SS examples have been judged by Peninsular Spanish speakers again.

3 Although this study did not benefit from a large empirical study, all the examples used in the text were consulted with native speakers of the relevant dialect. The data collection was performed at different stages and some participants did not judge all examples. Typically, data sets related to some grammatical property were created and sent electronically to native speakers. Each data set was judged by more than five speakers and the grammaticality results reported here are the ones overwhelmingly represented in the answers.

4 In all the examples, I represent unpronounced subjects as the relevant personal pronoun or expletive in parentheses.

5 Through the entire chapter, I make explicit the variety of Spanish represented in the examples with the use of subscripts. Namely, Puerto Rican Spanish is represented as $_{PRSp}$ and Standard Spanish is represented as $_{SS}$.

6 As one anonymous reviewer makes me note, the additional meaning does not need to be just contrast, it may well be clarification, as the examples in (i) illustrate:

(i) a. Liliana y José viven en Nueva Jersey. #Estudia inglés.
      Liliana and José live-3pl in New Jersey. Study-3SG English
      'Liliana and Jose live in New Jersey. # S/he studies English'
   b. Liliana y José viven en Nueva Jersey. Él estudia inglés.
      Liliana and José live-3pl in New Jersey. He study-3SG English
      'Liliana and Jose live in New Jersey. He studies English'

7 Note that the Montalbetti effects are sensitive to the linear word order of the subject, and show an asymmetry between preverbal (SV) and postverbal (VS) subjects. The differences between pre- and postverbal subjects will be discussed in Section 3 below.

8 See also example in (2b), which includes postverbal pronominal subjects.

9 Villa-García et al. (2010) note and quantify examples of postverbal subjects in child PRSp.

10 Although there are some other properties that have been repeatedly associated to null-subject languages, they are not considered here given the mixed reports on the grammaticality of these constructions in SS. For instance, long wh-extraction examples, illustrated in (i), have been used to classify languages as null-subject languages.

(i) L'uomo che mi domando chi abbia visto
    The man that CL wonder who has seen
    'The man who I wonder who he has seen'

                                  (Chomsky 1981: 240)

However, the relevant examples were judged ungrammatical by both SS and PRSp speakers.

11 Note that this does not mean that PRSp subjects are excluded as topics (cf. Gutierrez-Bravo 2008 and Section 4 below for a discussion of the topic properties of PRSp subjects).

12 Note that all these examples are marginal in SS only when the left dislocated elements are quantificational.

13 Note that, as one anonymous reviewer notes, OPC data are affected by stress/intonation patterns. Given that the grammatical judgments reported here did not take into

consideration the different stress/intonation patterns in PRSp, further research should re-evaluate this argument, including this factor.

14 There are proposals (Barbosa 2009; Ticio 2004, among many others) that argue in favor of parameterizing the EPP. According to this line of research, some languages, among them null-subject languages, would not carry an EPP feature. For the sake of the exposition, the current proposal assumes the universal existence of EPP and departs from these proposals.

Bibliography

Barbosa, P. (2009). Two kinds of subject pro. *Studia Linguistica*, *63*, 2–58.

Camacho, J. (2013). *Null-subjects*. Cambridge: Cambridge University Press.

Camacho, J., & Elías-Ulloa, J. (2010). Null-subject systems in Shipibo switch-reference. In J. Camacho, R. Gutiérrez Bravo, & L. Sánchez (Eds.), *Information structure in languages of the Americas* (pp. 65–85). Berlin: Mouton de Gryter.

Chomsky, N. (1981). *Lectures on government and binding*. Dordrecht: Foris.

Chomsky, N. (1995). *The minimalist program*. Cambridge, MA: MIT Press.

Cole, M. (2010). Thematic null-subjects and accessibility. *Studia Linguistica*, *64*, 271–320.

Comínguez, J. P. (2011). Occurrence and interpretation of subject pronouns in temporal embedded clauses in L2 English near-native speakers of L2 Spanish. Ms. Rutgers University, New Brunswick, NJ.

Comínguez, J. P. (2013). Puerto Rican Spanish as a partial pro-drop language: Evidence from wh-questions. Paper presented at *Hispanic linguistics symposium*. University of Ottawa, October 17–20, 2013.

Gutiérrez-Bravo, R. (2008). Topicalization and preverbal subjects in Spanish wh-interrogatives. In J. B. de Garavito & E. Valenzuela (Eds.), Selected proceedings of the 10th hispanic linguistics symposium (pp. 225–236). Somerville, MA: Cascadilla Proceedings Project.

Huang, C. J. (1984). On the distribution and reference of empty pronouns. *Linguistic Inquiry*, *15*, 531–574.

Jaeggli, O. (1986). Arbitrary plural pronouns. *Natural Language and Linguistic Theory*, *4*, 43–76.

Lizardi, C. (1993). Subject position in Puerto Rican wh-questions: Syntactic, sociolinguistic and discourse factors (PhD dissertation). Cornell University, New York.

Luján, M. (1987). Los pronombres implícitos y explícitos del español. *Revista Argentina de Lingüística*, *3*, 19–54.

Montalbetti, M. (1984). *After binding* (PhD dissertation). MIT Press, Cambridge, MA.

Morales, A. (1986). La expresión de sujeto pronominal en el español de Puerto Rico. In A. Morales (ed.), *Gramáticas en contacto: análisis sintácticos sobre el español de Puerto Rico* (pp. 89–100). San Juan, Puerto Rico: Editorial Playor.

Morales, A. (1988). Infinitivo con sujeto expreso en el español de Puerto Rico. In R. M. Hammond & M. Resnick (Eds.), *Studies in Caribbean Spanish dialectology* (pp. 85–96). Washington, DC: Georgetown University Press.

Morales, A. (1999). Anteposición de sujeto en el español del Caribe. In L. Ortiz López (Ed.), *El Caribe Hispánico: Perspectivas lingüísticas actuales* (pp. 77–98). Vervuert Verlag: Frankfurt.

Morales, A. (2007). Procesos discursivos del español de Puerto Rico. Paper presented at *La norma policéntrica del español* in Simposio de La Lengua Española, Cartagena. Retrieved from http://congresosdelalengua.es/cartagena/ponencias/seccion_3/default.htm#sec31

Muñoz-Pérez, C. (2014). Dominican Ello as a non-deleted null-expletive. *Borealis: An International Journal of Hispanic Linguistics*, *3*(1), 155–161.

Navarro, T. (1948). *El Español de Puerto Rico*. Rio Piedras: Editorial Universitaria.

Ordóñez, F., & Treviño, E. (1999). Left dislocated subjects and the pro-drop parameter: A case study of Spanish. *Lingua*, *107*, 39–68.

Pollock, J-Y. (1989). Verb movement, universal grammar, and the structure of IP. *Linguistic Inquiry, 20*, 365–424.

Rizzi, L. (1982). *Issues in Italian syntax*. Dordrecht: Foris.

Roberts, I. (2010). A deletion analysis of null-subject. In T. Bibehauer, A. Holmberg, I. Roberts, & M. Sheehan (Eds.), *Parametric variation: Null-subjects in minimalist theory*. Cambridge: Cambridge University Press.

Rodrigues, C. (2004). *Impoverished morphology and A-movement out of case domains* (PhD dissertation). University of Maryland, Maryland.

Shlonsky, U. (2009). Hebrew as a partial null – subject language. *Studia Linguistica, 63*, 133–157.

Suñer, M. (1983). pro*arb*. *Linguistic Inquiry*, *14*, 188–191.

Suñer, M. (1986). Lexical subjects of infinitives in Caribbean Spanish. In O. Jaeggli & C. Silva (Eds.), *Studies in romance linguistics* (pp. 189–203). Dordrecht: Foris.

Ticio, E. (2004). On the position of subjects in Puerto Rican Spanish. In M. Rodríguez-Mondoñedo & E. Ticio (Eds.), *The University of Connecticut Working Papers in Linguistics (UCONNWPL)*, *12*, 77–92.

Toribio, A. J. (2000). Setting parametric limits on dialectal variation in Spanish. *Lingua*, *110*(5), 315–341.

Uribe-Etxebarria, M. (1991). On the structural positions of the subjects in Spanish, their nature and their consequences for quantification. Ms., University of Connecticut, Storrs.

Villa-García, J. (2013). On the status of preverbal subjects in Spanish. *NELS*, *42*, 245–256.

Villa-García, J., Snyder, W., & Riqueros-Morante, J. (2010). On the analysis of lexical subjects in Caribbean and Mainland Spanish: Evidence from L1 Acquisition. In K. Franich, K. M. Iserman & L. L. Keil (Eds.), *BUCLD 34: Proceedings of the 34th annual Boston University conference on language development* (pp. 333–344). Somerville, MA: Cascadilla Press.

Language variation

6 A variationist account of Puerto Rican subject personal pronoun expression

Laurel Abreu

1 Introduction

In Spanish, the subject position may be expressed or null in most contexts. This phenomenon has been widely investigated and documented, first from the perspective of generative grammar, in which characterizing the properties of the Null Subject Parameter was an early goal (Camacho 2013; Chomsky 1981). Researchers in that tradition later began to address variation in the occurrence of the overt subject, particularly in Caribbean Spanish and Brazilian Portuguese (e.g., Duarte 2000; Gupton & Lowman 2013; Toribio 2000). In recent years, multiple researchers have approached variable subject expression from the variationist perspective. Adopters of a variationist perspective take the stance that language is variable, changing, and characterized by "structured heterogeneity" (Weinreich, Labov, & Herzog 1968: 99–100). Variable patterns in naturally occurring discourse are not random; instead, they are conditioned by underlying linguistic and/or extralinguistic, or social, constraints. Variationist work has been done with a number of languages and areas of language use. Careful study has revealed internal and external influences involved in variable phenomena in Spanish, such as the choice between *ser* and *estar* (e.g., Silva-Corvalán 1994) and periphrastic versus synthetic future tense usage (e.g., Aaron 2007).

With regard to subject expression, much work has been done on subject forms, with the bulk of work focused on the appearance of overt subject personal pronouns (SPPs). This work will be reviewed below, with a particular emphasis on Puerto Rican Spanish (PRSp), in keeping with the focus of this volume. The present study sheds new light on subject expression in PRSp through the contribution of data from an area outside the often-studied metropolitan area of San Juan. Furthermore, the study included a range of linguistic factor groups not previously analyzed in the literature. The implications identified suggest that Puerto Ricans are fairly homogeneous in their use of overt SPPs in terms of both rate and constraints.

2 Background

As evident in recent studies of SPP expression, the phenomenon has been widely studied from various perspectives. The varieties of Spanish that have been investigated include Puerto Rican, Dominican, Colombian, Venezuelan, Mexican, and Peninsular Spanish; and in the United States, Spanish in New York, New Jersey, Florida, California, and New Mexico, among others. The use of the SPPs in Spanish as a first and second language has been studied, mainly among adults, but also among children (e.g., Bayley & Pease-Álvarez 1997; Lapidus Shin 2012). Work in the generativist tradition has attempted to characterize the properties of the Null Subject Parameter, or what properties of a language allow it to have null subjects (see Camacho 2013, and references therein). However, research that takes a variationist approach has sought instead to establish what linguistic and extralinguistic factors condition the appearance of null and overt subjects, since variation is understood to be systematic. This review will focus on the latter perspective, as the present study takes a variationist approach to investigating SPP use.

Within the variationist literature, rates of overt SPP expression have been identified for many places in the Spanish-speaking world. Previous work has uncovered several linguistic constraints that operate in the expression of SPPs and often pattern similarly, despite disparate rates, which have been attributed to priming effects (Cameron & Flores-Ferrán 2004; Mayol 2012) and changes in progress (Ávila-Jiménez 1995; Mayol 2012; Toribio 2000), though the latter does not find widespread support (see, for example, Claes 2011). Research has shown that no one factor can explain all SPP use, but rather that factors interact and are affected by each other. Person and number, switch-reference, priming effects, verb characteristics, verb semantics, frequency effects, and pragmatic weight are some of the factors that have been determined; many of these will be reviewed in more detail below, with a focus on research on PRSp.

Person and number appears to be the strongest constraint operating on SPP expression, with singular SPPs expressed more often than plural and, in general, first and second person SPPs expressed more often than third person (Claes 2011; Enríquez 1984; Otheguy, Zentella, & Livert 2007). After person and number, switch-reference, defined as the relationship between the referent of a clause and the one that preceded it, appears to be the most important factor. Operationalizations of this construct have varied across studies. Cameron (1995) considered both the relationship between two adjacent clauses and reference chains involving multiple clauses, finding that speakers express subjects that differ from the ones that came before them, and that this tendency increases with the distance between referents in spoken discourse. Holmquist (2012) examined switch-reference as formulated by Cameron, finding the same tendencies for PRSp in Castañer, a small region in the central mountains of the island. Additionally, the position of the referent – in the same sentence, in the same turn, or in the prior discourse – played an important role in conditioning speaker selection of overt expression of the subject.

Work based on reference relations by Paredes Silva (1993) in Brazilian Portuguese inspired researchers in Spanish (e.g., Ávila-Shah 2000; Balasch 2008; Hurtado 2005) to broaden the conception of reference relations to include different types of relationships, with various degrees between coreferentiality and noncoreferentiality. Nuanced models of reference relations have contributed an advanced understanding of accessibility of referents and a deeper understanding of when speakers choose to express SPPs. In general, as the connection between referents is weakened, subjects are expressed more often in Spanish.

Another factor that is often cited as important for SPP expression is the semantics or lexical content of the verb, with increased expression of subjects, and in particular *yo*, with so-called cognitive verbs (e.g., *yo pienso*) (Enríquez 1984; Hurtado 2005; Morales 1997 – but see Bentivoglio 1987 for an exception). Posio (2011) noted the confusion that resulted from multiple studies' consideration of verb classifications in various ways. He analyzed first and second person singular pronouns separately and found that focusing of attention is responsible for varying rates of SPP expression. Lower transitivity related to the focusing of attention on the subject, while higher transitivity related to focusing attention on the object or the action expressed by the verb. Travis and Torres Cacoullos (2012) proposed that cognitive, mechanical, and construction effects combined to constrain the expression of *yo* in their study of the first person singular pronoun in conversations among Colombian Spanish speakers. The significant factor groups were as follows: semantic class of verb (cognitive versus other); intervening human subjects; realization of previous coreferential first person singular subject; realization of subject of immediately preceding clause; and verb tense, aspect, and mood (TAM). Travis and Torres Cacoullos (2012) identified the phrases *yo creo* and *no sé* as the most frequent first person singular verb forms in a conversational Colombian Spanish corpus, finding that they represent "prefabs"; they affirmed the lack of an effect of coreferentiality or priming on *yo* expression in *yo creo*. Claes (2011) also found significant effects in the PRSp of San Juan for TAM, after person and number; continuity of the referent was third; and the lexical content of the verb was fourth. These results, in comparison with the results for the Spanish of Barranquilla, Colombia, in Orozco and Guy (2008), led him to posit that the Antilles cannot be considered one dialectal zone.

All of the factors described above have to do with discourse itself or interaction; social factor groups do not appear to be as strongly related to SPP expression in Spanish, though some evidence has been provided for a few varieties. Orozco and Guy (2008) found that increased age was related to increased use of overt pronouns on the Colombian coast, and Holmquist (2012) found that farmers in central Puerto Rico used fewer overts than nonfarmers. In Ávila-Jiménez's (1995) study of PRSp, those with lower levels of schooling, professional or unknown occupation, and of the ages 10 to 19 or over 50, were each found to use fewer overts than other participants.

Apart from Holmquist's (2012) study, the research on subject expression in PRSp (e.g., Cameron 1993; Fernández Díaz 1990; Morales 1997) has traditionally focused on the Spanish spoken in San Juan, the capital, which has a population of 395,326, 15 percent of whom do not identify themselves as Puerto Rican (U. S. Census Bureau 2010a). Also, the studies on PRSp have not included the full range of factor groups identified for other varieties of Spanish as constraints on subject expression. Unlike past studies, the present one analyzes subject expression in a new location and includes a wide range of factor groups. The research questions that guided this study are as follows:

1   What is the overall rate of SPP expression in a city in western Puerto Rico that is not near the metropolitan area of San Juan?
2   What linguistic and social factors are related to SPP expression in PRSp?
3   How do these factors relate to previous research on SPP?

3 Methods

3.1 Participants

The participants in the study were 10 residents of Isabela, Puerto Rico, a town of 45,631 inhabitants on the northwestern coast of the island. The town is about eight-and-a-half times smaller than San Juan, and approximately 98 percent of the population identifies itself as Puerto Rican (U. S. Census Bureau 2010b). The participants were recruited by personal contact from the interviewer. There were six women and four men, and their ages ranged from 27–64.

3.2 Task

In keeping with the methodology used in the majority of variationist studies of SPP expression, sociolinguistic interviews (Labov 1984) were performed in the summer of 2008.[1] The interviews, approximately one hour in duration, were carried out with individuals by a Puerto Rican male in his late twenties who was acquainted with all the participants, as they were members of his extended family or friends of his family; while the use of this social network (cf. Milroy 1980) led to a more homogeneous participant group than desired, it was deemed best for achieving the recording of the most informal style of speech possible. Topics included such themes as politics and remembering past events.

All participants filled out a questionnaire that had two purposes: to gather background information on the participants, such as the demographics reported above, and to ensure that their contact with English was as minimal as possible. Participants were asked to quantify their contact with English in various aspects of their daily lives, such as watching television or movies, speaking to family members, and working at their jobs. Though all had had the obligatory English classes in their schooling, none used English in their daily lives and none claimed to have knowledge of the language.

3.3 Data extraction, coding, and analysis

With the goal of capturing the participants' speech when they might be less conscious of being recorded, the interviews were transcribed beginning at minute 30:00. A ten-minute portion of each interview was used for data extraction, since this period was determined to be the length of time it took each person to produce approximately 150 subjects, overt or null. Each site for the appearance of a null or overt SPP was extracted and coded for person and number and the remaining linguistic factor groups, each of which will be explained further below: priming between speakers and in the same speaker; reference relationship with the previous clause; TAM of the co-occurring verb; continuity of tense and of mood with respect to the previous clause; polarity; clause type; co-occurring reflexive verb; lexical content of the verb; and whether the subject occurred in a quote.

The background portion of the questionnaire revealed that the participants differed in terms of sex and age, and so a separate analysis took into account those two extralinguistic factor groups in relation to the use of overt SPPs.

In keeping with the literature, various contexts in which SPPs may not occur or do not vary were excluded from the analysis. These included meteorological verbs (e.g., *llover*, *hacer calor*), any clause with the verb *haber*, and experiencer verbs such as *gustar* and *encantar*. Abandoned and incomplete utterances were also not included, following Travis (2007), nor were SPPs that co-occurred with non-finite verbs and participles, although these were originally included as sites for SPP expression in the present analysis. However, they were infrequent in the data, and their removal facilitated comparison with other studies that also excluded SPPs in this context (e.g., Bayley & Pease-Alvarez 1997; Flores-Ferrán 2002). The obligatoriness of SPPs in constructions of contrast has been debated in recent studies. Amaral and Schwenter (2005) wrote that though overt SPPs are typically considered to be required in these cases, they are not the only option for denoting contrast; adverbs or adverbial phrases such as *aquí* and *por mi parte* are able to stand in for overt SPPs (p. 118, p. 120). Furthermore, Posio (2011) and Travis and Torres Cacoullos (2012) noted the low frequency of contrastive constructions in actual discourse. Travis and Torres Cacoullos tested three operationalized definitions of contrast, concluding that "expressed pronouns are not contrastive in general" (p. 724). During the coding process of the current study, contrast was held present as a possibility, but its frequency was indeed found to be low – only one token was ruled out as a clear case of contrast in which the SPP was not optional.

The subject of the discourse marker (*tú*) *sabes* was initially extracted and coded because it was determined to be a variable context in PRSp. However, it was eventually excluded, based on Travis (2005), which specified that discourse markers are not subject to referential relations like other subjects. This eliminated 17 tokens from the SPPs produced by the participants and left 1,200 for the analysis of the linguistic factor groups.

All grammatical persons and numbers were included in the analysis; additionally, both specific and nonspecific second and third persons were distinguished. While previous research (e.g., Travis & Torres Cacoullos 2012) has advocated for the analysis of just one person, including them all at once allowed the true strength of the person and number constraint to be observed.

All forms of verb TAM were coded, and it was initially noted in two other factor groups whether there was continuity of tense and continuity of mood from the previous clause. In an attempt to determine whether a functionalist hypothesis could be supported, potential ambiguity, both morphological and contextual, was coded for as well. Whether or not the verb was reflexive was included in another factor group. The final verbal characteristic taken into account in the coding was lexical content, with the following classifications, largely based on previous work: cognition (e.g., *pensar* 'think', *creer* 'believe'); volition (e.g., *dejar* 'let', *querer* 'want'); stative (e.g., *ser* 'be', *estar* 'be'); possession (e.g., *tener* 'have'); communication (e.g., *decir* 'say'); other (e.g., *mirar* 'look').

Two factor groups were designed with the goal of examining priming effects in the data. The first factor group, deemed intraspeaker priming, referenced the previous mention of the subject under analysis in the speaker's own discourse and whether it had been null, overt, or lexical, or if it was the first mention. The limit for looking back in the discourse was set at 10 clauses, since Travis (2007) found that priming effects were shorter-lived in conversational interaction than in narratives. The second priming factor group took into account possible priming effects through interaction with the interviewer, with the following classifications: occurred in first clause after interviewer used same overt SPP; occurred in first clause after interviewer used different overt SPP; occurred in first clause after interviewer used same null SPP; occurred in first clause after interviewer used different null SPP; occurred in first clause after interviewer and interviewer did not produce an SPP; occurred elsewhere.

In consideration of the various ways in which textual distance and reference relations had been measured in previous work, multiple measures were initially included in the study. These included the number of clauses between the token and the previous mention of the same subject (same referent occurred in previous clause; occurred two clauses back in the discourse; occurred within last three to five clauses; occurred six to 10 clauses back; occurred more than 10 clauses back; no previous mention) and the syntactic function of the previous mention of the referent (subject; direct object, indirect object, object of preposition; possessive; no previous mention). Switch-reference was itself measured in multiple ways to test out Cameron's (1995) findings, including switch-reference from one clause to another; reference chains that included the penultimate and antepenultimate noun phrases (NPs); and set-to-elements saliency, or the relationship between plural subjects and the members they comprise. Finally, a more complex model of reference relations derived from Ávila-Shah (2000), which was itself modified from Paredes Silva (1993), was designed in order to examine discourse-level reference relations. The various levels are represented in Table 6.1.

As can be observed in Table 6.1, the factors considered are maintenance of the referent, verb TAM, ambiguity, and maintenance of topic. The main difference between this model and that of Ávila-Shah (2000) is the introduction of Levels 5 and 6, which separate ambiguous and unambiguous cases of switch-reference.

Three characteristics at the level of the clause or greater formed the final component of data coding. Clause type, coded as matrix or subordinate, was one group. Another group was based on initial impressions of the data in which it seemed that participants used overt SPPs to quote themselves or other people. Finally, the polarity (positive or negative) of the clause where the SPP occurred was coded.

Table 6.1 Levels of discourse connectedness

Level 1: same referent maintained from previous clause and same verb TAM
Level 2: same referent is maintained, but change in TAM
Level 3: change in referent, but intervening subject is impersonal or [-human]
Level 4: change in subject; referent performed other syntactic function in previous utterance
Level 5: change in referent, but reference is unambiguous
Level 6: change in referent; there is another possible candidate for subject
Level 7: same referent maintained, change in topic
Level 8: both discourse topic and referent are changed

Goldvarb X (Sankoff, Tagliamonte, & Smith 2005), a program that performs logistic regressions and is often used in variationist research, was used to carry out multivariate analyses. The overt SPP was the application value. Goldvarb considers each factor group in relation to the variable in a step-up/step-down analysis and provides a ranking of the constraints that indicates the strength of their operation in the appearance of the application value. Each factor group is assigned a probabilistic weight that can vary from 0 to 1; weights over .50 indicate that the application value's appearance is favored in that context, while weights under .50 indicate the contrary. Finally, the magnitude of effect is obtained in the form of the range, which is calculated by subtracting the lowest probability weight from the highest. These numbers then indicate the ordering of the constraints in the analysis (Tagliamonte 2006).

The initial coding of the data was detailed – what Tagliamonte (2006) described as an "'elaborated factors' strategy" (p. 201). This strategy can lead to cells with little or no data, making it necessary to combine factors. "The important theme underlying this honing process is to arrive at the most logical configuration, the configuration that most adequately captures the trends and patterns in the data" (p. 206). Therefore, factors in this study were combined only where linguistically principled, and only when doing so helped to avoid empty cells and interactions among the data. Furthermore, finding the best model to explain the data guided the analysis and this meant that related factor groups were run separately. Then, by comparing the indicators of model fit – that is, log likelihood and Chi-square per cell of different runs (Young & Bayley 1996: 272–73) – some factor groups were removed from consideration in the analysis. This will be discussed further in the next section.

4 Results

The results are presented in three subsections. First, the overall rate of SPP expression is given, followed by a breakdown by person and number, as both of these are commonly reported in studies of SPP expression; both are compared with previous work. Next, the findings of the multivariate analysis are presented and, subsequently, more detailed information on various factor groups that were identified as significant.

4.1 Rate of subject personal pronoun expression

Table 6.2 provides the rate obtained in the present study in comparison with those reported in previous work that employed interviews as the method of data elicitation and analyzed both singular and plural SPPs. "% overt" refers to the proportion of overt SPPs reported in each study, and the final column gives the total number of overt SPPs.

As shown in Table 6.2, the overall rate found for the participants in this study was 38 percent, which is fairly in line with the rates found for PRSp in other studies. Multiple authors have pointed out that an overall rate can mask differences in expression of different persons and numbers; for instance, *yo* expression has often been found to exceed the overall rate. Therefore, a breakdown according to person and number is presented in Table 6.3.

One advantage of such a detailed breakdown is that differences between specific and nonspecific second and third person pronoun usage can be

Table 6.2 Rate of expression of overt SPPs by monolinguals in previous studies and present analysis

Variety	Source	% overt	N
San Juan, Puerto Rico	Cameron 1992	45	950
Puerto Rico (26 municipalities)	Avila-Jiménez 1995	40	1902
San Juan, Puerto Rico	Claes 2011	39	1048
Isabela, Puerto Rico	*Present study*	*38*	*457*
New York Puerto Ricans[a]	Otheguy and Zentella 2007	35	1332[b]
New York Puerto Ricans[c]	Flores-Ferrán 2002	31	247
Castañer, Puerto Rico	Holmquist 2012	28	793

[a] "Recent arrivals," who had spent under five years in the city (p. 281).
[b] Obtained by calculating percentage of overt pronouns from tokens contributed by Puerto Ricans.
[c] "Recent arrivals," who had spent under five years in the city (p. 97).

Table 6.3 Rate of expression of overt SPPs by person/number

SPP	% overt	N	% of data
yo (1st person singular)	50	239	40
tú (2nd person singular, specific)	56	44	7
tú (2nd person singular, nonspecific)	54[a]	30	5
usted (2nd person singular, formal)	60	3	<1
él/ella (3rd person singular)	31	108	29
nosotros (1st person plural)	19	15	7
ustedes (2nd person plural, formal/informal)	41	9	2
ellos/ellas (3rd person plural, specific)	10	5	4
ellos (3rd person plural, nonspecific)	5	4	7
Total	38	457	100

[a] Does not include tokens containing the discourse marker *tú sabes* 'you know'; total with this usage is 58% (N = 42).

observed, even though these did not account for much of the data. *Usted* and *ustedes* were particularly infrequent. As shown in Table 6.3, it was the first and third person singular that were used most commonly, together comprising 69 percent of the total data. The results here confirmed previous work: singular persons were expressed more than plural persons, and first and second person more than third person. While *ustedes* was frequently overt, at 2 percent of the data, there aren't enough tokens to enable any kind of generalization regarding this tendency.

In addition, the position of SPPs was considered in the present analysis. Typically, preposed subjects have been much more numerous in the data sets of previous work in Spanish than postposed subjects (Orozco & Guy 2008; Otheguy, Zentella, & Livert 2007). This pattern also appeared in the data of this study: 96 percent (N = 438) of the 457 overt SPPs were preposed and only 4 percent (N = 19) were postposed.

4.2 Social factor groups

Linguistic and social factors were considered separately in Goldvarb X. The social factors are presented first, in Table 6.4. The third column provides the factor weight, described in the previous section. The fourth and fifth columns list the percentage and number of overt SPPs for that context, respectively. The final column specifies the percentage of data that corresponds to the factor.

Social factors did not seem to be strongly related to SPP expression, as evidenced by the failure of the factor group of age to reach significance and the fairly low magnitude of effect (indicated by the range of 8) obtained for the significant factor group of gender. In addition, though females slightly favored overt SPPs and males slightly disfavored them, the probability weights for that factor group hover close to .50, which means that the effects of the factors are more or less neutral.

Table 6.4 Variable analysis of the contribution of social factors to the probability of overt SPP expression. Input probability: 0.39 (39%); N = 469/1217

Factor group		Prob	% overt	N	% of data
Gender					
	Females	.53	42	299	59
	Males	.45	34	170	41
	Range	8			
Age					
	50 or over	[.52][a]	39	264	56
	Under 50	[.48]	38	205	44

Log likelihood = -807.583; p = 0.008; χ^2/cell = 1.3702

[a] Brackets indicate that the effect of the factor group did not reach statistical significance.

4.3 Linguistic factor groups

The results of the analysis of the linguistic factors are summarized in Table 6.5; the factor groups selected as significant are described following the table. The total number of pronouns in this particular analysis was 1,200, rather than 1,217, and the overall rate is just slightly lower, because the tokens that occurred in the discourse marker *tú sabes* were not included in this statistical run, based on the fact that they are not subject to reference relations, as described above.

4.4 Person and number

Person and number was found to exert the strongest influence on the appearance of the overt SPPs, as evidenced by the range value of 58. The highest weights were obtained for second person (.67) and first person (.64), respectively. As expected, the trend was more frequent use of overt SPPs in these contexts, and more infrequent use of them with the third person. The weight for third person singular was near neutral at .49, and third person plural had the lowest weight at .09. Specific and nonspecific second and third person SPPs were found to pattern similarly and thus were combined for the purpose of the statistical analysis.

4.5 Discourse connectedness

After the multiple measures of textual distance and switch-reference described in the previous section were coded and analyzed, each was run separately in statistical analysis with the other factor groups. It was then determined that discourse connectedness provided the best explanation of the data. The factors patterned largely as expected, with increased favoring of overt SPPs as the connection to the referent became weaker. The percentages of overt SPP expression are represented in Table 6.6.

The only level at which overt SPPs were favored was Level 5 (.65), in which the subject is switched in relation to that of the previous clause but unambiguous in reference. This level is exemplified in (1) below:

(1)   Y ya políticamente políticamente <u>Aníbal ya está</u> muerto <u>yo no sé</u> porque <u>él se queda</u> en esa estupidez. (5, F, 53)[2]
      'Politically, <u>Aníbal is</u> already dead, <u>I don't know</u> why <u>he keeps</u> on with that stupidity.'

Levels 3 (the referent is changed but the intervening subject is impersonal or inanimate) and 4 (the referent performed another syntactic function in the previous utterance) were combined for the sake of the analysis because of numbers and their direction of effect; their influence on the overt SPP was neutral, at .50. Level 3 is displayed in (2).

(2)   Por más coraje que <u>yo tenga</u> por lo que me haiga pasado a mí Ø siempre <u>me mantengo</u> callao. (7, M, 53)
      'However much anger <u>I feel</u> because of what has happened to me <u>(I)</u> always <u>keep</u> my mouth shut.'

Table 6.5 Variable rule analysis of linguistic factors contributing to the appearance of overt SPPs. Input probability: 0.32 (38%), N = 457/1200

Factor group[a]		Prob	% overt	N	% of data
Person/number					
	2nd person singular (specific & nonspecific) and plural	.67	53	86	13
	1st person singular	.64	50	239	40
	3rd person singular	.49	31	108	29
	1st person plural	.34	19	15	7
	3rd person plural (specific & nonspecific)	.09	7	9	11
	Range	*58*			
Discourse connectedness	Level 5	.65	50	201	33
	Levels 3–4	.50	41	79	16
	Level 2	.46	35	71	17
	Level 1	.37	26	101	32
	Levels 6, 8	.33	26	5	2
	Range	*32*			
Verb TAM					
	Present and present perfect subjunctive	.58	43	16	3
	Present indicative, imperfect	.53	42	315	63
	Preterit	.48	33	113	29
	Future, conditional, imperfect subjunctive	.27	21	13	5
	Range	*31*			
Intraspeaker	Previous mention of same referent was overt	.65	54	181	40
	Previous mention of same referent was null	.40	25	129	60
	Range	*25*			
Reflexive verb	Not reflexive	.53	40	409	85
	Reflexive	.35	29	51	15
	Range	*18*			

Log likelihood = -660.831; p = 0.007; χ^2/cell = 1.0614

[a] The effects of the following factor groups did not reach statistical significance: verb class; clause type; quote; tense continuity; mood continuity; and polarity.

Beginning with Level 2 (same referent is maintained, but there is a change in TAM), we begin to see a slight disfavoring of the overt SPP (.46), and this continues with Level 1 (same referent is maintained from the previous clause and verb TAM is the same) with a weight of .37. Surprisingly, Level 6 (change in referent and there is another possible candidate for subject) also patterned this way, with a weight of .33. This context, together with Level 8, represented just 2 percent of the data. There were no examples of Level 7 and very few of Level 8 in the data.

Table 6.6 Rates of expression of overt SPPs by level of discourse connectedness

Level	Description	% overt	N	% of data
1	Same referent, same TAM	27	104	32
2	Same referent, different TAM	35	71	17
3	Intervening clause(s), but no rival subject	42	38	8
4	Change in subject; referent performed other syntactic function in previous utterance	40	41	9
5	Change in referent	50	201	33
6	Change in referent; there is another possible candidate for subject	29	2	<1
7	Same referent maintained, change in topic	-	-	-
8	Both discourse topic and referent changed	25	3	1

4.6 Verb TAM

This factor group displayed the third highest range value in the analysis. Some forms were infrequent in the data and had to be combined with other factors. For example, the conditional and the imperfect subjunctive, which both represent the hypothetical, were found to pattern similarly and were merged.

As can be seen in Table 6.7, the present indicative, the preterit, and the imperfect were the most frequent verb forms in the data set; this was not surprising, given the context of data collection, in which participants spoke of their lives, past and present. The present and the imperfect are both imperfective tenses, and they were found to behave similarly ($\chi^2 = 0.0474$, p = 0.828). Therefore, they were combined for the purpose of a more fitting model for the data. In previous research, the present tense had been reported to hover around .50, and the imperfect had been found to favor the overt SPP (Silva-Corvalán 2001).

4.7 Priming

The factor group of priming displayed a clear trend: when the preceding coreferential SPP had been null, the overt SPP was disfavored, with a weight of .40, and when the preceding coreferential SPP had been overt, the overt SPP was favored, with a weight of .65.

Two factors from the intraspeaker priming group could not be included in the multivariate analysis, due to interactions with other factor groups. Therefore, the results for these factors are provided in Table 6.8 in the form of percentages. Additionally, the results for interspeaker priming are displayed there; there were not enough tokens in different contexts for the group to be included in the statistical analysis.

As can be seen in Table 6.8, the majority of the SPPs analyzed in the factor group of interspeaker priming occurred in a context outside the first clause after the interviewer's turn, which was to be expected – in the sociolinguistic interview, the goal is to elicit as much speech from the participant as possible. Nonetheless,

Table 6.7 Rate of expression of overt SPPs by tense, aspect, and mood (TAM)

TAM	% overt	N	% of data
Present subjunctive & present perfect subjunctive	46	16	3
Present indicative	42	233[a]	47
Imperfect & imperfect progressive	42	76	15
Conditional	40	2	<1
Preterit & preterit progressive	34	105	26
Present progressive	33	6	2
Present perfect indicative	29	5	1
Imperfect subjunctive	20	4	2
Past perfect indicative	21	3	1
Synthetic & periphrastic future	18	7	3

[a] Does not include tokens containing the discourse marker *tú sabes* 'you know'; total with this usage is 246, or 43% (48% of the data).

Table 6.8 Rates of expression of overt SPPs for the factor groups of inter- and intra-speaker priming[3]

Factor group	Factor	% overt	N	% of data
Intraspeaker priming	Previous mention was overt SPP	54	181	28
	Token is first mention of referent	46[a]	128	23
	Previous mention was lexical	28	19	6
	Previous mention was null SPP	25	129	43
Interspeaker priming	Occurred in 1st clause after interviewer used same overt SPP	74	14	2
	Occurred in 1st clause after interviewer used different overt SPP	70	16	2
	Occurred in 1st clause after interviewer; interviewer did not produce SPP	48	24	4
	Occurred elsewhere	37	387	88
	Occurred in first clause after interviewer used same null SPP	31	12	3
	Occurred in first clause after interviewer used different null SPP	24	4	1

the patterning of the other tokens is noteworthy: when the interviewer ('I') used an overt SPP, the participant often used an overt SPP, as in (3):

(3) I: Pero Ø no sé si él es tan bueno como <u>yo</u>
   6: No qué mucho <u>yo gritaba</u> en esos juegos (6, F, 42)
   I: 'But (I) don't know if he is as good as I (was)
   6: No how <u>I used to yell</u> at those games'

The same trend held for null SPPs, shown in (4):

> (4) I: Y después Ø volvieron de nuevo?
>   10:   Y Ø se casaron a los diez y ocho meses Ø se casaron. (10, F, 64)
>   I: 'And then (they) got back together again?
>   10:   And (they) got married after eighteen months (they) got married.'

4.8 Reflexive verbs

The fifth and final significant factor group had to do with whether or not the verb that co-occurred with the SPP was reflexive. Reflexive verbs disfavored the overt SPP (.35) and nonreflexive verbs slightly favored it (.53). An analysis was undertaken of potential lexical effects (cf. Erker & Guy 2012) that might have affected the reflexive verbs. Three of the most frequent verbs composed 29 percent of the data: *irse* ('to leave') was the most frequent (N = 21) of the 175 reflexive verbs, with 19 percent overt pronouns (N = 4); *acordarse* ('to remember') occurred 15 times, 20 percent (N = 3) of the time with overt pronouns; and *quedarse* ('to stay, keep') also occurred 15 times, with 47 percent overt pronouns (N = 7). Therefore, no particular lexical effects could be identified for these verbs.

5 Discussion and conclusions

The organization of this section follows that of the research questions. The first question had to do with the overall rate of SPP expression in the Spanish spoken in the western part of Puerto Rico. The rate found, 38 percent, is well in line with rates reported for San Juan, as well as for Puerto Ricans termed "recent arrivals" in locations on the mainland, with the one exception of the rate of 28 percent in Holmquist (2012) for Castañer. This may provide further evidence for Holmquist's assertion that there is an interior, more conservative dialect of PRSp that contrasts with coastal PRSp, at least in terms of subject expression. Mayol (2012) and Holmquist (2012) both attribute higher rates of SPPs in PRSp to contact with African or bozal varieties of Spanish during colonial times. This assertion seems to need more exploration and should be investigated further in future research. The rate identified here is in line with the general tendency identified for varieties of Spanish, in that Caribbean Spanish typically displays higher rates than those of Peninsular Spanish.

Another contrast with Holmquist's (2012) data is the finding in this study that gender plays a role, if a somewhat limited one, in usage of the overt SPPs. Holmquist's study identified an effect for the social factor of farmer versus nonfarmer, but not for gender; in fact, no other study has found effects for gender in PRSp subject expression. It isn't clear why this is the case, then, in the present study. Further stratification of participants in terms of social factors such as education, socioeconomic status, or other as yet unidentified categories may help to elucidate these findings, since the participants' demographic information was fairly homogeneous in the present analysis due to the fact that the participants could all be considered members of the same social network.

With regard to linguistic factor groups, the findings in part confirmed what had been identified before for PRSp, and for other geographical varieties in general, while also contributing new factor groups not previously considered. Since person and number had previously been identified as an important constraint on subject expression across several varieties of Spanish, it was expected that it would form part of the set of factor groups that would be selected as significant in the analysis. Although it is true that there are different options for subject expression for the third person, for instance, that do not exist for the first person, and therefore, some researchers have argued that the SPPs should be studied individually, the results identified here and in previous work for priming effects demonstrate the existence of a subject slot that people fill when speaking, and that priming exerts effects on all SPPs.

It was also to be expected that discourse connectedness would play an important role in constraining SPP expression, because, following person and number, switch-reference is generally considered the most important factor; this has been identified in both generative (cf. Avoid Pronoun Principle, Chomsky 1981) and variationist research (e.g., Cameron 1995; Otheguy, Zentella, & Livert 2007). The findings here indicated that the simple construct of switch-reference is able to give an account of the most basic tendency observed: when subjects change, speakers tend to express them. However, the level of detail provided in the model of discourse connectedness in this study contributes an advanced understanding of how reference relations play out in SPP usage in this variety of PRSp. As the distance between two referents becomes greater, and even when verb TAM changes, subject overtness increases. When the same referent is mentioned in adjacent clauses and verb TAM is the same, speakers tend to use more null pronouns. Two exceptions to the trend occur at Levels 6 and 8, at which there are fewer overts than at the previous levels; however, due to the small number of tokens for each of these categories (together, they make up less than 2 percent of the data), the exceptions are not completely reliable and more data is needed to see if the results are upheld.

In general, the results of this study are very similar to those found by Ávila-Shah (2000) for the Cuban monolinguals in her study. Holmquist (2012) included a somewhat similar measure of textual distance between a subject and the clarification of its referent, with those occurring in prior discourse (outside the turn of the speaker) favoring the overt expression of the subject. However, it is somewhat difficult to compare the results of the present study to Holmquist's, because there is no indication of the magnitude of effect, nor of the ordering of factor groups. Claes (2011) found that referential continuity was ranked third for San Juan PRSp; the overt SPP was favored when it was switched in reference in comparison to the previous subject and disfavored when it was coreferential with the object of the previous verb or the previous subject. Travis and Torres Cacoullos (2012) reported that intervening human subjects between mentions of coreferential first person singular subjects favored overt *yo*. In short, the importance of reference relations in SPP expression cannot be overstated.

In Spanish, priming can be observed both within the same speaker and between speakers in the course of conversational interaction. This study appears to be only the third to consider intraspeaker priming for PRSp on the island, after Cameron (1994) and Cameron and Flores-Ferrán (2004), both of which analyzed San Juan PRSp. In the present study, a range value of 25 was obtained and the factor weights clearly show evidence of repetition effects. Based on Travis and Torres Cacoullos (2012), it is hypothesized that, had only first or second person singular subjects been included, this factor group might have displayed a larger magnitude of effect, since third person subjects in particular can take many forms, as noted previously, and therefore may prime subsequent subjects in different ways. Among Puerto Ricans in New York, when the previous mention was an overt SPP, the factor weight was .65 for overt SPPs (Flores-Ferrán 2002: 70), the same weight obtained in this study. Travis (2007) reported the same direction of effect: when the previous mention had been overt, the overt SPP was favored for both the New Mexican narrative data and the Colombian conversational data, and when the previous mention had been null, the overt SPP was disfavored.

With regard to priming effects between the interviewer and the participants, the trend is clear, even though the numbers in each category are small: use of an overt SPP by the interviewer tended to be followed by an overt SPP in the interviewee's response, while a null SPP produced by the interviewer tended to be followed by another null, as in (3) and (4). These results resemble in part what Travis and Torres Cacoullos (2012) found in their analysis of coreferential and noncoreferential first person singular SPPs. Further research into priming in Spanish will be helpful in understanding how speaker turns may prime subsequent expressions of SPPs.

With regard to verb TAM, Silva-Corvalán's (2001) hypothesis regarding foregrounding and backgrounding of information and subsequent effects on subject expression seems to provide an explanation for SPP usage in this data set: the preterit disfavors the overt SPP, while the imperfect indicative (along with the present indicative) and the present subjunctive favor it. Nonetheless, the tendencies, whose factor weights are close to .50, are not as strong as expected. In previous studies, the imperfect had been found to favor the overt SPP, while the present had been reported to hover around a factor weight of .50 (Silva-Corvalán 2001). Flores-Ferrán (2002) reported weights of .61 for the imperfect and .54 for the present tense, and the weights reported in Claes (2011) were similar. The future, imperfect subjunctive, and conditional strongly disfavored the overt SPP in this study; however, the token numbers for these forms were quite small. It is hypothesized that a larger data set, perhaps from a genre other than the semidirected interview (e.g., narrative), would be required in order to make more confident generalizations about SPP usage with these forms.

The final finding, that reflexive verbs disfavor the overt SPP, had not been considered in previous analyses of PRSp. In the analysis of Colombian Spanish in Hurtado (2005), reflexiveness of verbs was not selected as a significant factor; however, in their study of subject expression among Mexican-descent children, Bayley and Pease-Álvarez (1997) reported the same factor weight obtained in this study for non-reflexive verbs, and a slightly higher weight, but one that still disfavored the overt SPP, for reflexive verbs. They noted the following:

In the case of nonambiguous verbs, the reflexive pronoun provides a redundant marker of person and thus lessens the need for an overt subject. In the case of ambiguous verbs, a reflexive pronoun provides an unequivocal means of retrieving a null first or third person subject and of distinguishing between first and third person subjects.

(Bayley and Pease-Álvarez 1997: 95)

However, ambiguity did not seem to factor into the participants' use of SPPs in this study, as preliminary analyses failed to select a prior ambiguity factor group as significant. Posio (2011), in his discussion of the three-argument verb *dar*, noted that the pronominal arguments compete for the preverbal position with the subject, but, unlike the subject, they cannot be omitted. This perhaps indicates a general tendency among Spanish speakers. Reflexive pronouns occupy a space to the left of the verb, the canonical subject position; this may lead speakers to simply avoid adding an SPP to the equation when that slot is already filled.

Regarding the limitations of this analysis, this research could have been made stronger with the inclusion of more social factors, had the participant group been more varied. Nonetheless, previous research has identified far more linguistic than social constraints on subject expression. The other main limitation of the study relates to the small numbers of tokens in some categories, particularly for such factor groups as interspeaker priming and discourse connectedness. Future studies of PRSp, should they include highly detailed coding, will need to analyze a larger data set than that of this study, so that all coded factor groups are able to be entered into the multivariate analysis.

Despite these limitations, this study has provided very detailed information about linguistic constraints on SPP expression in the PRSp of a coastal location that had not previously been analyzed. The results coincide with previous studies of PRSp and indicate that, despite differing rates reported of overt SPPs, underlying constraints are similar. Person and number, discourse connectedness, verb TAM, priming, and the presence of a reflexive verb all conspire to influence the production of overt SPPs in this variety of PRSp. Of these factor groups, verb reflexiveness and discourse connectedness had not been analyzed in connection to PRSp in prior studies. Furthermore, additional factor groups that were not included in the final multivariate analysis described in the previous section provided further nuanced information about subject expression in discourse and priming effects between speakers of PRSp.

Notes

1 The Center for Latin American Studies of the University of Florida supported the data collection for this research with an Interdisciplinary Field Research grant.
2 The numbers in parentheses following the examples refer to participant number, gender, and age, respectively.
3 The data in this table were previously reported in Abreu (2012).

Bibliography

Aaron, J. (2007). Epistemic future and variation: Grammaticalization and the expression of futurity since 1600. *Moenia*, *13*, 253–274.

Abreu, L. (2012). Subject pronoun expression and priming effects among bilingual speakers of Puerto Rican Spanish. In M. Díaz-Campos & K. Geeslin (Eds.), *Selected proceedings of the 14th hispanic linguistics symposium* (pp. 1–8). Somerville, MA: Cascadilla Proceedings Project.

Amaral, P. M., & Schwenter, S. A. (2005). Contrast and the (non-) occurrence of subject pronouns. In D. Eddington (Ed.), *Selected proceedings of the 7th hispanic linguistics symposium* (pp. 116–127). Somerville, MA: Cascadilla Proceedings Project.

Avila-Jiménez, B. I. (1995). A sociolinguistic analysis of a change in progress: Pronominal overtness in Puerto Rican Spanish. *Cornell Working Papers in Linguistics*, *13*, 25–47.

Avila-Shah, B. I. (2000). Discourse connectedness in Caribbean Spanish. In A. Roca (Ed.), *Research on Spanish in the United States* (pp. 238–251). Somerville, MA: Cascadilla.

Balasch, S. (2008). La conectividad discursiva en el discurso interactivo. In J. Bruhn de Garavito & E. Valenzuela (Eds.), *Selected proceedings of the 10th hispanic linguistics symposium* (pp. 300–311). Somerville, MA: Cascadilla Proceedings Project.

Bayley, R., & Pease-Álvarez, L. (1997). Null pronoun variation in Mexican-descent children's narrative discourse. *Language Variation and Change*, *9*, 349–371.

Bentivoglio, P. (1987). *Los sujetos pronominales de primera persona en el habla de Caracas*. Caracas: Universidad Central de Venezuela.

Camacho, J. A. (2013). *Null subjects*. Cambridge: Cambridge University Press.

Cameron, R. (1992). Pronominal and null subject variation in Spanish: Constraints, dialects, and functional compensation (Unpublished doctoral dissertation). University of Pennsylvania.

Cameron, R. (1993). Ambiguous agreement, functional compensation, and nonspecific *tú* in the Spanish of San Juan, Puerto Rico, and Madrid, Spain. *Language Variation and Change*, *5*(3), 305–334.

Cameron, R. (1994). Switch reference, verb class and priming in a variable syntax. In K. Beals (Ed.), *Papers from the 30th regional meeting of the Chicago Linguistics Society: Volume 2: The parasession on variation in linguistic theory* (pp. 27–45). Chicago, IL: Chicago Linguistics Society.

Cameron, R. (1995). The scope and limits of switch reference as a constraint on pronominal subject expression. *Hispanic Linguistics*, *6–7*, 1–27.

Cameron, R., & Flores-Ferrán, N. (2004). Perseveration of subject expression across regional dialects of Spanish. *Spanish in Context*, *1*(1), 41–65.

Chomsky, N. (1981). *Lectures on government and binding*. Dordrecht: Foris.

Claes, J. (2011). ¿Constituyen las Antillas y el Caribe continental una sola zona dialectal? Datos de la variable expresión del sujeto pronominal en San Juan de Puerto Rico y Barranquilla, Colombia. *Spanish in Context*, *8*, 191–212. doi: 10.1075/sic.8.2.01cla

Duarte, M. E. (2000). The loss of the avoid pronoun principle in Brazilian Portuguese. In M. A. Kato & E. Negrão (Eds.), *Brazilian Portuguese and the Null Subject Parameter* (pp. 17–36). Frankfurt: Vervuert-Iberoamericana.

Enríquez, E. V. (1984). *El pronombre personal sujeto en la lengua española hablada en Madrid*. Madrid: Consejo Superior de Investigaciones Científicas, Instituto Miguel de Cervantes.

Erker, D., & Guy, G. (2012). The role of lexical frequency in syntactic variability: Variable subject personal pronoun expression in Spanish. *Language*, *88*, 526–557. doi: 10.1353/lan.2012.0050

Fernández Díaz, M. (1990). *El pronombre personal sujeto en el español de San Juan* (Unpublished doctoral dissertation). Universidad de Puerto Rico, Río Piedras.

Flores-Ferrán, N. (2002). Subject personal pronouns in Spanish narratives of Puerto Ricans in New York City: A sociolinguistic perspective. Munich: Lincom Europa.

Gupton, T., & Lowman, S. (2013). An F projection in Cibeño Dominican Spanish. In J. Cabrelli Amaro, G. Lord, A. de Prada Pérez, & J. E. Aaron (Eds.), *Selected proceedings of the 16th Hispanic Linguistics Symposium* (pp. 338–348). Somerville, MA: Cascadilla Proceedings Project.

Holmquist, J. (2012). Frequency rates and constraints on subject personal pronoun expression: Findings from the Puerto Rican highlands. *Language Variation and Change, 24*, 203–220. doi: 10.1017/S0954394512000117

Hurtado, L. M. (2005). Syntactic-semantic conditioning of subject expression in Colombian Spanish. *Hispania, 88*, 335–348.

Labov, W. (1984). Field methods of the project on linguistic change and variation. In J. Baugh & J. Sherzer (Eds.), *Language in use: Readings in sociolinguistics* (pp. 28–66). Englewood Cliffs, NJ: Prentice Hall.

Lapidus Shin, N. (2012). Variable use of Spanish subject pronouns by monolingual children in Mexico. In K. Geeslin & M. Díaz-Campos (Eds.), *Selected proceedings of the 14th hispanic linguistics symposium* (pp. 130–141). Somerville, MA: Cascadilla Proceedings Project.

Mayol, L. (2012). An account of the variation in the rates of overt subject pronouns in Romance. *Spanish in Context, 9*, 420–442.

Milroy, L. (1980). *Language and social networks*. Oxford: Basil Blackwell.

Morales, A. (1997). La hipótesis funcional y la aparición de sujeto no nominal: El español de Puerto Rico. *Hispania, 80*, 153–165.

Orozco, R., & Guy, G. R. (2008). El uso variable de los pronombres sujetos: ¿Qué pasa en la costa Caribe colombiana? In M. Westmoreland & J. A. Thomas (Eds.), *Selected proceedings of the 4th workshop on Spanish sociolinguistics* (pp. 70–80). Somerville, MA: Cascadilla Proceedings Project.

Otheguy, R., Zentella, A. C., & Livert, D. (2007). Language and dialect contact in Spanish of New York: Toward the formation of a speech community. *Language, 83*, 770–802.

Paredes Silva, V. L. (1993). Subject omission and functional compensation: Evidence from written Brazilian Portuguese. *Language Variation and Change, 5*, 35–49.

Posio, P. (2011). Spanish subject pronoun usage and verb semantics revisited: First and second person singular subject pronouns and focusing of attention in spoken Peninsular Spanish. *Journal of Pragmatics, 43*, 777–798. doi: 10.1016/j.pragma.2010.10.012

Sankoff, D., Tagliamonte, S., & Smith, E. (2005). *Goldvarb X: A variable rule application for Macintosh and Windows*. Toronto, Canada: Department of Linguistics, University of Toronto.

Silva-Corvalán, C. (1994). *Language contact and change: Spanish in Los Angeles*. Oxford: Clarendon Press.

Silva-Corvalán, C. (2001). *Sociolingüística y pragmática del español*. Washington, DC: Georgetown University Press.

Tagliamonte, S. A. (2006). *Analysing sociolinguistic variation*. Cambridge: Cambridge University Press.

Toribio, A. J. (2000). Setting parametric limits on dialectal variation in Spanish. *Lingua, 110*, 315–341.

Travis, C. E. (2005). Discourse markers in Colombian Spanish: A study in polysemy. Berlin: Mouton de Gruyter.

Travis, C. E. (2007). Genre effects on subject expression in Spanish: Priming in narrative and conversation. *Language Variation and Change, 19*, 101–135.

Travis, C. E., & Torres Cacoullos, R. (2012). What do subject pronouns do in discourse? Cognitive, mechanical and constructional factors in variation. *Cognitive Linguistics, 23,* 711–748. doi: 10.1515/cog-2012–0022

U. S. Census Bureau. (2010a). *Profile of general population and housing characteristics: 2010 demographic profile data.* Retrieved July 23, 2014, from http://factfinder2.census. gov/faces/tableservices/jsf/pages/productview.xhtml?pid=DEC_10_DP_DPDP1

U. S. Census Bureau. (2010b). Annual estimates of the resident population for selected age groups by sex for the United States, states, counties, and Puerto Rico commonwealth and municipios: April 1, 2010 to July 1, 2013. Retrieved July 23, 2014, from http:// factfinder2.census.gov/faces/tableservices/jsf/pages/productview.xhtml?src=bkmk

Weinreich, U., Labov, W., & Herzog, M. (1968). Empirical foundations for a theory of language change. In W. P. Lehmann & Y. Malkeil (Eds.), *Directions for historical linguistics: A symposium* (pp. 95–188). Austin: University of Texas Press.

Young, R., & Bayley, R. (1996). VARBRUL analysis for second language acquisition research. In R. Bayley & D. R. Preston (Eds.), *Second language acquisition and linguistic variation* (pp. 253–306). Amsterdam: John Benjamins.

7 Interaction among cognitive constraints

The case of the pluralization of presentational *haber* in Puerto Rican Spanish

Jeroen Claes

1 The pluralization of presentational *haber*

Normative Spanish presentational *haber* ('there is/there are') is an impersonal construction. This means that in expressions such as example (1), no grammatical subject can be identified. Rather, the only nominal argument (*clases* 'classes' in the example) functions as a direct object. This is evident from the fact that the noun encliticizes as an accusative pronoun (see example 2). As a result, in both examples the verb represents third person singular verb agreement, even though the NP is plural.

(1) (Los huracanes) Significaban que no *había* clases, que tú tenías tres, cuatro días sin clases (SJ09H12/SJ1086).[1]
    '(Hurricanes) meant that *there weren't*$_{sg}$ classes, that you had three, four days without classes.'

(2) El tren, e, estas vías aquí, no las había antes. E, están arreglando el Martín Peña, el caño. Lo están dragando, están bregando (SJ20H11/SJ2308).
    '(The train, er, these streets here, *there*$_{Acc}$ *weren't*$_{sg}$ before. Er, they're fixing the Martín Peña, the natural channel. They're dredging it, they're working.'

However, in many varieties (e.g., Bentivoglio & Sedano 2011: 172–174), including Puerto Rican Spanish (e.g., Claes 2014; Brown & Rivas 2012; Holmquist 2008; Rivas & Brown 2012, 2013; Vaquero 1996: 64), presentational *haber* displays patterns of variable verb agreement with the NP (see example 3). This phenomenon is known as the 'pluralization of presentational *haber*'.

(3) *Habían* dos pisos, o sea que, *habían* como como veinticinco salones, un poco más (SJ03H22/SJ310-SJ311).
    '*There were*$_{pl}$ two floors, that is to say, *there were*$_{pl}$ like, like twenty-five classrooms, a bit more.'

In an earlier paper (Claes 2014) I have shown that in San Juan, the pluralization of presentational *haber* constitutes an ongoing language change from below. Particularly, against the background of Goldberg's (2006) Cognitive Construction Grammar, I have indicated that *haber* pluralization can be conceptualized as an argument-structure change: the non-agreeing argument-structure construction <**AdvP** *haber* **Obj**>, which has a direct object NP, is being replaced by a novel, agreeing argument-structure construction (<**AdvP** *haber* **Subj**>), which has a subject NP. In that same paper, I have also shown that this change is conditioned by three domain-general cognitive constraints on language that are assumed in Cognitive Linguistics: markedness of coding, statistical preemption, and structural priming (see Section 4). However, the relative strengths associated with these cognitive constraints and the ways they interact still remain to be explored.

Therefore, in this chapter, I will focus on the following questions:

1   Do markedness of coding, statistical preemption, and structural priming interact? In what ways?
2   Which of these cognitive constraints have a deeper impact on *haber* pluralization: markedness of coding, statistical preemption, or structural priming?

To answer these questions, I use three types of statistical analyses (mixed-effect logistic regression, conditional inference tree, and conditional variable permutation in a random forest) performed on a large number of presentational *haber* tokens drawn from transcribed recording sessions. Before turning to the results, let us first consider the methods that were applied in collecting and processing these data.

2 Methods

2.1 The sample

The analyses are based on a corpus of approximately 24 hours of recording sessions with 24 residents of the San Juan Metropolitan Area who are native speakers of Puerto Rican Spanish. As is shown in Table 7.1, the data is stratified by three social parameters: age (25–35 years versus 55+ years), academic achievement (without university degree versus with university degree), and gender (female versus male).

Table 7.1 Configuration of the sample

	25–35 years		55+		Total
	Male	*Female*	*Male*	*Female*	
Without university degree	3	3	3	3	12
With university degree	3	3	3	3	12
Total	6	6	6	6	24

To obtain more variable contexts, I structured the recording sessions into three sections:

1) Interview. Speakers were interviewed for about 30 minutes on a variety of topics related to their day-to-day life. To investigate the effect of comprehension-to-production priming, a set of questions containing presentational *haber* (see example 4) was included in the interview format. In these questions, the variants were used randomly.

(4)   Interviewer: ¿Y *habían* castigos por no llevar el uniforme?
'And *were there*$_{pl}$ pun, punishments for not wearing the uniform?'
Participant: Sí, por ser una escuela católica, sí *había* (SJ06H12/ SJ758-SJ759).
'Yes, as it was a Catholic school, yes, *there were*$_{sg}$.'

2) Story-reading task. After the first section, the participants were handed a two-page children's story (*Juan Sin Miedo*, '*John Without Fear*') containing 31 selection contexts of the type exemplified in (5) (20 trials, 11 fillers). Without previous preparation, they were instructed to read aloud the text and to select the variant that matched their own idiom.

(5)   En una pequeña aldea, *había/habían* un anciano padre y sus dos hijos . . .
'In a small village, *there were*$_{sg}$/*there were*$_{pl}$ an old father and his two sons . . . '

3) Questionnaire-reading task. Finally, the interviewees were given a multiple choice sentence completion task consisting of 45 items (32 trials, 13 fillers) preceded by a description that evoked the appropriate context for the interpretation of the trial sentence (see example 6). Without previous preparation, the participants had to read aloud the questionnaire and fill in the blanks with the variants that corresponded with their own usage. Whenever a participant had difficulties completing the story-reading or questionnaire-reading task, I read the tests to her/him and asked her/him which form s/he preferred.

(6)   A Inés le acaban de robar el carro, que tenía aparcado en algún callejón obscuro. Aunque no es la cosa más sensata que se pueda hacer, una amiga trata de consolarla diciendo: "No es culpa tuya, es que siempre_____ unas personas malas."
a) habrá   b) habrán

'They have just stolen Inés's car, which she had parked in a dark alley. Although this is not the most intelligent thing to do, a friend tries to comfort her, saying: "It is not your fault, ____always be a few bad people."'
a) There will$_{sg}$ b) There will$_{pl}$.

2.2 Envelope of variation

Most previous sociolinguistic studies of *haber* pluralization did not find any variation involving the present tense *hay*. However, my corpus provides 21 tokens of the vernacular plural *hayn*, which had already been documented in earlier investigations of Puerto Rican Spanish (Holmquist 2008: 28; Vaquero 1996: 64). As a result, if we want to keep up the 'Principle of Accountability' (see Labov 1972: 72), the alternation between *hay* and *hayn* cannot be excluded from the scope of this investigation. Additionally, some surveys have treated first person plural *haber* (see example 7) as an instance of presentational *haber* pluralization (e.g., DeMello 1991; Freites-Barros 2008; Holmquist 2008).

(7)   Y *habíamos* bastantes, bastantes estudiantes en, e, los salones de clase (SJ03H22).
'And *we were*, plenty, plenty of students in, er, the classrooms.'

However, first person plural *haber* includes the speaker in the *presentatum*, as can be seen in example (7). This is not the case for third-person plural *haber*, as is exemplified by the constructed third person plural variant of example (7) provided in example (8). Since there is a clear difference in meaning between *habían* 'there were$_{pl}$' and *habíamos* 'we were' in these examples, the first person plural forms of *haber* were left outside of the envelope of variation.

(8)   Y *habían* bastantes, bastantes estudiantes en, e, los salones de clase (constructed example).
'And *there were*$_{pl}$ a lot, a lot of students in, er, the classrooms.'

2.3 Statistical toolkit: mixed-effect logistic regression, conditional inference tree, and conditional variable permutation in a random forest model

After transliteration, all 1,655 tokens of *haber* + plural NP (69 tokens per participant) were selected from the corpus and submitted to three complementary types of statistical analysis: mixed-effect logistic regression with the *lme4* package (Bates, Maechler, Bolker, & Walker 2016) in R (R Core Team 2016), conditional inference tree analysis, and conditional variable permutation in a random forest model with the *party* package (Hothorn, Hornik, & Zeileis 2006). Let us, briefly, consider these three statistical tools.

2.3.1 Mixed-effect logistic regression

This investigation uses mixed-effect logistic regression with the *lme4* R package to trace the overall effects of the three general cognitive factors on *haber* pluralization (see Johnson 2009; Tagliamonte 2012: 137–138). In the mixed-effect model, the individual speakers and the lexical items that occur with *haber* were included as crossed random effects. To select a parsimonious model, I started out with a full model including both the random intercepts and all the fixed effects I hypothesized to have an impact on presentational *haber* pluralization. Then, I recombined the fixed effects into all possible subsets with the *pdredge* function of the *MuMIn* package for R (Bartón 2016). The output of this computation-intensive 'dredging' procedure is a list of candidate models ordered by their AICc score.[2] The model with the lowest AICc value was selected as the basis for the final model. Subsequently, I evaluated for which of the predictors interaction terms and random slopes were appropriate. To do so, I started adding interactions and random slopes one by one. If the addition of the interaction or random slope lowered the AICc value of the model with two units or more (Burnham & Anderson 2002: 70) with respect to the model without the added information, I was prepared to include the interaction or random slope in the final model, provided that the model converged (i.e., provided that the regression function could calculate a result) and that the inclusion of the slope or interaction did not result in overfitting (i.e., a model that included more predictors than the data could support).

2.3.2 Conditional inference tree

Although the unequally distributed datasets typically used in sociolinguistic research are "the epitome of the type of data that mixed models are designed to handle" (Tagliamonte, 2012: 139–141), mixed-effects regression models may become less accurate when the data are distributed highly unevenly across regressor levels and represent multiple interactions between predictors and/or empty data cells (Baayen 2014: 363–364; Levshina 2015: Chapter 14). This sort of data structure is often present in sociolinguistic corpora. Therefore, for our present purposes it will be useful to combine mixed-effects logistic regression with another statistical approach that rests upon completely different distributional assumptions (Baayen 2014: 364; Tagliamonte & Baayen 2012: 161). If we achieve similar results with both approaches, we can be more confident that they are not due to distributional biases. Additionally, although a mixed-effects model provides insight into the influence of individual predictors while taking all others and intergroup variation into account, it says little about the way these predictors jointly determine speakers' behavior (Tagliamonte & Baayen 2012: 163).

These two concerns can be addressed at the same time with conditional inference tree models (Baayen 2014: 364; Tagliamonte & Baayen 2012: 161, 164), which can be generated in R with the software package *party* (Hothorn, Hornik, Strobl, & Zeileis 2014). According to Baayen:

> [C]onditional inference trees estimate a regression relationship by means of binary recursive partitioning. The *ctree* algorithm begins with testing the global null hypothesis of independence between any of the predictors and the response variable. The algorithm terminates if this hypothesis cannot be rejected. Otherwise, that predictor is selected that has the strongest association to the response, as measured by a *p*-value corresponding to a test for the

partial null hypothesis of a single input variable and the response. A binary split in the selected input variable is carried out. These steps are recursively repeated until no further splits are supported.

(2014: 364)

2.3.3 Conditional variable permutation in a random forest model of the variation

Tagliamonte (2013: 130) states that "similarities and differences in the significance, strength, and ordering of constraints" (i.e., predictors) "provide a microscopic view of the underlying grammatical system". Therefore, to investigate the constraints that govern morphosyntactic variation, variationists perform regression analyses and describe the significance of the predictors, their effect sizes and directions, and their relative contribution to explaining the variation, which is assessed by calculating the range between the highest and the lowest regression estimate that is generated for each predictor.

Even though this method has provided interesting insights into the behavior of different alternations across various communities (see Tagliamonte 2012: 166, 2013 for overviews), from a statistical point of view it is somewhat problematic to assess the relative importance of predictors based on coefficient ranges. That is, while this procedure may provide insight into the size of the effect of a particular predictor and even though predictors with large effect sizes tend to be among the most important ones for explaining the variation, this need not be the case. For instance, for predictors with more levels, there is a greater probability of obtaining large effect ranges by chance alone.

Therefore, in this chapter, I will use a random forest model of the variation to assess the relative importance of predictors. According to Baayen, this type of statistical models unites

> [a] large number of conditional inference trees, resulting in a (random) forest of conditional inference trees. Each tree in the forest is grown for a subset of the data generated by randomly sampling without replacement from observations and predictors. The predictions of the random forest are based on a voting scheme for the trees in the forest: each tree in the forest provides a prediction about the most likely class membership, and the class receiving the majority of the votes is selected as the most probable outcome.

(2014: 366)

In R, random forests can be grown with the software package *party*. Once we have a random forest model of the variation, we can derive the relative importance of the different predictors by calculating the loss in prediction accuracy of the model when the levels of a predictor are randomly permuted, breaking the associations between the dependent variable and the levels of the predictor. This can be achieved with the function *varimp* of the same software package. The greater the loss in prediction accuracy, the more important a predictor is (Baayen

2014: 366; Tagliamonte & Baayen 2012: 160). Let us now turn to the theoretical framework of this study.

3 Theoretical approach

3.1 Cognitive Construction Grammar

Cognitive Construction Grammar is a theoretical framework that forms part of the Cognitive Linguistics functionalist theoretical movement. Like other Cognitive Linguistics theories, Cognitive Construction Grammar takes a usage-based approach to language. This entails that language is recognized to represent variability and change at any moment in time (Bybee & Beckner 2010: 830). Additionally, the framework advocates an experiential view of semantics, meaning that knowledge of language is considered to include knowledge of the quantitative patterns in this variability, including which type of speakers uses what variants preferentially (Bybee & Beckner 2010: 846; Goldberg 2006: 10). Most importantly, Cognitive Construction Grammar proposes that language constitutes entirely of form-function pairings ('constructions') of different degrees of schematicity. As such, no distinction of principle is assumed between the regularities (for example, argument structure) and the exceptional facets of language (for example, lexical items and idioms), because both are approached as pairings of form and meaning.

For instance, in a brief utterance such as example (9), no less than five constructions, each with its own meaning, can be identified: *Fulano*, *compra*, *un*, *bacalaíto*, and <**Subj** Verb **Obj**>.

(9) Fulano compra un bacalaíto (constructed example).
    'Fulano buys a bacalaíto.'

The meanings of the lexical items *Fulano, compra, un,* and *bacalaíto* are rather transparent and specific. In contrast, <**Subj** Verb **Obj**> communicates a more abstract meaning, which, according to Langacker (1991: Chapter 7) refers to the conceptualization of a transfer of energy from the subject argument to the object argument.

As this meaning refers to an event type that minimally requires two participants to take place, the transitive construction determines that there will be two profiled participants: the subject and the object. Additionally, the construction establishes which argument role these participants fulfill in the event type, what their syntactic function in the clause will be, and how information will be distributed over the clause. In sum, in Cognitive Construction Grammar, argument-structure constructions, rather than individual verbs, are taken to determine argument structure.

3.2 Cognitive Construction Grammar description
of **haber** *pluralization*

As noted above, in another paper (Claes 2014) I have shown that in Puerto Rican Spanish, the agreeing presentational *haber* construction (<**AdvP** *haber*

Subj>) is replacing its non-agreeing variant (<**AdvP** *haber* **Obj**>). The meaning of these two can be described as referring to a conceptualization of an event type in which the speaker points out the existence of some entity to the hearer, while situating it in a 'mental space' (Lakoff 1987: 490).[3] This is captured by the POINTING-OUT Idealized Cognitive Model (ICM, henceforth):

> It is assumed as a background that some entity exists and is present at some location in the speaker's visual field, that the speaker is directing his attention at it, and that the hearer is interested in its whereabouts but does not have his attention focused on it, and may not even know that it is present. The speaker then directs the hearer's attention to the location of the entity (perhaps accompanied by a pointing gesture) and brings it to the hearer's attention that the entity is at the specified location.
>
> (Lakoff 1987: 490)

Since both variants of the presentational *haber* construction refer to the same ICM, they also display the same pragmatic and semantic properties. Particularly, because POINTING-OUT only describes the act of bringing a referent under the attention of the hearer, the referent of the NP is merely present in the scene that is being presented through the construction. Therefore, it is probably safe to assume that it is assigned a 'zero' argument role (Langacker 1991: 288). When it comes to information status, the ICM also implies that the felicitous use of presentational *haber* requires that the hearer is unaware of the entity brought under her/his attention. Indeed, presentational expressions only welcome NP arguments that are new to the hearer (in the sense of Prince 1992) or can be construed as such (see Ward & Birner 1995).

Even though the two variants of the presentational *haber* construction refer to the same ICM, two conceptual-semantic differences can be hypothesized to exist between them. First, since Cognitive Linguistics considers that "the grammatical behavior used to identify subject and object do not serve to characterize these notions but are merely symptomatic of their conceptual import" (Langacker 2008: 364), the variant with a subject can be hypothesized to grant more conceptual and formal prominence to the NP, as this is the primary function of subjecthood (Langacker 1991: 294). Second, earlier research on Puerto Rican Spanish supports that the social and the stylistic value of the two alternatives is not at all identical. Unfortunately, space limitations impede addressing these aspects of the variation; instead the reader is referred to Claes (2014, 2016: Chapter 8), where these matters are given their due consideration.

Turning now to the adverbial phrase that appears frequently in presentational expressions (e.g., Meulleman & Roegiest 2012), Lakoff (1987: 542–543) argues that with the English presentational *there is/there are* construction this element denotes the nature of the mental space that is set up by the expletive *there*. Examples such as (10) suggest that in Spanish *haber* clauses the adverbial phrase (e.g., *En mi salon* 'In my classroom') fulfills a similar function. However, the difference between English and Spanish presentationals appears to be that, as the presentational *haber* constructions do not involve expletive subjects, the adverbial does not only set up the mental space, it also specifies its nature.

(10)   <u>En mi salón</u> *habían* treinta o treinta y un niños, sí (SJ12M12/SJ1404).
'<u>In my classroom</u> *there were$_{pl}$* thirty or thirty-one children, yes.'

Syntactically, this implies that the presence of the adverbial expression cannot be considered completely optional. The conceptual incompleteness manifested by isolated examples such as (11), which leaves us wondering against which setting we must interpret the assertion, suggests that this is the case. Let us turn now to the cognitive constraints that will be the main focus of this chapter.

(11)   *Podrían haber* días en que yo tenía dos horas libres entremedio (SJ13H11/SJ1566).
'*There could be$_{pl}$* days that I had two hours of free time in between.'

3.3 Cognitive constraints on morphosyntactic variation

Following connectionist models in psycholinguistics (e.g., Dell 1986), Cognitive Linguistics proposes that language production initiates with speakers forming a highly rich conceptualization (Langacker 2008: 31–34). As the conceptualization takes form, domain-general categorization processes compare it to the conceptual import of constructions. In most cases, this rough first pass activates multiple constructions to the degree they match the conceptualization. These start competing for further activation, while also feeding back into the way the conceptualization is structured; this is called 'spreading activation' (e.g., Dell 1986; Langacker 2007: 421, 2008: 228–229). Eventually, one construction reaches the highest level of activation and becomes selected to categorize the conceptualization (Langacker 2007: 421, 2008: 228–229).

Of course, given a particular conceptualization, not all constructions will have equal probability of serving as a target for categorization. Since Cognitive Linguistics claims that speakers rely on domain-general cognitive abilities to retrieve constructions from long-term memory, it seems only fair to assume that domain-general cognitive constraints will also condition the probability of activation of constructions. In this regard, three such factors have been mentioned in the Cognitive Linguistics literature (Langacker 2010: 93): markedness of coding (Langacker 1991: 298), statistical preemption (Goldberg 2006: 94), and structural priming (Goldberg 2006: 120–125).

Regarding the first of these constraints, the notion of spreading activation entails that the better the conceptualization matches the conceptual import associated with the construction, the more the representation of the construction will become activated. Indeed, in morphosyntax it has been found that a "notion approximating an archetypical conception [tends to be] coded linguistically by a category taking that conception as its prototype" (Langacker 1991: 298). In Cognitive Linguistics, this prototype effect is called 'markedness of coding'; 'unmarked coding', referring to a close correspondence between form and meaning, is preferred (Langacker 1991: 298).

A second constraint that influences a representation's level of activation is statistical preemption. This notion indicates that, when the representations of words and constructions are activated frequently together, the compositional expression becomes stored as a single node in the network; this is called 'entrenchment' (Bybee 2001: Chapter 5). In turn, because this entrenched expression is more detailed and can be activated faster, it is "preferentially produced over items that are licensed but are represented more abstractly, as long as the items share the same semantic and pragmatic constraints" (Goldberg 2006: 94).

Thirdly, language users tend to pick up and recycle (unintentionally and unconsciously) construction patterns they have (heard) used before, without necessarily repeating the specific words that appear in these structures (e.g., Szmrecsanyi 2006). In the psycholinguistic literature, this tendency is called 'structural priming'. Psycholinguistic research into structural priming has revealed that the phenomenon can be accounted for as a residual activation effect: once a particular representation has been visited, it remains more activated than others for a period of time, giving it a head start over its competitors. At the same time, structural priming also appears to be a mechanism of implicit learning, which permanently adapts the ease of activation of constructions to observed patterns of usage (e.g., Goldberg 2006: 120–125; Pickering & Ferreira 2008: 447). Let us investigate now how these three constraints condition *haber* pluralization.

4 Hypotheses and coding

In Section 3.1, I proposed that the variation between agreeing and non-agreeing presentational *haber* can be conceived of as a competition between two nearly synonymous, abstract argument-structure constructions: <**AdvP** *haber* **Obj**> and <**AdvP** *haber* **Subj**>. If these two variants compete for more or less the same functional space, the cognitive constraints introduced in the previous section can be used to make the following predictions about the variation patterns of *haber* pluralization.

Markedness of coding

Cognitively more prominent entities will be encoded more frequently as subject, triggering the use of <**AdvP** *haber* **Subj**>.

Statistical preemption

If a particular third person singular tense form of *haber* occurs primarily in <**AdvP** *haber* **Obj**> construction, occurring only sporadically outside of this construction, then this verb tense will disfavor <**AdvP** *haber* **Subj**>, provided that the conceptual import can be encoded with an entrenched instance of the first construction (i.e., provided that it does not call for aspectual or modal auxiliaries).

Structural priming

If a speaker has just used or processed <**AdvP** *haber* **Subj**>, s/he will be more likely to use <**AdvP** *haber* **Subj**> in the following variable context, provided this context occurs within a fairly narrow time window.

Of course, these predictions remain rather abstract, but with additional theoretical support from Cognitive Linguistics, they may be made concrete and specific enough as to be coded into contextual features. Particularly, the Cognitive Linguistics literature defines cognitive prominence in relation to the speaker's center of attention: clausal participants on which s/he has her/his attention focused are said to be prominent (Langacker 1991: Chapter 7). In turn, Myachykov and Tomlin (2015) show that agents tend to attract more attention than any other type of clausal participants. Therefore, to operationalize markedness of coding, semantic role would be a good candidate.

Nevertheless, the NP of existential expressions cannot be agentive, as the construction presents it as merely being present in a static situation. Still, as argued in earlier work (e.g., Claes 2014, 2016), it is inarguably the case that some entities (say, a lumberjack) are intrinsically more likely than others (say, a tree) to play the agentive role in events. Therefore, with constructions such as existential *haber*, all things being equal, entities such as *lumberjack* may be perceived as more potential agents than entities such as *tree*, for which the former will be relatively more prominent than the latter.

In Cognitive Linguistics, the semantic roles 'agent' and 'patient' are defined in relation to what Langacker (1991: 283–285) calls the 'canonical event model' or the 'action-chain model': the head initiates physical activity, resulting "through physical contact, in the transfer of energy to an external object" (Langacker 1991: 285) and an internal change of state of that entity, the tail of the chain. The semantic roles of agent and patient, in turn, are defined as, respectively, 'action-chain head' and 'action-chain tail'. Additionally, events take place in a particular setting, such that the event model minimally includes three elements: action-chain head/agent, action-chain tail/patient, and setting. To classify nouns according to these categories, I relied on the question in (12).

(12)   Is *the referent of the noun highly likely to cause an internal change of state to a second entity without being affected by a third entity first?*
       Yes: Typical action-chain head (i.e., more potential agent; e.g., *temblor* 'earth quake', *madre* 'mother', *carro* 'car')
       No: Typical action-chain setting or tail (i.e., more potential setting or patient; e.g., *actividad* 'activity', *víctima* 'victim', *daño* 'damage')

Another linguistic feature that correlates closely with speaker's selective attention is definiteness and specificity (Langacker 1991: Chapter 7). As was mentioned in Section 3.1, because of the discourse function of presentational *haber*, the NP can only refer to specific indefinite referents (Prince 1992). However, when we negate a presentational expression (e.g., *No hay osos en Puerto Rico* 'There are no bears in Puerto Rico'), we suspend the reference of the NP (Keenan 1976: 318). As a result, a generic expression emerges, which can be paraphrased as "the category *x* does not exist in *y*". In other words, under negative polarity, the NP becomes "identifiable only as a type, not as a specific instance or token" (Croft 2000: 132), for which it will be less likely to attract the speaker's attention (Langacker 1991: 308). Therefore, markedness of coding was operationalized further by coding for polarity.

Let us turn now to statistical preemption. Operationalizing this constraint requires some metric that expresses the relative degree of entrenchment of the different tense forms of *haber* in <**AdvP** *haber* **Obj**>. To this end, I will rely on ΔP (*delta*-P), a measure derived from associative learning theory (e.g., Ellis & Ferreira-Junior 2009). Applied to *haber* pluralization, this metric expresses the probability of observing a third person singular form of *haber* in the presence of <**AdvP** *haber* **Obj**> minus the probability of observing this form in the absence of that construction. Of course, for this measure to be meaningful, it must be calculated for frequencies derived from a large corpus that contains samples of multiple registers of both spoken and written language. Therefore, I turn to the twentieth-century section of the *Corpus del español* (20 million words; Davies 2002) as an ancillary data source.

The resulting ΔP scores are resumed in Figure 7.1. These data suggest that *hay* and *hubo* rarely occur outside of <**AdvP** *haber* **Obj**>, whereas all other forms

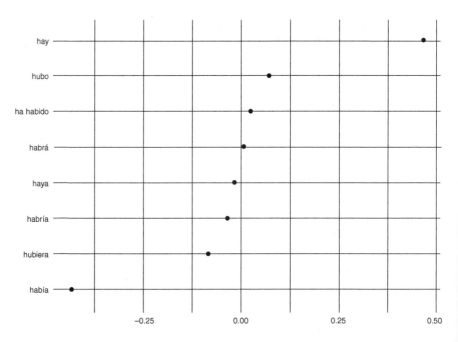

Figure 7.1 ΔP scores for the different tensed forms of *haber*

are either neutral with respect to their preference for occurring in or outside this construction or, in the case of *había*, display a marked preference for occurring outside of this construction. Also, the ΔP scores support that *hay* and *hubo* are more than twice as deeply entrenched in <**AdvP** *haber* **Obj**> as any other form of the verb. Therefore, the specific prediction that follows from statistical preemption is that the present and the preterit tense will disfavor <**AdvP** *haber* **Subj**>, unless encoding the conceptualization requires aspectual or modal auxiliaries, which would bypass the entrenched instances of <**AdvP** *hay* **Obj**> or <**AdvP** *hubo* **Obj**>. For this reason, statistical preemption was operationalized as: present and preterit tense without aspectual/modal auxiliaries versus all others.

Finally, as for structural priming, the data were coded for the type of last token that was uttered by the interviewer (comprehension-to-production priming) and the participant (production-to-production priming) and the number of conjugated verbs that occur between these tokens and the case at hand. Since the initial results displayed long-lasting priming effects independent of lexical repetition, structural priming was operationalized as follows: first occurrence/distance 20+ clauses, primed with <**AdvP** *haber* **Subj**>, and primed with <**AdvP** *haber* **Obj**>.

5 Results

5.1 Cognitive constraints

Overall, the top row of Table 7.2 (labeled *intercept*) shows that *haber* pluralization is a frequently occurring phenomenon in Puerto Rican Spanish. Still, the figures reported here do not match those that were documented in earlier sociolinguistic investigations of the phenomenon, which typically document agreeing *haber* in about 54 percent to 82 percent of the cases (Bentivoglio & Sedano 2011: 173). However, this appears to be due to the fact that I did not exclude the present tense *hay–hayn* from the scope of the investigation. Without these two forms, the rates of *haber* pluralization raise as high as 54.3 percent (N = 661/1217), which is significantly higher than the 44 percent (N = 83/190) of agreeing forms obtained by Brown and Rivas (2012: 329) for Caguas, Cayey, and San Juan. Yet, these fluctuations could be due to the fact that Brown and Rivas (2012: 330) base their conclusions on a limited number of tokens (total N = 190) derived exclusively from semi-directed interviews.

Let us review now the results that were obtained for the cognitive constraints with the three statistical tools. First, I will briefly go through the regression results in Table 7.2 in order to establish that the three cognitive constraints condition *haber* pluralization. Then, we will get to the main topics of this chapter, namely, the interaction among these constraints and their relative impacts on the variation. As anticipated earlier, Table 7.2 indicates that speakers are more likely to use the agreeing presentational *haber* construction with nouns that refer to typical action-chain heads (exemplified in 13), while they prefer the non-agreeing

Table 7.2 Logistic generalized linear mixed-effects models of presentational *haber* pluralization in San Juan (sum contrasts): numbers, percentages, and coefficients for agreeing presentational *haber*

Fixed effects	San Juan		
	n	*%*	*Coefficient*
(intercept)	684/1655	41.3	−0.974
Verb tense			
All others	622/1014	61.3	1.766
Synthetic expressions in present or preterit tense	62/641	9.7	−1.766
Production-to-production priming			
Agreeing presentational haber construction	352/558	63.1	0.597
First occurrence/distance 20+ clauses	88/246	35.8	−0.155
Non-agreeing presentational haber construction	244/851	28.7	−0.442
Comprehension-to-production priming			
Agreeing presentational haber construction	92/175	52.6	0.452
Non-agreeing presentational haber construction	30/125	24	−0.266
First occurrence/distance 20+ clauses	562/1355	41.5	−0.186
Typical action-chain position of the noun's referent			
Heads	350/773	45.3	0.418
Tails and settings	348/882	37.9	−0.418
Negation			
Positive	559/1225	45.6	0.341
Negative	125/430	29.1	−0.341
Model summary			
C-index of concordance			0.89
Pseudo-R2			0.62
aic$_c$			1517.9

Notes: Besides the predictors that appear in this table, the regression model also includes gender and education. Space restrictions inhibit us from discussing these results. The reader is kindly referred to Claes (2016: Chapter 8) for a discussion of the social covariates of *haber* pluralization in Puerto Rican Spanish. [b] I report Nakagawa's and Schielzeth's (2013) conditional pseudo- R.[2][c] In computing the models, the *bobyqa* optimizer for *glmer* was used.

presentational *haber* construction with nouns that refer to typical tails, as in example (14), or settings (see example 15).

(13)   Humans such as *madre* 'mother', natural phenomena such as *huracán* 'hurricane', self-propelling objects such as *carro* 'car'

(14)   Concrete objects such as *libro* 'book', animate beings that undergo an action such as, for example, *víctima* 'victim' and *invitado* 'invitee'

(15)   *Lugar* 'place', *año* 'year', nominalized events such as *actividad* 'activity', *discusión* 'discussion'

Similarly, Table 7.2 shows that the presence of negation disfavors the agreeing presentational *haber* construction, which is also evident from contrastive examples such as (16).

(16) *Habían* menos, no *había* tantos salones (SJ07H21/SJ886).
      '*There were$_{pl}$* less, *there weren't$_{sg}$* as many class rooms.'

Turning now to the results for statistical preemption, Table 7.2 shows that the agreeing presentational *haber* construction is unlikely to be used with the present or preterit (for which Figure 7.1 suggests an entrenched instance of <**AdvP** *haber* **Obj**>) when the coding of the conceptual import does not call for aspectual or modal auxiliary constructions. This is exemplified in (17), where the speaker simply points out that there have been tsunamis in San Juan in the past.

(17) Y aquí *hubo*, este, maremotos (SJ04M22/SJ493).
      'And here, er, *there have been$_{sg}$* tsunamis.'

For presentational *haber* expressions that involve other tenses or aspectual or modal auxiliaries, Table 7.3 shows that the non-agreeing presentational *haber* construction is unlikely to be used.

As noted in Section 4, statistical preemption requires that both the entrenched alternative and the novel expression could encode the conceptualization equally well. Therefore, we would not expect to document its effects with complex conceptualizations that cannot be expressed with <**AdvP** *hubo* **Obj**> or <**AdvP** *hay* **Obj**>. Table 7.3 suggests that this is the case, because in expressions involving aspectual or modal auxiliary constructions, agreeing presentational *haber* is used as frequently with the present and the preterit tense as with other tenses.

Finally, Table 7.3 shows that whenever speakers have used an agreeing presentational *haber* clause, they are more prone to use another one. This is the case whether or not they repeat the specific verb form, provided the next variable context is situated within a 20-clause range. The same results were obtained for the non-agreeing presentational *haber* construction. Similarly, when speakers have processed an agreeing presentational *haber* clause, they are more likely to utter an expression based on the agreeing construction pattern and vice versa.

Table 7.3 Present- and preterit-tense tokens of presentational *haber*, by absence/presence of aspectual or modal auxiliary constructions: numbers and percentages for the agreeing presentational *haber* construction

Type of expression	N	%
Presentational *haber* expressions in the present and preterit tense without auxiliary constructions	62/641	9.7
Presentational *haber* expressions in the present and preterit tense involving auxiliary constructions	84/124	67.7

5.2 Interaction among the cognitive constraints

Up until now, the discussion has been concerned with the way the individual cognitive constraints shape presentational *haber* pluralization when they are considered jointly with the others, with social constraints, and with the random variation due to individual participants and nouns. What has not been considered is the way these cognitive constraints work in tandem to promote one of the variants or, conversely, interact to cancel each other's effect. As Tagliamonte and Baayen (2012: 163–164) observe, disentangling this complex interplay of constraints goes beyond the capabilities of a mixed-effects regression model, but conditional inference tree models are very well suited for such a task.

Figure 7.2 displays such a model. On the left-hand side of the figure, nodes [3], [4], and [7] suggest an interaction between the two modalities of structural priming and typical action-chain position with tenses other than the synthetic present and preterit. Particularly, the bar plots in nodes [5], [6], [8], and [9] suggest that that both modalities of structural priming and typical action-chain position reinforce each other with these tenses. For instance, in example (18), the earlier use of the agreeing presentational *haber* construction by the interviewer and the speaker, together with the fact that *muchachos* 'kids' is a typical action-chain head, probably tipped the balance in favor of this construction.

(18)   Interviewer: ¿Y que tú recuerdes, *habían* más padres como los tuyos, los tuyos?
'And, as far as you remember, *were there*$_{pl}$ more parents likeyours, yours?'

Participant: E, ¿que yo recuerde? Pues en el internado había de todo. *Habían* estudiantes que tenían unos padres que no existían, que lascuidaban las nanas, los cuidaban los . . . *Habían* <u>unos much, muchachos de mucho dinero</u> (SJ04M22/SJ454-SJ457).
'Er, as far as I remember? Well, in the boarding school, there wasa bit of everything. *There were*$_{pl}$ students that had parents that didn't exist, who were looked after by the nannies, they were looked after by . . . *There were*$_{pl}$ <u>ki, kids with a lot of money.</u>'

Similarly, nodes [2] and [10] suggest that the tendency to use the agreeing presentational *haber* construction in contexts primed by the speaker with this variant is reinforced by the absence of negation (bar plot in node [12]), as in example (19).

(19)   Y *habían* de aquí. De Puerto Rico, *habían* <u>dos matrimonios</u>, tres, tres matrimonios y no, no nos conocíamos porque eran de la isla, de por ahí (SJ15M21/SJ1853).
'And *there were*$_{pl}$ from here. From Puerto Rico *there were*$_{pl}$ <u>two couples</u>, three, three couples and we didn't, we didn't know each other, because they were from the island, from around there.'

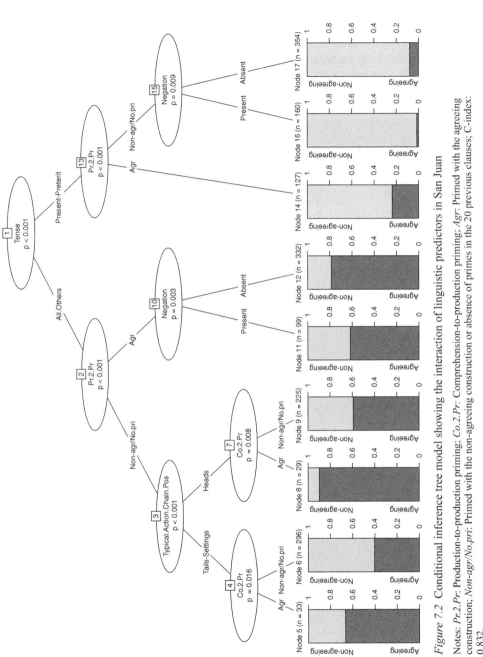

Figure 7.2 Conditional inference tree model showing the interaction of linguistic predictors in San Juan

Notes: *Pr.2.Pr*: Production-to-production priming; *Co.2.Pr*: Comprehension-to-production priming; *Agr*: Primed with the agreeing construction; *Non-agr/No.pri*: Primed with the non-agreeing construction or absence of primes in the 20 previous clauses; C-index: 0.832.

In turn, the right-hand side of Figure 7.2 shows that, for synthetic expressions in the simple present and preterit tense, production-to-production priming appears to operate more independently (node [13]), because in contexts primed by the speaker with the agreeing presentational *haber* construction, neither the noun's typical action-chain position nor comprehension-to-production priming impose constraints (bar plot in node [14]). In example (20), for instance, the interviewer's earlier mention of *hay* and the fact that *fiesta patronal* 'patron saint celebration' refers to a typical action-chain setting do not cause the speaker to use an expression based on <**AdvP** *haber* **Obj**>. Rather, she continues with the agreeing presentational *haber* construction, which she had already used multiple times before in the immediate context.

(20)   Participant: Se pueden comer en todos los momentos, porque, por lo menos en mi casa *hayn* pasteles todos, toda la sem, todo el año. Pero, este, sí, *hayn* platos como que es, específicos de diciembre. Como el arroz con gandules, el lechón, el pastel, las, el arroz con dulce, tembleque.

'They can be eaten at all times, because, at least at my home, *there are$_{pl}$ pasteles* every, all week, all year round. But, er, yes, *there are$_{pl}$* dishes that, spe, specific to December. Like rice with pigeon peas, suckling pig, *pastel*, the, rice pudding, *tembleque*.'

Interviewer: ¿Y que tú recuerdes siempre ha sido así o *han habido* cambios a este respecto?

'And as far as you remember, has it always been like that or *have there been$_{pl}$* changes in this regard?'

Participant: Pues, e, cuando yo era más pequeña se mataba el lechón en casa, mi casa de mi abuela. Se compró todos los, lechones y se mataban allí, y allí los hacían.

'Well, er, when I was smaller, they killed the suckling pig at home, my home of my grandmother. They bought every, suckling pigs and they killed them over there and there they made them.'

Interviewer: ¿Y los asaban?

'And you grilled them?'

Participant: Y los, exactamente, ahora no, ahora, pues, ellos los compranhechos.

'And them, exactly, not nowadays, nowadays, they buy them ready-made.'

Interviewer: ¿Y *hay* otras tradiciones por acá, este, fiestas patronales, carnavales?

'And *are there$_{sg}$* other traditions around here, er, patron saint celebrations, carnivals?'

Participant: Aquí *hayn* <u>fiestas patronales</u> en todos los municipios (SJ05M12/SJ653-SJ657).

'Here *there are$_{pl}$* patron saint celebrations in every town.'

Finally, nodes [13] and [15] suggest an interaction between the absence/presence of negation, production-to-production priming, and tense. Specifically, for synthetic expressions in the present and preterit tense, the absence/presence of negation is only a relevant constraint in unprimed contexts or contexts primed by the speaker with non-agreeing presentational *haber*. In these cases, the absence of negation attenuates the tendency to use the non-agreeing presentational *haber* construction (bar plot in node [17]).

5.3 Constraint ranking

In the previous section, it was already observed that statistical preemption and production-to-production priming emerge from the conditional inference tree as the most important constraints on *haber* pluralization. This is confirmed by Figure 7.3, which plots the conditional permutation variable importance for the different predictors. Additionally, as was already evident from the conditional inference tree, comprehension-to-production priming is one of the least influential constraints on the variation. In fact, only the absence/presence of negation ranks lower, which is consistent with Langacker's (1991: 312) observation that definiteness/specificity is among the least central characteristics of prototypical subjects.

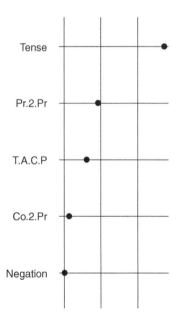

Figure 7.3 Constraint ranking for the linguistic predictors
Note: T.A.C.P: Typical action-chain position.

6 Discussion and conclusions

In this chapter, I have shown that markedness of coding, statistical preemption, and structural priming interact to a large extent. Particularly, the data suggest an antagonistic relationship in (this) language change between statistical preemption and the other two cognitive constraints: whereas the first encourages speakers to stick to the usage patterns they have observed, the other two incite speakers to extend the agreeing presentational *haber* construction to more (and new) conceptual regions. As a result, every time markedness of coding and structural priming tip the balance in favor of the agreeing presentational *haber* construction for the encoding of a present- or preterit-tense POINTING-OUT conceptualization without aspectual or modal nuances, the use of an expression based on this construction weakens the strength of the representations of the entrenched non-agreeing instances. This, in turn, debilitates their preemptive effect, which, eventually, will result in the less constrained use of <**AdvP** *hayn* **Subj**> and <**AdvP** *hubieron* **Subj**>. The results obtained from the conditional permutation of predictors in the random forest model corroborate this characterization of the interaction between the three cognitive factors.

The antagonistic relationship between, on the one hand, statistical preemption and, on the other, structural priming and markedness of coding reminds of the roles these cognitive constraints play in language acquisition and innovation. That is, in language acquisition, statistical preemption has been shown to be the mechanism that prevents children from overgeneralizing (Goldberg 2006: Chapter 5), whereas structural priming has been argued to promote the extension of perceived structures to new conceptualizations of the same type (Pickering & Ferreira 2008: 449–450). Regarding language innovation, Croft (2000: Chapter 5) argues that the tendency to maximize unmarked coding is the prime motivation for form-function reanalysis, which reforms established constructions or, put differently, overrules their preemptive effect.

The results also corroborate that structural priming is modality-independent, as has been argued in the psycholinguistic literature (Pickering & Ferreira 2008: 440–441). However, at the same time, the conditional permutation of factors in the random forest model and the conditional inference tree show that production-to-production priming has a deeper impact than comprehension-to-production priming on naturally occurring language use. This does not confirm the results of earlier work in experimental psycholinguistics, which found the magnitude of the priming effect to be comparable for both modalities (Pickering & Ferreira 2008: 440–441). On a methodological note, the importance of structural priming in this variation also suggests that priming effects should not be neglected in analyses of language variation and change, even more so because psycholinguistic inquiry has shown that virtually all levels of linguistic analysis (including phonology, for example, syllable structure) display priming-like phenomena (Pickering & Ferreira 2008: 429).

Finally, this chapter has illustrated how Cognitive Linguistics may contribute to establishing psychologically plausible and empirically adequate theoretical models of the quantitative patterns in linguistic variation. Particularly, I have shown that domain-general cognitive constraints on language that are assumed in Cognitive Linguistics lead to empirically correct predictions about the distribution of agreeing and non-agreeing presentational *haber*. This invites further research into these constraints and their effects on linguistic variation.

Notes

1 Conventions: the codes at the end of the examples identify the cases in my corpus: SJ = San Juan; 09 = informant number 9; H = male informant (M = female); 1: 20–35 years of age (2 = 55+ years of age); 2: university graduate (1 = less than university). The code behind the backslash is the identifier of the example in the database. Angled brackets identify construction schemas. The profiled proportions of the event frames of constructions (i.e., their conceptually indispensable participants) are printed in boldface. Construction schemas do not specify the linear ordering of constituents. This is handled by specialized word order constructions.

2 AICc (second-order Akaike's Information Criterion) is a sample-size adjusted statistic that expresses the tradeoff between model fit and model complexity. If we add predictors to the model that do not contribute to the fit, the AICc rises. Models with lower AICc scores are generally assumed to be more adequate for the data (see Burnham & Anderson 2002).

3 Fauconnier defines 'mental spaces' as "small conceptual packets constructed as we think and talk for the purpose of local understanding and action" (Fauconnier & Turner 1996: 113), and as such, they belong to the realm of working memory. In other words, mental spaces are novel, temporal conceptualizations that organize the information speakers and hearers are presented with in usage events.

Bibliography

Baayen, H. R. (2014). Multivariate statistics. In R. Podesva & D. Sharma (Eds.), *Research methods in linguistics* (pp. 337–372). Cambridge, MA: Cambridge University Press.

Bartón, K. (2016). *MuMIn: Multi-model inference.* Retrieved from http://cran.r-project.org/web/packages/MuMIn/index.html

Bates, D. M., Maechler, M., Bolker, B., & Walker, S. (2016). *lme4: Linear mixed-effects models using Eigen and S4.* Retrieved from http://cran.r-project.org/web/packages/lme4/index.html

Bentivoglio, P., & Sedano, M. (2011). Morphosyntactic variation in Spanish-speaking Latin America. In M. Díaz-Campos (Ed.), *The handbook of Hispanic sociolinguistics* (pp. 123–147). Oxford: Blackwell.

Brown, E., & Rivas, J. (2012). Grammatical relation probability: How usage patterns shape analogy. *Language Variation and Change, 24*(3), 317–341.

Burnham, K. P., & Anderson, D. R. (2002). *Model selection and multimodel inference.* New York: Springer.

Bybee, J. (2001). *Phonology and language use.* Cambridge, MA: Cambridge University Press.

Bybee, J., & Beckner, C. (2010). Usage-based theory. In B. Heine & H. Narrog (Eds.), *The Oxford handbook of linguistic analysis* (pp. 827–856). Oxford: Oxford University Press.

Claes, J. (2014). A cognitive construction grammar approach to the pluralization of presentational *haber* in Puerto Rican Spanish. *Language Variation and Change, 26*(2), 219–246.

Claes, J. (2016). Cognitive, social, and individual constraints on linguistic variation: A case study of presentational haber pluralization in Caribbean Spanish. Berlin & Boston, MA: De Gruyter.

Croft, W. (2000). Explaining language change: An evolutionary perspective. London & New York: Longman.

Davies, M. (2002–). *Corpus del español*. Retrieved from www.corpusdelespanol.org/

Dell, G. S. (1986). A spreading-activation theory of retrieval in sentence production. *Psychological Review, 92*(3), 283–321.

DeMello, G. (1991). Pluralización del verbo *haber* impersonal en el español hablado culto de once ciudades. *Thesaurus, 46*, 445–471.

Ellis, N. C., & Ferreira-Junior, F. (2009). Constructions and their acquisition: Islands and the distinctiveness of their occupancy. *Annual Review of Cognitive Linguistics, 7*, 187–220.

Fauconnier, G., & Turner, M. (1996). Blending as a central process of grammar. In A. E. Goldberg (Ed.), *Conceptual structure, discourse and language* (pp. 113–129). Stanford, CA: CSLI Publications.

Freites-Barros, F. (2008). Más sobre la pluralización de *haber* impersonal en Venezuela. El estado Táchira. *Lingua Americana, 12*(22), 36–57.

Goldberg, A. E. (2006). Constructions at work: The nature of generalization in language. Oxford: Oxford University Press.

Holmquist, J. (2008). Gender in context: Features and factors in men's and women's speech in rural Puerto Rico. In M. Westmoreland & J. A. Thomas (Eds.), *Selected proceedings of the 4th workshop on Spanish sociolinguistics* (pp. 17–35). Somerville, MA: Cascadilla.

Hothorn, T., Hornik, K., & Zeileis, A. (2006). Unbiased Recursive Partitioning: A Conditional Inference Framework. *Journal of Computational and Graphical Statistics, 15*(3), 651–674.

Hothorn, T., Hornik, K., Strobl, C., & Zeileis, A. (2014). *Party: A laboratory for recursive partytioning*. Retrieved from http://cran.r-project.org/web/packages/party/index.html

Johnson, D. E. (2009). Getting off the GoldVarb standard: Introducing Rbrul for mixed-effects variable rule analysis. *Language and Linguistics Compass, 3*(1), 359–383.

Keenan, E. (1976). Towards a universal definition of subject. In C. N. Li (Ed.), *Subject and topic* (pp. 305–333). New York: Academic Press.

Labov, W. (1972). *Sociolinguistic patterns*. Philadelphia, PA: University of Pennsylvania Press.

Lakoff, G. (1987). Women, fire, and dangerous things: What categories reveal about the mind. Chicago, IL: Chicago University Press.

Langacker, R. W. (1991). Foundations of cognitive grammar. Volume 2: Descriptive application. Stanford, CA: Stanford University Press.

Langacker, R. W. (2007). Cognitive grammar. In D. Geeraerts & H. Cuyckens (Eds.), *The Oxford handbook of cognitive linguistics* (pp. 421–462). Oxford: Oxford University Press.

Langacker, R. W. (2008). *Cognitive grammar: A basic introduction*. Oxford: Oxford University Press.

Langacker, R. W. (2010). Cognitive grammar. In B. Heine & H. Narrog (Eds.), *The Oxford handbook of linguistic analysis* (pp. 87–110). Oxford: Oxford University Press.

Levshina, N. (2015). How to do linguistics with R: Data exploration and statistical analysis. Amsterdam & Philadelphia, PA: John Benjamins.

Meulleman, M., & Roegiest, E. (2012). Los locativos en la valencia de la construcción existencial española. ¿Actante o circunstante? *Zeitschrift für Romanische Philologie, 128*, 57–70.

Myachykov, A., & Tomlin, R. S. (2015). Attention and salience. In E. Dabrowska & D. Divjak (Eds.), *Handbook of cognitive linguistics* (pp. 31–52). Berlin & Boston, MA: De Gruyter.

Nakagawa, S., & Schielzeth, H. (2013). A general and simple method for obtaining R2 from generalized linear mixed-effects models. *Methods in Ecology and Evolution, 4,* 133–142.

Pickering, M. J., & Ferreira, V. S. (2008). Structural priming: A critical review. *Psychological Bulletin, 134*(3), 427–459.

Prince, E. (1992). The ZPG letter: Subjects, definiteness, and information-status. In W. C. Mann & S. A. Thompson (Eds.), *Discourse description: Diverse linguistic analyses of a fund-raising text* (pp. 295–326). Amsterdam & New York: John Benjamins.

R Core Team. (2016). R: A language and environment for statistical computing. Retrieved from www.R-project.org/

Rivas, J., & Brown, E. (2012). Stage-level and individual-level distinction in morphological variation: An example with variable *haber* agreement. *Borealis: An International Journal of Hispanic Linguistics, 1*(2), 73–90.

Rivas, J., & Brown, E. (2013). Concordancia variable con *haber* en español puertorriqueño. *Boletín de Lingüística, 24*(37–38), 102–118.

Szmrecsanyi, B. (2006). Morphosyntactic persistence in poken English: A corpus study at the intersection of variationist sociolinguistics, psycholinguistics, and discourse analysis. Berlin & Boston, MA: De Gruyter.

Tagliamonte, S. (2012). Variationist sociolinguistics: Change, observation, interpretation. Oxford: Wiley-Blackwell.

Tagliamonte, S. (2013). Comparative sociolinguistics. In J. K. Chambers & N. Schilling-Estes (Eds.), *The handbook of language variation and change* (pp. 128–156). Oxford: Wiley-Blackwell.

Tagliamonte, S., & Baayen, H. R. (2012). Models, forests, and trees of York English: *Was/were* variation as a case study for statistical practice. *Language Variation and Change, 24*(2), 135–178.

Vaquero, M. (1996). Antillas. In M. Alvar-López (Ed.), *Manual de dialectología hispánica: El español de América* (pp. 51–67). Barcelona: Ariel.

Ward, G., & Birner, B. (1995). Definiteness and the English existential. *Language, 71*(4), 722–742.

Pragmatics

8 Mitigation and indirectness in Puerto Rican, Dominican, and Mexican Spanish in an institutional discourse setting

Nydia Flores-Ferrán

1 Introduction

This socio-pragmatic study investigates mitigation and indirect speech employed by Spanish-speaking clients in an institutional discursive setting where they discuss depression, treatment, and medication. In particular, the study addresses pragmatic variation and whether dialect and age condition the use of mitigating devices in Puerto Rican, Dominican, and Mexican Spanish dialects. The study is informed by Labov's and Fanshel's (1977) seminal study on mitigation in a therapeutic discursive setting.

There has been a great deal of discussion relating to mitigation and indirect speech. In his seminal research on conversational mitigation, Fraser (1980: 341) defined mitigation as a modification of a speech act that reduces the unwelcoming effects that the act may have on its hearer. He suggests that it is not a speech act but that it involves a certain effect that arises from a given speech act (342). In defining mitigation, Briz (2004) suggests that it serves as a negotiating tool since it minimizes what has been said by softening or reducing the illocutionary force of an utterance and repairing or masking the real intention of the speaker. Furthermore, Labov and Fanshel (1977: 346) maintain that mitigating strategies are also employed to mediate conflict.

With these definitions in mind, this study views mitigating devices and indirect propositions as strategies used by speakers to attain goals while maintaining an attenuated posture. In particular, the study examines the realization of hedges, bushes, shields, epistemic disclaimers, tag questions, parenthetical verbs, the use of the diminutive *-ito*, hypothetical utterances, and indirect utterances related to *el qué dirán* and *guardar las apariencias* (Placencia 1996) with the purpose of determining whether these strategies vary from dialect to dialect.

Pragmatic variation has received little attention in the field of sociolinguistics (Barron & Schneider 2009: 426). For example and with respect to Spanish, new research has drawn attention to the ways in which indirectness manifests among Spanish speakers with regard to age, gender, dialects, and between distinct languages (e.g., Félix-Brasdefer 2009; Márquez-Reiter 2002; Márquez Reiter & Placencia 2005). Many studies have also addressed mitigation in Spanish discourse (e.g., Bravo 1999, 2008; Bravo & Briz 2004; Chodorowska-Pilch 2004;

Haverkate 1990, 1994; Hernández-Flores 1999; Koike 1994; Murillo Medrano 2002; Placencia 1996). These and other studies have mostly reported on how variation emerges with regard to speech acts (e.g., refusals, requests). However, to date, only a few studies have attended to indirectness and mitigation in Spanish medical-related institutional discursive contexts (e.g., Cordella 2003, 2007; Delbene 2004; Flores-Ferrán 2009, 2010a, b), 2012).

The significance of this study resides within several concerns. First, the study centers on linguistic mitigation and indirectness in Spanish in an under-investigated institutional discursive setting. Second, since cultures have been found to differ with regard to how language is employed in distinct social and situational contexts, the study attends to mitigation and indirectness in three Spanish dialects. Finally, the study explores how cultural notions posited by Placencia (1996) (i.e., *el qué dirán* and *guardar las apariencias*) are issued, a concern which has not been fully attended to under the scope of pragmatic variation.

The chapter is organized as follows: Section 2 discusses theoretical considerations and related literature (i.e., institutional discourse, mitigation, pragmatic variation). This section is followed by Section 3, the methodology. Sections 4 and 5 discuss the qualitative and quantitative analyses. Finally, these sections are followed by Sections 6 and 7, the summary and discussion.

2 Theoretical considerations and related literature

In this section, several theoretical considerations are discussed: institutional discourse (i.e., motivational interviews), mitigation, and pragmatic variation.

2.1 Institutional discourse: motivational interviews

Bardovi-Harlig and Hartford (2005: 13) define *institutional discourse* as "spontaneous authentic language used by speakers who are speaking as themselves, in genuine situations, with socio-affective consequences". In other words, the discourse is not motivated by experimental prompts (e.g., discourse completion tasks) that guide speakers' talk. Agar (1985) maintains that institutional discourses are characterized as instances in which one person who represents an institution encounters another for its services. He also notes that institutional discourse accomplishes three things: first, the institution must diagnose the client. Second, the institution identifies specific clients, their problems, and the solutions (i.e., institutional frames). Third, there is a diagnosis, that part of the discourse where a representative adheres to the client's ways of talking. Clients, on the other hand, come to an institution with a variety of ways of thinking about themselves, their problems, etc. Given the common characteristics of institutional discourses (e.g., the clientele, diagnosis), this institutional discursive context is appropriate for an examination of mitigation and indirect speech since the linguistic behavior of the speakers is framed within one theme and, thus, allows for the data to reveal variation.

In this particular study, mitigation and indirectness are examined in Motivational Interviewing (MI) or Motivational Enhancement Therapy. These interviews are known as a change-inducing strategy, a modality that aims at enhancing client motivation towards change (Von Wormer 2007). It is considered a systematic intervention approach for evoking change (Miller & Rollnick 2002), a practice which was informed by motivational psychology with the purpose of producing rapid internal change in individuals. The treatment is not designed to guide or train clients. Rather it employs the client's own resources to enhance change; namely, the discourse is mainly generated by the client and is unguided.

2.2 Mitigation

Mitigation refers to words, phrases, linguistic forms, devices, and strategies speakers employ to attenuate, soften, or downgrade the strength of an utterance. In other words, these strategies contribute to modifying the illocutionary force of a message, thereby reducing the effects of directness. Blum-Kulka (1987: 132) has noted that indirect propositions tend to be more polite since "they increase the degree of optionality and because the more indirect an illocution is, the more diminished and tentative its force tends to be".[1] For instance, Labov's and Fanshel's (1977) examination of therapeutic conversations reported how breaches in social relations were mitigated successfully by the use of several linguistic devices such as syntactic alterations that mitigated requests and demands and the use of distinct intonation contours.

It should be noted that researchers who investigate mitigation in several Spanish dialects have argued that mitigation is not always related to politeness and 'face'-saving concerns (Bravo 1999; Briz 2004; Hernández-Flores 1999; Placencia 1996, among others). For instance, Placencia (1996: 21) also posits that the lexical choices speakers make do not necessarily have face-saving motivations and that it may be more precise to say that people want to save their public self-image. She maintains that the cultural concepts of *el qué dirán* 'what people will say' and *guardar las apariencias* 'to keep up appearances' represent ways in which people need to hold a 'good image' or conform to group expectations. Therefore, cultural values intersect with indirectness (Watts 2003).

Delbene's (2004) study merits special mention since it was one of the first to examine mitigation in a medical institutional discourse. The study investigated this phenomenon in medical interviews that dealt with a stigmatized disease (i.e., HIV). Among the many findings Delbene reported that male physicians exhibited the most frequent use of mitigating devices, especially when interacting with female patients, in instances where negative prognoses were forthcoming.

2.3 Pragmatic variation

Pragmatic variation examines how language use varies in specific sociocultural or situational contexts. Barron and Schneider (2009: 425) maintain that since "language use in interaction is shaped by cultural values, pragmatic similarities may occur across languages, while pragmatic differences may occur across varieties of the same language". Barron's and Schneider's framework, which can be conceived as an intersection between pragmatics and sociolinguistics, assumes two components: one distinguishes at the macro level the influence of the social factors on a linguistic feature under observation (e.g., age, gender, dialect) and the other component assumes the micro factors, related factors as power-distance, formal versus informal language, etc.

2.4 Research questions

The study was guided by the following research questions:

1   What mitigating devices and indirect propositions are employed by the speakers?
2   Can intra-lingual pragmatic differences be detected?
3   Do the social variables of age and dialect condition the use of indirectness and mitigation?

3 Method

3.1 The participants

Data were gathered from MIs conducted during 2006–2009. A convenience sampling of 12 residents of New Jersey (i.e., Puerto Ricans, Dominicans, and Mexicans) was extracted from a larger pool of client recordings. Each participant was interviewed twice. The participants' ages ranged from 28 to 51 years. They were subscribed to two sessions in which their medication intake was checked and the effects of the medication and treatment were discussed. The clients had varying levels of education and SES, and all were native Spanish speakers. The interviews varied in length from 30 to 45 minutes.

3.2 The corpus and analysis

There are several reasons why MI discourse was selected to investigate mitigation and indirectness. First the interview protocol was systematic and consistent for all participants. In using a step-by-step approach, it allowed the researcher to identity the linguistic features related to mitigation and indirectness in a systematic manner. Second, the clients all had a similar condition: depression, a stigmatized illness (Interian et al. 2007). Therefore, the MIs discussed similar concerns. Third, because of the stigma attributed to this illness, it was hypothesized that the clients would make negative associations and therefore employ mitigating strategies to indirectly express discomfort with the treatment. Another reason why this particular discourse was of interest had to do with the type of interaction that is unique to MI: the client does most of the speaking. Furthermore, the discursive organization of the interaction was found to be consistent: to motivate the client to adhere to treatment. Thus, from a discourse analytic perspective, this type of interaction lent itself to draw comparisons among the three dialects.

A convenience sampling of Spanish-speaking clients was extracted from a larger corpus of therapeutic interviews held at a clinic. The interviews were digitally recorded and held between a client and the same therapist in a clinic. To enable the study, approvals were obtained from two institutions: the university in which the researcher was employed and the clinic which was affiliated to another institution. To guarantee privacy between the therapist and each client, and to ensure reliability in the interpretation of the discourse, the researcher was not present for any of the interviews. The therapist forwarded the interviews digitally to the research. Each motivational session was approximately 20–45 minutes in duration. The recordings were later transcribed and coded by the researcher's assistant and researcher, respectively.

The analysis of each transcription consisted of a thorough examination of every clause produced in order to determine the presence of a mitigating device and indirect proposition. To analyze the corpus, the study employed aspects of an Interactional Sociolinguistics approach to capture how each participant's identity and dialect intersected with mitigation and indirectness.

A mixed-method approach was used to analyze the data: the qualitative analysis informed the quantitative analysis and vice versa. For the qualitative approach, mitigating devices and indirect utterances were first identified. This analysis generated themes in which mitigating devices were realized and identified indirect propositions that could not be undertaken by the quantitative analysis (i.e., proverbial saying). For the quantitative analysis variables were coded: the dialect and age of the speaker; the type of mitigating device as a hedge, shield, parenthetical verb, epistemic disclaimer; the use of mood and aspect to express uncertainty; and the theme in which the mitigating device was issued. A statistical analysis using SPSS[2] was then conducted to uncover the tendencies generated by the three dialects. Thus, the study addresses transferability, the extent to which these results can be extended to other contexts, and generalizability, the extent to which gross tendencies could characterize the linguistic behavior of the three distinct dialects.

4 Qualitative analysis

To respond to the first research question, this section addresses the types of mitigating devices and indirect propositions that emerged in the corpus. It should be noted that when examining large amounts of data, Schegloff (1993: 102–103) has argued that researchers are looking at multiple or aggregates of single instances. Although the study uses quantitative analysis to describe tendencies, it also takes into account a single instance of mitigation, since it represents a relevant occurrence.

In general, the devices and indirect propositions attested in the corpus which will be discussed were: hedges (e.g., *más o menos* 'more or less'); bushes (e.g., *como* 'as', 'like', and several constructions containing *como*); shields (e.g., *uno* 'one', epistemic disclaimers *según he leído* as 'as I have read'), hypothetical propositions, tag questions, parenthetical verbs (e.g., *creo que* 'I think'), proverbial sayings, and the -*ito* diminutive morphology (e.g., Bravo 1999; Briz 2004; Caffi 1999; Chodorowska-Pilch 2004; Flores-Ferrán 2010; Fraser 1980, among others).

The next section defines the mitigating strategy, contextualizes it, and exemplifies the use of the strategy according to speaker dialect.

4.1 Tag questions

Tags are propositions (e.g., declaratives) that are turned into questions. Labov and Fanshel (1977: 85) maintain that tag questions serve to mitigate. Their analysis of tag questions suggests that they mitigate more than an assertion. In other words, they are formulated in such a way that an order or demand is mitigated by a question, as in *¿Me puedes ayudar con esto, verdad?* 'You can help me with this, right?'

In excerpt (1) the client observes the therapist while the therapist scans the medication bottle to determine frequency of intake[3]:

Puerto Rican: 4, MI2L15

(1) Desde que los [medicamentos] recogí no se me ha olvidado ninguna dosis, ¿Verdad que no?
'Since I picked them [medications] up (I)[4] haven't forgotten any doses, right?'

The tag question issued by the client served to indirectly state that she was not sure whether she had followed the therapist's recommendations. To attenuate she converted her assertion into a question.

In excerpt (2) a Mexican client indirectly asks about the therapist's credentials:

Mexican: 8, MI2L203

(2) Una pregunta . . . y usted es doctor, ¿Verdad?
'A question . . . and you are doctor, right?'

In excerpt (2) there were three indirect strategies that operate as mitigators. First, she announced or inserted a preparatory formula: *una pregunta* 'a question', an epistemic disclaimer. Second, she employed the formal second person pronoun *usted*, which created distance between her and the therapist. Finally, she converted her assertion to a question, an indicator of politeness. A statement (e.g., 'Are you a doctor?') would have been considered impolite.

In the excerpt that follows the client was asked what she could attribute her more favorable condition to after reporting that she felt better:

Dominican: 3, MI2L131–132

(3) Pues me supongo que la medicina porque yo no estoy tomando sino esa y no más, ¿Verdad?
'Well, I guess that the medication because I am only taking just this one and nothing else, right?'

While she doubtfully attributed her improvement to the medication, she also indirectly expressed that she was only taking this one medication when both the client and therapist knew that she was only prescribed one medication. The client could have directly indicated that there was nothing else other than the one medication. By employing '*verdad*' at the end of her clause she was indirectly seeking confirmation.

In sum these three excerpts are illustrative of how clients of the three dialects employed the same mitigating device at the end of an assertion to express doubt and to seek confirmation.

4.2 Parenthetical verbs

These verbs relate to opinion, belief, thought, (e.g., *pienso* 'I think', *opino* 'my opinion is', *creo* 'I think', *considero* 'I consider'). Schneider (2004) points out that parenthetical verbs such as *me imagino* 'I imagine', *supongo* 'I suppose' operate as inserted verbs and do not have a syntactic connection to the host sentence. That is they serve a discursive function and are considered optional.

In (4) the client describes how she feels about her condition:

Puerto Rican: 30, MI1L295

(4)   A veces, de vez en cuando, cuando me siento triste así . . . pienso que no
      sirvo para nada o que no tengo todas las suficientes, eh, que no soy tan
      inteligente para ir a un sitio y que me den trabajo porque no tengo esas
      cualificaciones.
      'Sometimes, once in a while, when (I) feel sad like that . . . (I) think that
      I am good for nothing or that (I) don't have all sufficient, um, that (I) am
      not as intelligent to go to a place and (they) give me work because I don't
      have the qualifications.'

In (4) the client softened the impact of her statement by employing *pienso que* '(I) think that' in addition to expressing *a veces* 'sometimes' and *de vez en cuando* 'once in a while'. Her option to express 'I am good for nothing' would have been considered conflictful and direct. Thus, she masked her inability to change, something which the therapy was purposefully designed to do.

In excerpt (5) the client describes how her condition affects the people that surround her:

Mexican: 8, MI2L140

(5)   Eso es lo que, me da una gran satisfacción también, sentirme bien con-
      migo misma y sí con los demás. Ya no estarles como proyectándoles está
      tristeza también a ellos, porque ellos también a verme así, pues también
      me imagino que se sentían un poco tristes al verme así, me pasaba ahí
      llorando y enojada y ahora pues está cambiando mi vida y la vida de
      los . . . de los que me rodean.
      'That is what gives me great satisfaction too, feeling good with myself
      and also with others. Not projecting this sadness also to them, because
      they also seeing me, well, also (I) imagine that (they) feel a bit sad to see
      me that way, (I) would cry there and mad and now well my life is chang-
      ing and the life of . . . of those that surround me.'

Here the parenthetical verb *me imagino* '(I) imagine' along with the discourse marker, *pues* 'well' was used to downgrade the impact of how she was affecting her family. The syntactic position of the parenthetical verb, located before the conflict-related assertion, illustrates how she attempted to reduce the severity of her statement.

In the next excerpt a client discusses how she feels about her condition and how she was treated by her partner:

Dominican: 29, MI1L187–189

(6)   <u>Pienso</u> eso, que como que siempre voy a estar, con ese dolor y pensando, en todo lo que él me hizo, porque yo confiaba en él y de la manera que él me trataba, <u>pienso que</u> si él que decía que me quería mucho, me hizo eso, ¿Qué no me hará otra persona que no me quiera?

'(I) think that, that like (I) will always be, with this pain and thinking, in all that he did to me, because I trusted him and the way he treated me, I think that if he that would say that he loved me very much, (he) did that to me, what would another person do who doesn't love me.'

In (6) the parenthetical verb *pienso* 'think' was issued twice. In the first clause, the client could have directly affirmed by indicating 'yes' instead of *pienso* '(I) think' to indicate her pain was going to be indefinite. She also softened her message in using *como que* 'like'. The second instance of *pienso* also served to attenuate how poorly she was treated.

With regard to parenthetical verbs the speakers of these three dialects employed a mental verb in a similar manner: The verb decreased the impact of a harsher message and was employed in a conflictful context.

4.3 Hedges/bushes, 'como constructions', and shields

The study was partially guided by Brown's and Levinson's (1987: 45) definition of hedges to code these forms. They suggest that a hedge is "a particle, word, or phrase that modifies the degree of membership of a predicate or noun phrase in a set; it says of that membership that it is *partial*, or true only in certain respects". For example, *si mal no recuerdo* 'if I remember well' . . . *Si no me equivoco* 'if I'm not mistaken' . . .

Excerpt (7) is illustrative of how a client describes her improved condition:

Mexican: 8, MI2L68

(7)   Sí (.) de verdad sí, pues, <u>generalmente,</u> sí yo ya me siento ahí un poquito más tranquila, amm . . . no como con esa ansiedad.

'Yes (.) Really, yes, well, generally, yes I now feel there a bit more at ease, umm, not like with that anxiety.'

In (7) while the client attempted to agree about her improvement and used defini- tive terms *de verdad* 'really' and *sí* 'yes', she mitigated her assertion by issuing

generalmente, which suggests that her statement is partially true. The diminutive
-ito and *como* 'as if' also added vagueness to the clause.

In the following excerpt (8) the hedge *si no me equivoco* 'if I'm not mistaken'
was issued to describe how the medication is contributing to her well-being:

Puerto Rican: 30, MI2L515

(8)   Sí porque yo me la bebo y, <u>si no me equivoco</u>, me ayuda a controlar los
      problemas y . . .
      'Yes because I take it, and if I'm not mistaken, it helps me control my
      problems and . . . '

The hedge *si no me equivoco* 'if I'm not mistaken' contributed to decrease the
exactitude of the statement *me ayuda a controlar los problemas*. In other words,
while the cause-effect of the medication may be inappropriately stated, the client
cautiously indicated that the medication was helping her somewhat.

A Dominican client defiantly explains that she does not like taking medication
because she considers it addicting:

Dominican: 3, MI1315

(10)   A mi no me gusta. ¿A quién le gusta ser adicto a una medicina? A nadie,
       a nadie, supuestamente. A mi personalmente no me gusta.
       'I don't like it. Who likes to be addicted to a medication? No one, no
       one, supposedly. Personally, I don't like it.'

To reduce what could be considered non-adherence to medication behavior the client
employed the hedge *supuestamente* 'supposedly'. It operates as a cautionary measure since it decreases the commitment to the truth of the proposition *a nadie* 'no
one'. Noted also is the redundant uses of 'a nadie', which is indicative of adversity.

In sum the hedges in these three excerpts exhibit similarities: they were inserted
items and they modified the degree of membership and truth condition of the clients' statements.

4.3.1 Bushes

For bushes, the study was informed by Caffi (1999). Caffi (2007: 98) character-
izes 'bushes' as a reduction in the precision of the propositional content such as
is the use of 'kind of'. However, this study only coded approximators (i.e., *como*
'as if' 'like', *más o menos* 'more or less'). Caffi maintains that these mitigators
affect the propositional content of an utterance. The most frequently employed
bush in the corpus of this study was *como* 'as', *como que* 'sort of', *tal como*
'just like', *como+verb* (i.e., *como diría* 'like (I) would say'), and *como si fuera*
'as if'.[5]

In excerpt (11) a Mexican client employs *como que* 'sort of' to explain how the
medication has helped her condition:

Mexican: 45, MI1L433

(11)   Pues ee (.) que que, o sea que sí . . . me [medicamento] ha ayudado yo
pienso que me ha ayudado porque <u>como que</u> yo estoy cambiando.
'Well, um (.) that that, that is that if yes . . . [medication] has helped me
I think because, I am sort of changing.'

The use of *como que* 'sort of' operated as a vagueness-generating device indicating that her changed condition was not fully complete. In this instance the
client hinted that the medication was not serving a definitive purpose. The use
of *que que, o sea que sí*, and *yo pienso* were also indicative of the client's
ambivalence.

The following excerpt obtained from a Puerto Rican client shows how *como*
'sort of' is employed to indicate that she has experienced a mild improvement:

Puerto Rican: 5, MI1L176

(12)   Me he sentido <u>como</u> un poco más tranquila.
'I have felt sort of a bit calmer.'

In this example forms *como* 'sort of' and *un poco* 'a bit' combined produce vagueness.
In essence the client indirectly expressed that the treatment has not helped much.

In excerpt (13) the use of the bush '*como que*' employed by a Dominican client
to mitigate the impact that the depression has had on her life:

Dominican: 29, M11L110

(13)   Y pienso que me, que esto . . . <u>como que</u> nunca se me va, <u>como que</u>
nunca ee, voy a olvidar esto [condición], porque [] . . .
'I think that, this [depression] . . . like (it) will never leave, like never,
uhm, I'm going to forget this [condition] because [] . . .'

The use of *como que* 'like' affected the propositional content of the client's statement. The form served to attenuate the gravity of her condition and indirectly
expressed hopelessness.

In sum all three excerpts are representative of how bushes were employed and
co-occurred with other devices to produce vagueness regardless of dialect.

4.3.2 Shields

Shields are known as impersonal mechanisms, (e.g., the use of 'one', 'as we know',
generic 'you' and 'we') (Flores-Ferrán 2009; Haverkate 1990). In some instances,
they can serve to substitute for the first person 'I', the first person pronoun.

Excerpt (14) exemplifies the use of *uno* 'one' as a shield in the three instances
in which it was produced:

Mexican: 8, MI2L151

(14) Porque pues . . . sentirse triste no le de nada ni ganas a <u>uno</u> de hablar
      con la gente, estar ahí <u>uno</u> encerrado solo y pues ahora <u>uno</u> se siente con
      energía, con ganas de salir a la calle, al parque, a la tienda.
      'Because well . . . feeling sad it doesn't give one any will to speak to
      people, there one locked up and so now one feels with energy, with a
      will to go out to the street, to the park, to the store.'

In referring to herself the client employed *uno* 'one'. The form operated as a
shield in that she could have used *yo* 'I'. The first two instances show how *uno*
was issued in a conflict-related assertion. The third instance was employed to
generalize her condition to the hearer.

In describing the effects of the medication, the next excerpt shows how a client
explains her physical reaction:

Puerto Rican: 2, MI1L189

(15) Eso es horrible. Como que me voy a morir, siente <u>uno</u> como que se va
      a morir, una cosa en el pecho como que te vas a morir, es algo horrible,
      horrible.
      'That is horrible. As if I'm going to die, one feels as if (one) is going to die,
      a thing in the chest as if (you) are going to die, (it) is horrible, horrible.'

In (15) the client avoided using *yo* 'I' in the context of this conflictful clause. In
addition, she employed other mitigating devices: *como que* is an approximator
that produces vagueness. Furthermore, by impersonalizing the subject she indirectly generalized the feelings of anxiety to include the therapist. Noticeable
here is the use of *te*, an informal reflexive pronoun as opposed to *se* the formal,
a pragmatic choice which reduced the distance between the speaker and hearer.

In the next excerpt (16) a client describes how she feels when mixing beer with
the medication:

Dominican: 42, MI1L805

(16) Cuando <u>uno</u> se toma dos cervezas uno se siente bien, no es verdad <u>uno</u>,
      mira, <u>uno</u> se siente bien, se relaja, entonces sí yo sé, que voy a sentirme
      bien . . . ¿Me entiendes?
      'When one drinks two beers, one feels good, right one, look, one feels
      good, (one) gets relaxed, then yes I know, that (I) am going to feel
      good . . . (You) understand?'

The use of *uno* is particularly interesting in this excerpt since the client also used
yo as a subject in another clause and a null subject. The first instance of *uno* is
illustrative of how she avoided using *yo* 'I' to directly express how good she

felt when mixing medication and alcohol. The second instance she claimed how relaxing mixing was. Thus, the use of *uno* is emblematic of how she generalized this practice to include the hearer ensuring that this mixing is common practice. However, she employed *yo* to directly express how good she felt, defiantly (i.e., this statement in the audio file exhibited a raised voice).

Thus, in these three excerpts *uno* operated as a shield to avoid using *yo*, to engage the interlocutor, or to generalize the message to other individuals.

4.4 Epistemic disclaimers

Epistemic disclaimers are mitigating devices that serve as preparatory formulas (Caffi 2007: 67), such as "If I'm not wrong . . . " (*si mal no recuerdo, si no me equivoco*), and non-epistemic disclaimers, for example, "I hate to do this, but . . . " (*Siento decirte esto pero . . .; odio tenerte que decirte . . .*), or "If you don't mind" (*si no es molestia*). They tend to express a form of knowledge, opinion, or attitude.

In excerpt (17), the client expresses *eso es verdad* 'that is true' to reiterate her position when she refused to seek further assistance:

Mexican: 8, MI2L622

(17) Eso es verdad. Yo dije 'no' porque es mucho la ayuda que he recibido y tanto los beneficios y como yo me he sentido . . . y no, no sé, yo no sé. 'That is true. I said "no" because it is too much help that I have received and so many benefits and since I have felt . . . and no, (I) don't know, I don't know.'

In stating that *eso es verdad* 'that is true', the client inserted a preparatory formula that warned the hearer of the forthcoming clause. The response represented an indirect refusal to seek additional assistance.

In the excerpt that follows an epistemic disclaimer is employed when indicating that the medications have not helped much:

Puerto Rican: 4, MI1L4

(18) Siento decirle que yo siento que eso [medicamentos] no me ayudan por la razón de que sigo con mucho estrés . . . ¿Tú me entiendes? 'Sorry to tell you that I feel that that [medications] don't help me for the reason that I still continue with stress . . . Do you understand?'

The client forewarned the therapist by using *siento decirle* 'sorry to tell you'. This mitigating device reduced the negative effects of the report that indicated the treatment had not been effective. The use of the informal second person pronoun *tú* was used to decrease distance between her and the therapist.

In excerpt (19) a disclaimer *en realidad* 'in reality' is employed by a client:

Dominican: 51, MI1L73

(19) Bueno (.) que sí, que eso <u>en realidad</u>, eh (.) esta forma [con tratamiento]
a uno le da más conocimiento y (.) que por medio de esto [medicamen-
tos y terápia] yo he entendido que sí, que necesito más [ayuda].
'Well (.). that yes, in reality, um (.) this way [through treatment] one gets
more knowledge and (.) in this manner [medication and therapy] I have
understood that yes, I need more [help].'

In excerpt (19) the client first admitted that the treatment provided her with more
knowledge. By issuing the disclaimer *en realidad* 'in reality' she softened the
message in which she admitted to needing more treatment. In this excerpt the use
of the generic *uno* again was issued to refer to herself and to engage the hearer of
the forthcoming: a request for more treatment.

In all three excerpts differences are not found in the use of epistemic disclaimers: they were employed to express knowledge, opinion, or attitude, and as preparatory formulas.

4.5 The use of subjunctive and conditional forms

Fraser (1980) has noted that verbs in the subjunctive mood or conditional aspect
tend to make statements imprecise. They make actions hypothetical and therefore
are used to indirectly convey an idea.

4.5.1 The subjunctive mood

In excerpt (20) the client describes how she feels with regard to the medication
and its benefits:

Puerto Rican: 4, MI2L122

(20) Sí. No claro que sí. Si no <u>fuera</u> por la medicina yo ya <u>estuviera</u> muerta
¿Sabes? [la medicina] tiene sus efectos y sus cosas que estamos tratando
de mejorar pero si no <u>fuera</u> por la medicina, yo no <u>estuviera</u> aquí, no
<u>estuviera</u> tratando de seguir adelante.
'Yes. Of course, yes. If it wouldn't be for the medication, I would already
be dead. You know? [The medication] has its effects and its things that
we are trying to improve but if it weren't for the medication, I wouldn't
be here, (I) wouldn't be trying to get ahead.'

Even though the client explicitly indicated that the medication had side effects,
she offset that assertion by indirectly claiming she would not be alive if it were
not for the treatment, implicitly indicating that she would have committed
suicide.

In (21) a client discusses how she hopes to continue with the medication:

Mexican: 8, MI1L280

(21)   Yo quisiera que mi vida siguiera como ahora. Entonces creo que sí estoy
       dispuesta a tomármela [la medicina] el tiempo que <u>sea</u> necesario.
       'I would like that my life continue as it is now. Then, I believe that yes
       (I) am willing to take it [medication] as long as it is necessary.'

In excerpt (21) the client did not directly agree to take the medication. Rather she
suggested that she would be willing to continue it as long as needed. Again, the
hypothetical proposition functioned to create ambiguity.

   In response to the effects of the medication a client expresses the conditions in
which she will continue to adhere to treatment:

Dominican: 3, MI1L410

(22)   Mientras que no me <u>afecte</u> [la medicina], no <u>sea adicta</u>, no hay prob-
       lema. Mientras que no <u>sea</u> que si no me la [medicina] <u>tomo</u> me, me, me
       pongo toda paranoica, no hay problema.
       'As long as it [medication] doesn't affect me, not make me an addict,
       there's no problem. As long as it [medication] isn't that if I don't take it
       [medication], I, I, become paranoid, there's no problem.'

In (22) the client did not overtly say that she will stop taking the medication.
Instead she indicated the conditions in which she would agree to take it, conditions which are all hypothetically situated.

4.5.2 The use of the conditional aspect

This excerpt is illustrative of how a client employs the conditional form to mitigate:

Puerto Rican: 5, MI1L153

(23)   Es lo que te <u>podría</u> decir. Ha sido como un escape para quitarme de la
       mente las preocupaciones.
       'That's what (I) would say. (It) has been like an escape to remove my
       worries from my mind.'

Instead of directly indicating how the medications have helped, the client employed
the conditional aspect which positioned the utterance as semantically non-definitive.
In one part of the clause she indicated that the medication may have contributed to
her well-being, albeit as an escape mechanism. Yet she still described the effects of
the medication using a bush *como* 'like', also indicative of ambivalence.

   In describing her anxiety and depression a client uses the conditional aspect:

Mexican: 45, MI2L24

(24)   de pronto me daba una ansiedad . . . así <u>quería</u> salirme corriendo y andar
       corriendo en las calles

'suddenly (I) would get anxious . . . thereby wanting to go out running and running in the streets'

The client's urge to leave her environment running in the streets was indicative of the depressive state she was in, but the intensity of her feelings was diminished by the use of the conditional.

To explain whether she will continue with her medication a Dominican client also employs the conditional form:

Dominican: 29, MI1L949

(25)   La [medicina] <u>dejaría</u> de tomar a ver si me siento bien, y no <u>tendría</u> que seguirla tomando.
'I would stop taking it (medication) to see if (I) feel good, and (I) wouldn't continue taking it.'

In excerpt (25) the client expressed probability, possibility, or suggestion to indicate non-adherence to medication and treatment.

All six excerpts are illustrative of how the subjunctive and conditional forms were employed to create hypotheticals and non-definitive propositions.

4.6 The diminutive -ito

When speakers employ -*ito*, the proposition can be considered mitigating. For instance, Murillo Medrano (2002) suggests that the use of this form operates as an attenuating strategy by reducing a threat and shifting the focus of an imperative utterance to the object being requested. For example, direct speech acts as requests in combination with the diminutive, as in *Préstame un poquito de dinero* 'Lend me a little bit of money', downgrades an order or request. It should be noted that the corpus did not contain any instance in which the diminutive form was employed to mitigate by the Dominicans.

A client describes the side effects from the medication:

Puerto Rican: 4, MI2L29

(26)   Un <u>poquito</u> mal, el cuerpo un <u>poquito</u> caliente pero no como cuando tengo así fiebre alta.
'A bit bad, the body a bit warm but not like when (I) have a high fever.'

In (26), two instances of *poquito* 'a little' downgraded her message, which could otherwise be considered serious.

When describing change a Mexican client employs the diminutive to express the degree to which she feels she has changed:

Mexican: 14, MI2L204

(27)   Trato de pensar positivo ahora, porque antes tal vez era un <u>poquito</u> negativa.
'(I) try to think positive now, because before maybe (I) was a [little] bit negative.'

In excerpt (27) the use of *tal vez* 'maybe' and *poquito* 'a little' contributed to soften the message. Furthermore, the client opened her statement with *trato* '(I) try', a verb which semantically also added ambivalence regarding the change in her behavior.

4.7 Proverbs and metaphorical sayings: other mitigating strategies

Orwenjo (2009: 145) suggests that proverbs "offer one of the most accessible and efficient means of avoiding direct critique by alluding to the criticized manner in an indirect, less aggressive manner". In addition, Seitel (1972: 137) in citing Firth (1926: 137) has noted that proverbs "[b]y virtue of their being expressed in objective terms, they [proverbs] influence without forcing and, their objectivity carries more weight than an emotion outburst."

In excerpt (28) a Mexican client employs a saying to indicate how she felt with regard to her depression:

Mexican: 8, MI2L201

(28)   mi cuerpo ya estaba como vulnerable a que, a que pasara a cualquier cosa, una neumonía, una pulmonía, una simple gri gripe me podía matar, una infección, que me cortara algo, me podría infectar podría, succederme algo más, entonces estaba como un poquito asustada porque digo, es como, <u>como ir a la guerra sin armas</u> [] . . .
'My body felt sort of vulnerable to, that something would happen, pneumonia, a pneumonia, a simple col cold could kill me, an infection, if something would cut me, (it) could infect me, something else could happen, before (I) was a bit scared because, (let's) say, (it) was like being in a war without weapons . . . '

In expressing her vulnerabilities to illnesses the client completed her statement by indirectly stating that she felt totally unprotected from whatever could have happened to her. There were multiple mitigating devices that contributed to downgrading her message: the use of the conditional, a hypothetical *me podría infectar*, a bush *como*, the subjunctive mood *que me cortara*, and the diminutive *-ito*.

In (29) a Puerto Rican client expresses a proverbial-like saying to indicate that she needs to seek additional help:

Puerto Rican: 3, MI1L456

(29)   Porque dice también un refrán, dice "<u>Ayúdate que yo te ayudaré</u>". Porque dice "<u>Todo lo que pidáis en mi nombre, y cree que ya lo vas a recibir, lo tendrás</u>" todo eso lo dice. Y en combinación con la voluntad de, del médico también.
'Because there's a saying, "Help yourself and I will help you." Because (it) says "Everything you ask in my name, and (you) believe in eventually

(you) will receive, (you) will receive", all that is said. And in combination with the will of the doctor also.'

Interestingly the client employed this saying to indicate that she needed to ask for help (from divine intervention). However, she added the final clause *en combinación con la voluntad del médico también* so that the therapist would not feel excluded.

In (30) a client fears that her co-workers will find out about her condition and criticize her. This excerpt exemplifies how a proverbial saying is employed to say she is hiding her condition:

Dominican: 4, MI2L245

(30)   Mjm. Porque, claro, en el trabajo, <u>Ojos que no ven, corazón que no siente.</u>
       Si no saben nada de eso [my condition] no me criticarán.
       'Uhu. Because, of course, at work, [what] is out of sight, the heart
       doesn't feel' [Out of sight, out of mind]. If they know nothing about it
       [condition], (they) won't criticize me.'

In this excerpt the saying was realized to attenuate a direct statement as in 'I haven't told my co-workers'. In other words, the client revealed to the therapist that she hides her condition at work, a saying which intersects with *el qué dirán* 'what others will say'.

4.8 *Other indirect strategies:* **guardar las apariencias** *(Placencia 1996)*

These utterances reflect ways in which speakers can refuse or express a dispreferred response. For instance, the socio-cultural concepts of *el qué dirán* 'what others will say' and *guardar las apariencias* 'keep up appearances' posited by Placencia (1996) and attested in the corpus of therapeutic discourse by Flores-Ferrán (2009) suggest that these concepts intersect with indirectness.

In the following three excerpts (30, 31, and 32), indirectness related to *guardar las apariencias* 'to guard one's public image' and *el qué dirán* 'what others would say' are found. These narratives point to ways in which the clients of all three dialects saw themselves in a negative manner. Yet they do not explicitly assert that position in their statements. The narratives also suggest that their treatment (medication and therapy) was not seen as a positive feature in their lives.

All three narratives are mediated by *la imagen* and *el qué dirán* 'image' and 'what others would say':

Puerto Rican: 42, MI1L501

(30)   Ahí está la cuestión, no no no, yo nunca tengo miedo, yo no tengo miedo
       de que la gente me vea ee, que yo no esté, cantando ni bailando, miedo
       tengo del efecto del medicamento. Yo lo que tengo miedo <u>como de que</u>

la gente se dé cuenta de que, eee, o me estoy, bueno normalmente la persona que usa un medicamento antidepresivo [] . . .

'There's the point, no no no, I never am afraid, I'm not afraid that people see me, um, that I not be singing or dancing, the fear (I) have is the effect of the medication. I what frightens me is like that people realize that, um, (I) am, well, normally the person that uses anti-depressive medication.'

Mexican: 12, MI1L12

(31)   La semana pasada no pude venir, pero ya decía yo ya voy a ir, me hace falta ir, conversar, (.) porque a nadie más le puedo conversar lo que me está pasando, porque siento que, se ríen, se burlan más que nada, (.) dicen que estoy loca, que, terapia a veces que es para locos, o qué sé yo, (..) y como siempre me han tratado que estoy loca, desde pequeña, me trataban que estaba loca . . .

'Last week I couldn't come [for treatment], but I would say that I was going to come, (I) missed coming, talking (.) because no one else (I) can converse with and tell what is happening [to me], because (I) feel that they laugh, they make fun of me more than anything, (.) (they) say I am crazy, that, therapy is sometimes for crazy people, or what do I know, (..) and since (I) have been treated as insane, since a child, (they) treated me that I was crazy . . . '

Dominican: 29, MI1L498

(32)   Lamentablemente vivimos en un mundo, desde que, e por ejemplo alguien se da cuenta, o alguien sabe que tú estás tomando medicamentos andi antidepresivos o, o para la ansiedad, ee tú puedes dar con personas que dicen que no son antidepresivos o que se deprimen, sino que es para la gente que está loca, aa esas usan medicina.

'Unfortunately we live in a world, since that, um, for example someone notices or someone knows that you are taking anti-depressive medications, or, or for anxiety, um, you can encounter persons that say that (they) are not antidepressants or that they get depressed, but (it) is for people that are crazy, am, (they) use that medicine.'

5 Results: quantitative analysis

In this section the diverse mitigating devices found in the corpus are quantitatively analyzed. The section first addresses the frequency in the use of mitigating devices (MDs), and then it examines the devices used according to dialect and age group.

5.1 Results: quantitative analysis

To expand on the first research question that addressed the type of mitigating devices employed by clients, Table 8.1 is presented. It shows the gross frequencies in which the devices and utterances were employed by the clients' dialect.

Table 8.1 The raw frequencies in distribution of mitigating devices according to dialect

Dialect	# of mitigating devices produced	% of mitigating devices
Puerto Rican	761	11.5
Mexican	1248	18.8
Dominican	4626	69.7
Total	6635	100.0

Table 8.2 The distribution of mitigation devices and indirect speech according to dialects

Mitigation device	Participant dialect			
	Mexican	Dominican	Puerto Rican	Total
Hedges	2.2%	0.5%	4.2%	1.3%
	(27)	(25)	(32)	(84)
Bushes (*como*+)	38.1%	95.6%	18.3%	75.9%
	475	(4422)	(139)	(5036)
ParenthVerbs	7.6%	0.1%	9.7%	2.6%
	(95)	(4)	(74)	(173)
Shields	12.6%	0.1%	18.0%	4.5%
	(157)	(5)	(137)	(299)
Epistemic Dis	1.2%	0.8%	0.1%	0.8%
	(15)	(35)	(1)	(51)
Tag questions	0.2%	2.1%	6.0%	2.2%
	(3)	(98)	(46)	(147)
Diminitivo -*ito*	7.7%	0.0%	7.5%	2.3%
	(96)	(0)	(57)	(153)
Proverbials	0.7%	0.3%	0.3%	0.4%
	(9)	(15)	(2)	(26)
Guardar/El qué	22.0%	0.3%	2.8%	4.7%
	(274)	(15)	(21)	(310)
Other	7.8%	0.2%	33.1%	5.4%
	(97)	(7)	(252)	(356)
Total	100.0%(1248)	100.0%(4626)	100.0%(761)	100.0%(6635)

Note: p = .000

Table 8.1 shows that most of MDs were produced by the Dominican clients. That is of the 6,635 tokens, 69.7 percent were produced by the Dominicans, followed by the Mexicans, 18.8 percent, and the Puerto Ricans, 11.5 percent. These gross frequencies only reflect the contribution of MDs made by the three dialect groups to the entire corpus. In order to capture distinct tendencies by client dialect, a more detailed analysis is presented in Table 8.2.

Table 8.2 shows, as in the forthcoming tables, that the distribution of mitigating devices according to dialect is statistically significant at ($p = .000$). That is, there is a correlation between the realization of a device or indirect speech and the dialect in which the device was employed.

Several observations can be made from these data. First the device with the highest frequency of use was bushes (e.g., *más o menos* 'more or less', *como*+ constructions).

This device was employed to attenuate in 75.9 percent of the 6,635 devices represented in the corpus. The Dominicans issued most of these devices. Second, another preference to express indirectness was realized by employing the cultural notions of *guardar las apariencias* and *el qué dirán*. These indirect utterances were employed by the clients in 310 instances in the entire corpus, or 4.7 percent of the total. However, the Mexican clients exhibit the highest use of these strategies: 22.0 percent.

While the Puerto Rican clients issued fewer mitigating and indirect utterances as a group, the data show that, in proportion to their contribution of tokens, they favor a wider range: the use of parenthetical verbs (e.g., *creo* '[I] think') (9.7 percent), shields (e.g., *uno* 'one') (18.0 percent), and tag questions (e.g., *¿verdad?* 'right?') (6.0 percent).

The data also show that several strategies were not favored. For instance, the diminutive *-ito* was not employed to mitigate by the Dominican clients (0.0 percent). Furthermore, proverbial expressions were also not favored by all three dialect groups; Mexican clients employed these expressions in only 0.7 percent of their utterances and the Dominican and Puerto Rican clients 0.3 percent and 0.3 percent respectively.

In sum the Dominicans exhibit a favoring to employ bushes and the Puerto Rican clients employed a wider variety of MDs. Finally, to attenuate their statements, the Mexican clients employed the diminutive and the cultural notions of *guardar las apariencias* and *el qué dirán* more frequently than the other two groups.

Table 8.3 shows how hypothetical propositions were used to attenuate speech. Hypothetical propositions were employed by clients of all three dialects in varying frequencies. The conditional aspect, as noted in Table 8.3, was employed to attenuate by Puerto Rican clients in 9.2 percent of their indirect utterances and, by Mexicans, in 7.8 percent. The Dominican clients employed this verb form to attenuate with a lower frequency (1.5 percent). The subjunctive mood, however, a form found to be in decline among Spanish speakers (e.g., Silva-Corvalán 2001) was realized in this institutional discursive setting (11.3 percent), and the data reveal

Table 8.3 The use of hypotheticals to mitigate: conditional and subjunctive according to dialect

Hypotheticals	Participant dialect			
	Mexican	Dominican	Puerto Rican	Total
Conditional	7.8%	1.5%	9.2%	3.6%
	(97)	(69)	(70)	(236)
Subjunctive	22.4%	6.2%	24.2%	11.3%
	(279)	(289)	(184)	(752)
Neither	69.9%	92.3%	66.6%	85.1%
	(872)	(4268)	(507)	5647
Total	100.0%	100.0%	100.0%	100.0%
	(1248)	(4626)	(761)	6635

Note: $p = .000$

Table 8.4 The distribution of mitigating devices according to client age groups

	Participant age				
Mitigation device	20s	30s	40s	50s	Total
Hedges	1.3%	2.0%	0.7%	4.0%	1.3%
	(33)	(20)	(21)	(10)	(84)
Bushes (*como+*)	73.4%	70.8%	84.6%	19.5%	75.9%
	(1806)	(705)	(2476)	(49)	(5036)
ParenthVerbs	2.2%	2.0%	2.9%	5.6%	2.6%
	(55)	(20)	(84)	(14)	(173)
Shields	5.7%	4.8%	1.9%	21.9%	4.5%
	(141)	(48)	(55)	(55)	(299)
Epistemic Dis	1.3%	0.4%	0.5%	0.0%	0.8%
	(33)	(4)	(14)	(0)	(51)
Tag questions	1.4%	4.4%	2.2%	1.2%	2.2%
	(35)	(44)	(65)	(3)	(147)
Diminitivo *-ito*	3.3%	2.3%	0.9%	9.2%	2.3%
	(81)	(23)	(26)	(23)	(153)
Proverbials	0.2%	0.8%	0.3%	6.8%	4.7%
	(6)	(0.8)	(88)	(17)	(310)
Guardar/El qué	8.3%	0.1%	3.0%	31.1%	5.4%
	(204)	(1)	(87)	(78)	(356)
Other	2.8%	12.3%	3.0%	31.1%	5.4%
	(68)	(123)	(87)	(78)	(356)
Total	100.0%	100.0%	100.0%	3.8%	100.0%
	(2462)	(996)	(2926)	(251)	(6635)

Note: p = .000

that the Mexican and Puerto Rican clients employed this form more frequently (22.4 percent and 24.2 percent respectively) than the Dominicans (6.2 percent).

Next, data relating to the social stratification of indirectness and mitigation according to age is revealed. This next table addresses the third research question, which focuses on whether the use of mitigating devices and indirect speech are conditioned by age.

Since the *p* value is *.000* indicates that there is a correlation between the use of mitigation and indirectness and age, Table 8.4 is discussed. Recall earlier that bushes were employed in high frequencies. A detailed examination of the use of bushes produced among all age groups shows that clients in their twenties, thirties, and forties employed bushes to attenuate in over 70 percent of their indirect speech. For instance, speakers in their forties employed bushes in 84.6 percent of their devices. Nonetheless the data also reveal that clients in their fifties surpassed their counterparts in the frequencies in which they employed hedges (4.0 percent), parentheticals (5.6 percent), shields (21.9 percent), the diminutive (9.2 percent), proverbials (6.8 percent), and the cultural notions of *guardar las apariencias* and *el qué dirán* (31.1 percent). These data also point to an elevated frequency in the use the cultural notions of *guardar las apariencias* and *el qué dirán* (31.1 percent). In sum while claims can be made that suggest mitigation and indirectness is characteristic of all age groups, with caution it is suggested here that clients in their fifties seem to exhibit a different tendency; namely, they seem to have mitigated their utterances more than other age groups, an observation requiring further investigation.

6 Summary

This study set out to determine the mitigation devices and indirect speech employed by Puerto Rican, Dominican, and Mexican clients in an institutional discursive setting. The study used a mixed method approach to investigate pragmatic variation.

The first research question focused on the kinds of MDs employed by clients. The qualitative analysis yielded multiple findings: first the speakers of the Puerto Rican, Dominican, and Mexican dialects attenuated their utterances in a similar manner by means of similar MDs and indirect utterances. Second, the data also showed co-occurrences of devices and these co-occurrences were found common in all three dialects. Third, proverbial-like sayings and a reliance on *el qué dirán* was attested in the three dialects. The only noticeable difference among the three dialects is that the diminutive form *-ito* was not employed by the Dominican clients to mitigate.

Proverbial sayings were found to be limited in the corpus. They represented a modification to what would be considered a direct speech act and, as such, they remain relevant to the findings.

Another research question attended to intra-lingual pragmatic differences in the realization of mitigation and indirectness. The qualitative analysis showed that MDs and indirect utterances were employed with similar pragmatic functions: to attenuate, reduce or downgrade a message; to reduce distance between speaker and hearer; or to minimize what could have been considered a complaint or a negative outcome related to treatment. The analysis also showed that MDs were often employed in similar syntactic positions.

The third research question attended to the social variables of age and dialect. The quantitative analysis revealed that there were unique preferences among the clients' dialects. For example, the Puerto Ricans exhibited a tendency to employ parenthetical verbs, shields, and tag questions while the Dominicans showed a stronger preference to employ bushes compared to their counterparts. Dominicans also exhibited a tendency to disfavor the use of the diminutive form to mitigate. Furthermore, the Mexican clients favored the use of the cultural notions *el qué dirán* and *guardar las apariencias* to express indirectness more than their counterparts.

Hypotheticals were used by the three groups to express indirectness. However, the Mexican and Puerto Rican clients exhibited a favoring of the conditional aspect and subjunctive mood. The Dominicans' use of these verb forms was not as pervasive.

Only subtle differences were detected with regard to the clients' age and the use of mitigation and indirectness. Clients in their fifties employed more hedges, parentheticals, shields, the diminutive form, proverbials, and cultural notions than any other age group in proportion to their contribution of tokens. This age group did not favor the use of epistemic disclaimers and employed fewer tag questions and bushes than any other age group, a finding that requires further investigation.

In sum the only claim resulting from these analyses is that preferences to favor several MDs over others were detected among the three dialects but pragmatic variation was not found.

7 Discussion

While studies in Hispanic pragmatics have been conducted in either one dialect or contrasting dialects of Spanish and other contrasting languages (e.g., Félix-Brasdefer 2008; Placencia 1994, 1996; Márquez Reiter 2002), most of them have drawn our attention to the use of speech acts (e.g., refusals, requests) to examine mitigation and indirectness in service encounters and in other discursive contexts. Studies have employed various protocols (e.g., discourse completion tasks, role plays, prompted telephone conversations) to determine pragmatic differences and have reported inter- and intra-lingual pragmatic variation.

This study departs from other studies and expands research that investigates mitigation and indirectness in Spanish in an institutional discursive setting. With regard to concluding remarks, several points are made here: what it means to investigate mitigation and indirectness within the dimensions of institutional discourses, and the intersection between sociolinguistics and pragmatic variation. In brief, the study was able to show how speakers of three distinct Spanish dialects expressed indirect resistance to treatment.

Labov and Fanshel (1977: 31) have noted that the distinct character of the therapeutic interview is that B goes to A for help and it is B who will benefit. They also note that a person who requires therapy is socially stigmatized.

> If the patient could express simply and clearly what she felt and could give a perfectly accurate view of her relations with others, the therapist's problem would be simple ... the most difficult problem for the therapist is, therefore, to see through the many forms of masking and mitigating behavior that prevent the patient from seeing her own problem clearly and explaining it to others.
>
> (1977: 31)

Labov and Fanshel (1977: 335) go on to say that participants use a rich variety of mitigating devices "which transform the surface appearance of the speech actions they are performing and the propositions that they are using". That is, without these devices, social interactions would be found direct, abrasive, and abrupt. For example, Blum-Kulka (1987) maintains that the most indirect requests are not judged as necessarily polite. In this current study mitigating devices and indirect propositions in Spanish are perhaps no different from those employed in any other language in this type of institutional discursive context. However, an exception should be made with regard to the socio-cultural notions of Placencia's (1996) *guardar las apariencias* and *el qué dirán*. While these notions may mask resistance or represent ways in which the clients indirectly expressed discomfort with their condition, medication, or treatment, these notions operate in a different manner. They do not reduce the effects of a breach in a social interaction; they reveal the real intention of the speaker who is asserting how she is seen by others, first. Second, they point to ways of indirect resistance, hinting at opposition (Weizman 1985). Therefore, caution must be taken to distinguish these types of strategies from those that attenuate.

With regard to intra-lingual differences, the macro-social variables of age and dialect only pointed to subtle preferences. That is, speakers generally behaved in a similar manner with exception to the use of the diminutive *-ito*. While this form was employed by speakers of the three dialects, the Dominican clients did not employ the form in indirect utterances to mitigate. In his investigation of politeness routines in Costa Rican Spanish, Murillo Medrano (2002) has suggested that this form appears to be required in instances in which a speaker issues a directive. Unrelated to mitigation and institutional discourse, Mendoza (2005) adds that the diminutive has gone through a process of grammaticalization, namely, from referring to size (e.g., *¿Me ofreces un cafecito?* 'Can you offer me a little coffee?') to a crucial role related to politeness and more abstract concepts as intensification and approximation bringing forth concerns related to social relations. Mendoza goes on to argue that *-ito* serves as a pragmatic hedge, which can be used to soften or weaken the illocutionary force of an utterance. Therefore, while its realization was evident as a mitigation device in all but the Dominican clients, further investigation is needed to determine if this dialect employs this morphological ending as a mitigating device.

On closer inspection, the use of the shield *uno* 'one' in this study perhaps exemplifies what Labov (1966) considers a sociolinguistic variable. That is, it represents "two ways of saying the same thing". Flores-Ferrán (2009: 1821) reported that *uno* was employed most often in psychotherapeutic discourse rather than in oral narratives of personal experience. The study also suggested that *uno* served a discursive function: to generalize a proposition to other entities or to engage the hearer in the proposition. Furthermore, the study revealed that this form's use was conditioned by the age of the speaker. That is, the older the speaker, the stronger the tendency to use *uno*. This current study is aligned with those of Flores-Ferrán (2009) in that *uno* was found to have similar discursive functions. In addition, the form was employed as a shield by clients of the three Spanish dialects. Lavandera (1978: 181) posits that researchers should "relax the condition that the referential meaning [of two forms] must be the same for all the alternants and substitute for it a condition of functional comparability". In following that angle then the alternate use of *uno* as opposed to *yo* still remains a linguistic variable both in the Labovian sense and the Lavandera perspective. Therefore, the results obtained from this current study confirm that the use of *uno* in this institutional discursive context was pragmatically motivated but, more importantly, its use did not pragmatically vary among the dialects.

Schneider and Barron (2008: 1) conceptualize variational pragmatics as the intersection between pragmatics and variational linguistics. In fact, Schneider and Barron problematize an assumption that suggests speakers of the same language behave similarly with regard to their pragmatic choices. In looking at the macro- and micro-factors of this study within this particular institutional discursive setting, relatively similar behavior across three dialects of Spanish was indeed found.

Therefore, one may question whether the similarities generated are conditioned by the institutional discourse. Thus, future research must address whether similar findings can be obtained when investigating mitigation and indirectness in other institutional discursive settings.

Notes

1 When speakers employ strategies to mitigate, they may be issuing a polite response. But, in this institutional discursive therapeutic setting, it is noted here that the mitigating strategies are not always employed to be polite. See Blum-Kulka, House, and Kasper (1989) for a further discussion on this matter.
2 SPSS is a statistical package.
3 To check for adherence to treatment, the therapist scanned bottles to determine whether the client had taken medication.
4 In instances in which a subject was not expressed (since Spanish is a null subject language) the explanations distinguish whether the use of the null subject forms part of an indirect proposition. Furthermore, in translating into English, null subjects appear in parentheses (e.g., *no tengo problemas con las pastillas*\. '(I) don't have any problem with the pills').
5 The diverse uses of *como* throughout the chapter are referred to as '*como* constructions'.

Bibliography

Agar, M. (1985). Institutional discourse. *Text*, *1*, 147–166.

Bardovi-Harlig, K., & Hartforf, B. (2005). Institutional discourse and interlanguage pragmatics research. In K. Bardovi-Harlig & Beverly Hartford (Eds.), *Interlanguage pragmatics: Exploring institutional talk* (pp. 7–36). Mahwah, NJ: Lawrence Erlbaum.

Barron, A., & Schneider, K. P. (2009). Variational pragmatics: Studying the impact of social factors on language use and interaction. *Intercultural Pragmatics*, *6*(4), 425–442.

Blum-Kulka, S. (1987). Indirectess and politeness in requests: Same or different. *Journal of Pragmatics*, *11*, 131–146.

Blum-Kulka, S., House, J., & Kasper, G. (1989). Investigating cross-cultural pragmatics: An introductory overview. In S. Blum-Kulka, J. House, & G. Kasper (Eds.), *Cross-cultural pragmatics: Requests and apologies*. Norwood, NJ: Ablex.

Bravo, D. (1999). ¿Imagen 'positiva' vs. imagen 'negativa'? Pragmática cociocultural y componentes de FACE. *Oralia*, *2*, 155–184.

Bravo, D. (2008). The implications of studying politeness in Spanish-speaking context: A discussion. *Pragmatics*, *18*(4), 577–603.

Bravo, D. & Briz, A. (Eds.). (2004). Pragmática sociocultural: Estudios sobre el Discurso de Cortesía en Español. Barcelona: Ariel Lingüística.

Briz, A. (2004). La cortesía verbal codificada y cortesía verbal interpretada en la conversación. In D. Bravo & A. Briz (Eds.), *Pragmática sociocultural: Estudios sobre el Discurso de la Cortesía en Español* (pp. 67–92). Madrid: Ariel.

Brown, P., & Levinson, S. P. (1987). *Politeness. Some universals in language usage*. Cambridge: Cambridge University Press.

Caffi, C. (1999). On mitigation. *Journal of Pragmatics*, *31*(7), 881–909.

Caffi, C. (2007). *Mitigation*. Amsterdam: Elsevier.

Chodorowska-Pilch, M. (2004). The conditional: A grammaticalised marker of politeness in Spanish. In R. Márquez Reiter & M. E. Placencia (Eds.), *Current trends in the pragmatics of Spanish* (pp. 57–75). Amsterdam: Benjamins.

Cordella, M. (2003). En el corazón del debate: El análisis del discurso en la representación de las voces médicas. *Oralia, 6*, 146–168.

Cordella, M. (2007). 'No, no I haven't been taking it doctor': Compliance, face threatening acts and politeness in medical consultation. In M. Placencia & C. García (Eds.), *Linguistic politeness in the Spanish-speaking world* (pp. 191–212). Mahwah, NJ: Lawrence Erlbaum.

Delbene, R. (2004). The function of mitigation in the context of a socially stigmatized disease: A case study in a public hospital in Montevideo, Uruguay. *Spanish in Context, 1*, 241–267.

Félix-Brasdefer, J. C. (2008). Sociopragmatic variation: Dispreferred responses in Mexican and Dominican Spanish. *Journal of Politeness Research, 4*, 81–110.

Félix-Brasdefer, J. C. (2009). Pragmatic variation across Spanish(es): Requesting in Mexican, Costa Rican, and Dominican Spanish. *Intercultural Pragmatics, 6*(4), 473–515.

Firth, R. (1926). Proverbs in native life with special reference to those of the Maori. *Folklore, 37*, 134–153.

Flores-Ferrán, N. (2009). Are you referring to me? The variable use of UNO and YO in oral discourse. *Journal of Pragmatics, 41*(9), 1810–1824.

Flores-Ferrán, N. (2010a). An examination of mitigation strategies used in Spanish psychotherapeutic discourse. *Journal of Pragmatics, 42*, 1964–1980.

Flores-Ferrán, N. (2012). Pragmatic variation in therapeutic discourse: An examination of mitigating devices employed by Dominican female clients and a Cuban American therapist. In J. C. Félix-Brasdefer & D. Koike (Eds.), *Pragmatic variation in first and second language contexts: Methodological issues: Impact studies in language and society* (pp. 81–112). Philadelphia: Benjamins.

Fraser, B. (1980). Conversational mitigation. *Journal of Pragmatics, 4*, 341–350.

Haverkate, H. (1990). Politeness and mitigation in Spanish: A morphosyntactic analysis. University in Diversity. Papers presented to Simon C. Dik on his 50th birthday (pp. 107–131). Netherlands: Foris Publications.

Haverkate, H. (1994). *La Cortesía Verbal: Estudio Pragmalingüístico.* Madrid: Editorial Credos.

Hernández-Flores, N. (1999). Politeness ideology in Spanish colloquial conversation: The case of advice. *Pragmatics, 9*(1), 1018–2101.

Interian, A., Martínez, I., Guarnaccia, P. J., Vega, W. A., & Escobar, J. (2007). A qualitative analysis of the perception of stigma among latinos receiving antidepressants. *Psychiatric Services, 58*, 1591–1594.

Koike, D. (1994). Negation in Spanish and English suggestions and requests: Mitigating effects. *Journal of Pragmatics, 21*(5), 513–526.

Labov, W. (1966). *The social stratification of English in New York City.* Washington, DC: Center for Applied Linguistics.

Labov, W., & Fanshel, D. (1977). *Therapeutic discourse: Psychotherapy as conversation.* New York: Academic Press.

Lavandera, B. (1978). Where does the sociolinguistic variable stop? *Language in Society, 7*(2), 171–182.

Márquez Reiter, R. (2002). A contrastive study of conventional indirectness in Spanish: Evidence from Peninsula and Uruguayan Spanish. *Pragmatics, 12*(2), 135–151.

Márquez Reiter, R., & Placencia, M. (2005). *Spanish pragmatics*. New York: Palgrave Macmillan.

Mendoza, M. (2005). Polite diminutives in Spanish: A matter of size? In R. Lakoff & I. Sachiko (Eds.), *Broadening the horizon of linguistic politeness* (pp. 163–173). Amsterdam, Netherlands: John Benjamins.

Miller, W. R., & Rollnick, S. (2002). *Motivational interviewing: Preparing people for change*. New York: Guilford Press.

Murillo Medrano, J. (2002). La cortesía verbal en el español de Costa Rica. *Kañina*, *26*(2), 109–118.

Orwenjo, D. O. (2009). Political grandstanding and the use of proverbs in African political discourse. *Discourse & Society*, *20*(1), 123–146.

Placencia, M. E. (1994). Pragmatics across Spanish varieties. *Donaire*, *2*, 65–76.

Placencia, M. E. (1996). Politeness in Ecuadorian Spanish. *Multilingua*, *15*(1), 13–34.

Schegloff, E. (1993). Reflections on quantification in the study of conversation. *Research on Language in Social Interaction*, *25*(1), 99–128.

Schneider, S. (2004). Pragmatic functions of Spanish parenthetical verbs. In P. Garcés Conejos, R. Gómez Morón, L. Fernández Amaya, & M. Padilla Cruz, *Current trends in intercultural, cognitive and social pragmatics* (pp. 37–52). Sevilla: Universidad de Sevilla – Research Group of Intercultural Pragmatic Studies.

Schneider, K. P., & Barron, A. (2008). Where pragmatics and dialectology meet: Introducing variational pragmatics. In K. P. Schneider & A. Barron (Eds.), *Variational pragmatics* (pp. 1–32). Amsterdam: John Benjamins.

Seitel, P. (1972). *Proverbs and the structure of metaphor among the Haya of Tanzania* (Unpublished doctoral dissertation). University of Pennsylvania.

Silva-Corvalán, C. (2001). *Sociolingüística y Pragmática del Español*. Washington: Georgetown U. Press.

Von Wormer, K. (2007). Principles of motivational interviewing geared towards stages of change: A pedagogical challenge. *The Journal of Teaching Social Work*, *27*(1–2), 21–35.

Watts, R. (2003). *Politeness*. Cambridge UK: Cambridge University Press.

Weizman, E. (1985). Towards and analysis of Opaque utterances. *Theoretical Linguistics*, *12*(2–3), 153–163.

9 Respect and politeness in marketing and advertising documents in Mayagüez, Puerto Rico

Diane R. Uber

1 Introduction

Utilizing the theory of verbal politeness (Brown & Levinson 1987; García 1992), and the concepts of power and solidarity (Brown & Gilman 1960), this chapter will present results of a study of the usage of the singular forms of address, *tú* and *usted*, in marketing and advertising documents in Mayagüez, Puerto Rico. Spanish-language address forms reflect the concepts of respect and politeness in the workplace. With age and higher rank comes respect, which would dictate usage of the more formal address (*usted* along with its corresponding verb forms). People with whom a worker is not acquainted are also addressed with *usted*, such as walk-in clients. Norms of politeness dictate that one should be accommodating toward the addressee: "Be nice, so that the customer does not lose face." This politeness can be manifested in the form of the respectful, deferential *usted*. Alternatively, politeness also can dictate informal usage (*tú*, along with its corresponding verb forms) for the following:

1 toward those sharing equal social status, in all types of situations;
2 to show confidence and solidarity toward the consumer in business encounters, advertising, and marketing.

The use of examples from marketing and advertising documents and signs will illustrate these different usages geared toward different audiences (following Kaul 2010; Uber 2012). For example, advertisements from newspapers employ different address forms for different target markets. Ads directed toward business executives, wealthier clients, and mature or elderly people tend to use *usted*, to show respect. *Usted* is also used in signs on store doors and signs issuing direct orders (prohibiting certain activities or behavior). On the other hand, the following situations tend to show *tú* usage: public service announcements, to establish confidence and to show solidarity and togetherness; ads directed toward women, young people, students or families, showing informality; and ads directed toward local consumers or in-group members, showing local group unity ("you are one of us", "you belong here").

2 Forms of address in Spanish

In Spanish, as well as English, the title plus family name (*Señor García*) is considered a more formal type of address than the first name (*Pablo*), which is more informal. Generally, the formal address is used with strangers, with people who are older than the speaker, and with someone worthy of respect. However, a conflict arises if the stranger is a child, or if the older person lives next door, or if the professor is a close family friend. In such situations, speakers of both English and Spanish must decide which form of address to use (Uber 2011: 244).

In addition to first and last names, second person pronouns are also forms of address. In English there exists only one form, *you*, in both singular and plural (plus the dialectal variants *y'all*, *you guys*, and *yinz* in the plural). However, in Spanish one must choose between *tú*, *vos* (in some parts of Latin America), and *usted* for the singular. For more information on the use of *vos* (the *voseo*), consult Uber (2008). For the plural, in parts of Spain, a speaker must choose between *vosotros/vosotras* and *ustedes*, while only *ustedes* is used for the plural in Latin America (Uber 2011: 244–245).

3 Previous studies

Most studies of forms of address in European languages begin with Brown and Gilman (1960), who state that address is governed by the concepts of power and solidarity. For a discussion of the history of Spanish forms of address, a description, and norms of usage of the forms employed in present-day Spanish, see Uber (2011: 248–250; 2015: 620–626). Other recent works include Bishop and Michnowicz (2010), Millán (2011), Weyers (2014), and Rosales Lagos and Moyna (2016).

Regarding politeness in business address, Candia (2001) discusses the business letter and email, stating that an elegant style is used, along with the *usted* form of address, and the conditional tense to soften requests. Research studies on forms of address in the workplace in several Spanish-speaking cities are reviewed in Uber (2011: 256–259). Findings are summarized in Table 9.1.

4 The community

Mayagüez is a port city located on the central western coast of the island of Puerto Rico. According to Wikipedia, over the last century, it has suffered serious destruction from almost every type of natural disaster, including earthquakes, fires, hurricanes, lightning strikes, and floods (Mayagüez, Puerto Rico. September 25, 2016. Retrieved October 10, 2016 from Wikipedia). Aguiló Ramos describes the great fire of 1841, which destroyed some 660 houses (1986: 28); the earthquakes and tsunami of 1918, which destroyed 735 houses (1986: 65–57); and the 1919 fire, during the showing of a film in the Yagüez Theatre, in which approximately 300 people perished (1986: 57). Reconstruction occurred

Table 9.1 Variables that favor informal or formal address in the workplace

	Informal *(tú; vos* in Buenos Aires; verbal *voseo* in Santiago, Chile)	Formal *(usted)*
Age of interlocutor	Similar or younger	Older
Gender of interlocutor	Similar, especially among women	Opposite
Profession of interlocutor	Similar or lower in status	Higher in status
Relative ranks of interlocutors in the workplace (supervisor/ employee, professor/student)	Similar or lower	Higher
Working with/being a colleague of interlocutor	Yes	No
Acquainted with interlocutor for a few weeks/months/years	Yes	No
Friend of interlocutor	Yes	No
Interlocutor is a client	No	Yes
Type of business	Factory, office, workshop	Customer service, financial company
Topic of discussion	Daily tasks, social interaction	Contracts, agreements, giving quotes or prices
Speaking by telephone	No (before interlocutor is identified)	Yes
Personal style (*the wild card*)	Depends on individual	Depends on individual

during the 1920s (1986: 58). More recently, given Puerto Rico's economic crisis of 2015–2016, Mayagüez has undergone a reduction in population. This has occurred on the heels of an almost 10 percent loss of population during the decade of 2000–2010 due to the closure of textile factories and tuna canneries. Another consequence has been the closure of many stores and restaurants, leaving a large number of abandoned buildings and homes in the downtown area, known as Mayagüez Pueblo (Mayagüez, Puerto Rico. September 25, 2016. Retrieved October 10, 2016 from Wikipedia).

The remaining population of Mayagüez is somewhat older than that of the San Juan metropolitan area, so that many buildings are now occupied by health care facilities to serve these older residents. The residents of the city are very friendly individuals, many of whom struck up conversations with me on trolleys or as I just walked down the street. They are also very respectful, always addressing me with *usted*, but some combined it with seemingly intimate vocatives, such as *mi amor, mi reina, mi corazón* (literally, 'my love', 'my queen', 'my heart'); the more formal *doña* ('lady'); or even the younger-sounding *Miss*. Some language students from western Puerto Rico informed me that these vocatives are quite common in this part of the island. A previous study carried out in the San Juan metropolitan area (the northeastern part of the island) did find these vocatives used by female speakers there, in combination with either *tú* or *usted*, but *usted* was found to accompany the vocatives more frequently than *tú* (Uber 2000).

5 Examples of documents

Representative examples of different types of document will be given below, including advertisements from newspapers, magazines, signs, and promotional literature. There is an overall predominance of informal, familiar address. For example, a count of address usage in a sample of magazine and newspaper advertisements and flyers shows that 30 of the ads address the reader with *tú* (T), while 12 use *usted* (U).

Given that local residents and families would buy cable television services, their ads use T to show local group unity:

¡Disfruta de estos canales con tu triple pack! choicecable.com
Llévate el KIT DIRECTV PREPAGO
'Enjoy these channels with your triple pack! Choicecable.com'
'Take the DIRECTV prepaid'

By the same token, a restaurant offering children's birthday parties also shows T:

VEN Y CELEBRA TU CUMPLEAÑOS EN NUESTRO SALON [SIC] PRIVADO EN HAPPY LAND YOGUFRUTI MAYAGÜEZ
'Come and celebrate your birthday in our private banquet room in Happy Land Yogufruti Mayagüez'

Cell phone ads follow a similar pattern:

Libérate con T-Mobile
'Free yourself with T-Mobile'

Similarly, in a print advertisement, a political candidate would wish to address residents of the island with T:

Endosa el cambio antes del 15 de Febrero
'Endorse change before February 15'

Puerto Rico Ponte de pie
'Puerto Rico Stand up'

These results correlate with those discussed in Uber (2014), where T was found in advertisements directed toward local consumers, and in public service announcements, in Madrid, to try to establish solidarity and togetherness with local residents (p. 4). Similarly, advertisements directed toward local consumers, and public service documents, tend to use the familiar *vos* in Buenos Aires, as found in ads for caterers, an Argentine folk music restaurant, and ads on subway tickets (Uber 2012: 1788–1791).

In contrast, advertisements directed toward the elderly frequently use the respectful *usted* (U). In a print public-service announcement, older people in Puerto Rico are advised to prepare for Medicare:

¡Prepárese para Medicare!
'Prepare yourself for Medicare!'

Comuníquese con el agente de ventas certificado en Humana en su área para una consulta gratuita
'Communicate with the Humana certified sales agent in your area for a free consultation'

A formal newspaper ad for housing for the elderly also uses U:

. . . desea informarle que se están recibiendo solicitantes de vivienda . . .
' . . . would like to inform you that applications for housing are being accepted . . . '

Again, we see a parallel with results found in Madrid, where ads directed to business executives or to elderly people generally show respect and tend to use U (Uber 2014: 4). However, one ad for hearing aids in Mayagüez uses T, perhaps to soften the suggestion:

Evaluar tu audición, no es una opción . . . es una necesidad
'Testing your hearing is not a choice . . . it is a necessity'

Advertisements for prescription drugs use U, because they provide all of the formal instructions and warnings about the medication, and because they are not directed toward customers from a particular area:

No suspenda el uso de ELIQUIS. . . . El médico le dirá cuándo debe. . . . Si tiene que suspenderlo, el médico le puede recetar otro medicamento para ayudarle a evitar. . . . Usted puede correr un riesgo mayor de sangrado si toma ELIQUIS y usa otros medicamentos que aumentan su riesgo de sangrado. . . . **Informe al médico sobre** . . . Mientras tome ELIQUIS, usted puede ser más propenso a que se le formen . . . Procure atención médica si tiene . . .
'Do not stop using ELIQUIS. . . . Your physician will tell you when you should. . . . If you must stop, your doctor can prescribe another medication to help you to avoid. . . . You may be at greater risk if you take ELIQUIS and use other medications which increase your risk of bleeding. . . . **Inform your physician about** . . . While taking ELIQUIS, you may be more likely to form . . . Seek medical attention if you experience . . . '

Signs on store doors, such as this one seen on the door of Zapatería HQ, tend to employ U:

Empuje
Empuje
'Push
Push'

Signs in stores issuing direct orders (particularly prohibiting certain activities or behavior) also use U.
Service Department of Autoland (Mazda and Hyundai dealer), directed toward employees:

Aviso: Mantenga el área limpia y organizada.
'Notice: Keep this area clean and organized.'

Zapatería HQ, directed toward employees:

No entre con zapatos a la vitrina.
'Do not enter the display window wearing shoes.'

Zapatería HQ, directed toward clients:

Atención clientes: Sin recibos no se cambia, exija su recibo.
'Attention, customers: Without a receipt, no exchanges; ask for your receipt.'

Grand's, a store selling clothing and domestics, uses T on an ad for customers, but U on a sign prohibiting non-employees from entering a back room:

Decora tu hogar. T
'Decorate your home.'
No entre. Solo personal autorizado. U
'Do not enter. Authorized personnel only.'

These results also correlate with those of the Madrid study (Uber 2014), in which U tended to be used in more formal directives (26).
Most signs in the Mayagüez Mall show T usage:

LensCrafters: Aprovecha nuestra tarjeta. Aprovecha. Financiamiento disponible.
'Take advantage of our charge card. Take advantage. Financing available.'

Sears' appliances: Te servimos con rendimiento.
'We serve you with efficiency.'

General promotion for the mall: *Mayagüez Mall. Date el gusto!*
'Mayagüez Mall. Give yourself the pleasure!'

Dr. iPhone: Compra aquí tu teléfono desbloqueado.
'Buy your unblocked phone here.'

DirecTV: Si tu reintegro aún no llega . . . Además recibe gratis . . . Llévate los mejores equipos desde $4.14 al mes.
'If your repayment has not yet arrived . . . In addition, receive at no charge . . . Take home the best equipment starting at $4.14 a month.'

searspr.com: encuéntralo aquí
'Find it here'

However, a sign in Mayagüez Mall apologizing for construction uses the respectful U, saying that the mall's customers deserve new facilities:

Estamos construyendo nuevas facilidades, porque usted se lo merece. Nuestras disculpas por las inconvenientes.
'We are constructing new facilities, because you deserve it. Our apologies for the inconvenience.'

Advertising flyers obtained in the mall also use T, except for the formal credit card application, which uses U to deal with financial information:

An ad for the JCPenney credit card uses T: La tarjeta que te trata de maravilla. ¡Combínalo con otro cupón y ahorra aún más en la tienda!
'The card that treats you great. Combine it with another coupon and save even more in the store!'

However, on the form to fill out personal financial information, in order to be approved for credit, U is used:

Complete sólo para Solicitudes por Correo. Consulte la próxima página.
'Complete only for Applications by Mail. Consult the next page.'

Similarly, product labels and instructions were found to vary in Madrid. For example, a colorful sticker on the front of a product employs T. Instructions on the back of a label, and on the fold-up technical information use infinitives because they are addressed to no one in particular. A specific recommendation to the consumer uses U because it is more direct (Uber 2014: 4).

Two advertising brochures for sales of Hyundai autos in Mayagüez use T, trying to establish solidarity:

Lávalo. Tásalo. Manéjalo. ¡Sal con tu Hyundai nuevo!
LLÉVATELO NUEVO AL COSTO! ¡VISITANOS [sic] HOY, en menos de lo que imaginas sales con TU NUEVO HYUNDAI!

'Wash it. Rate it. Drive it. Leave with your new Hyundai! TAKE IT WITH YOU NEW, AT COST! VISIT US TODAY, in less than you imagine you leave with YOUR NEW HYUNDAI!'

In contrast, a brochure for auto insurance uses U consistently, perhaps because insurance is considered a more serious issue:

Protéjase del alto costo de las fallas mecánicas. No deje que le pase algo a su familia sin esta valiosa protección. Elija el plan Advantage que más le conviene. Lo último que quiere hacer en las vacaciones familiares es preocuparse del alto costo de una reparación inesperada. Puede financiar el programa Advantage junto con la compra de su automóvil.

'Protect yourself from the high cost of mechanical failure. Don't let something happen to your family without this valuable protection. Choose the Advantage plan most convenient for you. The last thing you want for your family vacation is to worry about the high cost of an unexpected repair. You can finance the Advantage program along with the purchase of your automobile.'

At the University of Puerto Rico – Mayagüez, a sign on the reception desk in the office of the College of Business Administration (*Administración de Empresas – ADEM*) uses a *tú* command:

Si eres estudiante de ADEM, regístrate en la computadora.
'If you are a student of UPRM Business (ADEM), sign in on the computer.'

This shows in-group solidarity directed toward the students of that College. These students are instructed to check in on the computer on the counter.

In contrast, visitors and students of other departments of the university are instructed to check in at a different location, and the sign uses the infinitive, instead of either a *tú* or *usted* command:

Visitantes y estudiantes de otros Departamentos, registrarse aquí ✐
'Visitors and students of other Departments, sign in here ✐'

Thus, we see that *tú* is used for students of the College of Business Administration served by that office, but the neutral infinitive is used for visitors and those who study in other departments of the university.

A sign on campus to recruit tutors in writing uses *usted* consistently throughout.

Se cree que sabe escribir?
'Do you think you know how to write?'
¿Es estudiante regular de nivel subgraduado?
'Are you a regular student at the undergraduate level?'
¿No tiene jornal y necesita 'unos chavitos extra'?
'Do you not have income and need some extra money?'
¿Tiene libre de 3:00 a 5:30 p.m. LW o MJ?
'Do you have MW or TTh from 3:00 to 5:30 free?'

¿EztAah ezkriitUra LE DUELE EN LO MÁS PROFUNDO DEL ALMA?
'Does this type of writing [spelled with many errors] HURT YOU IN THE DEPTHS OF YOUR SOUL?'
Desea hacer algo diferente y ayudar a motivar a niños y jóvenes a aprender?
'Do you want to do something different and motivate children and young people to learn?'
¡Pues siga leyendo!
'Well, continue reading.'
Para más información o una entrevista, escriba a. . . .
'For more information or an interview, write to. . . . '

The topic of formal writing and grammatical and stylistic correctness may contribute to the use of U in this notice.

6 Examples of switching (T~U)

Quite a lot of switching between T and U is also found. As seen above, in the case of JCPenney at the mall, the store's brochure uses *tú*, but a form to fill out for store credit (which is a more serious issue) uses *usted*.

A party planner's sample invitations use T for *quinceañera* parties (*Te invito a celebrar* . . . 'I invite you to celebrate . . . '; *Quiero compartir contigo* . . . 'I would like to share with you . . . ').

On the other hand, U (*invitarle* 'invite you') appears on the party planner's sample for wedding invitations, presumably because most participants in a wedding would be older than 15.
    However, not all switches are as easily explained as those presented above. For example, in a promotional brochure for the city of Mayagüez (*Guía Informativa Mayagüez Ciudad Universitaria*), we find T used in the following entries:

p. 2: MasterCard ad: Comienza a manejar tu crédito con . . . nuestra tarjeta MasterCard. Visita: www. . . .
'Start managing your credit with . . . our MasterCard. Visit: www. . . . '

p. 8: places of interest around the town: Diversos . . . te esperan para que deleites tus sentidos.
'Various . . . await you so that you can delight your senses.'

p. 17: yogurt ad: Yogurízimo: *Te esperamos*.
'We await you.''

p. 22: Mayagüez Medical Center: *Manos que te cuidan*.
'Hands that care for you.'

p. 28: brewery ad (Cervecera de Puerto Rico): Únete a nosotros en Facebook. 'Join us on Facebook.'

On the other hand, U is found in the following entries:

p. 4: the welcoming statement from the Mayor: . . . un maravilloso retiro que seducirá sus sentidos y traerá un nuevo significado a sus vacaciones. . . . le damos la más cordial bienvenida a la Ciudad de Mayagüez. . . .
' . . . a marvelous retreat that will seduce your senses and bring a new meaning to your vacation. . . . we give you the most cordial welcome to the City of Mayagüez. . . . '

p. 9: a natural food store, Natucentro: Su centro de productos naturales. Pase por cualquiera de nuestras dos tiendas o llámenos.
'Your center for natural products. Come in to either of our two stores, or call us.'

p. 14: how to obtain a more detailed map: Para un Mapa más grande y detallado sobre los puntos de interés que ofrece Mayagüez, escanee aquí con su celular.
'For a larger, more detailed map of points of interest that Mayagüez offers, scan here with your cell phone.'

p. 28: Mayagüez Ford ad directed toward students at the local campus of the University of Puerto Rico: Uno de nuestros ejecutivos le atenderá para presentarle todos nuestros servicios y le proveerá con una Oferta Especial para Estudiantes Universitarios.
'One of our executives will assist you to show you all of our services and will provide you with a Special Offer for University Students.'

In this brochure, one might expect T usage for yogurt, tourism, and the brewery, but not necessarily for a credit card or a medical center. If MasterCard uses T, why does a Ford dealership use U, given that both are directed toward university students?

Zales, a fine jewelry store at the mall, uses mostly U on their signs:

Ahorre hasta el 25% en seleccionadas joyas para novias. Declare Su Amor.
'Save up to 25% on selected jewels for brides. Declare Your Love.'

However, the next sign begins with two usages of U and concludes with a usage of T:

Reciba $100 en Zales premier rewards ¡por cada $300 que compre! ¡Redímelos ahora. [redimir = to redeem]
'Receive $100 in Zales premier rewards for every $300 that you purchase! Redeem them now!'

The optical shop, LensCrafters, as mentioned earlier, has two signs that use T:

Aprovecha nuestra tarjeta.
'Enjoy our charge card.'
Aprovecha. Financiamiento disponible.
'Enjoy. Financing available.'

However, another sign in the same LensCrafters uses U:

Programe su cita para un examen de la vista hoy.
'Schedule your appointment for an eye exam today.'

When I pointed out these examples of switching to the woman who accompanied me to the mall, she was at first surprised. Then, she expressed a negative attitudinal reaction by saying, "No somos un país muy culto. Debemos saber usar el *usted*." ['We are not a very cultured country. We should know how to use *usted*.']

At the large town market, Plaza del Mercado, one fast-food stand, Antojitos, used T on their signs:

Llama, ordena y recoge. Aprovecha nuestro menu [sic].
'Call, order and pick it up. Enjoy our menu.'

On the other hand, a paper flyer vacillated, beginning with U:

Llame, ordene y recoja.
'Call, order and pick it up.'

Then two lines below, it switched to T:

¡Antójate!
'Go ahead!'

A regional bilingual school switches throughout its flyer, which was posted on the bulletin board at the city's post office. The text begins with T, but then uses U three times on the page of text:

Acepta el reto y sé parte de nuestro selecto grupo de estudiantes. (T twice)
'Accept the challenge and be part of our select group of students.'
Busque ... (U)
'Look for ... '
Envíe un correo electrónio solicitando los documentos de admission [sic] a ... (U)
'Send an email requesting admissions documents to ... '
Puede llamar para más información al ... (U)
'You can call for more information to ... '

The flyer's cover pages show U used three times in the instructions for Facebook:

> Busque Bilingue Ramirez Hostos (sin diéresis ni acento)
> 'Look for Bulingue Ramirez Hostos (without dieresis or accent mark)'
> Solicite un "Friend Request"
> 'Ask for a "Friend Request"'
> Una vez aceptado solicite por inbox los documentos
> 'Once accepted, ask for the documents through the inbox.'

However, the email instructions use T:

> Escribe un email solicitando los documentos de admission [sic] a . . .
> 'Write an email asking for the admissions documents to . . . '

The final instructions in the flyer switch back to U:

> Para información adicional conuníquese a los siguientes números telefónicos: . . .
> 'For additional information call the following telephone numbers: . . . '

Interestingly, although we see a lot of switching between T and U, which would not be viewed favorably by prescriptive grammarians, below the school's crest on the cover, we see the slogan:

> UNA ESCUELA DE EXCELENCIA ACADÉMICA
> 'A SCHOOL OF ACADEMIC EXCELLENCE'

A newspaper advertisement for Sherwin-Williams paints uses T in the ad:

> Enamórate del color. Encuentra una tienda cerca de ti.
> 'Fall in love with the color. Find a store near you.'

However, just below this ad, U is used in a coupon for its products:

> ¡Traiga este cupón y ahorre! Ahorre 30% en pinturas, barnices y selladores de techo Koolseal. Ahorre 15% en accesorios para pintar.
> 'Bring in this coupon and save! Save 30% on paints, varnishes and Koolseal roof sealer. Save 15% on painting accessories.'

A brochure for prevention of teen pregnancy from Catholic Social Services uses T in its text:

> Ser feliz y realizarte en la vida es tu destino. Fuiste creado (a) para el triunfo, y la plenitud. Pero el triunfo no llega solo, debes buscarlo. No está lejos, está en tu interior y en el bien que puedas hacer a los demás.

'To be happy and fulfill yourself is your destiny. You were created for triumph and fulfillment. But triumph does not come on its own; you must search for it. It is not far away, it is within yourself and in the good that you may be able to do for others.'

On the other hand, the instruction for how to obtain more information uses U:

PARA MAS INFORMACION SOBRE EL PROGRAMA COMUNIQUESE AL: . . .
'FOR MORE INFORMATION ABOUT THE PROGRAM, CONTACT: . . . '

Some people have asked me whether it might the case that some people simply do not know the forms, and that this could explain the switching between T and U. However, I would argue that speakers do, in fact, know the forms of their language. Others have wondered if, perhaps, the U forms are disappearing from Puerto Rican Spanish, which is possible and should be investigated. I would suggest that formal directives, such as commands, may have become lexicalized in the U form. This would explain the usage of U in more direct types of instructions. A similar result was discussed in Uber (2012) for Buenos Aires, where the subway tickets all have a formal directive:

Conserve esta tarjeta en buen estado
'Keep this card in good condition'

But all of the advertisements on the tickets appear in the familiar *vos* form, showing group identity (1789–1791). Also, a sign that appears in all stores and restaurants in Buenos Aires uses U first:

Exija su factura
'Obtain your receipt'

This is a formal directive, instructing the customer to be certain to obtain a receipt. However, the remainder of the sign uses the familiar *vos* form:

✓ Pagás
✓ Pedís
✓ Ganás
'You pay. You ask for [your receipt]. You win.'

These verbs are not imperatives, but, rather, indicative forms, which explain to the consumer why there is a benefit from obtaining a receipt. Thus, the familiar forms are used to show solidarity with the local consumer.

7 Conclusions

We have seen that the concepts of respect and politeness are reflected in the forms used to address different consumers. Politeness dictates usage of *usted* in advertisements directed toward older and wealthier clients, toward business executives, and in ads for financial assistance, in order to show respect. *Usted* is also used toward unknown consumers and in more formal directives, such as signs on store doors and signs issuing direct orders (prohibiting certain activities or behavior). These formal directives, such as commands, may have become lexicalized in the *usted* form. This would explain the usage of *usted* in more direct types of instructions.

Politeness also dictates usage of *tú* in advertisements directed toward women, young people, students, and families in order to show confidence, togetherness, and solidarity. *Tú* is also used in ads and public service announcements directed toward local consumers or in-group members in order to show local group unity ("You are one of us", "You belong here").

Ideological conflicts in Puerto Rico may help to explain the frequent switching between *tú* and *usted*. Certainly, it is possible that different people wrote different parts of some of the documents, such as the advertisement for Sherwin-Williams, on the one hand, and the coupon for its products right below the ad, on the other hand. However, most of the examples discussed here show switching of address forms within the same document (advertisement or brochure). Many Puerto Rican speakers are proficient at switching between languages (Spanish and English) and cultures (mainland and island). Address may present a similar conflict for some users, in terms of the politeness of respect versus the politeness of solidarity.

One line of future inquiry would be to elicit linguistic attitudes toward switching. Some Puerto Ricans have expressed surprise, or even disbelief, when made aware of switching between *tú* and *usted* in the same document. Also, the negative attitudinal reaction expressed by the woman who accompanied me to the mall shows a high degree of linguistic insecurity:

> "No somos un país muy culto. Debemos saber usar el *usted*." ['We are not a very cultured country. We should know how to use *usted*.']

A similar negative attitude was expressed in Buenos Aires by some speakers toward their *porteño* Spanish. After friends congratulated me on my ability to use *vos*, they then said that they preferred *tú* over *vos* because they thought it was prettier (Uber 2012: 1791): *Yo prefiero el 'tú'. Es más bonito.* ['I prefer *tú*. It's prettier.']

Another example of a negative attitude toward language usage in Mayagüez is the sign on campus to recruit tutors in writing, which suggests that the person who drafted the sign has seen examples of writing in this fashion:

> **¿EztAah ezkriitUra** LE DUELE EN LO MÁS PROFUNDO DEL ALMA?
> 'Does this type of writing hurt you in the depths of your soul?'

Future studies are suggested along these lines as well, to examine linguistic ideologies and attitudes in a more systematic way.

Acknowledgements

I would like to acknowledge the Faculty Research and Study Leaves Program of The College of Wooster for having granted me a one-year research leave to carry out this research project. In addition, I acknowledge a generous grant from the Henry Luce III Fund for Distinguished Scholarship to pay a large portion of the travel expenses. Finally, my most profound thanks goes to Professor Melvin González-Rivera (Estudios Hispánicos, Universidad de Puerto Rico – Mayagüez), undergraduate student Yarelmi Iglesias (Estudios Hispánicos), and graduate student Becky Andújar (Administración de Empresas).

Bibliography

Aguiló Ramos, S. (1986). *Mayagüez: Notas para su historia* (2nd ed.). San Juan, PR: Oficina Estatal de Preservación Histórica.

Bishop, K., & Michnowicz, J. (2010). Forms of address in Chilean Spanish. *Hispania, 93*, 413–429.

Brown, P., & Levinson, S. C. (1987). *Politeness: Some universals in language usage* (Studies in Interactional Sociolinguistics 4). Cambridge: Cambridge University Press.

Brown, R., & Gilman, A. (1960). The pronouns of power and solidarity. In T. A. Sebeok (Ed.), *Style in language* (pp. 253–276). Cambridge, MA: MIT Press.

Candia, R. (2001). The business letter in Spanish: A cultural perspective. *Global Business Languages, 6*(9). Retrieve from http://docs.lib.purdue.edu/gbl/vol6/iss1/9

García, C. (1992). Refusing an invitation: A case study of Peruvian style. *Hispanic Linguistics, 5*, 207–243.

Kaul de Marlangeon, S. (2010). Voseo, ustedeo y cortesía verbal en folletos de propaganda argentinos. In M. Hummel, B. Kluge, & M. E. Vázquez Laslop (Eds.), *Formas y fórmulas de tratamiento en el mundo hispánico* (pp. 993–1011). México, DF: El Colegio de México.

Millán, M. (2011). Pronouns of address in informal contexts: A comparison of two dialects of Colombian Spanish (Unpublished doctoral dissertation). University of Illinois, Urbana, IL.

Rosales Lagos, M., & Moyna, M. I. (2016). Second-person address forms in comtemporary Uruguayan children's literature. *Hispania, 99*, 320–337.

Uber, D. R. (2000). 'Addressing' business in Puerto Rico: Tú vs. usted. In A. Roca (Ed.), *Research on Spanish in the United States: Linguistic issues and challenges* (pp. 310–318). Somerville, MA: Cascadilla Press.

Uber, D. R. (2008). Creo que entiendo el uso de *tú, usted, ustedes,* y *vosotros.* Pero, ¿qué hago con *vos*? In J. Ewald & A. Edstrom (Eds.), *El español a través de la lingüística: Preguntas y respuestas* (pp. 50–60). Somerville, MA: Cascadilla Press.

Uber, D. R. (2011). Forms of address: The effect of the context. In M. Díaz-Campos (Ed.), *The handbook of hispanic sociolinguistics* (pp. 244–262). Chichester, UK: Blackwell Publishing Ltd.

Uber, D. R. (2012). La unidad grupal, el respeto y la cortesía: Fórmulas de tratamiento en los negocios en el español porteño. In A. M. Cestero Mancera, I. Molina Martos, & F. Paredes García (Eds.), *La lengua, lugar de encuentro: Actas del XVI Congreso Internacional de la ALFAL* (pp. 1783–1792). Alcalá de Henares: Servicio de Publicaciones de la Universidad de Alcalá.

Uber, D. R. (2014). Spanish forms of address in advertising and marketing documents in Madrid: Respect and politeness. In *Proceedings of the 2014 Hawaii University international conference on arts, humanities and social sciences*. Retrieved from www.huichawaii.org/assets/uber_diane_spanish_forms_of_address_in_advertising_ahs2014.pdf

Uber, D. R. (2015). Formas de tratamiento. In J. Gutiérrez-Rexach (Ed.), *Enciclopedia de lingüística Hispánica* (Vol. 1, pp. 620–629). London & New York: Routledge.

Weyers, J. R. (2014). The *tuteo* of Rocha, Uruguay: A study of pride and language maintenance. *Hispania, 97*, 382–395.

Applied linguistics

10 Text messaging and bilingual discursive practices of college students in Puerto Rico

Edward G. Contreras and Rosita L. Rivera

1 Introduction

Text messaging is both a communication tool and a language phenomenon, yet it remains a fairly new area of academic inquiry. There is little research on text messaging as it relates to the social, cultural, and linguistic processes of texting as a tool for communication. Recent studies have either focused on building a corpus of text messages to analyze linguistic features embedded in the messages (Tagg 2012) dynamics of mobile text messaging, or code switching in speech or written language (Ling & Baron 2007; Ling & Haddon 2003; Klamer, Haddon, and Ling 2000). However, the study of language choice and discourse in bilingual text messaging remains a new area of research in both the field of language and technology as well as the sociolinguistic context of Puerto Rico.

The aim of the study was to examine and discuss bilingual discursive practices and text messaging as a linguistic and social phenomenon. In this chapter, we analyzed the discursive practices used in text messages by college students in a university in Puerto Rico in order to better understand the relationship between language choice and the role of technology in redefining the boundaries around the use of two or more languages. We explored language use in text messaging by English language learners in a bilingual context. We also discuss how culture and language choices are intertwined. The following questions guided the study: (1) What language choices do Puerto Rican college students make when texting? (2) What does the language choice tell us about the message the learner wants to get across? (3) What factors influenced the use of English and/or Spanish?

2 Mobile phones, text messaging, and language use

Short message service (SMS), as defined within the Global System for Mobile communications (GSM) digital mobile phone standard, is a service which enables its users to send short text messages from one mobile phone to another, or to a mobile phone via the Internet (Hård af Segerstad 2002). Communication through SMS service is one mode of communication referred to as computer mediated communication (CMC). Although text messaging does have its benefits in saving time and does not require being online, which has made text messaging one of the preferred alternatives for communicating, the act of texting has been considered by some linguists to be corrupting the use of language. Humphrys (2007) describes this as "vandals who are doing to our language what Genghis Khan did to his neighbors 800 years ago. They are destroying it: pillaging our punctuation; savaging our sentences; raping our vocabulary. And they must be stopped" (p. 98). Although the view of text messaging language may be portrayed as one which is uneducated and unorthodox, the fact is that technology is influencing language, which is best explained by Carroll (2008), "throughout the industrialized world, technology, and specifically the internet, has overwhelmingly changed the way we think and talk about language" (98). Texters have changed language at all levels: lexicalization, morphology, phonology, and syntax.

Although text messages may be viewed by some scholars as a negative phenomenon affecting language use, it is not the only element categorized as endangering language. Incorporating fragments, phrases, or any lexical item from other languages is also considered to be a type of corruption of language as in the case of code switching.

The main argument posed by this study is that English language learners access their linguistic repertoire in two languages to get their message across when communicating through text messages. Thus linguistic repertoire is defined in this research as the resources on which texters draw to construct meaning and get their message across. It encompasses the use of more than one language in the case of the data collected from the participants who volunteered their text messages. We further argue that texting allows for the use of two or more languages to create a different persona, thus creating multiple identities as texters as they use discursive practices to manipulate the use of two languages either consciously or incidentally. This ability to use two or more languages when texting allows for creativity when communicating through text messages that is not possible in other contexts outside of the use of technology-enhanced communication. This notion of language use is also known as what Tagg (2012) and Butler (1995) called performativity. This concept provides a venue for the analysis of the text messages to further elaborate on the intention and the social factors influencing the language choices of the participants. It allows for a creativity that is unique of a bilingual or multilingual context due to the multiple options texters have when it comes to choosing how to convey their messages.

3   Contextualizing language use and texting

The context of this study places bilingualism and language use in a sociocultural continuum, which is constantly evolving. Thus, this study draws from a culturally situated perspective of bilingual practices. This dynamic nature allows researchers to further re-evaluate the current beliefs about language use and new means of communication as a result of new available technologies such as text messaging. We study and define bilingual discursive practices as socially structured patterns and resources that form the core of everyday activity and allow researchers to analyze these patterns and technology use from a contextualized cultural and social setting (Thorne 2013). From this perspective, we examine texting language practices in their cultural and social contexts and how these socially constructed interactions determine the form and choices made by language users. Bilingualism then becomes a tool to access different linguistic repertoires rather than a limitation when texting in more than one language. García (2009) poses a similar argument in terms of how bilingualism is not a parallel or systematic equal knowledge and use of two languages, but rather a dynamic conceptual process which involves different discursive practices. Based on this view of language use, texting is conceptualized in this study as a particular technologically enhanced context in which different discursive practices emerged based on the social interaction of those exchanging messages.

This research looks at mobile phones as a technology tool to communicate in what Crystal (2004) and Tagg (2012) called "a third medium of communication" in order to demonstrate how an understanding of texting can be used and adapted in a bilingual context for pedagogical purposes. This "third medium" views text messaging as a hybrid of both speaking and writing that blurs the line between speech and text. As such, new linguistics varieties are used for the purpose of not only conveying a message, but also creating and affirming an identity as texters (Tagg 2012). These identities salient in discursive practices are also based on factors such as gender and topic discussed by texters. Using Tagg's and Crystal's concept of this "third medium" as a framework for looking at texting as a hybrid of speaking and writing, the present study exemplifies this theoretical construct.

4 A framework for bilingualism and text messages in the Puerto Rican context

Bilingualism, language use, and code switching of Puerto Rican youth and college students have been documented by researchers from a social and anthropological perspective (García, Flores & Chu 2011; Zentella 1997; Mazak & Herbas-Donoso 2014). García et al studies how Puerto Rican teenagers in two high schools in the United States used hybrid practices in English and Spanish to negotiate agency in their available linguistics repertoires. Zentella (1997) poses the argument of how Puerto Ricans also negotiate meaning through their linguistics repertoires and discourse strategies available in both languages through "Spanglish". She advocates for literacy practices that allow learners to expand on those repertoires in English and Spanish, as opposed to the view of code switching as a negative aspect of bilingualism. Most recently Mazak and Herbas-Donoso expanded on the use of English and Spanish in content courses in college as an advantage and not a negative aspect of higher education science courses. These studies view bilingualism as a tool for language users to convey their messages in two languages and a resource for Puerto Ricans and bilinguals to access their available linguistics repertoires to convey information as well as to attest to their identities in two different languages. This perspective views bilingualism and code switching as positive and not detrimental for the users. We examine the data through this standpoint and apply it to the context of Puerto Rico, college students, and text messaging.

Text messaging as a communication tool by young adults has been explored in order to better understand texting as a language phenomenon. Ling and Baron

(2007) reported that teens are responsible for popularizing the mainstream use of text messaging. Corpus linguists have also analyzed the body of the text messages and use the corpus to unravel text language and how this is present in bilingual language contexts (Tagg 2012). We argue for the use of two or more languages as a tool for communicating as opposed to the view of texting as a corruption of language. We view text messaging in two or more languages as the combination of linguistics repertoires available to bilinguals and multilingual speakers in order to get a message across in this third medium of communication.

Corpus linguistics and sociocultural approaches when analyzing data in computer mediated communication research are a current trend in the field of linguistics. This trend is evident in the case of texting and language use. Tagg (2012) collected a substantial corpus of text messages in order to examine the use of language and linguistic features based on Crystal's concept of texting as a "third medium of communication" and the postructuralist view evidenced in performativity as defined by Butler (1995). She examined pattern-forming creativity as a repetition and an involvement strategy manifested in the everyday conversation of text messaging. Based on her study of pattern-forming creativity defined by Carter (2004) and Tannen (1989), Tagg argues that texters create a persona and use language both consciously and incidentally as they manipulate their choices based on the receiver of their messages. Thus, this dynamic functions as a tool to create different identities with different texters. This has further implications when we add to the use of one language a bilingual or multilingual context. The present study also illustrates with examples from the discourse how texters make language choices in order to convey a message and to affirm their identity or their position with regard to the message receiver. However, Tagg study only examined the role of monolingual texters.

There are very few studies on the merging of both text messaging and language used. Thus fields such as sociolinguistics, CMC, and multiple types of language use and technology may benefit from the findings of this study. In the context of Puerto Rico, this phenomenon has not been empirically documented, yet this is a daily practice for young adults to communicate on a daily basis due to the availability of such technologies. For instance code switching, which is a language phenomenon, is occurring in numerous media outlets and it will continue to be a nuisance for those who see language as a pure entity. We also argue that rather than wrecking the language, young texters at the cutting edge of both language use and CMC, as they are aware of the dynamic nature of discourses. Finally, this chapter supports the notion that the nature of the social relationship and interaction among texters as well as the topic being discussed rather than proficiency are factors that may influence language choices made by those exchanging messages.

5 Methodology

5.1 Methods for data collection

This study used a survey designed to elicit quantitative and qualitative data of how participants use their mobile phone for the purpose of examining language use and bilingual discursive practices among college students in Puerto Rico. This two-part data collection survey and analysis included (1) a Mobile Phone Use Survey, which is the quantitative data analysis; and (2) a corpus of text messages provided by the participants answering the survey, which is the qualitative component of the data analysis.

5.2 The corpus: a cautionary word on text messages

The corpus included 502 text messages provided by the participants as part of the questionnaire (see Appendix A). The language use and composition of the text messages is included in the data analysis section. We collected eight to 10 text messages from each participant. Names and any information that might identify the participant were removed for ethical and personal reasons. Also, jokes or chain messages were not counted as text messages because the person did not write them; they are usually the result of a forwarded message. This study does not attempt to make any generalizations regarding the use of language in text messages by bilingual students, but rather it seeks to showcase an example of how language learners in a bilingual context access their linguistic repertoires when text messaging in two languages.

5.3 Participants

The participants of the study were first-year college students at a major public university on the west coast of Puerto Rico named West University for anonymity purposes. This study addressed issues of proficiency and language use as well as sociolinguistics factors when text messaging, as such students were selected based on proficiency levels. The study was conducted with two sections at each language proficiency level: pre-basic English, basic English, intermediate English, and advanced English. Table 10.1 shows the demographic data of the participants. The students' College Board Entrance Examination scores determined the level of proficiency for a student at this university. The maximum score is 800. Table 10.2 shows the proficiency levels and the score used to place students in the courses.

The AP exam is not a requirement for high school students. In most cases it is offered to those who were in advanced courses during their senior year and want to get some credits approved before they begin university studies. This study

Table 10.1 Participants according to gender and English proficiency level

Gender	Total (74)	Percentage (100%)
Male	38	52
Female	36	48
English track		
Pre-basic	14	19
Basic	25	33
Intermediate	17	23
Advanced	18	25

Table 10.2 Proficiency levels at West University

Proficiency level in English	CBEE cut-off points
Pre-basic	469 or less
Basic	470–569
Intermediate	570 or more
Advanced	Scored a 4 or 5 on the Advanced Placement (AP) English Exam

analyzed all English level proficiency groups at this institution due to the multiple language proficiency levels that provided a variety of language use and discursive practices of these participants.

5.4 Proficiency level and placement in Spanish courses at West University

Placement of students in Spanish courses at West University differs from English in that the university does not have pre-basic or intermediate tracks in their program. Students are placed in basic Spanish if they take the CEEB or they are placed in advanced Spanish courses if they take the AP for Spanish and pass with a 4 or 5. By advanced Spanish courses, we mean courses other than basic Spanish. They could be literature, writing, or language courses.

In order to analyze the use of both English and Spanish in bilingual text messages, a survey was designed to elicit demographic data and the mobile phone history of the participants. The text messages were analyzed through the lens of discourse analysis (Fowler 1996) in order to better understand and identify discursive practices and patterns of language use in the text messages.

5.5 Data analysis of survey

All surveys were initially grouped by language proficiency and then were tallied and analyzed based on emerging categories. A code system was developed in order to categorize the different patterns salient in the data. The categories coded based on language use were: (1) code switching, (2) text talk, (3) stock phrases, (4) spelling variation, (5) all English, and (6) no English. Data analysis also involved the counting of Spanish and English words, phrases, or sentences and tallying up a percentage using the system previously outlined by Al-Khatib and Sabbah (2008).

Table 10.3 provides the definitions and examples of the categories tallied up and the language use.

5.6 Analysis of text messages

Messages were analyzed and interpreted in relation to their sociocultural background through the lens of discourse analysis to provide a micro-level perspective on the language choices made by participants in the text messages. The following

Table 10.3 Type of language used and definitions

Types of language used	Definition
Code switching	'The ability of multilingual speakers to shuttle between languages, treating the diverse languages that form their repertoire as an integrated system' (Canagarajah 2011: 401) (e.g., *jajaja that's not easy … voy a jugar loto deskiciadamente …*)
Spelling variation	Words that have been modified phonetically to fit the need of the host language (e.g., *jangear*)
Text talk	Abbreviations to decrease the number of keystrokes one has to make in order to write a word, phrase, or emoticons (e.g., *lol*)
Stock phrase	A string of words that count as one lexical item such as idioms or popular phrases used in the media or everyday life (e.g., *see you tomorrow*)
All English	Using only English in the text
No English	Using only Spanish in the text

categories emerged from the data and operational definitions were provided for each one of them.

Coding of text message for discourse patterns:

1 *Over-lexicalization* – the availability of many words for one concept, and it indicates the prominence of the concept in a community's beliefs and intellectual interests (Fowler 1996); that is, the repeated use of terms of endearments such as *honey, baby*, and sweetie when texting someone informally, such as a friend or significant other.

2 *Spelling variation and abbreviation of words* – lexical items spelled in the discourse of the text messages in non-standard forms and abbreviated to economize characters in the text messages. The data includes examples from both English and Spanish; for example, *please* is spelled in a message as *plis* and the Spanish word *loca* is spelled in a message as *loka*.

If the text messages for some reason were not decipherable, they were presented as the participants wrote them. Although a large corpus of text messages was gathered, only some examples relevant to the research questions will be discussed in this study. The text message presented and analyzed in the results section will show discourse patterns salient in the data based on language use and the participants' social and cultural context. These issues are linked to the research questions guiding the study.

6 Results

6.1 Type of language use in text messages

Table 10.4 provides a summary of the language use in text messages across proficiency levels.

Table 10.4 Type of language used in text messages across proficiency levels

Types of language used by participant	Total	Percentage
Code switching	17	23%
Spelling variation	15	20%
Text talk	13	18%
Stock phrase	27	36%
All English	2	3%
No English	27	36%

6.2 Code switching

The first category to be analyzed is code switching. Generally described as a person using one language and then switching to another language, code switches can be placed in any part of the sentence: beginning or end. Due to the different definitions and forms of code switching, we have adapted Canagarajah's (2011) definition (cited in Table 10.3) and Zentella's code switching categories to help analyze the corpus. The following is an example of a text message that has a code switch:

(1)   jajaja that's not easy . . . voy a jugar loto deskiciadamente . . .
       'hahaha that's not easy . . . I am going to play lotto like crazy . . . '

The switch is done but it is not using a borrowed word, it is an actual phrase from one language (in this case English); the phrase is in English and then the texter goes back to Spanish. Thus, written in English this phrase would translate to: *jajaja that's not easy . . . I'm going to play lotto like crazy*. Within this category, 17 out of the 74 participants used code switching in their text messages. According to Zentella (1997) code switches may occur at the boundary of complete sentences (inter-sententially) or within sentence boundaries (intra-sententially). Some examples of inter-sentential code switching from the corpus are:

(2)   *Not much*, te iba invitar pa vega baja pero veo que tienes mucho trabajo
       'Not much, I was going to invite you to vega baja but I see you have a lot of work'

(3)   *So I'll tell you the truth* . . . estoy adicta a ti . . .
       'I am addicted to you'

There were also accounts of intra-sentential code switching:

(4)   Ta bn mamita, *I got test too*, ps un día después del examen y dentro del lunes; cdt mamita!!!
       'ok mamita I got test too then a day after the exam and on Monday; take care mamita!'

(5) Mira, dime si me puedes ver *online* en *chat* de Facebook pq hoy pusieron internet en mi apt y kiero ver si funciona
     'Look, tell me if you can see me online in the chat because I got Internet access today and I want to see if it works'

(6) Baby voy a *the church* te llamo cuando salga TAM!!
     'Baby I am going to church I'll call you when I leave TAM!!!'

Just under one-fourth (23 percent) of the sample used code switching. These participants used a variety of different ways of code switching. It is worth noting that code switching has been defined and given different criteria over the years to help distinguish it from other forms of describing language use. Rivera and Mather (2015) highlight criteria that distinguished code switching and borrowing. Code switching involves entire phrases and clauses, different from borrowing that is usually associated with a single word or in some cases a short phrase. The authors also indicate that code switching is associated with high levels of fluency in both languages. Finally, they state that code switching maintains the phonology of each language, while spelling variation adapts phonetics and phonology of the host language. However, the dynamics of language and globalization have blurred the line between written and spoken use of language. Texting is a hybrid form of communication involving the written and spoken word (Crystal 2004). Thus when individuals communicate through texting, they may think of the word and type it, but there is no evidence of pronunciation on the part of the texter. Due to this difference between spoken and written language, we are using Canagarajah's definition of code switching, which states that code switching is "the ability of multilingual speakers to shuttle between languages, treating the diverse languages that form their repertoire as an integrated system" (Canagarajah 2011: 401). The following are examples of spelling variation.

6.3 Spelling variation

Within categories of language use, spelling variations have often been confused with code switching. Though many scholars have dealt with the processes of code switching, code mixing, and spelling variation, there is not one clear distinction for such use (Romaine 1989; Myers-Scotton 1990, 1993; Poplack 1980). This study categorizes spelling variation as words that have been modified phonetically; the spelling has been changed or modified to fit the need of the host language. For instance, a word would have to be taken from the second language, which in this case is English, and would be used in Spanish, but the word will have been modified to fit the linguistic rules of the host language, in this case Spanish. For instance, the English verb "to hang out" has been borrowed Spanish and is now used commonly in Puerto Rican Spanish as the verb "janguear"; they both mean the same thing, but the latter is the borrowed version of the English phrase. It can be seen as borrowed, specifically because of the spelling and how it is modified. The word "jangueo" is a noun but by adding -ar, we turn it automatically into a verb. Many Puerto Ricans interpret such use of language as a form of corruption of Spanish. Nevertheless, it has not seemed to deter Puerto Ricans from using borrowed words and phrases in many of their daily functions. Some examples of text messages with spelling variations are:

(7)   El examen tah *chilin*
        'The test is *chilin*'

(8)   Conseguiste *parquearte*?
        'Were you able to park?'

(9)   Ya toy *ready*
        'I am ready'

(10)   Hermana *check* el periódico
        'Sister check the newspaper'

(11)   Okk dame un *break*
        'Ok give me a break'

Based on the definition previously discussed and the examples from the data, 20 percent of the participants used spelling variations in their text messages. Although some lexical items might be spelled the wrong way, their semantic value stays intact and those that are spelled exactly the same way in the second language are used within the host language's phonemic rules, to the extent that many of the users think its origin is from Spanish. In this next section, we discuss the number of participants who texted completely in English and those who did not send any text messages with a word in English.

6.4 Text talk

According to Crystal (2009), text talk is when the language user incorporates terms that have become popular throughout the texting and are often truncated or abbreviated to decrease the number of keystrokes one has to make in order to write a word or phrase. In some cases people will use symbols to portray facial expressions, which are known as emoticons. For the purpose of this study, emoticons will not be counted as a form of text talk; the only characteristic that will be depicted is the wording within the text. The following are some examples of text talk:

(12)   Is the blood drive *4 ur* sister *2day*

(13)   I am lost . . . *lol*

(14)   Te envio las *pics* por email
        'I'll send you the pics by email'

(15)   *U* welcome and happy *b-day* again

(16)   No not *rlly lolz* so how's my cutie

At the time of data collection, smart phones were not as common as they are nowadays. There was a limitation in the number of characters for texting. Thus with only 160 characters per text message, writing in the shortest possible code is essential to convey meaning and to save resources. Within the questionnaire, 13 out of the 74 (18 percent) of the participants had at least one token of text talk in their text messages. This was the language category that had the least number of tokens. Although participants used text talk, they did not use it as much as they used other categories, specifically, code switching and spelling variation, all English and stock phrases.

6.5 Stock phrases

Stock phrases accounted for the largest number of tokens. Stock phrases are categorized in this study as a string of words that count as one lexical item, such as catch phrases or popular phrases used within television or other common aspects of the media, popular culture, or one's everyday life. For the purpose of this study it is defined as a standard phrase that can be remembered and does not require spelling variation. Phrases or words that were part of the text message data that can exemplify this category are: *Random*, *Where are you? Me too*, *Love you*, *Happy Birthday*. Those are just some of the examples that were logged as stock phrases within the data collected. A total of 27 students used a stock phrase within their text messages. That is the equivalent of 36 percent of the entire group. Some examples pertaining to stock phrases within the corpus are the following:

   (17)   Ditto *sorry* toi muy llena pero grax *anyway*
          'Sorry I am full but thanks anyway'

   (18)   *Good Morning* primero que todo . . . necesito un favor, tu me prestas
          tu *laptop*
          'Good Morning first of all . . . I need a favor, would you let me borrow
          your laptop'

   (19)   Mira ven a la biblio para que hagas lo de la clase de Bio . . . *Please!*
          Please!
          'Look come over to the library so that you can work on the Bio class
          Please! Please!'

   (20)   Ok me too

   (21)   Yes, why?

While stock phrases seem to be popular among the Puerto Rican participants, an additional category that uses English words that have been blended into what are now considered to be 'adopted' Puerto Rican words was labeled spelling variations.

6.6 All English

Text messages completely in English were not common within this study. Out of the 74 participants, only two (3 percent) sent an entire text message in English; one example:

(22)   A bit tired but ok.
       Going to school?
       Yup

These are just some of the examples of text being sent completely in English. It could have been the case where the participant received a text message by some-one whose first language was English, but for the purpose of this study, they only provided the relationship they had with the person sending the text message. For a future study it would be noteworthy to explore the language background of both sender and receiver.

6.7 No English

When it came to text messages completely in Spanish, 36 percent of the messages were in Spanish. These results have implications for the way language is used by young bilingual texters and also serve as a catalyst to delve into the study of other variables such as gender (male versus female) or the analysis of schooling before the university (public versus private education).

6.8 Male and female language choices

The data also showed some patterns of language use by male and female partici-pants, as shown in Table 10.5.

Males code switched more while females used more stock phrases. Yet both males and females used English across proficiency levels. The following section provides examples of the lexical choices and spelling variation exemplified in the text messages to contextualize the results shown in Table 10.5. We provide some examples of lexical choices made by both males and females as they relate to over-lexicalization and spelling variation as part of the discourse analysis in the section below.

Table 10.5 Types of English use among males and female participants

English used by participants	Male (%)	Female (%)
Code switching	32%	14%
Text talk	23%	11%
Stock phrase	32%	42%
Spelling variation	29%	11%
All English	3%	3%
No English	32%	42%

6.9 Getting a message across in English and Spanish

The use of two different languages not only facilitates the conscious or incidental use of language, but also gives way to the use of different linguistics features within text messages. The text messages analyzed here showed different patterns that were evident in the discursive practices of the participants.

In the following section we discuss examples of discursive practices and linguistic features salient in the text messages. The examples show lexical choices and spelling variation among participants. The examples are also evidence of how language learners used both their L1 and L2 based on topics and how the social interaction and relationship of the sender and receiver of the text message may also influence lexical choices, specifically over-lexicalization and spelling variation.

6.10 Over-lexicalization

As previously defined in the methodology section, over-lexicalization is the availability of many words for one concept and it indicates the prominence of the concept in a community's beliefs and intellectual interests (Fowler 1996); for example, the repeated use of terms of endearments such as *honey*, *baby*, and *sweetie* when texting someone informally, such as a friend or significant other.

6.11 Females' use of adjectives and terms of endearment in English

The repetition of adjectives considered terms of endearment and adjectives appealing to emotions or over-lexicalization (Fowler 1996) was evident in both English and Spanish. It is worth noting that males and females used these lexical items repeatedly in either one language or another. For instance, female participants used English terms across proficiency levels when speaking to friends as well as significant relationships such as boyfriends or girlfriends. Further, females accounted for the use of the most stock phrases in English out of all the participants of this study. Within their group of 20 participants, nine of them had at least one token of stock phrases within their text messages. Most of these stock phrases were one or two words to express endearment or a type of sentiment. Some examples are:

(23)   OK *honey*

(24)   Estoy *super bored*

(25)   Ok! Thank you! Good nite *my love*!

(26)   Ok *baby*!

(27)   OK *sweetie*!

These text messages, although they do use English, do not necessarily require a great deal of language competency. The use of terms of endearment in everyday conversation is part of the Puerto Rican context. In fact, people in Puerto Rico use these lexical items on a regular basis, often to the extent that they have almost been adopted as the ever-emerging and changing Puerto Rican Spanish vernacular as English is introduced into different media. Ling and Haddon (2003) make the argument that the use of the mobile phone allows females to be away from home but in contact at the same time, which in the past would not have been possible. According to the data from the questionnaire, female participants did not use English in ways that would require a long train of thought. These are terms used or internalized in English. This is aligned with García's notion that discursive practices are used based on the social interaction of the discourse community and those involved in the interaction. Some text message examples that support this claim are the following:

(28) *Me too*!!

(29) Tell meeeee!!!

(30) Que *nice* tu!

Male participants, on the other hand, used many terms of endearment in Spanish when compared to their female counterparts. Below are some examples of terms of endearment used by male participants in Spanish:

(31) Bebe, Chikita, chiquita, golda, adoracion, mi cielo, amor, carino, mi reina

Although we cannot categorically state the reasons why males and females used these terms in either English or Spanish, there was a clear pattern in terms of the over-lexicalization of these terms in both languages. Females used English more often than males.

6.12 Males' use of adjectives as an expression of vulgar language

Men's language within text messages had a more informal tone and had message examples, which did not delve into much detail and in some cases portrayed more vulgar and English-filled text messages. Some examples of these are:

(32) Always bitch

(33) Chekeate el *trade* q te mande *rebounds* por *assists*
'Check the trade I sent you assist rebounds'

(34) *Infeliz* prestame el libro de quim *2morrow* pa studial
'*Infeliz* let me borrow the chemistry book tomorrow so I can study'

Colley et al. (2004) found in email writing men were less affectionate and had fewer personal inquiries than women. Similarly, within the current study, male participants used more English than women in the categories code switching, text talk, and spelling variation. Moreover, male participants from private institutions had more combined English tokens than any other group within this study. It seems to be the case that men use much more English in their text messages because of their constant engagement with media and to express a more informal and vulgar language among themselves in order to create a sense of identity or unspoken code when texting each other. For example: *"Tipo coje el fuckin cell. (Dude pick up your fucking phone)"*. This is aligned with Butler's performativity as a creative process in which texters create or reaffirm a persona while using this type of language. Colley et al. (2004) also asserted men use more offensive language in emails than women. Within the corpus of texts several males portrayed the characteristic of using "obscene" language. When males talked to each other, they chose lexical items considered in this particular context as offensive or vulgar. Below are some more examples of these adjectives.

(35) Estuvo *cabron*!
      'That was *cabron*'

(36) Coge el *fucking* telefono!
      'Pick up the *fucking* phone'

(37) *Infeliz* prestame el libro de química
      '*Infeliz* let me borrow your chemistry book'

In the context of the previous example, *cabrón* means great or awesome. However, the term is very offensive and vulgar when considered in other contexts in which the term is used in Puerto Rican Spanish. The use of *infelíz* is also a term used in this context to bond as opposed to simply insult the receiver of the message. Yet as in the case of *cabrón*, this term is also very offensive when used in other contexts. Therefore, the meaning giving in the text messages is one of bonding in the same way that the terms of endearments work for the interaction between males and females. These terms may represent an attempt to affirm an unspoken identity among texters and their relationship within their message exchange and getting their meaning across through performativity.

6.13 Abbreviations

Abbreviations were very common among both males and females and across proficiency levels. Below are some examples of how participants abbreviated, merged, and spelled Spanish and English words:

(38) **Male**:   *Q acs*? (Qué haces?)
                  'What are you doing?'

(39) **Female**: *Dond stas*? (Donde estás?)
                   'Where are you?'

(40) **Male**:   Llama *plis* te amo bye.
                  'Call me please I love you bye'

(41) **Male**:   no klases los viernes. Thats exelent
                  'No clases on Friday. That's excellent'

Abbreviation is one of the most relevant linguistic features salient in the corpus. Both males and females showed abbreviations in both English and Spanish. The choices of words were very similar and consistent across participants: *loka, stas, porq* showed that participants are comfortable using these variations in Spanish. Originally, texters and online communities used these abbreviations to economize characters. Yet, as the examples above show, in some cases they are not economizing characters, as in the case of *loka* instead of *loca*. Therefore these expressions show a difference in informal (*loka*) and formal (*loca*) register. It is becoming more common in social media as well as in texting to use this non-standard abbreviation of this word. Thus language is being reshaped by these interactions prompted by CMC and texters are creating their own identity as part of this interaction by the choices they make when spelling these words, which is aligned with Tagg (2012). These patterns also show how texting provides a space for multiple identities to emerge through performativity and creativity in language use.

The spelling of *please* as *plis* is another example of how participants chose to write a word in English based on the phonological sound of the word as opposed to the conventional spelling. Yet, they understood the meaning and continued to communicate their message. This is another spelling phenomenon in this particular context in which learners determine and use their own language rules.

Accessing these repertoires also requires a sense of identity and creativity that could be linked to the use of technology and texting; what Crystal coined as a "third medium of communication". It allows texters to convey their message while showing a distinctive tone that is not available when solely relying on speaking. These variations show that texters are able to use a discourse that only they understand as being part of a discourse community. They are co-creators of their own linguistics rules as they choose to communicate with different members of these communities. These choices (over-lexicalization and spelling variation) show how language learners in a bilingual context are constantly accessing different discourses and make metacognitive choices when interacting through text messages. Thus this opens possibilities for the use of both their L1 and L2 in creative ways that could be expanded and recontextualized in the L2 classroom. The following section expands on the main findings and presents the pedagogical implications of this study.

7 Discussion

Participants in the study used both Spanish and English in their text messages. They used word choice as well as spelling variation to reflect the influence of their linguistic landscape. The line dividing language use – in this case, Spanish and English in the context of Puerto Rico – is blurred and transferring to everyday practices. This raises the question as to how cultural practices and language use are being transformed into everyday practice.

The participants of this study potentially represent a generation of Puerto Ricans that are capable of manipulating the language in a way that is bilingual and unconsciously literate in text messages. Because of the implicit and explicit exposure to different multimedia outlets in English and Spanish, Puerto Ricans have developed the ability to process and manipulate language to fit their individual communication needs, and in the process creating their own bilingual discourse community.

7.1 Language choice

This chapter shows that English tokens are common in text messaging practices of Puerto Rican college students. Stock phrases, which was the most commonly used among both men and women participants, allows participants to embed a word or phrase that might evoke a more personal or implicit message. An example of this can be seen for the English word *happy birthday* or *happy bday*, which is more specific than a Spanish *felicidades*. Because *felicidades* is not a specific message, the person sending the message would have to use the specific Spanish expression *feliz cumpleaños*. The English expression for *happy birthday* or *happy bday* is not only shorter, but it also conveys the message directly as opposed to the Spanish form *feliz cumpleaños*, which is also considered to be very formal. Participants who wanted to convey a message using both languages but with longer English fragments would utilize the strategy of code switching.

Similar to the examples of messages with stock phrases, messages with spelling variation words were also short but included at least one English word. Contrary to stock phrases, abbreviated words can be linguistically modified to fit Spanish properties. Puerto Ricans over the years have taken English words and incorporated them in their daily speech. One common example of this is the word "check". The word check has been modified to be *chekeate – to check out*; *chekeamos – see you later, let's check*; *chequeaste – did you check out?* These examples highlight Puerto Ricans' ability to manipulate language to fit a Spanish need. In some linguistic views this might be viewed as poisoning or destroying the language, but it seems that Puerto Ricans have managed to adapt and change certain English words to the degree where they might be considered Spanish by native speakers of Puerto Rico. A future study could shed light on the ability of Puerto Ricans to distinguish borrowed terms and whether or not the view them as borrowed terms in the first place.

As mentioned before, code switching involves the alternation of two or more codes in one sentence. From this study we noticed that those who code switched had longer English phrases in their sentences than those who used stock phrases or spelling variations. Participants in this study portrayed examples of similar sentence patterns as those in Zentella's (1997) study. Learners took advantage of their understanding of both languages and placed English both intra- and inter-sententially. One set of examples show that code switching language choices occur because of the context that is being discussed. In a larger scale study it would be relevant to see if participants continue to code switch when referring to English webpages. One particular set of examples focus on a participant discussing NBA fantasy league and chooses tokens that are in English because the webpage is only in English (e.g., *Chekeate el trade q te mande rebounds por assists*). The words trade, rebound, and assists have Spanish equivalencies (trade = cambio, rebounds = rebotes, assists = asistencias) and are used in Spanish media; however because the outlet that they are referring to is solely in English, this particular participant chose to refer to them in English, even though the rest of the sentence is in Spanish.

Participants also code switched if they wanted to intensify their messages with English adjectives. This can be seen in the following example ("Lokis! Algún plan pa hoy, Haha estoy super bored") where the participant is looking to go out or do something, and intensifies her current state by switching to English and indicating that she is *super bored*. A similar example is also seen in the data, where another participant (No klases los viernes. Thats exelent) is indicating that there is no class in Spanish and intensifies her feeling by switching to English. These and more examples in the data show that when Puerto Rican college students want to intensify their feelings towards a given situation, they might code switch between Spanish and English. While performing these switches between languages, the participants of this study constructed larger sentences in the process.

The study illustrates that when the participants texted in English the message was shorter and more specific. The choice of adjectives and spelling variation in the text messages show that participants use certain language choices to manipulate language, which requires linguistics skills and knowledge of language as well as the different meanings assigned to one concept.

7.2 Factors influencing language choice

7.2.1 Relationship between texters

One major factor that determined language choice was the relationship between the person texting and the recipient. When texting friends or someone with whom the texter had a close relationship, such as a partner, there were more instances of use of both English and Spanish, as opposed to texting a parent, in which case the texter and recipient used in most cases one language. Another noteworthy aspect of language choice was the use of words that could be considered profanity in this context. Male participants' language within text messages had a more informal tone, which in some cases portrayed more vulgar and explicit language when using English and Spanish. Some examples of these are:

(42)   Always bitch

(43)   Tipo coje el fuckin cell

(44)   Infeliz prestame el libro de quim 2morrow pa studia

Furthermore, within this small-scale study it can be determined that language choice is not arbitrary; rather it is determined by the relationship shared between the person sending and receiving the message. English and a more informal tone are used with friends, while Spanish and more formal language is used with family and other closed relationships.

7.2.2 Topic

Topic was another factor that greatly influenced the amount of English used or not used in Puerto Rican participant text messages. For instance, the section that discussed stock phrase examples referred to fantasy sports. Because the language use and the identity of playing fantasy sports and the categories are used in English, it is fitting that the participants would want to communicate the concept as they are seeing it on the webpage. The identity of the texters as participants of this online community influences their identity as language users. English is the identity within this online social environment. The one grey area in regards to topic is that of terms of endearment. We can assert that terms of endearment in Spanish convey a different meaning; for instance, *te quiero* as opposed *te amo*. In English this distinction is not possible. However, this should be viewed as an advantage for bilingual writers and texters. It allows for a more specific meaning in a specific language. Although they use English in these text messages, it does not necessarily require a great deal of language proficiency. In fact people within Puerto Rico use these types of words or phrases on a regular basis, often to the extent that they have almost been adopted as the ever-emerging and changing Puerto Rican Spanish vernacular as English is introduced into different media sources. Thus proficiency levels are not a determining factor when choosing to use either English or Spanish in text messages.

8 Conclusions

Based on the data collected through the survey and the text messages analyzed in this study, it is evident that Puerto Rican youth are bilingual texters who draw from a variety of discourses and show spelling variation in both their L1 and L2. Furthermore, this study highlights a key demographic population of language users. Most teenagers and young adults have mobile phones and are using them to communicate using text messages. They are incorporating different language strategies and symbols to get across meanings that only those who receive and engage constantly with them could comprehend. For instance bilingual texters can use four stock phrases in a row and it can still be an intelligible message:

(45) Ok! Thank you! Good nite my love!

It is also worth mentioning how some use text talk while code switching:

(46) Pa saber mi Corazón. U wanna come 2 my house?
      'To know my love, you want to come to my house?'

Overall, many of these students know how to incorporate English within their text messages and they are doing it in a very clever manner. It also appears to be a very organic practice that may indicate metacognition processes and both conscious and incidental linguistic choices. Using two languages within Puerto Rican college students' text messages portrays to the users how they can communicate with one another in multiple ways, but also lets them know that they have a skill that is quite useful and makes them seem more attractive to their target audience as texters. They are recontextualizing the same practices they are using in text messaging in other types of CMC such as chatting and updating status and walls posts on Facebook and tweets on Twitter. This third medium of communication provides multiple outlets for the use of bilingual discursive strategies. This finding is aligned with Carroll's (2008) statement regarding the use of language in online communities on the island when he says that "Puerto Ricans on MySpace.com are part of a larger community of users, and thus many choose to present themselves as people who are able to communicate in a language of wider communication" (109). Puerto Ricans are boosting their image and letting the world know that they are far more than an island in the Caribbean, but are a part of the United States and more importantly a part of the world. Thus, the participants of this study, as well as other Spanish-speaking English-language learners around the world, are being influenced and are influencing the use and merging of two languages through CMC.

Although this is a small-scale study, based on the data we could make some assertions and recommendations regarding text messaging and bilingualism not only in Puerto Rico, but in other contexts with bilingual texters. Below is a summary of the main findings, which could be also future lines of inquiry to expand on the main issues discussed in this study:

Language use

- Language learners in a bilingual setting text cleverly and creatively in both languages.
- Learners across language proficiency levels are using both English and Spanish as evident in the lexical choices and linguistic repertoire salient in discourse.

Bilingual discursive practices

- Texters' socially and culturally constructed relationship influence the formality, lexical choices, and spelling variation of the text messages.

Below we discuss some implications regarding the use of both languages and text messaging.

This study has implications for language use and sociolinguistics as well as learning in ESL, EFL, or bilingual contexts. The language and discourse of text messages, if used in a creative, purposeful, and structured manner, can be developed into an excellent teaching tool for enhancing vocabulary or lexical items such as idioms, colloquial language, syntax, and morphology. The constant exchange of vocabulary serves for multiple functions within communication and could possibly be developed to signal differences between different types of language use, such as net speak, text talk, code switching, and spelling variation. Crystal (2004) suggests that there is more writing being done during this generation than in any other era because of the extensive use of text messages around the world. In addition, it is evident that texting is becoming a new medium for communication, which is substituting traditional writing and might lead to a new strategy to engage younger generations to benefit from this non-traditional style and in language learning settings to promote different styles of creative writing. However, this is not to say that this is detrimental to standard forms of academic writing. The argument we pose is that texters should be able to use these repertoires without understanding the use of that type of language as unacceptable in this particular context of texting. Standard forms of language will continue to be supported and college students will continue to learn the differences between the two if educators and researchers continue to explore how the two can coexist in the bilingual setting of contexts such as Puerto Rico.

A crucial point we argue here is that the perspective that text messages are a "corruption of language" needs to be reevaluated as language users and texters are constantly reshaping the language and influencing what goes on in the media as well as in other outlets of communication. Thus these college texters are a step ahead than the rest of the population that is not as familiar or maybe reluctant to use language and these linguistic repertoires evident in the text messages we analyzed in this study.

This research contributes to the growing body of literature addressing issues of language use and bilingual texting in Puerto Rico as well as other contexts. It will also add to the pedagogical uses of technologies such as text messages in the language classroom. It provides a perspective on how language choices are affected and modified by society's daily use and conventions.

Finally, adding to the literature in the field might lead to future studies on language in other countries and how computer mediated communication and language should not be considered to be monolingual, but rather a bilingual tool to gain access to different sociocultural contexts and discourse communities. Gaining insight into current topics discussed among teenagers will provide numerous different ideas for ESL and non-ESL materials, and will provide a better understanding to those who are not young adults or do not engage in the use of such technologies.

Bibliography

Al- Khatib, M., & Sabbah, E. (2008). Language choice in mobile text messages among Jordanian University students. *SKY Journal of Linguistics*, *21*, 37–65.

Butler, J. (1995). *Performativity and performance*. London & New York: Routledge.

Canagarajah, S. (2011). Translanguaging in the classroom: Emerging issues for research and pedagogy. *Applied Linguistics Review*, *2*(1), 1–28.

Carroll, K. (2008). Puerto Rico language use on Myspace.com. *CENTRO Journal*, *20*(1), 96–111.

Colley, A. Todd, Z., Bland, M. Holmes, M., Khanom, N., & Pike, H. (2004). Style and Content in e-mails and letters to male and female friends. *Journal of Language and Social Psychology, 23*(3), 369–378.

Crystal, D. (2009). 2b or not 2b? *The Guardian*. Retrieved from www.guardian.co.uk/books/2008/jul/05/saturdayreviewfeatres.guardianreview

Crystal, D. (2004). *The Language revolution*. Cambridge, MA: Polity Press.

Fowler, R. (1996). On critical linguistics. In C. R. Caldas-Coulthard, & M. Coulthard (Eds.), *Texts and practices: readings in critical discourse analysis* (pp. 3–14). New York: Routledge.

García, O. (2009). Bilingual education in the 21st century: A global perspective. Malden, MA and Oxford: Basil/Blackwell.

García, O., Flores, N., & and Chu, H. (2011). Extending bilingualism in U.S. secondary education: new variations. *International Multilingual Research Journal, 5*(1), 1–18.

Hård af Segerstad, Y. (2002). Use and adaptation of written language to the conditions of computer-mediated communication (Doctoral dissertation). Göteborg University, Göteborg, Sweden.

Humphrys, J. (2007). I h8 txt msgs: How texting is wrecking our language. *Daily Mail Online*. Retrieved from www.dailymail.co.uk/news/article-483511/I-h8-txt-msgs-How-texting-wrecking-language.html

Klamer, L., Haddon, L., & Ling, R. (2000). *The qualitative analysis of ICTs and mobility, time stress and social networking* (Report of EURESCOM P-903). Heidelberg, Germany: EURESCOM.

Ling, R., & Baron, N. S. (2007). Text messaging and IM linguistic comparison of American college data. *Journal of Language and Social Psychology, 26*(3), 291–298.

Ling, R., & Haddon L. (2003). Mobile telephony, mobility, and the coordination of everyday life. In J. E. Katz (Ed.), *Machines that become us: The social context of personal communication technology* (pp. 245–265). Piscataway, NJ: Transaction Publishers.

Mazak, C., & Herbas-Donoso, C. (2014). Translanguaging practices and language ideologies in Puerto Rican University science education. *Critical Inquiry in Language Studies, 11*(1), 27–49.

Myers-Scotton, C. (1990). Codeswitching and borrowing: Interpersonal and macrolevel meaning. In R. Jacobson (Ed.), *Codeswitching as a worldwide phenomenon* (pp. 85–110). New York, NY: Peter Lang.

Myers-Scotton, C. (1993). *Duelling languages: grammatical structure in codeswitching*. Oxford: Clarendon Press.

Poplack, S. (1980). Sometimes I'll start a sentence in Spanish y termino en español: toward a typology of code-switching1. *Linguistics 18*(7–8), 581–618.

Rivera, Y., & Mather, P. -A. (2015). Codeswitching and borrowing in Aruban Papiamentu: the blurring of categories. In S. Sessarego, & M. González-Rivera (Eds.), *New pespectives on Hispanic contact linguistics in the Americas* (pp. 155–176). Madrid: Iberoamericana.

Romaine, S. (1989). *Bilingualism*. Oxford: Basil Blackwell.

Tannen, D. (1989). *Talking voices: Repetition, dialogue, and imagery in conversational discourse* (Vol. 6). Cambridge: Cambridge University Press.

Thorne, S. L. (2013). Digital literacies. In M. Hawkins (Ed.), *Framing languages and literacies socially situated views and perspectives* (pp. 192–218). London & New York: Routledge.

Tagg, C. (2012). Discourse of text messaging: Analysis of SMS communication. New York: Bloomsbury.

Zentella, A. C. (1997). Growing up bilingual: Puerto Rican children in New York. Cambridge, MA: Blackwell.

Appendix A
Mobile phone use survey

Uso de celular/mensajes de texto

¿Por cuánto tiempo aproximado ha tenido su teléfono celular? Sea lo más específico posible.

  Menos de 2 años   entre 2–4 años   entre 5–6 años   entre 7–8 años   9 o más

¿Qué tipo de teclado usa para enviar mensajes de texto: QWERTY o tradicional? (circule el que usa)

Aproximádamente, ¿cuántos mensajes de texto envía y recibe por día? (Circule)
0   1–5   5–10   11–15   16–20   21–25   26–30   31–40   40 +

¿Quiénes son los receptores más comunes de sus mensajes de texto? (Circule no más de 2 opciones, si aplica).
  Mejores amig@s Padres Familiares Novi@/Jev@ Compañer@s de trabajo

Si usas inglés en tus mensajes de texto, ¿Porqué lo utilizas en lugar del español?

Por favor provea los últimos 10 mensajes de texto que ha recibido o enviado. Subraye si fue enviado o recibido e indique la relación que tiene con la persona de la que recibió o a la que envió el mensaje.

  Ejemplo1. Enviado   Recibido _Amigo_____ : Hey ! ¿como tas? Q vas hacer orita   Enviado Recibido_____ : Ehh no estoy sure, dame un call a ver, ttyl.

  1. Enviado _____
  2. Recibido _____
  3. Enviado _____
  4. Recibido _____
  5. Enviado _____
  6. Recibido _____
  7. Enviado _____
  8. Recibido _____
  9. Enviado _____
  10. Recibido _____

11 Language education policy issues in Puerto Rico

Alicia Pousada

1 Introduction

Puerto Rico is a Spanish-speaking territory that exists within a complicated political status with the United States known as Estado Libre Asociado (Free Associated State or Commonwealth). Language planning issues pertaining to both Spanish and English have received varying degrees of attention since the territory was taken over by the United States in 1898; however, overall, the situation has been characterized by a lack of organized language planning and the adoption of language education policies that respond more to the pressures of federal administration and insular party politics than to pedagogical prudence (Ostolaza Bey 2001).

All modern, industrialized states have to confront questions of language education policy (Shohami 2006; Gibson 2006). Language policy issues faced by educators worldwide fall into three general categories: language status, language corpus, and language acquisition (Wright 2004). These concerns overlap and may be addressed simultaneously by different types of language policies initiated and implemented by distinct groups. They are all observable in Puerto Rico.

Language status policies are generally the most controversial and overtly political in nature. They involve the official selection of one or more language varieties for use in the schools, government, and media, and the value explicitly or implicitly assigned to the given codes (Cooper 1990). Language status planning was a central issue in many of the decolonization movements of the 1960s and 1970s, particularly in Africa and the Pacific (Fishman, Ferguson, & Das Gupta 1968). Language status decisions are generally guided by sociopolitical ideologies such as nationalism, assimilationism, pluralism, or internationalism. The formal allocation of language resources is commonly made by governmental bodies but put into action and/or monitored by school administrators and teachers, as well as other language stakeholders such as the courts and the media.

In Puerto Rico, language status was the major concern between 1898 and 1948 when the US government controlled education and attempted to utilize English as the language of instruction in order to Americanize the island (Torres González 2002; Pousada 1999; Morris 1996; Algren de Gutiérrez 1987; Negrón de Montilla 1970). However, status issues have cropped up periodically even after Spanish became the sole language of instruction in 1949, mainly in connection with the waging of party politics and/or the proposal of bilingual programs (Schmidt 2014; Barreto 2001; Vélez 2000; Clampitt-Dunlap 2000).

Language corpus policies are concerned with paying attention to or engineering changes in the internal structure of the language(s) being used (Ferguson 2006), including the determination of standard norms versus non-standard usage, the revision and regulation of spelling and accentuation, the treatment of foreign loanwords and archaisms, the establishment of scientific and technological terminology, and the carrying out of lexicographic research for the preparation of dictionaries. Language corpus decisions are often made by language academies, linguists, publishers, or influential intellectuals and then put into effect by educational systems (Haugen 1983).

Overall, since both Spanish and English are highly standardized codes with extensive written literatures and prescriptive reference materials, there is little need for much corpus planning in Puerto Rico, in contrast to other countries in the Caribbean and Latin America where the existence of creole and indigenous languages necessitates the creation of official orthographies and grammars (Aceto & Williams 2003; Roberts 1994; Winer 1990). The Academia Puertorriqueña de la Lengua Española has primarily concerned itself with the preparation of specialized dictionaries of standard and non-standard Puerto Rican Spanish, Anglicisms, Puerto Rican regionalisms, and occupational jargon; the explanation of standard Puerto Rican Spanish grammatical norms; and the description and historical analysis of social dialects of Spanish on the island, but its public impact has been rather limited.[1]

Language acquisition policies refer to the design of curricula and materials for the development of linguistic proficiency in a language or set of languages, either as vehicles of instruction or as academic content (Tollefson 1981, 1991). They also include the recruitment of teachers and the training necessary for teachers to utilize the curricula and materials effectively. Language acquisition planning is primarily the work of educational planners, textbook companies, and administrators, although once again, it is implemented by classroom teachers. Universities are also involved, since much pre-service and in-service pedagogical training occurs through university degree and certificate granting programs.

Another language acquisition concern, which is also closely linked to language status planning, is the development of positive attitudes toward the process of learning other languages and toward the speakers of those languages. A number of studies of attitudes toward English in Puerto Rico indicate complex mixed emotions (Schenk 2011; Lugo 2002; Schweers & Vélez 1999; Clachar 1997b; López Laguerre 1989); however, this ambivalence has not been adequately addressed in educational planning. Other studies show an increasing willingness among young Puerto Ricans to learn English. Pizarro (2006) found that freshman UPR, Río Piedras students who had studied in a Spanish-medium high school maintained a high average in English at both the high school and university levels, held positive attitudes toward English (while not devaluing their Spanish), and planned to use their English to pursue professional careers. There is also recent research that indicates that in some areas of the island (e.g., Bayamón) a wholeheartedly positive attitude toward English is developing, accompanied by the very controversial notion that knowing Spanish may not be the defining feature of being Puerto Rican (Domínguez Rosado 2013).

It should be noted that there is no official body that directly addresses language planning issues in Puerto Rico. The Language Planning Institute, which resulted from a Senate investigation into language matters (Ostolaza Bey 2001), was approved on August 9, 2002 but never funded or convened. On July 29, 2010, the law authorizing the Institute was revoked because neither the political climate nor the economic situation of the island favored the creation of a new administrative body. In January of 2013, Senator Antonio J. Fas Alzamora presented PR Senate Bill 266 to restore the Institute, with the stated goals of protecting and maintaining the Spanish language, facilitating and accelerating the learning of English, and making possible the learning of other languages, particularly French and Portuguese. The new bill (which has not yet been passed)[2] included within the Institute's responsibilities the creation of language testing mechanisms, research comparing Spanish and English teaching results, and a study of the methods for foreign language teaching utilized at the university and lower levels (Fas Alzamora 2013; Propone restablecer 2015).

One government body that has been somewhat involved in language policy issues in Puerto Rico is the Instituto de Cultura Puertorriqueña (Institute of Puerto Rican Culture), whose website can be found at www.icp.gobierno.pr/. Its purpose (as set out in Law 89 on June 21, 1955) is to conserve, promote, enrich, and disseminate the cultural values of the Puerto Rican people and foment a deep understanding and appreciation of these values. Language is central to cultural values, and the ICP deals with language in some of its publications. Most notably, in 2004, it published in book format the study on language carried out by the Puerto Rican Senate titled *Informe sobre el idioma en Puerto Rico*.

Periodically, non-governmental organizations dedicated to language advocacy crop up. For example, on August 19, 2008, a lawsuit (*Diffenderfer v. Gómez-Colón*) was filed by American residents on the island to object to violations of the voting rights of non-Spanish speakers. Three weeks before the November 2008 elections, Federal District Court Judge José Antonio Fusté ordered that the ballots be printed in both Spanish and English because "the Spanish-only ballots violate the Voting Rights Act, the Equal Protection Clause, and the First Amendment" (*Diffenderfer*, 587 F. Supp. 2d at 343). He also certified the suit for class action and awarded the plaintiffs $67,550.34 in attorney fees. The lawsuit stimulated the formation of a coalition that succeeded on September 7, 2009 in obtaining the passage of an amendment (Law 90) to the electoral law of Puerto Rico, obligating the printing of thousands of bilingual ballots (Olivera-Soto 2010; Hernández Vivoni 2009).

From the opposite pole of public opinion, in 2009, a group of Puerto Rican lawyers and intellectuals created an association called *Unidos por Nuestro Idioma* to protest the utilization of English on public signage and police cars in locales like Guaynabo and to uphold Spanish as the "natural, everyday language of Puerto

Ricans."[3] They prepared a manifesto of 13 points that affirmed the importance of Spanish in Puerto Rican identity and culture, as well as its prominence world-wide, and stated unequivocally the need to preserve and defend it in the face of "progressive deterioration" of vocabulary, basic oral and written skills, and critical thinking. They clarified that they held no prejudice toward English; however, they were concerned about the mixing of Spanish and English, which they felt demonstrated inadequate knowledge and management of the two languages. They called for recognition of the primacy of Spanish and acknowledgement of the historically proven inefficacy of programs that force English upon Puerto Rican students. They closed by asserting that the Spanish language was a non-negotiable feature of Puerto Rican society, regardless of the political status of the island (*Manifiesto* 2009: 1; Rivera Quiñones 2009). The group succeeded in organizing an impressive march on the Capital, which nevertheless did not result in any appreciable change in the existing language policy.

The activism of such groups contrasts with the sociolinguistic reality of the island as described by a study carried out by Hispania Research Corporation in 1992, which confirmed that Spanish was used in most social domains on the island and that the greatest exposure to English came via books (i.e., schooling) and cable television. More recent research (Carroll 2008) indicates that the Internet has become the central arena for English language use in Puerto Rico, since Puerto Rican users of MySpace and Facebook create a bilingual linguistic continuum by code switching constantly between Spanish and English.[4] Neither of these studies supports the claims that Spanish is threatened by English or that English speakers are discriminated against in Puerto Rico.

2 Development of English proficiency

2.1 School-based instruction

In spite of significant effort, expense, and a plethora of overtly assimilationist language education policies between 1898 and 1948 (Torres González 2002), the US government was unsuccessful in making English the language of the Puerto Rican masses by obligating it as the medium of instruction (Clachar 1997b). Since 1949, instruction in the public schools has been almost exclusively in Spanish, with English as a required subject at all levels up through college. While the number of English speakers has steadily increased since then (see Figure 11.1), with 50 percent of the population indicating on the 1990 census some ability to speak English, in 2000, only 17.6 percent of islanders considered that they spoke English "very well" (U. S. Census Bureau 2000).

There have been many attempts to improve the quality of English instruction in Puerto Rico. Preferential pay scales for English teachers were set early in the twentieth century to attract English-proficient Puerto Rican instructors, and American teachers have been enlisted at different points to teach English on the island (Rodríguez Sanfiorenzo 2009; Osuna 1949). Nevertheless, the Puerto Rico Department of Education cannot compete with the considerably higher pay scales

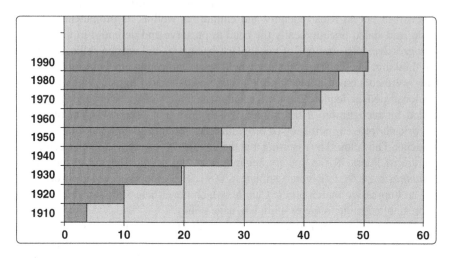

Figure 11.1 Percentage of Puerto Rican population aged 10 or older that speaks English to some degree, 1910–1990 (US Bureau of the Census figures reported in Torres Gonzalez 2002, p. 152)

in the United States, and English-proficient Puerto Rican teachers are regularly recruited to work in stateside bilingual programs (Velázquez 2013; Burgos 2013). Some of the teachers who stay behind on the island fall into the habit of teaching the English class in Spanish to accommodate the students' limited English skills. This furthers a common perception among students that English is a "Mickey Mouse" course that one can pass without really making an effort or learning the language. In addition, the English textbooks utilized in the public schools are designed for use among minority group ESL learners in the States and are not truly relevant to islanders' interests or needs. There are very few locally written books for young people in English. It appears that Puerto Rican youths are learning more English from the Internet, radio, and cable television than from classroom instruction.

To make things worse, English and Spanish are constantly characterized as combatants instead of as complements. Drops in Spanish test scores are often attributed to the time spent on English (Agencia F 1997). The College Board scores of high school seniors between 1985 and 2008 reveal two very clear patterns: 1) the public school students score lower in both Spanish and English than do the private school students; and 2) the Spanish scores among the public school students have been decreasing since 1985, while the English scores have remained fairly constant and slightly lower than the Spanish scores (College Board Puerto Rico y América Latina 2009). Blaming the decline in Spanish scores on the English classes is illogical since most public school students receive only an hour of English a day and carry out the rest of their academic endeavors in Spanish. Private school English scores have surpassed Spanish scores since 1995 probably because the private schools stress English strongly to comply with parental expectations; however, their Spanish scores never dip down as far as the public school students' scores, most likely due to the greater resources available in the private schools.

Despite the existence of various bilingual public schools and numerous private schools that teach in English only or in both languages,[5] the island lacks a cohesive language education policy with regard to bilingualism. Various schemes to create a bilingual citizenry have been tried, most notably that of Secretary of Public Education Víctor Fajardo in 1997 (Fajardo, Albino, Báez, et. Al. 1997) and that promoted by Governor Luis Fortuño in 2012 (Marcano 2012); however, their implementation was undermined by rushed or limited planning, opposition from teachers (Navarro 1997), shortages of trained personnel and materials, and lack of continuity and follow-through due to post-election administration changes.

2.2 English as tool of business and professional endeavor

Language-related issues abound in the commercial and professional arenas and have serious implications for education.[6] Strauch (1992) found that most Puerto Ricans "supervalorize" English as an instrument of socioeconomic ascent. Consequently, the use of English and Anglicisms is most common among upwardly mobile individuals such as doctors, scientists, pharmaceutical employees, engineers, business executives, lawyers, media personnel, and computer technicians (Alcina Caudet 2001; Cuadrado Rodríguez 1993; Huyke Freiría 1973; Mellado de Hunter 1961).

Most businesses in Puerto Rico have their own informal rules for language use. The tourist industry and US-based corporations usually hire employees with strong English skills, while local companies often include "bilingual" in their classified ads[7] but do little to evaluate or utilize these skills. Many jobs in Puerto Rico require only minimal English skills, but there is a strong popular conviction that English is equated with economic success. The media lend credence to this belief by depicting bilingual speakers on the island as trendy, modern consumers of luxury merchandise. Coupled with the current economic crisis (14.7 percent official unemployment rate), this presentation stimulates Puerto Rican youths to immigrate to the United States in search of work rather than remain at home and fight to improve the local state of affairs.

In addition, it is common practice in Puerto Rico to utilize English in naming businesses and promoting products, regardless of the nature of the business and its language demands (i.e., Quality Roofing, Smart Computer PR, Yoly's Hair Cut, Los Primos Auto Collision, etc.). The longstanding association of English with business success is further perpetuated by the multitude of American franchises (e.g., McDonald's, Sears, K-Mart, KFC, etc.).

Furthermore, most products sold in Puerto Rico come from the United States and are therefore labeled in English. Every trip to the supermarket, drug store, or mall exposes Puerto Ricans to English, although many of the product names may be hispanized and phonologically integrated into Spanish (e.g., *Visine* pronounced as vee-**see**-neh instead of vay-**zeen**). It should be noted that Puerto Rican consumers may not appreciate the full semantic content of product names (e.g., Tide, Pamper, Caress, Renuzit, etc.) due to limited English vocabularies but still develop product loyalty from the omnipresence of the merchandise in local stores.

Mazak (2008) carried out an ethnographic study of the uses of English text in a rural Puerto Rican community and discovered that rural adults utilized and wrote English texts that pertained primarily to the social domains of bureaucracy, health, and finances. Thus even in areas distant from the metropolitan center, English is linked to the acquisition of services and monetary benefits and cannot be ignored in the planning of language education policy.

2.3 English in the legal system

Puerto Rico has had two official languages, Spanish and English, since 1902 when the United States set up a civilian government on the island. The Official Language Act of 1902 was approved primarily for the benefit of the English-monolingual colonial governors and the implementation of a bald-faced Americanization plan. While the text of the law refers to treating the two languages "indistinctly," the fact is that English was the language of power, particularly in the local courts. In 1966, a law was passed enforcing Spanish as the language of the insular courts with special provisions made for non-Spanish-speaking individuals who came before the law. In 1991, under the administration of pro-Commonwealth Rafael Hernández Colón, Spanish was made the sole official language of Puerto Rico (Law 4, April 5, 1991), but this only lasted until 1993 when pro-statehood Pedro Roselló was elected governor and fulfilled a campaign promise to reinstate Spanish and English as co-official languages (Law 1, January 28, 1993). This was one of the most blatant illustrations of the intense interaction between party politics and language policy on the island.

Interestingly enough, the US federal court in Puerto Rico has always held its sessions in English (Pousada 2008). Interpreters are provided for witnesses and accused who do not speak English, and Spanish testimony is translated into English for the consideration of the bilingual jury members. English is the language of record, even though virtually all participants are native Spanish speakers. The official explanation is that this approach is necessary to facilitate the appeals process in the Boston Circuit Court; however, several cogent proposals have been made to translate only the contested parts of the testimony in the case of an appeal (cf. Justice Hiram Cancio's pronouncements in 1989, reported in Baralt 2004).

2.4 Concept of PR English

The English spoken in Puerto Rico does not always follow the rules of standard US English. Like the many "Englishes" spoken around the world, Puerto Rican English (PRE) has a flavor all its own. As would be expected, it is heavily influenced by the lexicon, semantics, phonology, and syntax of Puerto Rican Spanish. The official recognition of PRE would have important language policy implications, but this is highly controversial.

Back in 1971, Rose Nash coined the term *Englañol* to describe the English spoken by Puerto Ricans in PR. Englañol has false cognates used in a Spanish manner, loan translations, and spelling pronunciations. Some examples of *Englañol* would be:

1   My **assistance** [*asistencia* = attendance] in class has been poor this semester.
2   We need to **pass the vacuum** (*pasar el vacuum* = vacuum) before the party.
3   I'd like to **separate** [*separar* = reserve] that room for the meeting next week.

Nash considered Englañol to be "the true standard" in Puerto Rico: "With very few exceptions, it is Englañol rather than Standard English that is taught in the public schools, from the first grade through the university level" (1971: 121).

Later studies suggested the emergence of a new English along the lines of Indian English, Nigerian English, or Australian English. Schweers (1993) proposed the possibility of a Puerto Rican variety of English and recommended research to describe its users and its functional context. Walsh (1994) identified a number of features of PRE, such as de-spirantization of [ð] and [θ] to [d] and [t], de-affrication of [dʒ] to [ʒ] or [j], devoicing of [z], confusion of [ʃ] and [tʃ], and shifting stress to the last element of compound nouns (e.g., pronouncing ***dish**washer* as dish**washer**). She argued that the impact of Spanish and the fact that the majority of English teachers in Puerto Rico used the local dialect of English contributed to the maintenance of the two varieties of English. She recommended that teachers recognize the existence of local practices and adapt their English lessons to that reality (Ortiz Garcia 1997).

In 1997, Blau and Dayton carried out a study of the acceptability of PRE among 223 subjects, including UPR students in basic, intermediate, and honors English classes; Puerto Rican English teachers; and native speakers of English residing in the United States. Task 1 entailed reading real sentences containing lexical items that were posited as belonging to PRE. Participants had to correct any sentences they felt merited repair. The test sentences included false cognates such as *interpreted* (for "sang"), *domination* (for "mastery"), *approved* (for "passed"), and *celebrated* (for "held"). Task 2 consisted of multiple choice questions in which target words were replaced by blanks that respondents filled as they saw fit. The researchers also interviewed an island-raised English teacher, a return migrant English teacher, and an English native speaker. They found that native English speakers accepted the least number of PRE items. As student proficiency increased, students accepted fewer PRE items; in fact, at the honors English level, the students' scores equaled those of the teachers on the multiple choice task. There was additionally considerable difference between the acceptability rates of the PRE forms on the two tasks by the Puerto Rican teachers (61 percent and 30 percent) versus the native English speakers (28 percent and 3 percent). Given that English teachers are trained to teach standard language forms, they would be expected to approach native speaker levels; however, it appears that they are aiming at Puerto Rican English norms, rather than US English standards.

Fayer et al. (1998) and Fayer (2000) investigated linguistic reformulations of English in Puerto Rico based on Spanish models, such as inverted word order in noun clauses (e.g., *They tell me how important **is the bill** for them.*), new lexical creations based on Spanish forms, borrowings from Spanish (e.g., *There are many **urbanizations** [public housing projects] in Puerto Rico.*), and hybrid compounds utilizing English and Spanish words (e.g., *Many people were arrested at the **drug punto** [place drugs are sold]*). They considered that there was sufficient syntactic, lexical, and morphological evidence to propose the existence of PRE. This was further confirmed by Schweers and Hudders (2000), who also collected considerable lexical, phonological, and discourse level evidence of distinctive patterns in the English of Puerto Ricans.

Nickels (2005) considers that "the variety of English spoken in Puerto Rico is only beginning to be identified as a variety in its own right through research, but only time will tell whether Puerto Ricans will claim ownership of this variety" (234). She makes a very interesting point regarding the recognition of PRE and the teaching of English on the island.

Perhaps labeling English in Puerto Rico as Puerto Rican English would encourage learning of the language as "original" and without any resentments or feelings of betrayal to Hispanic heritage, thus allowing the teaching and learning of English to flourish and enter into the next stage in the life cycle of non-native varieties. (235)

3 Development of academic discourse structures in Spanish

3.1 The Language Academy

The Academia Puertorriqueña de la Lengua Española (the Puerto Rican Spanish Language Academy), directed by Dr. José Luis Vega, is at present the only agency that directly addresses language corpus issues on the island.[8] Its goal is to promote the correct use, conservation, and study of Puerto Rican Spanish. It carries out linguistic research to amend existing grammars, document historical changes, carry out spelling and accentuation revision, and contribute to an international Spanish language corpus project called CORPES. The Academy publishes grammars, general and specialized dictionaries, special editions of classic works, and tributes to significant literary figures. It is greatly concerned with the development of *lengua culta* (standard or cultured language) and carries out regular campaigns to increase linguistic awareness, including requests for local submissions to the *Real Academia Española* dictionary and a Facebook page that posts regular guides to standard Spanish usage (www.facebook.com/pages/Academia-Puertorrique%C3%B1a-de-la-Lengua-Espa%C3%B1ola/297768212160?fref=nf). One of the stated goals of the Academy is the early identification of foreign borrowings in order to provide native alternatives that facilitate linguistic uniformity. Its online journal called *Dilo* (Say it) informs the public on different aspects of language structure and usage and responds to questions regarding spelling, grammar, and word selection.

In December of 2010, the Academy initiated a campaign to popularize the use of typically Puerto Rican words called "*Español puertorriqueño: ¡Atrévete y dilo!*" (Puerto Rican Spanish: Dare to say it!). Fifty 30-second radio capsules were recorded by influential artists and public figures, and 75 Puerto Rican words were promoted during the campaign.

The Academia has a moderately normative effect upon the teaching of Spanish on the island since it serves as an authoritative voice and publishes reference books that are employed as source material for textbooks and other pedagogical documents. Nevertheless, its work is not widely known outside of academia despite occasional televised programs and the new Facebook page.

3.2 Effects of English contact on Puerto Rican Spanish

English loanwords are widespread in Puerto Rican Spanish, and being communicatively competent in Puerto Rico includes knowing how to use Anglicisms while speaking Spanish. English structures, usually phonologically and morphologically integrated into Puerto Rican Spanish, are an intrinsic part of the local lexicon. The loans can be single nouns or verbs (e.g., *dona* [donut], *matre* [mattress], *bómper* [bumper], *faxear* [to fax], etc.) or phrases (e.g., *Dame un breiquecito.* [Give me a little break. or Let me break into line/pass in front of you.]). Some occupational groups are more prone to use Anglicisms than others (e.g., auto mechanics, sports announcers, fashion/beauty consultants, and computer technicians), but everyone, regardless of English language proficiency, employs them on a daily basis.

It should be noted that the incorporation of English loans into local speech repertoires is a global trend. Linguists view borrowings non-judgmentally as an inevitable consequence of contact between speech communities and point to the ways in which they enrich vocabulary by increasing the number of synonyms and expressing nuances not present in equivalent native words. In and of themselves, they do not represent a danger to the native language.

Maria Vaquero (1990) carried out a study of Anglicisms in the Puerto Rican press and isolated various strategies for incorporating English forms into Spanish. Among these are: 1) creating a Spanish-looking word based on an English word form instead of its Spanish equivalent (e.g., *coincidentalmente* instead of *de forma coincidente*); 2) using Spanish words with English meanings (e.g., *bloques* [building blocks] for "street blocks" instead of *cuadras*); 3) translating literally from English into Spanish (e.g., *hacer sentido* to mean "make sense" instead of *tener sentido*); and 4) using an English word to refer to a specific aspect of the meaning of a particular referent (e.g., *magacín* for popular magazines and *revista* for news magazines and journals).

Humberto López Morales carried out a comparative study of the use of Anglicisms in Madrid, Mexico City, and San Juan, PR in 1992. Figure 11.2 shows how Puerto Ricans have the highest number of Anglicisms, but Madrid and Mexico City are not far behind.

In 1996, John Lipski wrote about a number of syntactic influences of English upon Puerto Rican Spanish. Among the Anglicized examples discussed were: *¿Cómo te gustó la playa?* [How did you like the beach?]; *El problema está siendo considerado.* [The problem is being considered.]; *Te llamo para atrás.* [I'll call you back.]; and *Él sabe cómo hablar inglés.* [He knows how to speak English.].

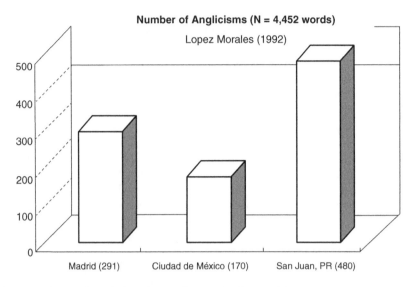

Figure 11.2 Use of Anglicisms in Madrid, Mexico City, and San Juan

Amparo Morales (1986, 1989, 2001) looked at the use of present continuous verbs such as *¿Qué estás haciendo?* [What are you doing?] instead of the simple present form *¿Qué haces?* to see if it had resulted from English contact. She concluded that such syntactic influences were low in frequency and could be found in other Hispanic speech communities, even those with little direct English influence. In some cases, they were retentions of older forms of Spanish. She pointed out that not every variation in Puerto Rican Spanish syntax was automatically due to English.

More linguistic research needs to be done on the influence of English on Puerto Rican Spanish to determine its current extent, its effects on the society, and how educators are dealing with it.

4 Eradication of functional illiteracy in Spanish

Literacy has long been a language policy issue in Puerto Rico, particularly in rural and urban working class neighborhoods. Table 11.1 presents the illiteracy figures from 1898 to 1990.

In 1898, when the Spanish ceded Puerto Rico to the United States, the illiteracy rate was 79.6 percent. In 1926, high school students from Vieques and Caguas volunteered to give night classes to illiterate adults. During the 1930s, the federal Puerto Rico Emergency Relief Administration (PRERA) operated 22 literacy camps around the island. During the 1940s, combatting illiteracy was an integral part of industrializing the island. By 1950, only 24.7 percent of Puerto Ricans

Table 11.1 Illiteracy in Puerto Rico based on Ortiz (1990)

Year	% of population
1898	79.6
1899	79.0
1910	65.5
1920	55.0
1930	41.4
1940	31.5
1950	24.7
1960	16.6
1970	10.8
1980	11.5
1990	10.4
2000	NA

remained illiterate. In 1954, the Literacy Program (*Programa de Alfabetización*) was created and, in 1958, the Program for Continuing Education. By 1970, illiteracy was reduced to 10.8 percent. During the 1980s, there were programs of peer teaching, education for the homeless, and library-based literacy classes.

In the island census of 1990, 10.4 percent of Puerto Ricans (245,291) indicated that they could not read and write in Spanish, their native tongue. It should be noted that this is still very high for a supposedly industrialized society. In 2000, the Puerto Rico census bureau began utilizing the US census questionnaire, which does not include a literacy question, so there are no data for that year. However, we do know from the 2000 census that more than 25 percent of island residents aged 25 and over had less than a ninth-grade education, which would imply a limited level of productive literacy. In 2000, a creative literacy curriculum called *Alfabetización: La Magia de Leer* (Literacy: The Magic of Reading) was put into effect. It featured reading, math, learning games, flexible hours, and alliances with other government agencies. By May of 2005, it had given service to 42,334 adults.

Disdier Flores, Pesante González, and Marazzi (2012) reported the findings of the 2010 Literacy Survey of Puerto Rico (*Encuesta de Alfabetización de Puerto Rico*). This survey (intended to provide the missing census data on literacy) was carried out via telephone interviews with a representative sample of 6,574 people aged 18 or older.[9] They were asked 11 questions related to literacy skills. Statistical analysis was made of 244 variables. The findings indicated that overall literacy stood at 92 percent,[10] with slightly lower figures for females and for the elderly.[11] More than six percent of the participants stated that they needed help to understand what they read. Only 45.8 percent reported reading books weekly, while 98.5 percent watched TV or listened to the radio. Among the men, 7.5 percent had trouble writing and 18.5 percent of the interviewees had children at home who had difficulties reading (1).

There was a strong correlation between poverty and illiteracy. In Adjuntas, where illiteracy was 30.0 percent, 79.0 percent of the people lived under the poverty level, and Maricao was a close second with 22.3 percent illiteracy and 71 percent poverty (17). Disdier Flores and Pesante González (2013) correlated literacy achievement with various health indicators and discovered that literate individuals were more likely to be healthy, have a lower incidence of diabetes, and be more active physically.

In 2012, the Education Commission of the House of Representatives in Puerto Rico reported that the literacy campaign of the Department of Education had failed in eradicating illiteracy since so many young people were dropping out of the schools and thus not completing their education. This points to a very serious problem. Functionally illiterate youths cannot operate effectively in a technologically advanced society and generally wind up among the permanently unemployed, the underemployed, or the criminally involved.

Literacy has many non-linguistic benefits. It helps to eradicate poverty, reduce infant mortality, control population size, promote gender equality, and guarantee sustainable development (UNESCO 2006). However, full societal literacy requires a good curricular design, adequate planning, continuous collection and publication of data, political and economic backing by the government agencies, and community support.[12] It also necessitates making school facilities available to communities during the evenings and weekends when adults and adolescents can attend classes. Conquering functional illiteracy will pay off in many ways and must not be ignored by educators and policymakers.

5 Education of immigrants and return migrants

While there is a general perception that Puerto Rican schools are relatively homogenous in ethnic makeup, the reality is that they receive increasing numbers of students from the Dominican Republic, Haiti, or other Caribbean islands, as well as return migrants who have been residing in the States. Dominicans speak a distinctive variety of Spanish, and Haitians and US return migrants may have little or no formal training in Spanish. Dominicans and Haitians generally have few or non-existent English skills, and the return migrants who are native speakers of English may speak non-standard varieties that are not accepted in the schools in Puerto Rico (Pousada 1994; Clachar 1997a).

The Department of Education of Puerto Rico operates the *Programa de Limitaciones Lingüísticas en Español e Inmigrantes* (Language Instruction for Limited Spanish Proficient and Immigrant Students), which is intended for all students who speak a language other than Spanish at home or who come from outside of the United States and its territories. This Spanish as a Second Language program, funded by Title III-A in compliance with federal No Child Left Behind policies, seeks to teach such students to read, write, speak, and understand Spanish; perform effectively in content areas; master the curricular standards for their grade; and integrate themselves into Puerto Rican society. Students are selected via a Home Language Survey and given a screening and placement test. Teachers receive special training for dealing with this population. In addition to classroom support, the program provides family literacy training, workshops for parents, tutoring, mentoring, and counseling.

However, this program is insufficient and does not reach the neediest immigrants, who may not be documented or may not participate in the school system.

Much more must be done to identify and give service to Puerto Rico's growing immigrant population. In addition, Puerto Rican return migrants may not qualify for this program since Spanish is spoken in their households, and many must depend on other means to get help with their sometimes limited or non-standard Spanish skills and their often challenging cultural adaptation to life on the island.

6 Teaching of additional foreign languages

Most public schools in Puerto Rico do not offer classes in foreign languages other than English. Private schools sometimes offer classes in French. The majority of students first encounter foreign languages at the university level. The UPR in Río Piedras is famous for its intensive foreign language courses in French, Italian, Portuguese, and German. It also offers courses in Japanese, Mandarin, Latin, and Haitian Creole on a less consistent basis, and the English Department of the College of Humanities offers a year-long course in Afro-Caribbean Creole English as part of its graduate program.

People often point to the successful learning of such foreign languages in a year or two and compare it to the far less stellar accomplishments of students in English despite many more years of instruction and exposure. However, there are various things to consider. First of all, the students who elect to study foreign languages are self-selected, intrinsically motivated, and strongly attracted to the "exotic" and "prestigious" nature of the languages. Second, these languages have not been pushed down their throats as an obligatory part of the school curriculum since elementary school and are not tainted with a history of colonial imposition on the island. Thus there are few attitudinal barriers to overcome, and that makes all the difference.

The essential tasks involved in teaching any additional language, regardless of whether it is conceived of as a second or a foreign language, are the same. The identical requirements of well-trained instructors, attractive teaching materials, and adequate exposure to or immersion in the language are operative. The only real pedagogical difference lies in the degree of availability of extra-curricular language resources. Typically, a second language program relies on ready access to real-life language learning situations outside the classroom, while a foreign language program has to seek out or create simulated or online interactional settings for language acquisition or provide travel opportunities to its students. Puerto Rico possesses aspects of both second and foreign language environments and needs to utilize them all in the teaching of both English and other foreign languages. A change in perspective to "X as an additional language" would go a long way in advancing the island beyond the unproductive wrangling over labels for language programs (Pousada 2003).

7 Conclusion

This article has attempted to present an overview of the myriad of language policy issues that educators in Puerto Rico encounter today and some of the efforts that have been made to resolve them over the years. The teaching of English has been a major concern in Puerto Rico for quite some time; however, the development of cognitive academic discourse skills in Spanish, the elimination of functional illiteracy in Spanish, and the education of immigrants and return migrants in Spanish have become increasingly problematic matters. Less frequently discussed issues are the evolution of Puerto Rican English as a distinctive variety and the teaching of foreign languages, but these should not be pushed off the language-planning agenda.

The need for structured and linguistically based language planning in Puerto Rico has been declared repeatedly over the years (cf. Ostolaza Bey 2001; Pousada 1996, 1985; Schweers 1993; Resnick 1993). Nevertheless, one of the biggest obstacles is the stranglehold that party politics and nepotism have over all aspects of public policy in Puerto Rico. Many creative language-related programs have been initiated and then abandoned with each new election. There is virtually no continuity of policy and very little evaluation of the effectiveness of any given policy. Therefore the wheel is constantly having to be reinvented and the frustration level of all stakeholders keeps rising. This leads to defeatist postures and acceptance of less-than-effective programs.

It is hoped that the brief review provided in this article will nourish an interest in the field of language planning and policymaking and provoke the sort of productive discussion that is needed for real changes to occur. Linguists must be involved in much of the work, particularly that involving language corpus revision and/or regulation; however, there must also be a recognition of the interdisciplinary nature of language policy and the unavoidable political factors that must be taken into account in coming to solutions that everyone can live with.

Notes

1   The Academia did address the language status issue in a small book in 1998; however, the major thrust of its work has been on language corpus matters.
2   The bill was filed on January 17, 2013 and referred to three Senate commissions that deal with education, culture, and public finances (Educación, Formación y Desarrollo del Individuo; Turismo, Cultura, Recreación y Deportes y Globalización; Hacienda y Finanzas Públicas). According to the Office of Legislative Services, it has progressed no further than the April 2, 2014 meeting of the Tourism and Culture commission (www.oslpr.org/legislatura/tl2013/tl_medida_print2.asp?r=PS266).
3   Original Spanish: "el lenguaje cotidiano y natural de los puertorriqueños."
4   It should also be noted that video gaming in Puerto Rico is another domain that favors interaction in the English language. Gamers often have surprisingly good vocabularies in English, especially those involved in role playing games (RPG). In fact, there is ongoing research into using video games pedagogically to improve English acquisition in Puerto Rico (Horowitz García 2013).
5   There are Protestant schools on the island which are taught exclusively in English due to the fact that they were set up by American missionaries.
6   Business and professional education at the university level typically emphasizes English, since it is required for communication with and certification by corporate headquarters and professional licensing boards in the United States.
7   Muntaner (1992) analyzed employment advertisements in Puerto Rican newspapers and ascertained that 80 percent called for English skills, and 36 percent sought completely bilingual candidates.

8 The College Board of Puerto Rico deals with the testing of language and math skills among all students in Puerto Rico and is therefore involved in the evaluation of language corpus planning. In its bulletin *Academia*, it regularly publishes test results. It also organizes conferences for teachers in which language issues are discussed and tests teachers for certification via the *Pruebas de Certificación de Maestros* (PCMAS).

9 It should be noted that using telephone interviews skews the data, since poor or homeless people may not have phones and are thus not represented in the sample. These are precisely the sector with the highest level of illiteracy.

10 This contrasts somewhat with the 2011 figure of 90.3 percent cited by the CIA's *World Factbook*.

11 Illiteracy was highest among the rural elderly (32.3 percent). It should also be noted that, in 2010, the World Bank indicated that the literacy rate among Puerto Rican youths (ages 15 to 25) was only 85 percent, meaning that 15 percent were unable to read and write (with understanding) a short, simple statement about their everyday life. Therefore the illiteracy problem existed both among the elderly and among the young.

12 Puerto Rico would profit from an examination of the highly effective literacy campaigns of Cuba and Nicaragua (e.g., Murphy 2012; Keeble 2002; Miller 1985; Hirshon 1984), which transformed those societies in a very short time.

Bibliography

Academia Puertorriqueña de la Lengua Española. (1998). *La enseñanza del español y del inglés en Puerto Rico: Una polémica de cien años*. San Juan: Academia Puertorriqueña de la Lengua Española.

Aceto, M., & Williams, J. P. (Eds.). (2003). *Contact Englishes of the Eastern Caribbean*. Amsterdam, Philadelphia: John Benjamins.

Agencia EFE. (1997, September 22). El bilingüismo en Puerto Rico amenaza con ser un "nilingüismo." *El País*. Retrieved from http://elpais.com/diario/1997/09/22/cultura/874879208_850215.html

Alcina Caudet, M. A. (2001). El español como lengua de la ciencia y de la medicina. *Revista Médico Interamericano*, *20*(1), 30–2.

Algren de Gutiérrez, E. (1987). *The movement against teaching English in the schools of Puerto Rico*. Lanham, New York & London: University Press.

Baralt, G. (2004). *History of the federal court in Puerto Rico*. San Juan: Publicaciones Populares.

Barreto, A. A. (2001). Statehood, the English language, and the politics of education in Puerto Rico. *Polity*, *34*(1), 89–105.

Blau, E., & Dayton, E. (1997). Puerto Rico as an English-using society. In R. M. Hammond & M. G. MacDonald (Eds.), *Linguistic studies in honor of Bohdan Saciuk* (pp. 137–148). West Lafayette, IN: Learning Systems, Inc.

Burgos, C. (2013, October 28). Estado de Florida recluta maestros en la Isla: La Universidad del Este es la anfitriona del reclutamiento de maestros certificados para el distrito escolar de Condado Polk, en Florida. *Metro Puerto Rico*. Retrieved from www.metro.pr/locales/estado-de-florida-recluta-maestros-en-la-isla/ pGXmjB!dviqMyfzKGJ4w/

Carroll, K. (2008). Puerto Rican language use on MySpace. *Centro Journal*, *20*(1), 96–111.

Clachar, A. (1997a). Ethnolinguistic identity and Spanish proficiency in a paradoxical situation: The case of Puerto Rican return migrants. *Journal of Multilingual and Multicultural Development*, *18*(2), 107–125.

Clachar, A. (1997b). Resistance to the English language in Puerto Rico: Toward a theory of language and intergroup distinctiveness. *Linguistics & Education*, *9*(1), 69–97.

Clampitt-Dunlap, S. (2000). Nationalism and native-language maintenance in Puerto Rico. *International Journal of the Sociology of Language, 142*, 25–34.

College Board Puerto Rico y América Latina. (2009). *Promedios de las Pruebas de Aprovechamiento Académico en Español e Inglés*. Programa de Evaluación y Admisión Universitaria. Retrieved from http://tendenciaspr.uprrp.edu/Educacion/Rendimiento_Academico/TABLAS_PEAU_ESC_PUBLICAS_PRIVADAS_1985_2008.pdf

Cooper, R. L. (1990). *Language planning and social change*. Cambridge: Cambridge University Press.

Cuadrado Rodríguez, D. (1993). *Bilingualism among Eastern professionals in Puerto Rico* (Unpublished master's thesis). University of Puerto Rico.

Disdier Flores, O. M., Pesante González, F., & Marazzi Santiago, M. (2012). *Encuesta de alfabetización de Puerto Rico*. Instituto de Estadísticas de Puerto Rico. Año natural 2010. San Juan: Estado Libre Asociado de Puerto Rico.

Disdier Flores, O. M., & Pesante González, F. (2013). La alfabetización de adultos y algunos aspectos de su relación con salud: Puerto Rico 2010. Paper presented at the *Congreso Puertorriqueño de Investigación en la Educación*, San Juan, PR, March 8, 2013.

Domínguez Rosado, B. (2013). Language and identity: The study of a possible ongoing change in attitudes towards American English and Puerto Rican Spanish in Puerto Rico (PhD dissertation). University of Puerto Rico, Río Piedras.

Fajardo, V., Albino, I, Báez, N. C. (1997). *Proyecto para formar un ciudadano bilingüe*. San Juan: Departamento de Educación, Gobierno de Puerto Rico.

Fas Alzamora, J. A. (2013). *Proyecto del Senado 266*. Retrieved from http://senado.pr.gov/Proyectos%20del%20Senado%202013/ps0266.pdf

Fayer, J. (2000). Functions of English in Puerto Rico. In C. Ramírez & R. Torres (Eds.), *Languages of former colonial power and former colonies: The case of Puerto Rico* (pp. 89–102). Berlin: Mouton de Gruyter.

Fayer, J., Castro, J., Díaz, M., & Plata, M. (1998). English in Puerto Rico. *English Today, 14* (1), 39–44.

Ferguson, G. (2006). *Language planning and education*. Edinburgh: Edinburgh University Press.

Fishman, J. A., Ferguson, C., & Das Gupta, J. (Eds.). (1968). *Language problems of developing nations*. New York: John Wiley and Son.

Gibson, F. (2006). *Language planning and education*. Edinburgh: Edinburgh University Press.

Haugen, E. (1983). The implementation of corpus planning: theory and practice. In J. Cobarrubias & J. A. Fishman (Eds.), *Progress in language planning: International perspectives* (pp. 269–289). Berlin: Mouton.

Hernández Vivoni, M. (2009). Letter to Thomas Rivera Schatz, president of the Puerto Rico Senate, certifying approval of Ley 90, September 7, 2009.

Hirshon, S. L. (1984). *And also teach them to read*. Westport, CT: Lawrence Hill & Co.

Hispania Research Corporation. (1992). *Memorando analítico sobre el estudio del idioma en Puerto Rico*. San Juan, PR: Hispania Research Corporation.

Horowitz García, K. (2013, Fall). Breaking with tradition: Video games as an alternative tool for ESL instruction in PR's public schools. *Hispanic Educational Technology Services Journal, 4*, 6–16. Retrieved from http://hets.org/journal/flash/vol4-1/pdf/VolIV-Fall.pdf

Huyke Freiría, I. (1973). *Vocabulario culto de San Juan: Cuatro campos léxicos* (Unpublished master's thesis). University of Puerto Rico.

Keeble, A. (2002). In the spirit of wandering teachers: The Cuban literacy campaign 1961. North Melbourne, Australia: Ocean Press.

Kerkhof, E. (2001). The myth of the dumb Puerto Rican: Circular migration and language struggle in Puerto Rico. *New West Indian Guide, 75*(3), 257–288.

Lipski, J. M. (1996). *El español de América*. Madrid: Cátedra.

López Laguerre, M. (1989). Bilingüismo en Puerto Rico: Actitudes sociolingüísticas del maestro. Río Piedras, PR: López Laguerre.

Lugo, N. (2002). Changes in perception toward learning English: A classroom investigation project. *Cuadernos de Investigación en la Educación, 17*. Retrieved from http://cie.uprrp.edu/cuaderno/ediciones/17/pdfcuaderno17/c17art2.pdf

Manifiesto de la entidad de ciudadanos Unidos por Nuestro Idioma. (2009). Retrieved from http://noticias.universia.pr/vida-universitaria/noticia/2009/05/05/131220/manifiesto-entidad-ciudadanos-unidos-idioma-(uni).html

Marcano, I. (2012, July 19). Fortuño's plan for English proficiency in Puerto Rico. *Dominican Today*. Retrieved from www.dominicantoday.com/dr/opinion/2012/7/19/44439/Fortunos-plan-for-English-proficiency-in-Puerto-Rico

Mazak, C. (2008). Negotiating *el difícil*: Uses of English text in a rural Puerto Rican community. *Centro, 20*(2), 51–71.

Mellado de Hunter, E. (1961). *Anglicismos profesionales* (Unpublished master's thesis). University of Puerto Rico, Río Piedras.

Miller, V. L. (1985). Between struggle and hope: The Nicaraguan literacy crusade. Boulder, CO: Westview Press.

Morales, A. (1986). Gramáticas en contacto: Análisis sintáctico sobre el español de Puerto Rico. San Juan, PR: Editorial Playor.

Morales, A. (1989). Algunas consideraciones sobre los fenómenos de convergencia lingüística en el español de Puerto Rico. *Asomante, 1*(2), 113–36.

Morales, A. (2001). *Diccionario de anglicismos en Puerto Rico*. San Juan: Editorial Plaza Mayor.

Morris, N. (1996). Language and identity in twentieth century Puerto Rico. *Journal of Multilingual and Multicultural Development, 17*(1), 17–32.

Muntaner, A. (1992). Política pública y planificación lingüística en el sector público en Puerto Rico. *Revista de Administración Pública, 24*(2), 117–33.

Murphy, C. (2012). *Maestra*. Produced by Women Make Movies. DVD.

Nash, R. (1971). Englañol: More language contact in Puerto Rico. *American Speech, 46*, 106–122.

Navarro, M. (1997, May 19). Puerto Rico teachers resist teaching in English. *New York Times*. Retrieved from www.nytimes.com/1997/05/19/us/puerto-rico-teachers-resist-teaching-in-english.html?pagewanted=all

Negrón de Montilla, A. (1970). *Americanization in Puerto Rico and the public school system*. Río Piedras, PR: Editorial Edil.

Nickels, E. L. (2005). English in Puerto Rico. *World Englishes, 24*(2), 227–237.

Olivera-Soto, A. L. (2010). English monolingual speakers in Puerto Rico: A new language minority group under the Voting Rights Act. *Saint Louis University Public Law Review, 30*(1), 139–169.

Ortiz, D. (1990). *Educación de adultos en Puerto Rico: Breve historia*. Retrieved from www.de.gobierno.pr/ofrecimiento-academico/191-educacion-de-adultos/441-historia-de-la-educacion-de-adultos

Ortiz García, A. L. (1997, February 25). El inglés en Puerto Rico: Balón político. *El Nuevo Día*. Retrieved from www.adendi.com/archivo.asp?num=278560&year=1997&month=2 &keyword=El%20ingl%E9s%20en%20Puerto%20Rico%20Bal%F3n%20pol%EDtico

Ostolaza Bey, M. (2001). *Informe final sobre el Idioma en Puerto Rico. En cumplimiento de la R. del S. 1 del 2 de enero de 2001*. San Juan, PR: Comisión de Educación, Ciencia y Cultura del Senado de Puerto Rico.

Osuna, J. J. (1949). *A history of education in Puerto Rico* (2nd ed.). Río Piedras: Editorial Universitaria.

Pizarro, V. (2006). The ethnolinguistic identity of the University of Puerto Rico, Rio Piedras Campus first year college students and their attitudes towards the learning of English as a Second Language (EdD dissertation). University of Puerto Rico.

Pousada, A. (1985). La planificación lingüística en Puerto Rico. *Plerus, 19*(1), 105–116.

Pousada. A. (1994). Achieving linguistic and communicative competence in two speech communities: The Puerto Rican return migrant student. In A. Carrasquillo & R. Baecher (Eds.), *Educación bilingüe en Puerto Rico/bilingual education in Puerto Rico* (pp. 51–59). Caguas, PR: Puerto Rican Association for Bilingual Education (PRABE).

Pousada, A. (1996). Puerto Rico: On the horns of a language planning dilemma. *TESOL Quarterly, 30*(3), 499–510.

Pousada, A. (1999). The singularly strange story of the English language in Puerto Rico. *Milenio, 3*, 33–60. Retrieved from http://aliciapousada.weebly.com

Pousada, A. (2003). El inglés en la universidad puertorriqueña: ¿Segunda lengua o lengua extranjera?: Perspectivas mundiales sobre un problema local. Paper presented at *Repensar las lenguas extranjeras*, University of Puerto Rico, Río Piedras, April 8–9, 2003.

Pousada, A. (2008, February 28). The mandatory use of English in the Federal Court of Puerto Rico. *Centro, 20*(2), 136–155.

Propone restablecer el Instituto de Planificación Lingüística. (2015, February 28). *Telemundo Puerto Rico*. Retrieved from www.telemundopr.com/noticias/local/Fas-Alzamora-propone-restablecer-el-Instituto-de-Planificacion_Linguistica-   294479811. html

Resnick, M. (1993). ESL and language planning in Puerto Rican education. *TESOL Quarterly, 27*(22), 259–275.

Rivera Quiñones, I. (2009, April 23). Unidos en la defensa del idioma español. *Primera Hora*. Retrieved from www.primerahora.com/noticias/puerto-rico/nota/ unidosenladefensadelidiomaespanol-292744/

Roberts, P. (1994). Integrating creole into Caribbean classrooms. *Multilingual and Multicultural Development, 15*(1), 47–62.

Rodríguez Sanfiorenzo, D. (2009).   Problems in the recruitment of english teachers from the United States by the Department of Education of Puerto Rico: 1900–1910 (Doctoral dissertation). San Juan, PR: University of Puerto Rico.

Schenk, E. (2011). Instrumental, integrative, and intrinsic: A self-determination framework for orientations towards language in a Puerto Rican community. *The Canadian Journal of Applied Linguistics, 14*(1), 155–176.

Schmidt, J. (2014). *The politics of English in Puerto Rico's public schools*. Boulder & London: FirstForum Press.

Schweers, W. (1993). Language planning for Puerto Rico. *TESOL-GRAM, 20*(4), 7–8.

Schweers, W., & Hudders, M. (2002). The reformation and democratization of English education in Puerto Rico. *International Journal of the Sociology of Language, 142*, 63–87.

Schweers, C. W., & Vélez, J. (1999). To be or not to be bilingual in Puerto Rico: That is the issue. *Milenio*, *3*, 23–32. Retrieved from http://uprb.edu/milenio/Milenio1999/10SchweersVelez99.pdf

Shohami, E. (2006). *Language policy: Hidden agendas and new approaches*. Oxford and New Yrok: Routledge (Taylor & Francis Group).

Strauch, H. (1992). The compelling influence of nonlinguistic aims in language status policy planning in Puerto Rico. *Working Papers in Educational Linguistics*, *8*(2), 107–131. Retrieved from www.wpel.net/v8/v8n2.html

Tollefson, J. T. (1981). The role of language planning in second language acquisition. *Language Learning*, *31*(2), 337–348.

Tollefson, J. T. (1991). *Planning language, planning inequality*. New York: Longman.

Torres González, R. (2002). *Idioma, bilingüismo y nacionalidad: La presencia del inglés en Puerto Rico*. San Juan, PR: La Editorial de la Universidad de Puerto Rico.

UNESCO. (2006). Why literacy matters. In *Education for all global monitoring report 2006* (pp. 135–145). Paris: UNESCO. Retrieved from http://unesdoc.unesco.org/images/0014/001416/141639e.pdf

U. S. Census Bureau. (2000). *Puerto Rico: Educational attainment: Population 25 years and over*. Retrieved from http://censtats.census.gov/data/PR/04072.pdf

Vaquero, M. (1990). Anglicismos en la prensa una cala en el lenguaje periodístico de San Juan. *LEA: Lingüística española actual, 12*(2), 275–288.

Velázquez, B. (2013, January 13). Reclutan maestros boricuas para trasladarlos a Texas: Los salarios y el bajo costo de vida son incentivos para muchos educadores. *El Nuevo Día*. Retrieved from www.elnuevodia.com/nota-1426088.html

Vélez, J. A. (2000). Understanding Spanish-language maintenance in Puerto Rico: Political will meets the demographic imperative. *International Journal of the Sociology of Language*, *142*, 5–24.

Walsh, M. T. (1994). Towards a Puerto Rican variety of English: An ethnographic study with implications for the English curriculum in Puerto Rico (EdD dissertation). University of Puerto Rico, Rio Piedras.

Winer, L. (1990). Orthographic standardization for Trinidad and Tobago: Linguistic and sociopolitical considerations in an English Creole community. *Language Problems and Language Planning*, *14*, 236–268.

World Bank. (2010). *World Bank indicators. Puerto Rico. Literacy rate of youth ages 15–24*. Retrieved from www.tradingeconomics.com/puerto-rico/literacy-rate-youth-total-percent-of-people-ages-15-24-wb-data.html

Wright, S. (2004). *Language policy and language planning*. New York: Palgrave Macmillan.

12 Puerto Ricans on the move in the Anglophone Caribbean

The case of Spanish in St. Croix, United States Virgin Islands

Alma Simounet

1 Introduction

The migratory movements of large numbers of Puerto Ricans to various urban centers in the continental United States since the 1940s have been documented for a number of years (Duany 2002). The fields of history, sociology, linguistics, literature, music and the visual arts, anthropology, and popular culture, to name a few, have served as the matrix for the analysis of the continued legacy of this group from the Hispanic Caribbean. In the literature on the subject, the states most frequently mentioned as recipients of these large contingencies are usually New York, New Jersey, Pennsylvania, and Chicago, although other cities in states from the eastern seaboard are also known to have experienced the arrival and settlement of Puerto Ricans. More recently, the city of Orlando has become the center of attention for those scholars who, like Duany (2002), follow emigrations from the island to the United States, although this latter group seems to include a different kind of migrant in terms of the individuals' perceived higher socio-economic and professional status. This is an element of the population that is different from the members of the original Puerto Rican migratory groups, which came predominantly from the working class socio-economic group in the island. The financial crisis that had its onset in 2009 has promoted an additional wave of migration from the island to the mainland in search for professional improvement and economic stability, not to mention a safer environment. From July 2010 to July 2013, the US Census reported that 110,703 islanders had left Puerto Rico (Melo 2014). Of these, the majority were identified as young, professional individuals. However, little mention has been made of the various waves of migratory groups of Puerto Ricans who moved to the island of St. Croix, the largest of the US Virgin Islands, in the 1920s, 1930s, and 1940s. A later move of individuals from different parts of Puerto Rico took place in the 1960s in relation to an opening for jobs in the oil refinery, but this occurred in much fewer numbers and for a limited time. Although the majority of the individuals in the first three groups came from the island of Vieques, a small island off the southeastern coast of Puerto Rico, others came from the island of Culebra, just to the north of Vieques. Both islands constitute part of the territorial integrity of Puerto Rico.

This study focuses on the diaspora group of Puerto Ricans in St. Croix, their impact on life and education on the island, their sociolectal variety of Spanish, and the present Spanish language situation in that community. It is the product of living, working, and engaging in research among the Puerto Ricans there for the past 30 years. The discussion begins by looking at the various waves of Puerto Ricans, mostly from the smaller island of Vieques, and examining the historical events that triggered the various moves. This is followed by a brief discussion of the ensuing sociocultural, linguistic, and educational impact these migrants had on the life and people of St. Croix. It then turns its attention to the particular variety of Spanish spoken by them. Next it brings into perspective the role of Spanish in the construction of Puerto Rican identity vis-à-vis the plurilingual nature of the speech community and the commanding place English has enjoyed as the language of communication for hundreds of years. Finally, it discusses the factors that make up the present sociolinguistic context of St. Croix with the purpose of providing an up-to-date description of the current language situation and the factors that either encourage or deter the use of Spanish. The study thus concludes with comments on Spanish language maintenance or language shift.

2 Brief history of St. Croix and the migratory moves from Vieques

The island of St. Croix is the largest of the US Virgin Islands. It was sighted by Columbus in his second voyage of 1493 and given the name of Santa Cruz. Like many other islands in the Caribbean, it often changed in sovereignty until the United States bought it from the Danish West India Company in 1917 for 25 million dollars. St. Croix has flown the flags of seven European entities, including that of a religious organization: Spain, Holland, England, France, Knights of Malta, Denmark, and the United States of America. Notwithstanding this history of continuous change in sovereignty, in addition to the documented movements of people from other countries and Caribbean islands and the forced migration of slaves, all reflecting differing linguistic backgrounds, English was and still is the predominant language in St. Croix (Dookhan 1974; Boyer 2010). This is explained by the lack of a permanent settlement in St. Croix on the part of the Spaniards early on during the period of colonization and by the constant presence of settlers from England.

The arrival of Puerto Ricans, mainly from the smaller Puerto Rican island of Vieques, into this plurilingual context began in the 1920s with the objective of helping the local labor force in the sugar cane industry (Senior 1947; Dookhan 1974). A second migratory wave of *Viequenses* ensued in the 1930s in the midst of a period of serious economic duress in Vieques caused by the fall of the sugar industry and the closing of local sugar factories. Concomitantly, in 1931 two important decisions were made by the US government concerning St. Croix: Congress appropriated funds in order to help small farmers and homesteaders in the newly acquired territory and President Roosevelt, deeply impressed by the deplorable economic situation he observed in his visit to the island, was instrumental in the establishment of the Virgin Islands Corporation with the purpose of pushing forward a general rehabilitation with the help of a grant of over one million dollars (Géigel 2013).

A third wave occurred in the 1940s, when the people of Vieques were faced with the governmental approval of the expropriation of 24,762 acres of land by the US Navy in 1941. This high number of acres erased 72.8 percent of the entire area of an island whose mainstay was agriculture (Géigel 2013; Silva 1988). Without any doubt, this was the most damaging event to the economy of this small island, for it brought about an exodus which had never been seen in the history of Vieques (Fabián 2013). Three-fourths of the island's territorial integrity was emptied of its population. A final migratory movement, although less dramatic in numbers, occurred in the 1960s with job opportunities made available at the Hess Oil Company refinery and with the recruitment of English-Spanish bilingual teachers to attend to the marked increase of Spanish-speaking students in the public school system.

Why did a majority of the displaced people of Vieques select St. Croix as their place of refuge? In addition to the economic incentives the island provided during all the decades of economic stagnation in Vieques, there was the added attraction of geographical proximity between the two islands, the possession of US citizenship, and the additional bonus of relatives who had already moved there and who could serve as their hosts (Fabián 2013). Although the censuses of St. Croix provide numbers for individuals of Puerto Rican ethnicity, the numbers are not believed to represent the reality of the matter. Nineteen percent is one such number (Simounet de Géigel 1990); however, island educators, government officials, and researchers in the area of Caribbean societies such as Lewis (1972) and Highfield (2009) believe that a higher percentage, perhaps 35 to 40, would be a more accurate figure. This is thus a migratory group that requires attention within the field of study of the Puerto Rican diaspora.

3 Sociocultural, linguistic, and educational impact of the migrants

The demographic profile of St. Croix at the moment of arrival of the largest wave of immigrants from Vieques in the 1940s reflected a population whose composition displayed diverse cultural and national backgrounds (Simounet de Géigel 1990). The population consisted mainly of the descendants of African slaves born in St. Croix, people from other Caribbean islands whose linguistic background included one or more languages such as Creoles, English, French, or Dutch; people of European ancestry (mainly Danish and English) and some US continental Americans; Arabs, mainly Palestinians; and Trinidadian Indians associated with business ventures. Filipino physicians settled there a number of years later, while immigrants from the Dominican Republic arrived in bigger numbers via other Caribbean islands such as St. Martin. All were to affect the sociocultural fiber of the island community by adding greater richness to the pluriculturalism that already was characteristic of the local population. It is important to note, however, that no single group could claim majority.

With this situation of a highly diverse community in mind, it is evident "that a harmonious co-habitation within such a limited amount of territory and resources is a difficult feat" (Simounet 2013a: 40). Besides, receiving small numbers of migrants, from various places, throughout a reasonable amount of time is a very different reality from receiving them in startling numbers, from the same source, and in a relatively short span of time. The latter is what the 1920s migration first and then the massive move in the 1940s of *Viequenses* meant to Cruzans, the people of St. Croix. In addition, the migrants' profile indicated that this was a community of Spanish-speaking farmers, with a limited amount of schooling and hardly any knowledge of English, even though this language and Spanish were and still are the official languages in Puerto Rico (Lawaetz 1991; Simounet de Geigel 1990). Although they were US citizens, Puerto Ricans were viewed as foreigners, as strangers who looked different, spoke a different language, and behaved in 'odd' ways. So were their children seen upon entrance into the St. Croix Public School System (Ríos Villarini & González 2010; Simounet 2013b).

The language problem at the school level was initially dealt with through the recruitment of bilingual teachers trained in Puerto Rico; this was a solution that in 1969 received formal recognition as the Bilingual Education Program on the island in response to the federal law that addressed similar problems in the education of students who spoke no English at the national level. Two studies published in 2009–2010, one by Hernández Durán and the other by Ríos Villarini and González, are related to the language situation in the schools of St. Croix during this period of heavy migration. They discuss the problem in greater detail, offering a more complete picture of this language-related educational challenge.

4 Variety of Spanish spoken by the migratory groups

It is important to begin this discussion by pointing out once more that the majority of the individuals that settled in St. Croix as a result of the three migratory waves mentioned above were members of the working class, who spoke the sociolect of this socioeconomic class. Generally speaking, they arrived with little, if no schooling, and did not speak English, despite the strong US influence in Puerto Rico since the 1898 invasion of the island (Simounet 1999). As I mentioned earlier, the diaspora group of Puerto Ricans in the Anglophone Caribbean has overwhelmingly been ignored by scholars interested in these groups, while they have focused their attention on those that have moved to different parts of the US mainland. The lack of presence of these migrants to St. Croix in the literature of the diaspora in general is a major reason for the void that is evident concerning studies about any aspect of this group, especially that of language. Although the books on the history of the US Virgin Islands, especially the section that discusses social and educational matters in St. Croix, devote a section to the Puerto Rican migration (see Dookhan 1974; Boyer 2010), except for Senior's publication in 1947 on the Puerto Rican migrant there, it is not until the 1970s that there is significant published material on this particular migration and the ensuing problems in education on the island (see Centro de Investigaciones Sociales 1970; Padgett

1983). Whatever the reason for this dearth in scholarship, the same scarcity of information applies to the language situation in St. Croix.

Although issues of language are mentioned in the studies just mentioned above in conjunction with problems of education, as for example, student retention, the formal aspects of language are not addressed. It was not until 1986, when Vaquero de Ramírez published an article in *Español Actual*, that some information of a linguistic nature was finally made available about the Spanish spoken not just in St. Croix but also in Curaçao, Trinidad, and St. Thomas. In this article, she acknowledges that despite the monumental size of the bibliography that is available on the Spanish of the Americas, there is a marked void in the information concerning the Antilles in which Spanish is a minority language. She posits an explanation for this void:

> The little importance that our language has in these islands, where it lives as an instrument of communication that is restricted to very concrete situations of business or family, has made joint studies about the function and status of Spanish in these territories nonexistent. Titles within bibliographies about the Spanish of the so-called Virgin Islands are hard to be found and those that do appear (Trinidad does have some important studies) do not have the purpose of establishing comparisons. As far as I know, never, until now, had there been any intention of carrying out research that concerned the status and function of the Spanish spoken in these islands, following a rigorous plan and applying the same questionnaire.
>
> (Vaquero de Ramírez 1986: 13; my translation)

In the fieldwork done in the four islands and reported by Vaquero de Ramírez, she utilized a questionnaire that had been prepared by Manuel Alvar and Antonio Quilis in 1984 for its use in the writing of the Linguistic Atlas of Hispanic America. The end in view of her study was to utilize the information gathered through this instrument about the Spanish in Cuba, the Dominican Republic, and Puerto Rico in addition to the information from the four smaller islands mentioned above, in order to produce an atlas of the Antilles. In her article, Vaquero de Ramírez emphasizes four aspects about the Spanish in the smaller islands visited: the function of Spanish, its degree of vitality, the linguistic elements affected by the interference from other adjoining languages, and the habitual way in which the language is acquired and/or transmitted.

As to the function of the language, Vaquero de Ramírez (1986) underscores the situation of Curaçao, the Papiamento-speaking Dutch island, versus that of the other three English-speaking islands. Spanish in the former is learned outside the home environment, while in the case of the other three, where English is the official language, the speakers learn it at home due to a number of reasons: their parents are themselves of Spanish origin; they have transmitted the language to their children at home and Spanish has been the language these new speakers use to communicate at home, a language they hear at the same time as the English that is spoken on the street and at school. As to the type of English used in the three islands, it must be pointed out that either Standard English or an English Lexifier Creole or both would have been heard by the speakers in this study. Vaquero de Ramírez acknowledges that in the case of St. Croix, Spanish is the native language of the Puerto Rican migrants and thus it lives "with a major or minor degree of vitality, as the family language from infancy and later as a language of diminishing advantage vis-à-vis English, the sole language of prestige" (1986: 14; my translation). In addition, the author underscores the finding that in St. Croix and St. Thomas not only is Spanish used at home, but business endeavors require knowledge of this language. As to this matter, she points out the following:

> [T]he Spanish of the Hispanic that is born in these islands also presents a large quantity of insecurities, lack of knowledge of vocabulary that is refined [*culto*] and specific, phonetic and syntactic interference from English and complete ignorance of the writing skills [in Spanish]. It could be said that it is a Spanish "for emergency situations," that is used to solve basic problems in basic communication.
>
> (Vaquero de Ramírez 1986: 14; my translation)

Another function that Vaquero de Ramírez identifies for Spanish in St. Thomas and St. Croix is that of understanding the Spanish language television channels they can get from Puerto Rico. This point in particular still holds, for local cable television companies in both islands include at least two Spanish language channels as part of their basic offer.

The author presents the linguistic features for the Spanish spoken in each of the islands in very general terms. In fact, she calls them 'notes' that entail the need for further studies that would take into consideration all of the levels of language. The notes on the Spanish in St. Croix are limited to two assertions: 1) that it follows the patterns of the Spanish spoken in Puerto Rico and 2) that it does not present as many examples of interference as the sample from St. Thomas. The two language phenomena are explained by appealing to extralinguistic variables. She believes this is the result of the impressive numbers of Puerto Ricans who reside in St. Croix on a permanent basis and their continuous interaction among themselves, friends, and family members (1986: 17). The fact that both Vieques and Culebra are of close geographical proximity to St. Croix makes it possible for the Puerto Rican communities from these islands to participate in a constant communicative mode in Spanish. Vaquero de Ramírez ends her comments about St. Croix by stating that the community of migrants use Spanish at home and that their children learn it as the family language; however, afterwards, they "impoverish their use of it and forget the vocabulary. This second generation feels more secure in English" (18).

Although the points that follow refer specifically to what Vaquero de Ramírez (17) identifies as the characteristics of the Spanish spoken by Puerto Ricans in St. Thomas, on the basis of my exposure to the Spanish used by the members of the Puerto Rican community in St. Croix for the past 33 years, I feel comfortable in stating that they may also be applied to refer to the latter speakers. First, as to her comments about the pronunciation patterns of this variety, she states that they represent the popular patterns of the Spanish spoken in the Hispanic Caribbean. In her discussion, for example, she explains that it exhibits "the systematic latelarization of the implosive liquids"; the use of the fricative [š] in place of the palatal affricate [č]; and the loss of final [s]. Second, in terms of morphemics, she affirms that there are many instances of lack of agreement and gives the example *mucho ave* instead of *muchas aves*. Moreover, she believes that there is "a total confusion as to gender in names, irregular verbs, and the use of verbal time and mood" (17). Third, she identifies a lack of knowledge concerning "vocabulario culto" or formal vocabulary and, in addition, she comments on the 'picturesque' manner in which her informants translated certain terms from English to Spanish. For example, *watermelon* became *agua de melón* instead of *melón de agua*. According to her, this easily gave way to the use of many loanwords from English in their Spanish discourse.

Although Vaquero de Ramírez does not delve into a detailed account of St. Croix Spanish in terms of the various levels of language, in response to the informative nature of the article, according to her, I must state here that many Puerto Ricans who visit the island express their dismay to me at hearing speakers use word forms such as *dijía, dijiera*, which they themselves believed were no longer in use. My own personal reactions to these forms occurred when I began to carry out interviews of the original migrants who moved from Vieques and their descendants in the 1980s. These forms are still prevalent.

Two other studies of Puerto Rican Spanish in St. Croix appeared more than 20 years later in a special issue of the journal *Sargasso* (Ríos Villarini & González Vélez 2009–2010), which focused solely on studies that discussed a variety of factors concerning the Vieques migration to St. Croix. One of the linguistic studies (González-Rivera 2009–2010) addresses the distribution of the morpheme *-ndo* in periphrastic constructions in the variety that he calls Porto Crucian Spanish. In my introductory comments to the articles in this issue, I state the following:

> Historically, language contact and imperfect acquisition have been utilized as the explanations for the use of certain structures in dialects of languages in close linguistic contact. González Rivera believes that it is the analysis of the internal linguistic system under scrutiny and, in his case in particular, the study of the grammatical system of Spanish, that should always be examined before seeking answers for the explanation of certain linguistic phenomena in extralinguistic sources. He concludes that this is the case of the construction he examined, that is, that linguistic factors within the internal grammatical system of Spanish bring about the use of the aforementioned morpheme; it is the sense of activity in the predicates utilized by the speakers that lead them to the use of the progressive construction and not the result of contact with English.
>
> (Simounet 2009–2010: 16)

The second linguistic study that appeared in the journal *Sargasso* examines the inclusion or omission of subject pronouns in the grammatical position of the subject by the population of heritage speakers, the terms Morales-Reyes decides to use to refer to the Porto-Crucians in the diaspora community in the island (2009–2010). Once again, on reviewing her contribution to this special issue, I expressed the following:

> The results of her analysis of Porto-Crucian Spanish show that semantic and progressive aspects together with the influence of English play an important role in the inclusion or omission of the third-person subject pronouns. In addition, she also found that in comparison to Puerto Rican Spanish, Porto-Crucian Spanish evidences a linguistic behavior that tends toward simplicity and generalization while the former reveals a preference towards a more restrictive use.
>
> (Simounet 2009–2010: 16–17)

Morales Reyes believes that the changes in the Spanish of these speakers result from the "internal processes of the language, but those changes are conditioned in great measure by L2" (17). From these two studies, it is evident that the situation of this former colony of Denmark is still rich as to what it can offer in terms of language contact. Morales Reyes herself manifests her concern about the need to continue doing research in St. Croix, a community she believes has so much to offer but has been "barely studied". The rest of this special issue of the journal *Sargasso* is devoted to some other issues of the Puerto Rican migration and other migrations from various Caribbean islands. For example, one essay discusses the historical relations between St. Croix and Vieques, another dramatic photo essay about Vieques and St. Croix focuses on the importance of viewing objects as representatives of the intertextuality between reality and the conceptual meaning for which they stand, and two studies analyze, one through a historical lens and the other through the eyes of the bilingual teachers, the problems that are inherent in a system with a clear lack of language planning that would deal with the cultural variety represented by the students of multiethnic backgrounds in the local schools.

5 Spanish and the construction of Puerto Rican identity in a plurilingual context

Before I delve into the role of Spanish in the construction of Puerto Rican identity, I would like to present my view as regards the elusive notion of ethnic identity. I must point out that in terms of its ethnic identity, a migrating group's response to new and more permanent cultural contexts should be viewed both from cognitive and social perspectives. Although both levels could be seen as opposing explanatory angles, they do not necessarily respond to a binary system. I believe they help in the understanding of the possibility of differing reactions to the contexts just mentioned above. At the cognitive level, it is important to be aware that the ethnic identity of a person can be understood as a dynamic state that can change "in response to the surrounding sociocultural environment" (Simounet 2013a: 142).

At the social level, it is also of value to underscore that when "a group of people of one's ethnic background exists as an ingroup in a particular context, one's ethnicity as a significant construct is aroused" (142). Both perspectives help in understanding the cultural changes or absence of them that migrating groups experience in their new social and cultural milieu. The first one allows for malleability and change to occur, notwithstanding the process of enculturation in the group's first experience with said process at the cognitive level, for it makes it possible for new cultural knowledge to develop new or additional roots that permit other pathways in terms of values, norms, beliefs, and social practices. The second one helps explain an initial reaction of resistance to the possibility of change or, more markedly, the eventual and complete rejection of it. As to the cognitive perspective, I reiterate the possibility of change, since it can also partially modify the original makeup, and with this alternate reaction, both comply with the first cultural mold and also become part of the new one; that is, become engaged in cultural hybridity. This means that the individuals allow the self to open itself to the passage of other realities, to the penetration of an 'otherness' that is an expression of a "cultural identity . . . that includes simultaneous themes of separation and desire for inclusion" (González 1990: 276). Bearing in mind both levels of understandings, then the attachment to one's ethnicity, the internalization of the other, or the integration of different ethnicities could also lead members of the group to divide into distinct identity choices. Rather than having a situation in which each member varies in ethnic identity according to time or place, in the case of migration groups, one could completely identify with the ingroup, a second one with the host group, and a third one with both (Mercer et al. 1998).

The diaspora group of Puerto Ricans encountered the situation described above from the start. Their ethnicity as Puerto Ricans became the axis of their existence in this new environment where Spanish was the first line of defense in their quest to preserve crucial and defining ethnic characteristics. Time must be allowed to pass in order to attempt to understand the different pathways to identity taken and the role that Spanish played in the selection. As the years went by and one generation followed another, the defining ethnic qualities of Puerto Ricans in Cruzan soil slowly changed in response to the different social and linguistic milieu that surrounded the group. In few words, the three possible outcomes of cultural confrontation in situations of migration as presented above were given, but in disparaging statistics. Spanish played and still plays a significant role in the ever-changing dimension of language contact in St. Croix among Puerto Ricans. I was able to attest to this continuity in a number of interviews I carried out there in March of 2014, in conjunction with Ana Fabián, a sociologist and researcher at the Institute of Caribbean Studies at the University of Puerto Rico.

However, I would like to share the results of a study I conducted in 1993 (Simounet 1999) that delved into the question of ethnic identity and the role that Spanish played in its construction, given the fact that the speech community of St. Croix was and still is characterized by the use of many languages. I based my work on Smolicz's theoretical stance (1992), which addressed his concern as to the end result of the ethnic identity and language maintenance of a number of cultural groups that had arrived in Australia. He was particularly interested in discovering, identifying, and describing the ethnic characteristics of the end product of the migratory groups to Australia and the matrix that brought it about. Smolicz based his study on the premise that language, as well as other central cultural elements, act as 'pivots' that constitute the core of a group and comprise the identifying values that are symbolic to the group, to the point that, if lost, it would imply the group's disintegration as a self-perpetuating social entity (279). In the case of the Puerto Ricans in St. Croix, my goal was to discover too what had happened to this group of individuals, who as Morris (1996) attested in her fieldwork, marked their identity in terms of the Caribbean variety of their language. In order to accomplish this, I utilized and modified a questionnaire used by Dorian (1981) in her study of Scottish Gaelic.

The results were surprisingly similar to those of Smolicz (1992). Of the 47 intermediate and high school students plus four university students who responded to and filled out the questionnaire completely, 15 percent considered themselves Puerto Rican, although they were born in St. Croix, because, as they stated, they belonged to a different culture and they lived according to the best Puerto Rican traditions. Despite the fact that they spoke Spanish frequently and believed in its importance, surprisingly, the majority did not believe that Spanish should be the sole marker of their ethnic identity. Thirty-eight percent identified themselves as Porto Cruzan, manifesting in this way a hybrid identity. They continued to promote Puerto Rican values through the use of Spanish; however, they admitted to having added new components to their cultural life by speaking Standard American English and the local Creole. Finally, almost 47 percent called themselves Cruzan. They strongly believed that, since they were born in St. Croix, they were 'automatically' Cruzan (Simounet 1999: 622, 627–628).

Out of curiosity, I carried out a survey at the St. Croix Campus of the University of the Virgin Islands among 72 students who had no Puerto Rican ethnic connection and asked them to write the ethnicity that they would ascribe to the Puerto Ricans in St. Croix. The results were unexpected in terms of their closeness to those presented above. Nine percent considered them to be Puerto Rican because their parents were Puerto Rican too; 42 percent viewed them as Porto Cruzan because, although they were born in St. Croix, they still celebrated their Puerto Rican cultural traditions; 49 percent believed they were Cruzan because they had been born in St. Croix, and this matter on being locally born is a very delicate matter on the island due to the cultural diversity of the island population. In a 1997 informal conversation I held with renowned socio-linguist Ana Celia Zentella concerning the close parallelism of both sets of results, she commented that these findings were in line with her belief that ethnic identity is forged as the result of the social interaction that takes place between the incoming group and the members of the base community. She strongly recommended that I include these additional findings.

> The construction of identity is, therefore, the product of a negotiation between these two constituencies of the Cruzan speech community. Puerto Ricans born in St. Croix have thus walked through three different roads in order to

forge their identity in the midst of a context which in itself has contributed to the formation of this construct that is not necessarily tied to just one language.

(Simounet 1999: 629)

Although the number of respondents in my study does not provide a platform for generalization, it is significant to mention that a thesis written by García Lozada in 2011 ratified my findings of 1993, 18 years later, with regards to the group's ethnicity and the corresponding view of the role of Spanish. This later work replicated my 1999 study, making some changes: a modified questionnaire, a smaller and older sample of participants, and a different instrument for the analysis of data.

Now, what impact did the use of English in the educational system of St. Croix have on the use of Spanish and its role as the marker of Puerto Rican ethnicity (Morris 1996)? As stated earlier, English is the language of St. Croix. Besides the people who speak other languages brought in by various settlers from foreign countries and other Caribbean islands, the majority of local islanders speak Cruzan English, the name that is given to the English Lexifier Creole of the island. The school age children who arrived in St. Croix as part of the two big waves of migration from Vieques encountered serious problems in the island public schools due to their lack of language skills in English (Hernández Durán 2009–2010). Moreover, they could not engage in conversation with other local children at school or in their new neighborhoods because these children spoke in Cruzan English. At home Spanish was still used and Puerto Rican cultural traditions were celebrated. On viewing the language patterns followed according to generation, the studies (Simounet 1990, 1999, 2005, 2013a; Villanueva 2006; García Lozada 2011; Veliz 2014) show that the migrant parents or first generation spoke only Spanish; the second generation, their offspring, spoke only Spanish at first but eventually learned Cruzan English from their peers at school and in the playground and also learned Standard English at school. This exposure led them to create a pattern of use characterized by Spanish at home, English in the classroom and Cruzan English both at school and in the neighborhood and the rest of the community. Among themselves they turned to Spanish-English codeswitching, especially in their adolescent years (Simounet 2005). The third generation spoke mostly in English, although they still used Spanish with older family members and whenever the situation called for it such as with incoming relatives from Vieques. The use of codeswitching, which had been evident in the earlier studies, especially among adolescents of Puerto Rican descent, continued to be present in the 2014 interviews mentioned above with second- and third-generation adults.

While the concept of ethnicity continues to be elusive and the pattern of language use in a plurilingual context to be characterized by an expected outcome at one moment and an unexpected one at another, it is the belief that it is perhaps best not to force its understanding but to allow it to 'float' without necessarily negating memories of past interaction nor pinpointing a particular variety of language (Banks 1988). It is best to focus on the analysis of ethnic identity and the indexing of language use at the moment of its occurrence and as part of the negotiation that takes place in a communicative interaction. In order to accomplish this, the need for further study cannot be considered an exaggerated requirement.

6 Current language situation: language maintenance or language shift?

The composition of the population of present day St. Croix is still pluricultural and plurilingual.

> [It] consists of Crucians, those who were born and raised on the island – usually of African descent, but also of European and mixed ancestry – as well as people who arrived more recently from the other Virgin Islands, Puerto Rico and Vieques, the Dominican Republic, St. Lucia, Guadeloupe, Trinidad, Haiti, Jamaica and other nations of the Caribbean, the United States, Venezuela and other nations of Central and South America, the Middle East, Asia, and Europe: indeed, the world.
>
> (De Jesús 2011: 12)

This richness of ethnicities in which each group is characterized by "its own rhythms, flavors, music, and language" (12) thus creates an ambience of distinctiveness, for people on the island respond in complex sets of different patterns of behavior, especially those related to language. Although the US Census provides important demographic data, its lack of background information concerning linguistic knowledge paints a picture of the language situation that is misleading. In its various collections of data classification of the languages spoken on the island, it arranged the statistics according to the 'ability to speak English', drawing a line between those who speak English only and those that speak a language other than English (12). As a result, it is easy to reach the false conclusion that the people on the island are monolingual either in English or in another language. Besides, other varieties of English spoken on the island such as Cruzan, Antiguan, Trinidadian, Jamaican, and their respective Creoles are simply ignored. By ignoring the plurality of languages spoken on the island, there is a total disregard of the presence of bilingualism and bi-dialectalism. In truth, French, French Creole, Spanish, Papiamento, Dutch, Arabic, Pilipino, and other Asian/Pacific languages are spoken in St. Croix (12–13).

Notwithstanding the social situation of plurilingualism on the island, the predominant language of use in the government, schools, mass media, and, most importantly, in the everyday interaction of the speech community is English, in its Standard variety or in its creolized form. In terms of the Puerto Rican diaspora, the question then is: given these linguistic circumstances, what is the future of Spanish? Once more, the studies that are available are very few: Vaquero de Ramírez (1986), Simounet (1993a,b, 1999, 2004, 2005), García Lozada (2011) and Veliz (2014).

Vaquero de Ramírez (1986) expressed doubts about the possibility for this migratory group to retain its language due to the overwhelming functions that English has on the island. She strongly believed that "eventually, with the extinction of the migrant communities, Spanish would also gradually disappear and find refuge in places of little or no importance at all" (18). Veliz (2014) reached the same conclusions as Vaquero de Ramírez.

However, throughout my continuous interest in the topic of Spanish maintenance in St. Croix and in the presentations I have made at various conferences, I have stated that language maintenance in general is a very difficult matter to predict. There are too many factors and combinations of them at work and, according to Myers-Scotton (2006), "maintenance and shift within a bilingual community fall on a continuum with those individuals who use only the L1 at one end to those who use only the L2 at the other end" (89). In fact, I have borrowed the terminology from meteorology for the predicted path or trajectory of a hurricane in order to describe the predictions that linguists wish to make about the behaviors of various languages. Hurricanes create their own pathways, despite the predictions made by recently developed computer programs and advances in technology, and languages and their speakers do likewise. Although, Puerto Ricans are now advancing to a fourth generation in an English-speaking environment, I believe that the following facts help to keep the lifeline to Spanish alive: there is an important influx of 'Dominicanos' on the island; there is continued travel between St. Croix and Vieques or Puerto Rico for medical purposes, shopping, special events, and traveling connections; newspapers from Puerto Rico are flown into St. Croix on a daily basis; television and radio stations from Puerto Rico are seen and heard there; there is a local Spanish radio station; different Protestant church denominations attend to the needs of the Spanish-speaking community (Simounet 2005) and the Catholic Church continues to have special mass services in Spanish. Besides, the young subjects in my 1999 study and the adult participants in García Lozada's study (2011) expressed their appreciation for and love of Spanish and their strong belief in the instrumental importance it holds in the island and in today's world of business and commerce.

The present economic situation in St. Croix can only be described as a devastating one. In the midst of the 2009 recession, the island was dealt a severe blow with the 2012 closing of the Hovensa Oil Refinery, the largest refinery in the Western Hemisphere, a joint product of Hess Oil Company and the Venezuelan government. This refinery was unquestionably the largest private sector employer on the island and, when it shut down, 2,600 people lost their jobs (Bram & Hastings 2013). Although the refinery re-opened under new owners in the summer of 2016, St. Croix is still in 2017 at one of its lowest points, economically speaking, since the island was bought from the Danish West India Company 100 years ago, in 1917. The situation is not clear as to the long-standing effects the closing had in reality, for thousands have already left and are still leaving the island as a result of the debacle.

On the basis of my number of years on the island, I am inclined to sit and wait a little before I make any predictions concerning the language situation for Spanish. Throughout these 33 years of contact with the Cruzan community, various factors have made the language context favorable for Spanish language maintenance while others have deterred its continuity.

What is evident from the limited number of studies discussed here is that work is urgently needed in order to present a thorough scientific description of the Spanish language spoken by Puerto Ricans in St. Croix. The same can be said concerning other language-related issues. Notwithstanding the research already carried out by students from the graduate programs in English and Linguistics at the University of Puerto Rico in situ, it covers merely a fraction of what is available. Moreover, the continuous migration of other Caribbean Spanish speakers from the Dominican Republic into St. Croix has not received the attention it merits from concerned scholars in language studies. The linguistic laboratory work that St. Croix offers is still waiting for the interest and commitment of linguists in general and for those whose interest lies in Hispanic linguistics. It is my hope that this article provokes such action.

Bibliography

Banks, S. (1988). Achieving "unmarkedness" in organizational discourse: A praxis perspective in ethnolinguistic identity. In W. B. Gudykunst (Ed.), *Language and ethnic identity* (pp. 15–34). Clevedon: Multilingual Matters.

Bram, J., & Hastings, J. (2013, November 15). A long road to economic recovery for the US Virgin Islands. Retrieved from http://libertystreeteconomics.newyorkfed.org/2013/11/a-long_road_to_economic_recovery_for_the_us_virgin_islands.html#.U7qu85;Wok4.email

Boyer, W. W. (2010). *America's virgin Islands: A history of human rights and wrongs* (2nd ed.). Durham, NC: Carolina Academic Press.

Centro de Investigaciones Sociales. Universidad de Puerto Rico. (1970). The educational setting in the Virgin Islands with particular reference to the education of Spanish-speaking children (Unpublished manuscript).

De Jesús, S. (2011). St. Croix: A pluri-lingual and pluri-cultural island. In M. Reyes-Laborde & B. L. Dominguez-Rosado (Compilators). *New perspectives on the languages, literatures and cultures of St. Croix* (pp. 11–31). Private offprint.

Dookhan, I. (1974). *A history of the Virgin Islands of the United States*. St. Thomas: Caribbean University Press.

Dorian, N. (1981). *Language death*. Philadelphia: University of Pennsylvania Press.

Duany, J. (2002). The Puerto Rican nation on the move: Identities on the Island and in the United States. Chapel Hill, NC: University of North Carolina Press.

Fabián, A. (2013, November). The importance of a transdisciplinary approach and the use of oral history for the study of migration people: Following the trail from Vieques to St. Croix. Paper presented at the *Annual Meeting of the Islands in Between Conference*, Aruba.

García Lozada, J. (2011). La comunidad de habla en Santa Cruz: un estudio sobre las actitudes y el mantenimiento de la lengua e identidad en los puertorriqueños (Unpublished master's thesis). University of Puerto Rico, Río Piedras, Puerto Rico.

Geigel, W. (2013, November). St. Croix, Vieques and Puerto Rico. Paper presented at the *Annual Meeting of the Islands in Between Conference*, Aruba.

González, A. (1990). Mexican "otherness" in the rhetoric of Mexican Americans. *Southern Communication Journal, 6*, 276–291.

González-Rivera, M. (2009–2010). El español de Puerto Rico en su contexto cruceño: el caso del morfema – *ndo*. *Sargasso, 2*, 51–70.

Hernández Durán, M. (2009–2010). The education of minorities in St. Croix. *Sargasso, 2*, 23–35.

Highfield, A. (2009). Apuntes históricos sobre las migraciones de puertorriqueños a la isla de Santa Cruz, Islas Vírgenes estadounidenses. Keynote address at the *Conferencia*

Magistral en Seminario para maestros: Memorias. Puerto Rico: Fundación para las Humanidades.

Lawaetz, E. J. (1991). *500 years: Pre-Columbus to 1990.* Denmark: Paul Kristensen.

Lewis, G. (1972). *The virgin Islands: A Caribbean lilliput.* Evanston: Northwestern University Press.

Melo, J. C. (2014, June 26). Puerto Rico sigue perdiendo población. *Metro Puerto Rico,* p. 6.

Mercer, L., Mercer, J., & Mears, A. (1988). Ethnic identity among young Asians in the community of Leicester. In W. B. Gudykunst (Ed.), *Language and ethnic identity* (pp. 112–129). Clevedon: Multilingual Matters.

Morales Reyes, A. (2009–2010). Pronombres de sujeto en Santa Cruz (y Puerto Rico): ¿Procesos semánticos/pragmáticos o influencia de L2. *Sargasso, 2,* 71–86.

Morris, N. (1996). Language and identity in twentieth century Puerto Rico. *Journal of Multilingual and Multicultural Development, 17,* 17–32.

Myers-Scotton, C. (2006). *Multiple voices: An introduction to bilingualism.* Malden, MA: Blackwell Publications.

Padgett, C. H. A. (1983). *Parent-client participation in the Bilingual Education Program in St. Croix, United States Virgin Islands.* U. S. Department of Education: Educational Resources Information Center (ERIC).

Reyes-Laborde, M., & Dominguez-Rosado, B. (Compilators). (2011). *New perspectives on the languages, literatures and cultures of St. Croix.* Private offprint.

Ríos, Villarini, N., & González Vélez, M. (2009–2010). Oral histories of bilingual education teachers from the Puerto Rican diaspora in St. Croix: Exploring ideological tensions inside and outside the classroom. *Sargasso, 2,* 35–49.

Senior, C. (1947). *The Puerto Rican migrant in St. Croix.* Facultad de Ciencias Sociales: Universidad de Puerto Rico.

Silva, F. (1988). *Movimientos migratorios: El caso de Vieques y Santa Cruz* (Unpublished student manuscript), Department of Sociology, University of Puerto Rico, Río Piedras, Puerto Rico.

Simounet de Géigel, A. (1990). The analysis of sales encounters in contexts of work situation in St. Croix: An ethnographic approach. In M. A. K. Halliday, J. Gibbons, & H. Nichols (Eds.), *Learning, keeping and using language* (pp. 455–492). Amsterdam: John Benjamin Publishing Co.

Simounet-Geigel, A. (1993a). The case of Puerto Ricans in St. Croix: Language maintenance or language loss? Paper presented at the *World Congress of the International Association of Applied Linguistics,* Amsterdam, The Netherlands.

Simounet-Geigel, A. (1993b). Focusing on the patterns of language use and social organization of a migrant community within a multicultural context. Implications for language curriculum development. Paper presented at the *Tenth World Congress of the International Association of Applied Linguistics,* Amsterdam, The Netherlands.

Simounet, A. (1999). Lengua e identidad: lazos que no siempre unen. In A. Morales, J. Cardona, H. López Morales & E. Forastieri (Eds.), *Estudios de lingüística hispánica. Homenaje a María Vaquero* (pp. 615–636). Río Piedras, Puerto Rico: Editorial de la Universidad de Puerto Rico.

Simounet-Géigel, A. (2004). Spanish language vitality in the context of language contact with English: The views of the migrant speaker in St. Croix. *La Torre: Revista de la Universidad de Puerto Rico. Caribe Anglófono 2003, 32*(9), 259–267.

Simounet, A. (2005). La religión y la retención lingüística: el caso de una iglesia pentecostal en Santa Cruz, Islas Vírgenes estadounidenses. In L. A. Ortiz & M. Lacorte (Eds.),

Contextos y contactos lingüísticos: El español en los Estados Unidos y en contacto con otras lenguas (pp. 263–270). Madrid: Iberoamericana/Vervuert.

Simounet, A. (2009–2010). Introduction. *Sargasso*, *2*, 9–18.

Simounet, A. (2013a). The construction of "otherness" in the Caribbean island of St. Croix and its pertinence to decisions about language and education policy for diaspora groups at the community and governmental levels: A socio-cultural and historical perspective. In E. Núñez Méndez (Invited Ed.), *Revista Internacional d'Humanitats*, *16*(27), 37–44.

Simounet, A. (2013b). The diaspora of Puerto Ricans in St. Croix: A socio-cultural and historical look at ethnicity, language and identity in a migratory group within a pluri-cultural context. In N. Faraclas, R. Severing, C. Weijer, E. Echteld & M. Hinds-Layne (Eds.), *Transcultural roots uprising: The rhizomatic languages, literatures, and cultures of the Caribbean* (pp. 137–149). Curaçao: Fundashon pa Planifikashon de Idioma and University of the Netherland Antilles.

Smolicz, J. (1992). Minority languages as core values of ethnic cultures: A study of maintenance and erosion of Polish, Welsh and Chinese languages in Australia. In K. Fase, K. Jaespaert & S. Kroon (Eds.), *Mainenance and loss of minority languages* (pp. 277–305). Amsterdam: John Benjamin.

Vaquero de Ramírez, M. (1986). La lengua española en Curaçao, Trinidad, St. Thomas y St. Croix. *Español Actual*, *46*, 11–19.

Veliz, M. C. (2014). *El español en Santa Cruz: factores que determinan su expectativa de vida* (Unpublished master's thesis). University of Puerto Rico, Río Piedras, Puerto Rico.

Villanueva, O. (2006). Language use among Puerto Ricans in St. Croix. *Focus*, *5*(1), 61–70.

Index

For Product Safety Concerns and Information please contact our EU
representative GPSR@taylorandfrancis.com Taylor & Francis Verlag GmbH,
Kaufingerstraße 24, 80331 München, Germany

Printed and bound by CPI Group (UK) Ltd, Croydon, CR0 4YY
01/05/2025
01858416-0004